THE SHAPE OF THE RIVER

THE SHAPE OF THE RIVER

LONG-TERM CONSEQUENCES OF CONSIDERING RACE IN COLLEGE AND UNIVERSITY ADMISSIONS

William G. Bowen and Derek Bok

IN COLLABORATION WITH

James L. Shulman, Thomas I. Nygren, Stacy Berg Dale, and Lauren A. Meserve

PRINCETON UNIVERSITY PRESS   PRINCETON, NEW JERSEY

Library of Congress Cataloging-in-Publication Data

Bowen, William G.
The shape of the river : long-term consequences of considering
race in college and university admissions / William G. Bowen and
Derek Bok ; in collaboration with James L. Shulman . . . [et al.].
p.   cm.
Includes bibliographical references and index.
ISBN 0-691-00274-6 (cloth : alk. paper)
1. Universities and colleges—United States—Admission—
Case studies. 2. Affirmative action programs—United States—
Case studies. 3. Afro-Americans—Education (Higher)—
Case studies. 4. Afro-American college graduates—Case studies.
I. Bok, Derek Curtis. II. Title.
LB 2351.2.B696   1998
378.1′61′0973—dc21   98-19900
                                                                CIP

"You've got to know the shape of the river perfectly. It is all there is left to steer by on a very dark night. . . ."

"Do you mean to say that I've got to know all the million trifling variations of shape in the banks of this interminable river as well as I know the shape of the front hall at home?"

"On my honor, you've got to know them better."

—Mark Twain, Life on the Mississippi

Contents

List of Figures

Chapter 4

Chapter 7

Chapter 8

Appendix C

List of Tables

STRETCHING FROM St. Paul to New Orleans, Mark Twain's Mississippi winds for twelve hundred miles through fog, rapids, slow eddies, sandbars, bends, and hidden bluffs. Drawing upon his own experiences on the Mississippi, Twain created an image of the river as both physically central to the United States and symbolically central to the progress of the country. The image of the river is also central to the story of our book, which is concerned with the flow of talent—particularly of talented black men and women—through the country's system of higher education and on into the marketplace and the larger society.

The image most commonly invoked in discussions of this process is the "pipeline." We often hear of the importance of keeping young people moving through the "pipeline" from elementary school to high school to college, on through graduate and professional schools, and into jobs, family responsibilities, and civic life. But this image is misleading, with its connotation of a smooth, well defined, and well understood passage. It is more helpful to think of the nurturing of talent as a process akin to moving down a winding river, with rock-strewn rapids and slow channels, muddy at times and clear at others. Particularly when race is involved, there is nothing simple, smooth, or highly predictable about the education of young people.

While riverboat pilots on the Mississippi navigated "point to point"— only as far as they could see into the next bend—they had to know every depth, every deceptive shoal, and every hidden snag of the river. Moreover, since the boats ran throughout the night, in high water and low, and both up the river and down it, these pilots had to know the river's features in every imaginable condition, and from either direction. Even though they could only steer through what they saw in front of them, they had to understand how the bend that they were navigating at any moment fit into the shape of a twelve-hundred-mile river.

The college admissions process and the educational experience that follows it are similarly complex. Most recently, debate about the use of race as a criterion has centered on the question of who "merits" or "deserves" a place in the freshman class. At this one bend in the river, prior grades and numerical test scores offer a tempting means of defining qualifications, since they are easily compiled and compared. But what do they really tell us, and what are we trying to predict? Much more, surely, than first-year grades or even graduation from one college or another. It is the contributions that individuals make throughout their lives and the broader impact of higher education on the society that are finally most relevant.

In this book, we seek to be helpful to both the "pilots" of this educational process—the parents of prospective students, the high school counselors, college admissions officers, faculty members, and administrators, trustees, and regents responsible for setting policies—and those future students who will some day have to navigate the river. We also hope this study will be useful to employers, legislators, and the public as a whole, since everyone has an interest in the development of talent and access to opportunity in our society. We need to know as much as we can about what has happened around bends and curves—in college, in graduate school, and then twenty years downstream—from the frozen moment in time when seventeen-year-olds from various races and backgrounds sat down with Number 2 pencils to take the SAT. This book is an attempt to chart what race-sensitive admissions policies have meant over a long stretch of the river—both to the individuals who were admitted and to the society that has invested in their education and that counts so heavily on their future leadership.

These questions are enormously important because this country is not yet where any of us would want it to be in terms of race relations. On this central point, liberals and conservatives often agree. Echoing W.E.B. Du Bois, John Hope Franklin has argued eloquently that "the problem of the twenty-first century will be the problem of the color line. . . . By any standard of measurement or evaluation the problem has not been solved in the twentieth century, and thus becomes a part of the legacy and burden of the next century."[1] The problem of "the color line" is so central to American life for reasons that are rooted in the disjunction between the values embedded in the Constitution and the realities of three centuries of collective experience. These reasons reflect a sense on the part of many that, despite all the progress made in the past fifty years, we have not yet succeeded in transcending a racial divide that too often discourages the development of ordinary relationships among individuals based on trust and mutual respect. They include as well persistent gross inequities in wealth, privilege, and position that are hard to explain away simply on the basis of differences in individual effort and initiative, significant as such differences are. Finally, there is a collective concern that we are failing to develop to its fullest the human potential of the country and a growing realization that our society, with its ever more diverse population, cannot ultimately succeed as a democracy if we fail to close the gaps in opportunity that continue to be associated with race.

The subject of race in America is as sensitive and contentious as it is

[1] Franklin 1993, p. 5.

important. Highly charged words, such as "fairness," "merit," "achievement," "preference," and even "race" itself, often take on very different connotations depending on the speaker and the context. (Note, for example, the radical differences in polling results when the wording of questions about race is changed in relatively minor ways.)[2] Language itself has been a casualty of heated debate; for this reason one aim of this study is to "unpack" the meaning of terms such as "merit," clarify their various possible meanings, and set forth the consequences of embracing one conception of what they signify rather than another.

Our country respects individual achievement, but it also recognizes that what people have achieved often depends on the families they have grown up in, the neighborhoods in which they have lived, and the schools they have attended, as well as on their own ability and hard work. People rightly seek a society in which racial prejudice no longer limits opportunities. But any close observer of American society cannot help but see the many ways in which, covertly and overtly, consciously and unconsciously, actively and as a consequence of inertia, racial differences that have been long in the making continue to thwart aspirations for an open and just society. Words reflect this reality. When an interviewer interested in nomenclature asked the distinguished social psychologist, Kenneth Clark, "What is the best thing for blacks to call themselves," Clark replied: "White."[3]

THE NATURE OF THIS STUDY

Many Americans are uncomfortable about the use of race as a factor in admitting students to selective colleges and professional schools. Critics have attacked the policy on several grounds. They maintain that it is wrong for universities to exclude white applicants with high grades and impressive test scores while accepting minority applicants with lower grades and scores. They point out that admissions officers sometimes accept minority applicants who are not disadvantaged but come from wealthier, more privileged homes and better schools than some applicants who are rejected. They claim that all such policies accentuate racial differences, intensify prejudice, and interfere with progress toward a color-blind society. They assert that admitting minority applicants with

---

[2] See Kravitz et al. 1996. A New York Times/CBS News Poll indicated that "the issue of affirmative action, much like abortion, is particularly sensitive to semantics" (Verhovek 1997b, p. A1). Even more recently, the rewording of a referendum in Houston seems to have played a major role in retaining that city's affirmative action program (Verhovek 1997a, p. A1).

[3] Roberts 1995, p. 7.

lower grades and scores may stigmatize and demoralize the very students that the policy attempts to help, by forcing them to compete with class-mates of greater academic ability.

Defenders of race-sensitive admissions respond with arguments of their own. They insist that such policies are justified to atone for a legacy of oppression and to make up for continuing discrimination in the so-ciety. They point out that admissions officers have long deviated from standardized test scores and prior grades to favor athletes, legacies, and other applicants with special characteristics that are deemed desirable. They argue that admitting a diverse class gives students of all races a better preparation for living and working in an increasingly diverse society.

Until now, the debate has proceeded without much empirical evidence as to the effects of such policies and their consequences for the students involved. The chapters that follow seek to remedy this deficiency by drawing on an extensive study of students from a number of academically selective colleges and universities—places where the debate over race-sensitive institutions has been played out in "real time." We are con-cerned primarily with the performance, in college and after college, of black and white students admitted to these schools.

In setting forth the "facts," as best we can discern them, we recognize that all data of this kind are subject to many interpretations. Moreover, even considering such questions can antagonize people on both sides of the argument who believe that the "right principles" are so compelling that no amount of evidence can change their minds. Plainly, data take us only so far in considering this subject. Individuals who agree on "the facts" may still end up disagreeing about what should be done because of overriding differences in values. As a result, we have no expectation that the analyses presented in this study will resolve complex issues to every-one's satisfaction. But we do hope that our research can inform the debate by framing questions carefully and presenting what we have learned about outcomes.

Of course, it is widely understood that in framing questions and testing hypotheses, investigators are always influenced by their own values and preconceptions. We know that we have been. It would be disingenuous not to acknowledge that both of us came to this study of race-sensitive admissions with a history of having worked hard, over more than three decades, to enroll and educate more diverse student bodies at two of the country's best-known universities. This does not mean that we have fa-vored quotas (we have not) or that we are unaware of how easy it can be for good intentions to lead people astray. Nor have we ever believed that all colleges or universities—including those with which we have been most closely involved—have always made the right choices or implemented every policy perfectly. Still, the fact remains that we are both strongly identified with what we regard as responsible efforts to improve educational opportunities for well-qualified minority students.

At the same time, in contemplating this study, we recognized that race-sensitive admissions policies rested on a set of assumptions that had not heretofore been tested empirically. Much basic information was lacking about such topics as the academic performance of minority students with higher and lower test scores in the most selective colleges and universities, the nature and extent of interaction among different races on campus, and the subsequent careers of minority students accepted through race-sensitive policies. When we began the study, we were far from certain what the data would reveal. Quite possibly, some important assumptions underlying the efforts to enroll more minority students would turn out to be unfounded. Nevertheless, we felt that after thirty years, it was surely time to discover the facts, insofar as it was possible to do so. It was important, we thought, to try to understand and come to terms with any disappointing results as well as to learn from positive outcomes. Now that we have completed our study, we can only say that we have learned a great deal along the way. The image of the river, with its twists and turns and muddy patches, as well as its occasional brilliant vistas, seems exactly right for describing an educational process that has turned out to be even more subtle and complicated than we had imagined it to be when we began our research.

SCOPE OF THE STUDY

This study is limited in several important respects. First, we are concerned solely with higher education. In our view, one problem with much of the debate over affirmative action is that it lumps together a large number of highly disparate areas and programs, ranging from the awarding of contracts to minority-owned businesses to policies governing hiring and promotion to the admissions policies of colleges and universities. The arguments that pertain to one area may or may not apply in other areas. It is noteworthy, for example, that the plaintiffs in the *Piscataway* case, which centered on the layoff of a white secondary school teacher, took pains in their final brief to ask the Supreme Court not to confuse the job-specific issues that confronted the plaintiff with the much broader, and rather different, sets of considerations that face educational institutions in deciding whom to admit.[4]

---

[4] A brief filed with the Court in October 1997 on behalf of the plaintiff states: "University admissions decisions . . . differ critically from local school boards' employment

Within the realm of higher education, we are concerned only with academically selective colleges and universities. The main reason is that the debate surrounding race-sensitive admissions is relevant primarily within these institutions. In colleges and professional schools that admit nearly every qualified applicant, there is little to debate (although there may be arguments over how "qualified" should be defined, and whether the same definition is applied to white and black candidates). It is when there are strict limits on the number of places in an entering class and far more qualified applicants than places, that the choices become difficult and the issue of whether to give weight to race comes to the forefront. Many very well-regarded public universities have broadly inclusive admissions policies at the undergraduate level, and the overall number of selective undergraduate schools is much smaller than many people assume (see Chapter 2). At the graduate and professional level, many schools also take almost every qualified applicant; however, the leading private and public institutions, including almost all accredited schools of law and medicine, select their students from an appreciably larger number of qualified candidates.

The scope of our study is limited in a third way: although we include information about Hispanic students, our work focuses principally on whites and African Americans (whom we usually refer to as "black"). We hope that other inquiries will be able to do full justice to the educational experiences of Hispanics along with those of Native Americans and Asian Americans. One reason for focusing on black and white students in this study is that so much of the debate over race-sensitive admissions policies

---

decisions. Unlike the nuanced, multifaceted decisionmaking process that many universities employ in deciding which students to admit—a process that arguably defies the standard 'underutilization' analysis of employment discrimination law—school boards are able to determine whether their employment decisions have an adverse impact on available, qualified members of minority groups without resorting to racial preferences." (Board of Education of the Township of Piscataway v. Sharon Taxman 1997, p. 40).

It is helpful, in our view, to think of admissions decisions as having many of the attributes of long-term investment decisions involving the creation of human and social capital. The considerations, and especially the risk/reward profiles, that are appropriate to such admissions decisions may be quite different from those that apply elsewhere within the academy itself, never mind outside it. For instance, it may make sense to accept considerably more risk, in return for the possibility of a very high long-term social return, in accepting an applicant for undergraduate study than in appointing a senior professor with tenure. Of course, there are many other differences between admitting students and hiring colleagues, as there are differences between layoffs and new hires. See Bok (1982) for a more general discussion of the differences between affirmative action in admissions and in faculty hiring.

has centered on black-white comparisons.⁵ There are also practical considerations. While Hispanics share many of the problems faced by blacks, there are so many differences in cultures, backgrounds, and circumstances within the broad Hispanic category that any rigorous study would need to make more distinctions than are possible within the confines of our database. Native Americans have also endured many handicaps and injustices and have benefited from race-sensitive admissions policies. Nevertheless, their representation at the academically selective colleges and universities is exceedingly small and does not permit proper statistical analysis in a study of this kind. Thus, however much we would have liked to include comparisons with a variety of groups of Hispanic and Native American matriculants, this was not a practical possibility.

Asian Americans differ from other minorities in important respects. Unlike the case of blacks and Hispanics, the percentage of Asian Americans in selective colleges and universities is far higher than their percentage in the population at large and continues to increase at the institutions included in this study. While there are important and sensitive issues associated with the enrollment of Asian American students (who, like Hispanics, are themselves highly diverse), these are different issues from those that confront admissions offices in considering black candidates.

Finally, our study addresses issues of educational policy. Our objective is not to analyze the development of constitutional law, the proper interpretation of civil rights legislation, or the present holdings of the courts in these areas. We are concerned with the admissions policies that colleges and universities have followed and with their consequences for the country.

THE COLLEGE AND BEYOND DATABASE

Much of the new content in this study derives from exploitation of a rich database called College and Beyond (C&B). This database was built by The Andrew W. Mellon Foundation over nearly four years (from the end of 1994 through 1997) as a part of the Foundation's broader interest in supporting research in higher education. A full explanation of its construction and its components, including links to data compiled by other researchers, is contained in Appendix A. In brief, the part of the database used in this study contains the records of more than eighty thousand undergraduate students who matriculated at twenty-eight academically

⁵ On the issue of which groups should be included in the discussion of race in America, see Shepard (1997); Shepard quotes scholars from the black, Hispanic, and Asian American communities. Shelby Steele is quoted by Shepard as having said: "The real racial divide in America was and remains black and white" (p. 11).

selective colleges and universities in the fall of 1951, the fall of 1976, and the fall of 1989. Created on the explicit understanding that the Foundation would not release or publish data that identified either individual students or individual schools, it is a "restricted access database."

The "in-college" component of the database was compiled from individual student records in collaboration with the participating colleges and universities. For each entering student (except those few cases where records had been lost or were incomplete), the database contains information available at the time the student was admitted, including race, gender, test scores, rank in high school class, and, for many students, information about family background. It also includes records of academic performance in college, compiled mainly from transcripts, which have been linked to the admissions data. Each student record was coded to indicate graduation status (when and if the student graduated), major field of study, grade point average, and whether the student participated in athletics or other time-intensive extracurricular activities.

For many of these same matriculants, we also have extensive survey data describing their subsequent histories (advanced degrees earned, sector of employment, occupation, earned income and family income, involvement in civic activities, marital status and number of children). The respondents were also asked to provide information about where else they applied to college, where they were admitted, whether they did or did not attend their first-choice school, how they now assess their experiences in college, and how satisfied they have been with their lives after college. Finally, for the '89 matriculants only, the survey sought information on the extent to which they interacted (during college and since college) with individuals of different races, political outlooks, socioeconomic backgrounds, and geographic origins. The individuals contacted through the survey were extraordinarily cooperative: the overall sample response rates were 80 percent for the '76 matriculants and 84 percent for the '89 matriculants (Appendix A).

The twenty-eight colleges and universities whose matriculants are included in the C&B database are:

Liberal Arts Colleges	*Research Universities*
Barnard College	Columbia University
Bryn Mawr College	Duke University
Denison University	Emory University
Hamilton College	Miami University (Ohio)
Kenyon College	Northwestern University
Oberlin College	Pennsylvania State University
Smith College	Princeton University

Swarthmore College   Rice University
Wellesley College   Stanford University
Wesleyan University   Tufts University
Williams College   Tulane University
                            University of Michigan at Ann Arbor
                            University of North Carolina at Chapel Hill
                            University of Pennsylvania
                            Vanderbilt University
                            Washington University
                            Yale University

Thus the database includes both liberal arts colleges and research universities, including four public universities, and it reflects some reasonable geographic spread. These colleges and universities are not, however, at all representative of American higher education. They were not intended to be. All of them share the attribute of being academically selective, though the degree of selectivity (as measured by the average combined verbal and math SAT score of the entering class) varies considerably.

In the fall of 1976, eight of the twenty-eight C&B schools had average combined SAT scores of more than 1250 (before the recentering of the scores by ETS which has raised all the scores). Nationally, we estimate that there were only twenty schools in this category, and the eight C&B schools enrolled 40 percent of all freshmen entering these extremely selective colleges and universities. Another thirteen of the C&B schools had average scores of 1150 to 1250; nationally, there were fifty-three schools in this range, and the thirteen C&B schools enrolled 34 percent of all their freshmen. The remaining seven C&B schools had average SAT scores in the 1000–1149 range, and they enrolled 7 percent of all freshmen who entered the 241 schools with SAT scores in this range.[6] In short, the C&B student population contains a sufficiently large fraction of the total number of matriculants at the most selective colleges and universities that we are reasonably confident that our findings apply generally to this set of institutions and especially to those with average scores above 1150.

In building the C&B database, the intention was to assemble data from a group of schools that were similar enough to permit in-depth comparisons, yet different enough to make such comparisons revealing. Being able to observe the full set of entering students at each of the

---

[6] See Appendix Table A.2 for the detailed derivation of these percentages. Estimates of the number of institutions in each SAT interval are based on data provided by the Higher Education Research Institute at UCLA.

participating institutions[7] is a great advantage in studying a subject such as race-sensitive admissions. The large size and census-like character of the database, the strong similarities among the institutions in curricula and admissions standards (with many overlapping applications for admission), and the ability to form coherent clusters of institutions (defined by degree of selectivity and type of school) combine to permit a closer, more intensive examination of black-white differences in outcomes than is possible in studies using national samples of individuals from a larger and more diverse array of institutions. We wanted to be able to examine in detail black-white differences among finely classified subgroups of students: men and women, those with lower and higher SATs, those majoring in a variety of fields, those going on to graduate study and those stopping after receipt of the BA, and so on. We believe that "the shape of the river" must be studied at this level of detail if its course is to be charted accurately.

The other side of the proverbial coin is that because the database was not designed to be "representative," we cannot extrapolate findings from these institutions to the whole of higher education. There are, however, national longitudinal databases that do permit researchers to work with sample data for schools that are much more representative of higher education in general.[8] The objective was to complement the existing longitudinal databases by creating a new resource that would permit more detailed analyses within a circumscribed set of institutions.

METHODS OF ANALYSIS

This study is highly quantitative. In describing and presenting our work, we have used the simplest techniques that are consistent with the obligation to report meaningful results. Most of the findings are presented in the form of tabulations or cross-tabulations, and we make extensive use of bar charts and other figures (from which the main story line of the book can be read).

We also use other standard techniques, primarily multivariate regres-

---

[7] This is a slight overstatement. We include the full entering cohorts at twenty-four of the twenty-eight institutions; for the other four institutions, we included all the black matriculants and a sample of approximately half of the white matriculants (see Appendix A).

[8] National longitudinal databases include: Beginning Postsecondary Student Longitudinal Study (BPS), Baccalaureate and Beyond (B&B), National Longitudinal Survey of 1972 (NLS), High School and Beyond Longitudinal Study (HS&B), and National Education Longitudinal Study of 1988 (NELS).

sions, to disentangle the many forces that jointly affect student performance in college, receipt of advanced degrees, and later-life outcomes. While we have no doubt failed to include enough of this finer-grained analysis to satisfy many empirically minded social scientists, we may well have included too much for readers who want only to know "the bottom line." (A considerable amount of explanatory material appears in footnotes.) Our goal has been to achieve the balance that allows us to isolate the effects of different variables—and to understand their interactions—without drifting too far from commonsense questions and answers. Throughout, we have done our best to explain our findings and our methods in language that lay readers can understand.

The methods used to analyze the data are described in Appendix B. We have also included a great deal of material in additional tables in Appendix D in an effort to make it as easy as possible for readers to check our interpretations, and, if they choose, to substitute their own. In due course, we expect others, using more sophisticated econometric techniques, to extend the analysis presented here. In many instances, the simple methods we employ can only suggest directions and permit what we hope are informed judgments concerning relationships.

We have devoted a great deal of effort to providing precisely defined national benchmarks that allow the results for the C&B schools to be seen in context. It is important, for example, to compare the earnings of the black graduates of the C&B schools with the earnings of all black holders of BAs who graduated at roughly the same time and to provide the same data for white graduates. In making all such comparisons (as well as comparisons among various groupings of schools included in the C&B database), we confront the problem of selection bias. The process by which students choose colleges and by which colleges choose students is, of course, anything but random, and such a complicated selection process produces outcomes that are independent of the variables we are able to study. We have done our best to deal with this problem by introducing appropriate controls and by attempting to calibrate some of the remaining effects of this double-selection process, but we do not claim to have found a full resolution to this often intractable problem.

In addition to the many statistics, figures, and tables, we have included in the book some brief personal reflections provided for the most part by individuals who participated in the C&B surveys. These accounts are intended to be only illustrative. Our hope is that they will provide some sense of the kinds of experiences and feelings that underlie the rather antiseptic numbers that appear in such abundance. We would have been reluctant to include these observations—even though many of them are quite revealing—had we not first built the statistical foundation upon which they rest. The stories are meant to amplify the empirical findings and to be thought-provoking, but not to "prove" or confirm any of our interpretations.

ORGANIZATION OF THE BOOK

Chapter 1 describes the origins and evolution of race-sensitive admissions policies in the context of other changes in American society.

Chapter 2 discusses the admissions process and describes how race affects the odds of being admitted to selective colleges. The chapter then proposes an operational definition of a "race-neutral" standard and develops estimates of how many black students in the '89 cohort would not have been admitted to certain C&B schools if such a standard had been applied.

Chapter 3 describes how 1976 and 1989 matriculants fared academically in college—the number who graduated, the majors they chose, how the grades of students varied with their SAT scores, and how black students performed in relation to how we might have expected them to do on the basis of pre-collegiate indicators.

Chapter 4 follows the '76 and '89 matriculants from college to graduate and professional schools and charts how many of them (classified by rank in class as well as race) went on to earn PhDs or degrees in professional fields such as law, medicine, and business.

Chapter 5 explores how the 1976 C&B matriculants have done in the marketplace—how many are employed, how much money they have earned, and how satisfied they are with their jobs. We compare blacks and whites, women and men, and C&B graduates with graduates of all colleges nationwide.

Chapter 6 is concerned with the lives of C&B matriculants outside of the workplace. We examine their civic contributions, marital status, family income, and their own assessments of how satisfied they are with their lives.

Chapter 7 describes the matriculants' responses when asked to look back and give their impressions of what they learned in college, and whether, given the opportunity, they would go back to the same school, choose the same major, and spend their time in the same ways.

Chapter 8 examines how much interaction took place across racial and other lines among the 1989 C&B matriculants and reports on the extent to which students from three different eras (those who entered in 1951, 1976, and 1989) agree or disagree with the degree of emphasis that their colleges have placed on recruiting a racially and ethnically diverse student body.

In Chapter 9, we draw together the major findings from the earlier chapters and discuss their implications for the principal arguments that have been used to criticize race-sensitive admissions policies.

Finally, in Chapter 10, we present our own conclusions concerning the role of race in the admissions process and how concepts such as "fairness" and "merit" should be interpreted.

ACKNOWLEDGMENTS

There is no way we can thank adequately the small army of people who have worked so hard on this study. The evident importance of the subject, and the privilege of being able, perhaps, to contribute something of value to a wrenching national debate, surely account in large measure for the willingness of all of those mentioned below, and others not mentioned, to go far beyond any definition of the call of duty.

We begin by thanking our four principal collaborators:

- James Shulman, The Andrew W. Mellon Foundation's Administrative and Financial Officer as well as a program and research associate, has had a hand (and a considerable brain) in every facet of the study. He deserves principal credit for having worked tirelessly with individuals at the institutions in the College and Beyond database, as well as with colleagues at the Foundation and others outside it, to guide the construction of a scholarly resource of immense value. He then participated actively in the analysis of the data, in the drafting and editing of chapters, and in the final passage of the manuscript through what must surely have seemed like an endless swamp rather than a smooth flowing river.
- Thomas Nygren, Director of the Princeton office of the Foundation and also the Foundation's Director of Technology (as well as the program officer responsible for grantmaking in South Africa), has overseen all of the technical work that went into the building of the C&B database with characteristic skill and patience. He has also been responsible for supervising the regression analysis and has taken a principal role (with Stacy Berg Dale) in drafting Appendix A and Appendix B and, more generally, in insisting that the subject deserves the most thoroughgoing effort to respect the underlying data.
- Stacy Berg Dale, a Research Associate in the Foundation's Princeton office, has mastered the intricacies of the C&B database. We have depended heavily on her unusual talent for thinking—by reflex, it seems—in terms of multivariate regressions. She has used this talent to challenge conclusions that might have been

accepted at face value, to range freely in exploring alternative hypotheses, and to keep to an absolute minimum the number of arbitrary assumptions and inconsistencies that intrude on any research of this kind.

• Lauren Meserve, a Research Associate in the Foundation's New York office, has worked tirelessly to ensure that the underlying empirical analysis was done correctly and to design the charts and figures that provide the main storyline for the analysis. She has an exceptional range of quantitative and qualitative skills and has been, from start to finish, tenacious in using these talents to improve the research and the presentation of the results.

It is no exaggeration to say that this study could not have been done without the crisp intelligence and unflagging dedication of these four collaborators.

Other colleagues at the Foundation also made valuable contributions. In the Princeton office, Susan Anderson checked and re-checked the text, made many suggestions for improving the exposition, assisted in the preparation of the list of references cited, and was our principal liaison with Princeton University Press. Douglas Mills was enormously helpful in providing advice on statistical questions and in extracting data from the Census and other national databases. Joyce Pierre, Dorothy Westgate, Jennifer Dicke, and Deborah Peikes all made important contributions to what was clearly a group effort. Earlier in the project, Fredrick Vars, now completing his studies at the Yale Law School, was instrumental in constructing the institutional files that underlie the C&B database and in doing initial empirical work on black-white differences in the relation between SAT scores and academic performance. In New York, David Crook also helped organize data and explore various empirical questions.

Still other Mellon Foundation staff members provided an unfailing stream of criticism and suggestions as they read versions of the manuscript. Foremost among this group is Harriet Zuckerman, who read more versions of the manuscript than anyone and did so much to improve the clarity of both the analysis and the exposition. Mary Patterson McPherson, T. Dennis Sullivan, Stephanie Bell-Rose, Jackie Looney, and Henry Drewry also read the manuscript carefully and made useful comments. Pat Woodford, Kamla Motihar, and Ulrica Konvalin proved over and over again their willingness to do whatever was needed to bring the project to conclusion. In Cambridge, Connie Higgins has been of enormous help in a project that tested the patience of all who were caught up in its wake.

We are very fortunate to have benefited from a close reading of the manuscript by outstanding scholars who contributed many valuable suggestions: David Featherman, Director of the Institute of Social Research at the University of Michigan; Randall Kennedy, Professor of Law at the Harvard Law School; Alan Krueger, Bendheim Professor of Economics at Princeton University; three other economists who are now college or university presidents—Richard Levin (Yale University), Michael McPherson (Macalester College), and Harold Shapiro (Princeton University); Michael Nettles, Professor of Education at the University of Michigan; Sarah Turner, Assistant Professor of Education and Economics at the University of Virginia; and Gilbert Whitaker, another economist who is now Dean of the Jones Graduate School of Administration at Rice University. Professors Richard Light of Harvard University, Daniel Kahneman of Princeton University, John Simon of the Yale Law School, and Claire Simon commented on particular chapters. Charles E. Exley, Jr., retired Chairman of NCR Corporation and a Trustee of The Andrew W. Mellon Foundation, also read the manuscript with great care and made extremely insightful comments—which he transmitted to us from the Sudan! At an earlier stage in the study, Professors David Card, now at the University of California at Berkeley, and Orley Ashenfelter of Princeton University, contributed to the shaping of the research design.

Robert K. Merton of Columbia University and Arnold Rampersad of Princeton University provided knowing advice concerning the title of the book and the preface. Alan Rosenbaum, Director of the Art Museum at Princeton, was heroic in his efforts to find just the right cover illustration (he succeeded, we think).

In our initial efforts to collect institutional records, we were joined by an exceptional group of people at the twenty-eight participating institutions, many of whom worked nights and weekends to generate the raw files we needed. It is only limitations of space that prevent us from thanking each of them, and their presidents, for having had the faith to participate so actively in the construction of the C&B database.

The survey component of the database, which plays such a vital role in the analysis, could not have been created without the thoughtful contributions of Herbert Abelson of the Survey Research Center of Princeton University and Geraldine Mooney and her colleagues at Mathematica Policy Research (the entity that administered the surveys so successfully, as is documented in Appendix A). We also want to thank the forty-five thousand individuals who took the time to complete the surveys so carefully and often volunteered additional comments. Many of these former students obviously care, and care deeply, about the questions we have been studying.

As a companion project, the Foundation commissioned the creation of a national control group survey (described in Appendix A); Norman Bradburn and Allen Sanderson of the National Opinion Research

Center in Chicago did yeoman work in completing this part of the project.

We were also able to link the core of the C&B database to two other large databases that complemented the information we were able to collect directly. Donald Stewart and his colleagues at the College Entrance Examination Board and the Educational Testing Service, and Alexander Astin, Director of the Higher Education Research Institute at UCLA, and his colleagues at the Cooperative Institutional Research Project, understood what we were trying to accomplish and were determined to help. In addition, Linda Wightman, former Vice President of the Law School Admission Council and now a faculty member at the University of North Carolina, Greensboro, went to extra efforts to provide detailed data on law school students.

In order to learn more at first hand about the interest of businesses and professional associations in the recruitment of minority students, we contacted many knowledgeable individuals. Thomas Schick at American Express, Ira Millstein and Marsha Simms at Weil Gotschal & Manges, Jeffrey Brinck and Christina Wagner at Milbank Tweed Hadley & McCloy, Richard Fisher and Marilyn Booker at Morgan Stanley, and Marc Lackritz at the Securities Industry Association in Washington, D.C., were all extremely generous with their time. Subsequently, Glenda Burkhart has been responsible for involving representatives of the business, professional, and academic communities in thinking about the implications of this research.

We have been fortunate, too, in our publisher. Walter Lippincott, Peter Dougherty, Neil Litt, and their colleagues at Princeton University Press made it clear from the outset that for them this project was in no way "business as usual." They have worked diligently to publish a complex book at their usual high standard under extraordinary time constraints.

Finally, we wish to thank the Trustees of The Andrew W. Mellon Foundation for their appreciation of what we have tried to do, their financial support, and their understanding (nay, their insistence) that we would, of course, come to our own conclusions. The arguments developed in this book represent our own thinking, and none of the Trustees of the Foundation, nor any of the others who provided so much advice and help, should be implicated in the results. Whatever faults remain, despite the efforts of so many to "get it right," are solely our responsibility.

William G. Bowen
Derek Bok

May 1998

THE SHAPE OF THE RIVER

CHAPTER 1

Historical Context

FEW PEOPLE today recall the full measure of the predicament in which African Americans found themselves prior to World War II. In 1940, most black men and women lived out of common view in rural communities, chiefly in the South. Approximately 90 percent lived in poverty (measured by today's criteria).[1] Their annual earnings were less than half those of whites. The education they received was markedly inferior in quality. African American children in the South went to predominantly black schools, in which (on average) pupil-teacher ratios were one-quarter greater than those in white schools, school terms were 10 percent shorter, and black teachers were paid half the salary of white teachers.[2] The median amount of education received by blacks aged 25–29 was about seven years.[3] Only 12 percent of blacks aged 25–29 had completed high school; less than 2 percent could claim a college degree.[4]

Very few blacks managed to enter the higher-paying occupations. Only 1.8 percent of all male professionals were black, and only 1.3 percent of all male managers and proprietors.[5] Blacks made up 2.8 percent of physicians, 0.5 percent of attorneys, and 0.5 percent of engineers. No more than thirty-three elected officials in the entire United States were black. Of these, one was a member of Congress, but there were no mayors, governors, or senators. Only a single African American sat on the federal bench.[6]

World War II brought an unprecedented demand for factory labor and a new wave of migration to the North, trends that did much to better the material circumstances of blacks. The sustained economic growth that followed the war accomplished even more. From 1940 to 1960, black poverty rates declined from roughly 93 to 55 percent, while expected lifetime earnings as a percentage of the prevailing levels for

---

[1] Jaynes and Williams 1989, p. 277.

[2] Card and Krueger 1992b, p. 167.

[3] Jaynes and Williams 1989, p. 334.

[4] U.S. Department of Education 1997, p. 17.

[5] Jaynes and Williams 1989, p. 273.

[6] Data on the professions are from the U.S. Bureau of the Census 1940, tab. 6; data on public service are from Jaynes and Williams 1989, pp. 240, 243.

whites rose from 42 to 50 percent for men and from 56 to 72 percent for women.[7]

Educational levels also increased as millions of blacks moved from the rural South to the urban North and as Southern states improved black schools in an effort to slow the outward migration of cheap labor. By 1960, even in the South, teachers' salaries and the length of the school term were approximately equal in black and white schools, and the high pupil-teacher ratios for black schools had declined to within approximately 10 percent of the average level in predominantly white schools.[8] Meanwhile, median years of schooling for blacks aged 25–29 grew from approximately 7 years in 1940 to 10.5 years in 1960.[9] Over the same period, the proportion of blacks aged 25–29 who had graduated from high school increased from 12.3 to 38.6 percent, and the percentage graduating from college rose from 1.6 to 5.4 percent.[10]

Despite these gains, little progress occurred in opening elite occupations to African Americans. The percentage of all professionals who were black rose to 3.8 percent for men and 6.0 percent for women, while the percentages of managers and proprietors who were black grew only to 3.0 percent for men and 1.8 percent for women.[11] The percentage of physicians who were black, only 2.8 in 1940, failed to increase at all during the ensuing 20 years. Meanwhile, the proportion of attorneys who were black rose only from 0.5 percent to 1.2 percent, while the percentage of black engineers remained the same.[12] The number of black elected officials jumped from 33 in 1941 to 280 in 1965, but even this total was only a tiny fraction of the thousands of elected offices throughout the nation. No more than four African Americans sat in Congress (less than 1 percent of all members), and there were still no senators. The largest gains came at the lower levels of government, with increasing numbers of blacks serving as state legislators (26 to 102), mayors (0 to 3), city council members (4 to 74), and school board members (2 to 68). In 1961, only four federal judges were black.[13]

The early postwar period also brought several Supreme Court rulings that changed the impact of the Constitution on African Americans. Most of these decisions involved educational opportunity. A 1938 Supreme

[7] Jaynes and Williams 1989, pp. 278, 295. The changes in the economic and educational status of blacks and Hispanics since 1940 have been described more recently by Reynolds Farley (1996, pp. 208ff.).

[8] Card and Krueger 1992, p. 168.

[9] Jaynes and Williams 1989, p. 335.

[10] U.S. Department of Education 1997, p. 17.

[11] Jaynes and Williams 1989, p. 273.

[12] U.S. Bureau of the Census 1940, 1960.

[13] Jaynes and Williams 1989, pp. 240, 243.

Court opinion had found that Missouri had violated the Equal Protection Clause of the Fourteenth Amendment by barring blacks from attending the state university's law school, giving them tuition money instead to attend an out-of-state law school.[14] In 1949, the Court went further, ruling that Texas could not satisfy the Fourteenth Amendment by establishing a separate law school for blacks.[15] Finally, in 1954, a unanimous Supreme Court handed down its celebrated decision in *Brown v. Board of Education,* putting an end to de jure school segregation in the South.[16]

As events unfolded, the early effects of *Brown* proved to be limited. Although the prohibition against segregation was quickly extended to public transportation and other state-owned facilities, these rulings were not widely enforced. Southern politicians uniformly denounced the school desegregation decision, and white citizens' councils sprang up in countless Southern communities to harass any black who advocated desegregation.

Responding to these developments, blacks began to organize.[17] The Montgomery, Alabama, bus boycott in 1955–1956 brought Dr. Martin Luther King, Jr., to prominence and launched a long series of efforts to desegregate public transportation, schools, and places of public accommodation throughout the South. During the rest of the decade, however, the federal government refused to take decisive action to secure the rights of blacks. Faced with open defiance by an Arkansas governor, President Eisenhower reluctantly sent federal troops to Little Rock to enforce a court order to integrate the schools, but the executive branch did little more to hasten the end of segregation. Congress did even less, passing a Civil Rights Act in 1957 that was too weak to have much effect in breaching the barriers to black voter registration in the South.

THE ORIGINS AND DEVELOPMENT OF RACE-SENSITIVE ADMISSIONS POLICIES

In 1960, then, the outlook for blacks seemed highly uncertain. Their economic position had improved greatly but was still vastly inferior to that of whites. Although they had acquired important new constitutional

---

[14] Missouri *ex rel.* Gaines v. Canada, 305 U.S. 337 (1938).

[15] Sweatt v. Painter, 339 U.S. 629 (1950).

[16] 347 U.S. 483 (1954).

[17] A succinct summary of the struggle for civil rights can be found in Thernstrom and Thernstrom (1997, esp. pp. 97–180). Among the many extended treatments, see Kluger (1975).

rights, these Supreme Court rulings had not yet produced much tangible change. Moreover, the role of blacks in the nation's power structure was virtually nonexistent. Very few African Americans held public office, and few had entered the elite occupations and professions. Virtually no blacks could be found in the country's leading corporations, banks, hospitals, or law firms. Erwin Smigel reported in his 1960s study of Wall Street law firms: "In the year and a half that was spent interviewing, I only heard of three Negroes who had been hired by large law firms. Two of these were women who did not meet the client."[18] Colleges and professional schools enrolled few black students. In 1965, only 4.8 percent of all U.S. college students were African American.[19]

The position of blacks in selective colleges and universities was, if anything, even more marginal than in higher education as a whole. Occasionally, a particular college demonstrated a desire to attract black students. As early as 1835, the Oberlin board of trustees declared that "the education of the people of color is a matter of great interest and should be encouraged and sustained in this institution."[20] Beginning in 1941, Antioch College took steps to recruit black students and managed to enroll 123 black undergraduates before discontinuing the program in 1955. Even before World War II, universities such as Rutgers and the University of California, Los Angeles, featured a Paul Robeson or a Jackie Robinson on their football teams. It is probably safe to say, however, that prior to 1960, no selective college or university was making determined efforts to seek out and admit substantial numbers of African Americans.

In the fall of 1951, black students averaged 0.8 percent of the entering class at the nineteen College and Beyond schools for which adequate records are available; the range was from zero at four schools to a high of 3 percent at Oberlin, and the percentage of black matriculants exceeded 1 percent at only five other C&B schools. Overall, there were 63 black matriculants in these nineteen entering classes.[21] The faces in the college yearbooks tell the same story graphically.

By the end of the 1950s, faint stirrings of interest had begun to appear.[21] In 1959, the director of admissions at Mount Holyoke College started to visit "schools which might provide promising Negro appli-

[18] Smigel 1969, p. 45.

[19] Hacker 1983, p. 247.

[20] Cited in Duffy and Goldberg (1997, p. 137). Chapter 5 of this book provides an informative account of the earliest beginnings of active recruitment of minority students by selective liberal arts colleges and is also the source of the account below of "stirrings of interest" at colleges such as Mount Holyoke and Wellesley.

[21] The College and Beyond database is described in the Preface and in Appendix A. The 0.8 percent figure cited in the text is an unweighted average of the percentages at the individual C&B schools.

cants," and the college actually enrolled a total of ten black students in 1964.[22] In 1963, Wellesley College introduced a junior-year program for black students attending colleges supported by the United Negro College Fund. Dartmouth, Princeton, and Yale all established special summer enrichment programs to prepare promising disadvantaged students for possible admission to selective colleges.

By the mid-1960s, amid a rising concern over civil rights, a number of schools began to recruit black students. Nevertheless, the numbers actually enrolled remained small, with blacks making up only 1 percent of the enrollments of selective New England colleges in 1965, according to one estimate.[23] The reasons were clear enough. As one author put it, "The selective colleges would rather be selective than integrated."[24] Accordingly, although they might recruit black students vigorously, they did not significantly modify their regular standards for admission and financial aid. Their academic requirements were too demanding to accommodate more than a tiny number of African American students, and their tuition and fees were more than most of those who were admitted could afford.

Similarly, few blacks were enrolled in the nation's professional schools. In 1965, barely 1 percent of all law students in America were black, and over one-third of them were enrolled in all-black schools.[25] Barely 2 percent of all medical students were African American, and more than three-fourths of them attended two all-black institutions, Howard University and Meharry Medical College.[26] It was in this context that Harvard Law School dean, Erwin Griswold (later solicitor general of the United States), undertook to increase the number of black students. Griswold was struck by the fact that law had come to play a crucial role in the lives of American blacks, yet virtually no black students were enrolled in the Harvard Law School or any other predominantly white law school. In 1965, therefore, he launched a special summer program for juniors from historically black colleges to interest them in attending law school. One year later, Harvard began admitting black students with test scores far below those of their white classmates. The strategy that Griswold employed was adopted by other law schools, and black enrollment began to rise.

Over this same period, the civil rights struggle had been intensifying throughout the country. In 1960, black students in North Carolina began a series of sit-ins to protest segregation at Woolworth stores and other

---

[22] Duffy and Goldberg 1997, pp. 138–39.
[23] Kendrick 1967, p. 6.
[24] Ibid.
[25] O'Neil 1970, p. 300.
[26] Nickens, Ready, and Petersdorf 1994, p. 472.

retail establishments. In 1961, black and white freedom riders boarded buses bound for the deep South to protest continued segregation in buses and other forms of public transportation. In 1962, a federal judge ordered the University of Mississippi to admit a black student, James Meredith, and violence erupted as Governor Ross Barnett ordered state troopers to block Meredith's entry. The following year, Governor George Wallace tried to keep two black students from attending the University of Alabama, the last remaining all-white state university. In 1965, police reacted with violence to a peaceful voting rights march in Selma, Alabama.

Meanwhile, as protests continued, public opinion in the country gradually shifted in favor of blacks. Eventually, Congress was moved to act. In 1964, President Johnson signed into law a Civil Rights Act committing the government to serious efforts to dismantle state-enforced segregation. In 1965, following the bloody police action at Selma, Congress passed a Voting Rights Act with real teeth. Almost immediately, black registration levels and election turnouts began to rise rapidly throughout the South.

As the 1960s progressed, the government's efforts on behalf of blacks grew more determined. A policy of simple nondiscrimination gave way to a requirement that companies contracting with the federal government make deliberate efforts to identify and consider minority applicants for employment. In June 1965, at Howard University, President Johnson delivered his now famous justification for moving beyond nondiscrimination to a more vigorous, affirmative effort to provide opportunities for black Americans: "You do not take a person who, for years, has been hobbled by chains and liberate him, bring him up to the starting line in a race and then say, 'you are free to compete with all the others,' and still justly believe that you have been completely fair."[27] Soon, the Office of Federal Contract Compliance and the Equal Employment Opportunity Commission were requiring federal contractors to submit elaborate plans that included goals and timetables for assembling a workforce reflecting the availability of minority employees in the relevant labor market. Before long, these requirements were extended beyond the recruitment of black workers to include Hispanics, Asian Americans, and Native Americans.

In the years that followed, almost all leading colleges and professional schools came to believe that they had a role to play in educating minority students. Often spurred by student protests on their own campuses, university officials initiated active programs to recruit minority applicants

---

[27] Reprinted in Rainwater and Yancey 1967, p. 126.

and to take race into account in the admissions process by accepting qualified black students even if they had lower grades and test scores than most white students. A few universities said that they were acting out of a desire to rectify past racial injustices. As the chapters that follow will elaborate, however, most college and university leaders adopted these policies for two other reasons, both closely related to the traditional aims of their institutions. To begin with, they sought to enrich the education of all their students by including race as another element in assembling a diverse student body of varying talents, backgrounds, and perspectives. In addition, perceiving a widely recognized need for more members of minority groups in business, government, and the professions, they acted on the conviction that minority students would have a special opportunity to become leaders in all walks of life.

These efforts soon bore fruit. According to one study, the percentage of blacks enrolled in Ivy League colleges rose from 2.3 in 1967 to 6.3 in 1976, while the percentages in other "prestigious" colleges grew from 1.7 to 4.8.[28] Meanwhile, the proportion of black medical students had climbed to 6.3 percent by 1975, and black law students had increased their share to 4.5 percent.[29]

Much had changed, however, from the early efforts to recruit black students to the approaches followed at the time the '76 C&B matriculants were admitted. The exuberance and strong ideological commitment that were so evident in the late 1960s and early 1970s had led many colleges to place an emphasis on recruiting truly disadvantaged students from the ghettos. It was frequently assumed that once minority students were admitted, they would fit in "naturally," as earlier groups of newcomers had done. In fact, however, the absorption of black students into higher education did not prove to be a simple matter.[30] Some black students were disillusioned by their experiences in white institutions, and there was considerable debate on many campuses about admissions criteria, support programs, residential arrangements, and curricular offerings. Student protests in the late 1960s and early 1970s—which were closely tied to the Vietnam War—were but a visible manifestation of recurring efforts to reconcile differences in perspectives and priorities.

While selective colleges and universities continued to work hard to recruit minority students—often increasing their admissions staffs for this purpose—the numbers of black matriculants at these schools began to plateau. Also, by the mid- to late 1970s, many liberal arts colleges had

[28] Karen 1991, pp. 208, 217.

[29] Blackwell 1987, pp. 103, 290.

[30] See Peterson et al. (1978), for a detailed analysis of the period 1968–1975.

"discontinued their initiatives aimed at enrolling high-risk or under-prepared blacks," while adopting other modes of minority recruitment.[31] The '76 C&B matriculants reflect this shift in emphasis.

The law had played little part in increasing minority enrollments. In fact, some university administrators worried that race-sensitive admissions might run afoul of Title VI of the Civil Rights Act, which states: "No person in the United States shall, on grounds of race, color, or national origin, . . . be subjected to discrimination under any program or activity receiving Federal financial assistance." By the early 1970s, however, federal officials had incorporated reports on student enrollment into the affirmative action plans they required of universities, thus seeming to make race-conscious admissions not merely permissible but mandatory.

In 1978, a challenge to the legality of such admissions policies under Title VI of the Civil Rights Act finally reached the Supreme Court in the *Bakke* case, involving a white student who claimed that he had been wrongfully excluded from the medical school of the University of California, Davis, to make room for minority applicants with inferior academic records.[32] The Court was sharply divided. Four justices found that the system of racial quotas used by the medical school was discriminatory, and hence violated "the plain language" of Title VI. Four justices upheld the admissions procedure as a necessary device to overcome the effects of past discrimination, with Justice Blackmun writing, "In order to get beyond racism, we must first take account of race."[33] The deciding opinion was written by Justice Lewis Powell. Powell condemned the use of rigid quotas in admitting minority students and found that efforts to overcome "societal discrimination" did not justify policies that disadvantaged particular individuals, such as Bakke, who bore no responsibility for any wrongs suffered by minorities. At the same time, as a means to secure the educational benefits of a student body of diverse backgrounds and experience, he ruled that admissions officers could "take race into account" as one of several factors in evaluating minority applicants in comparison with other candidates.

On the authority of Justice Powell's decisive opinion in *Bakke*, virtually all selective colleges and professional schools have continued to consider race in admitting students. The period from 1975 to 1985, however, was a difficult one for many colleges and universities because of the severe financial pressures brought about by the oil crisis and stagflation. These pressures affected financial aid budgets at many institutions, drove up

---

[31] Duffy and Goldberg 1997, p. 152.

[32] 438 U.S. 265 (1978).

[33] Ibid., p. 407.

tuition, and in general made it harder to build on previous efforts to enroll a more diverse student population. As a general rule, black enrollments did not decline as a percentage of total enrollment, but they did stop increasing.

As the economic circumstances of colleges and universities improved in the latter half of the 1980s, there was "a resurgence in recruitment."[34] It was not only administrators, faculty members, and current students who stressed the need to continue—and, if possible, augment—efforts to enroll talented minority students. For example, John Anderson, the dean of admissions at Kenyon College, recalled that parents would comment that Kenyon was "too sheltered" and that their children needed to be exposed to people from different backgrounds.[35] At the same time, competition for places at the most selective colleges and universities was intensifying; black students were now competing not only with rising numbers of extremely well-qualified white candidates but also with much larger numbers of well prepared Asian Americans and Hispanics. The result was that the percentages of black students remained largely constant through the 1980s, while the relative numbers of Asian Americans and Hispanics increased.[36]

Looking back over the whole period from the beginning of the civil rights movement to the present day, we see that the percentage of black students graduating from colleges and professional schools has grown enormously. From 1960 to 1995, the percentage of blacks aged 25 to 29 who had graduated from college rose from 5.4 to 15.4 per-

---

[34] Duffy and Goldberg 1997, p. 155.

[35] Quoted in Duffy and Goldberg 1997, p. 156.

[36] During the 1960s, most universities seeking to enroll a more racially diverse student body concentrated on black students. It was soon apparent, however, that other groups, especially Hispanics, also suffered from inferior schools, low enrollments in colleges and universities, and scant representation in management and the professions. In 1970, more than half of all Americans over the age of twenty-five had completed high school, but less than one-third of all Hispanics possessed a high school diploma. Whereas 10.7 percent of whites had graduated from colleges, only 4.5 percent of Hispanics possessed a BA (U.S. Bureau of the Census 1997, tab. 243, p. 159). Only 2 percent of all managers and administrators and less than 1 percent of all lawyers were Hispanic (Reddy 1995, p. 506). Against this backdrop, students began to protest the failure of selective colleges and professional schools to seek out Hispanic applicants. By the early 1970s, almost all of these institutions had responded by expanding their minority recruitment programs to include not only Hispanics but Native Americans as well. Along with the admission of women to traditionally single-sex colleges, the rapid rise in applications from Asian Americans, and the influx of many more foreign students, the growth in the number of minority students was a major element in the enrollment of much more diverse student bodies in all selective institutions.

cent.[37] In the nation's law schools, the percentage of blacks grew from barely 1 percent in 1960 to 7.5 percent by 1995.[38] Similarly, the percentage of medical students who were black climbed from 2.2 percent in 1964 to 8.1 percent in 1995.[39] Although figures for Hispanics are not available for years prior to 1970, the percentage of Hispanics twenty-five years of age or older with a college degree more than doubled, from 4.5 percent in 1970 to 9.3 percent in 1995; since 1981, their share of professional and doctoral degrees has nearly doubled.[40]

SOCIETAL CONSEQUENCES

These trends have led to striking gains in the representation of minorities in the most lucrative and influential occupations. By 1996, blacks made up 8.6 percent of all male professionals and 13.1 percent of all female professionals (up from 3.8 percent and 6 percent in 1960). They also accounted for 8.3 percent of all male executives, managers and administrators and 9.6 percent of all females in such positions (up from 3 percent and 1.8 percent).[41] From 1960 to 1990, blacks almost doubled their share of the nation's physicians and almost tripled their share of attorneys and engineers.[42] From 1965 to 1995, black representation in Congress increased from four to 41 members, and the total number of black elected officials rose from a scant 280 in 1965 to 7,984 in 1993.[43] Hispanics also made impressive gains. From 1983 to 1996, they increased their share of executives, managers, and administrators from 2.8 percent to 4.8 percent and their proportion of professionals from 2.5 percent to 4.3 percent.[44]

The growing numbers of blacks graduating from colleges and professional schools, and the consequent increase in black managers and professionals, have led to the gradual emergence of a larger black middle class. In 1990, 20 percent of blacks were managers or professionals, up from only 5 percent in 1950.[45] The proportion of blacks earning more than $50,000 per year rose from 5.8 percent in 1967 to 13 percent in

[37] U.S. Department of Education 1997, p. 17.
[38] Nettles and Perna 1997, p. 330.
[39] Nickens, Ready, and Petersdorf 1994, p. 472; Association of American Medical Colleges 1996, p. 73.
[40] U.S. Bureau of the Census 1997, pp. 159, 194.
[41] Jaynes and Williams 1989, p. 273; U.S. Bureau of Labor Statistics 1998.
[42] U.S. Bureau of the Census 1960, 1990.
[43] Jaynes and Williams 1989, p. 240; U.S. Bureau of the Census 1997, pp. 281, 286.
[44] U.S. Bureau of the Census 1997, p. 405.
[45] Hochschild 1995, p. 43.

1992.[46] These developments contrasted sharply with the condition of blacks possessing only a high school education or less. From 1967 to 1992, the share of total black income received by the most affluent 20 percent of blacks rose from 44.6 percent to 48.8 percent, while the share received by the poorest fifth fell from 4.7 percent to only 3 percent.[47] After the rate of economic growth declined sharply in the early 1970s, the incomes of the most affluent 20 percent of blacks continued to rise at virtually the same rate as the incomes of their white counterparts, while the bottom 20 percent of blacks saw their incomes fall at more than twice the rate for similarly situated whites.[48]

With all the progress that has occurred since the 1960s, the black middle class is still much smaller proportionately than the white middle class. Blacks are less than half as likely as whites to earn $50,000 a year. Moreover, their economic position is even more precarious, since even the highest-earning blacks have less than a quarter of the net financial assets of whites earning comparable incomes.[49] Still, the entry of so many highly educated blacks into the ranks of managers and professionals must count as the principal success story for African Americans in the past twenty-five years.

The growth of minority managers and professionals has been encouraged by a widespread recognition of the pressing need for greater diversity at all levels of responsibility and in all walks of life. Evidence of this recognition is provided by the actions of leaders throughout government, business, and the professions. It is reflected in the efforts of every U.S. president since Lyndon Johnson to appoint a diverse cabinet and to achieve diversity in other federal appointments. It is manifest in the programs initiated by the American Bar Association and the American Medical Association to attract more minoritiy lawyers and doctors into their professions and into leading law firms and hospitals. It is underscored by the policies and practices of major companies. As Louis V. Gerstner, Chairman and CEO of IBM, has said: "Inclusion is a time-honored aspect of our corporate culture. We're a diverse organization by design, not mandate. The practices and policies we follow . . . were in place many years before required by law. . . ."[50]

The reasons why diversity has become so important at the highest levels of business, the professions, government, and society at large are readily apparent. By the year 2030, approximately 40 percent of all Amer-

[46] Ibid., p. 44. Income reported in constant 1992 dollars.
[47] Hochschild 1995, p. 48.
[48] Ibid., p. 49.
[49] Oliver and Shapiro 1995, p. 101.
[50] Executive Leadership Council 1998, p. 59.

icans are projected to be members of minority groups.[51] It will surely be more difficult for government officials to produce enlightened policies and harder still to enjoy the confidence of the minority community if an overwhelmingly white cabinet and Congress are making the decisions affecting the lives of such an increasingly diverse, multiracial society.

Similar considerations apply to business. More than $600 billion in purchasing power is generated by minorities and more than one-third of all new entrants to the workforce are persons of color. In this environment, a diverse corporate leadership can be valuable both to understand the markets in which many companies sell and to recruit, manage, and motivate the workforce on which corporate performance ultimately depends. Two statements by corporate CEOs make these points forcefully:[52]

> At The Coca-Cola Company, we remain focused on taking actions that serve us best over the long run. That includes building strong management teams and a diverse workforce. As a company that operates in nearly 200 countries, we see diversity in the background and talent of our associates as a competitive advantage and as a commitment that is a daily responsibility.

> At Chrysler Corporation, we believe that workforce diversity is a competitive advantage. Our success as a global community is as dependent on utilizing the wealth of backgrounds, skills and opinions that a diverse workforce offers, as it is on raw materials, technology and processes.

In addition, business executives often stress another reason for seeking diversity at all levels. Ultimately, they say, corporations will not be healthy unless the society is healthy, and a healthy society in the twenty-first century will be one in which the most challenging, rewarding career possibilities are perceived to be, and truly are, open to all races and ethnic groups.

Other important opportunities exist for highly trained minority managers and professionals in meeting the pressing needs in predominantly minority communities. At present, minority groups are disadvantaged in government and politics because they are less likely to vote than the rest of the population. This is especially true in poor communities, where voting rates have been falling for three decades and are now far below the national average. Because these communities have such a vital stake in public policies involving health care, welfare, law enforcement, job training, education, and other areas, it is especially important that they have well-trained, articulate leaders to represent them in the political arena.

[51] U.S. Bureau of the Census 1997, tab. 19, p. 19.

[52] M. Douglas Ivester (Chairman and CEO of The Coca-Cola Company) and Robert J. Eaton (Chairman and CEO of Chrysler Corporation), in Executive Leadership Council 1998, pp. 10, 34.

Urban minority communities are also in need of business leadership to help offset the loss of jobs resulting from the movement of employers from the cities to the suburbs. Jobless rates for black males have been double those of whites. Minority enterprises can play a distinctive role in helping to overcome this problem, because the record shows that minority-owned businesses—whether they are located in the central city or the suburbs—are much more likely than white-owned companies to hire minority employees.[53]

Finally, many minority neighborhoods suffer from a shortage of doctors and from a lack of ready access to high-quality health care. Minority doctors are not the only physicians capable of meeting these needs, and one recent study of the medical school at the University of California at Davis found that there was no significant difference in the ethnic mix of patients treated by graduates (mostly minority students) recruited through a "special" process and graduates recruited through the regular admissions process.[54] But more comprehensive investigations have found that black and Hispanic physicians are much more likely to serve minority communities and to include minorities and poor people among their patients.[55] According to one study, minority physicians are twice as likely to work in locations designated as health manpower shortage areas by the federal government.[56] Another study revealed that minority patients are more than four times as likely as whites to receive their regular care from a minority physician.[57]

Despite widespread recognition of the value of diversity, efforts to increase the number of minority professionals through race-sensitive admissions policies have never been fully accepted. For almost two decades, the *Bakke* case seemed to have settled the issue from a legal standpoint. Still, large segments of the public continued to object to the use of race as a factor in deciding who should gain entry to selective institutions. As the competition to enter leading colleges and professional schools continued to intensify, this opposition became more vocal.

In 1989, and again in 1995, Supreme Court opinions involving other aspects of affirmative action signaled a possible shift in the attitudes of the Justices toward race-based policies.[58] In 1996, the Court of Appeals

---

[53] Bates 1993, pp. 90–91. For unemployment data, see Jaynes and Williams 1989, p. 308.
[54] Bronner 1997.
[55] See, e.g., Komaromy et al. 1996, p. 1305.
[56] Keith et al. 1985, p. 1521.
[57] Moy and Bartman 1995, p. 1515.
[58] City of Richmond v. J. A. Croson Co., 488 U.S. 469 (1989); Adarand Constructors, Inc. v. Peña, 515 U.S. 200 (1995).

for the Fifth Circuit ruled in the case of *Hopwood v. Texas* that the University of Texas law school could not take race into consideration in admitting students unless such action was necessary to remedy past discrimination by the school itself.[59] Although the court could have invalidated the law school's admissions policy on the ground that it did not meet the *Bakke* test, a majority of the judges chose instead to declare that *Bakke* no longer represented the view of the Supreme Court and that "the use of race to achieve a diverse student body . . . simply cannot be a state interest compelling enough to meet the steep [constitutional] standard of strict scrutiny."[60]

At about the same time, the Regents of the University of California issued a ruling of their own, announcing that the nine universities in the state system would no longer be permitted to take race into account in admitting students. This policy was subsequently affirmed by the voters of California in a statewide referendum.

By now, therefore, the efforts of selective institutions to increase the number of black, Hispanic, and Native American students have come under heavy fire. Lawsuits have been filed in several other states challenging the race-sensitive admissions policies of public universities. All signs suggest that the controversy is moving toward some new authoritative review and resolution. Clearly the time is ripe for a careful accounting of how race-sensitive admissions policies have been applied during their thirty-year history, and what their consequences have been.

[59] 78 F.3d 932 (5th Cir. 1996), *cert. denied,* 116 S.Ct. 2581 (1996).
[60] Ibid., p. 948.

CHAPTER 2

The Admissions Process and "Race-Neutrality"

THE AIMS AND VALUES of an educational institution are often revealed most vividly by the choices it makes in selecting its students. That being so, what purposes and values have led virtually all highly selective colleges and professional schools to try so hard to enroll substantial numbers of black and Hispanic students? How have these efforts been related to other institutional objectives? How much weight have these colleges and universities attached to race in order to achieve their goals, and what would happen to the racial composition of their student bodies if race-neutral policies were mandated?

Before attempting to answer these questions, we need to clear up two misconceptions that frequently creep into discussions about the role of race in the admissions process. One of the most common misunderstandings concerns the number of institutions that actually take account of race in making admissions decisions. Many people are unaware of how few colleges and universities have enough applicants to be able to pick and choose among them. There is no single, unambiguous way of identifying the number of such schools, but we estimate that only about 20 to 30 percent of all four-year colleges and universities are in this category. Nationally, the vast majority of undergraduate institutions accept all qualified candidates and thus do not award special status to any group of applicants, defined by race or on the basis of any other criterion.[1]

---

[1] Both *Peterson's Guide* and *Barron's* classify colleges and universities by their degree of selectivity, using a combination of test scores, high school grades, and acceptance rates. The 1998 edition of *Peterson's Guide* placed only 212 four-year colleges and universities, or about 12 percent of all the U.S. institutions they classified, in one of their top two categories—the categories that include almost all of the undergraduate schools in the College and Beyond universe. The top two categories used by *Barron's* in 1982 include 90 institutions, and the top three include 229 schools.

Using regression analysis, Thomas J. Kane (forthcoming) has estimated that a marked degree of racial preference is given within only the top 20 percent of all four-year institutions; he found a very limited degree of preference in the next quintile and none in the remaining 60 percent of all four-year institutions. Michael T. Nettles and his collaborators have used a similar methodology and arrived at similar conclusions (Nettles, Perna, and Edelin [forthcoming], pp. 32ff).

A second source of confusion has to do with how one measures the degree of advantage that black applicants receive when they apply to a genuinely selective institution. The most obvious approach, comparing average SAT scores of black and white students, is seriously flawed and should not be used *for this purpose*. The fact that, nationally, blacks are very underrepresented at the higher SAT levels and very overrepresented at the lower levels ensures that they will have substantially lower average SAT scores even if a college were to use precisely the same SAT cut-off in admitting white and black students.[2] For example, if a school admitted every applicant with SAT scores over 1100 and none with lower scores, the white students would still have a higher average SAT score than the black students because relatively more of them score at the upper end of the SAT distribution. This result obtains even though *no* racial preference was given in this hypothetical situation.[3] A colleague has suggested an analogy based on male-female differences in height. Suppose all applicants over five feet tall were admitted, and no others. The average height of the male students would exceed that of the women simply because there are more tall men. The same would be true if the minimum height were set at 5′6″ or at 6 feet.

Clearly, differences in average scores (or average heights) can be highly misleading if used as indicators of the degree of preference extended to one group or another in the admissions process. Similarly, it would make no sense to use averages as a way of defining a race-neutral standard of admission. The only way to create a class in which black and white students had the same average SAT score would be to discriminate *against* black candidates. Of course, the fact that average SAT scores are

[2] There is, for all of the obvious reasons, a tremendous degree of interest in test scores and especially in the racial gaps in test scores. See, e.g., Ethan Bronner's front-page article in the *New York Times* (Bronner 1997) and the ensuing correspondence (*New York Times*, November 14, 1997, p. 34). Jencks and Phillips (forthcoming) contains the best available summary of recent research on trends in test score gaps and what is known about their causes and consequences. The hypotheses reviewed include the alleged effects of genetic differences, environmental and cultural forces, sociopsychological phenomena, and bias in test design.

[3] The same result would be obtained if high school grades were used as the sole criterion for admissions. Thus, Kane estimates that "if a college relied entirely on high school GPA to rank students and admitted only those in the top third of their class, its white freshmen would score 180 points higher on the combined verbal and math SAT than its black freshmen." Similarly, Kane has estimated that at the 20 percent of the nation's colleges with the lowest test scores, where open admissions are the norm and there is little if any selectivity, average scores for blacks are 135 points below those of whites—a difference roughly comparable to the black-white gap of 146 points found within the top 20 percent of all colleges. See Kane (forthcoming) and the earlier, extended, version of this paper (Kane 1997).

poor indicators of the degree of preference given to minority students, which is best measured "at the margin," does not mean that averages are not useful for other purposes. For example, they serve as convenient summary measures of overall differences between groups (men are, on average, taller than women), and therefore serve also as measures of changes over time in such differences between groups. We use average SAT scores for precisely these purposes later in the chapter. As is always the case, the usefulness of any measure depends on the question being asked.

To obtain a more accurate sense of the actual degree of preference given to black applicants and to define a race-neutral standard of admissions in an operational way, it is necessary to enter the admissions process itself: to examine applicant pools, to understand the criteria used to select students and the purposes they are designed to serve, and, finally, to consider differences between black and white applicants in "yield" (the percentages of those offered admission who decide to enroll). This kind of detailed analysis requires access to the complete admissions records used to select a class, including information about those not offered admission, those offered admission who did not enroll, and those who in fact matriculated. There were five colleges and universities within the College and Beyond universe that were able to provide the full range of data used to admit and enroll their 1989 entering cohorts, and the following analysis is based on these school-specific records; the key results are then checked against national reference points.[4]

At the conclusion of this analysis, we return to the twin questions of

---

[4] The five institutions for which we have detailed admissions data include three private universities and two coed liberal arts colleges. These five schools represent a range of conditions (size, location, degree of selectivity), and they are roughly representative of the C&B universe of schools. They were not chosen, however, to be statistically representative of this set of schools—much less of the far larger universe of less selective schools. Detailed admissions data of the kind analyzed here are hard to obtain, and these five schools were chosen in part because all had well-documented electronic files that they were willing to make available. The average combined SAT scores of *applicants* to these schools ranged from the low 1200s at one of the liberal arts colleges to the high 1200s at two of the universities; the average SAT scores of their *matriculants* ranged from about 1240 to roughly 1350. (These scores all predate the recentering in 1995 of the test score means; after recentering, national mean test scores increased by roughly 75 points for the verbal SAT and 25 points for the math SAT.) The summary statistics for the five schools presented here are simple averages of the data for the individual applicants and matriculants. We cannot identify these schools, or present data for them individually, because of the need to respect promises of confidentiality. We have, however, analyzed the data for each school individually to satisfy ourselves that the averaging process has not produced misleading results. Overall, the patterns are remarkably consistent.

how much of an effect race-sensitive admissions had on the composition of entering classes and how much preference black applicants can be said to have been given. These questions are related, but they are not the same. The best way to measure the degree of preference given is by comparing the credentials of those black students who presumably would not have been enrolled under a race-neutral standard (once the size and characteristics of that group have been estimated by simulating the effects of a race-neutral policy) with the credentials of an equivalent number of rejected applicants (mostly white) who would have been admitted under a race-blind procedure. We will show later, using law school data, that such comparisons "at the margin" of the admissions process indicate much smaller differences in test scores and grades than do comparisons based on averages for all students.

APPLICANT POOLS

Who is admitted to selective schools depends, of course, on who applies. The five schools whose records we studied received over 40,000 applications for admission to their '89 entering cohorts to fill 5,166 places. More than 2,300 applications were submitted by candidates who identified themselves as black. These applicants were highly self-selected.[5] Most presumably knew the academic standards of the schools to which they were applying and had at least some reason to believe that they had a chance of being admitted. In many cases, they were surely encouraged to apply to these schools by parents, teachers, guidance counselors, or representatives of the colleges and universities themselves. The resulting applicant pools are, therefore, not only large, but of very high quality; only a small fraction of all college-bound seniors in the United States are inclined even to enter the competition for admission to such selective schools.

The evidence of high qualification is clear. Of the black applicants, over 90 percent scored above the national average for all black test-takers on both the verbal and math SATs, considered separately. The large majority of these black applicants handily outscored not only the average black test-taker, but also the average white test-taker. More than 75 percent of the black applicants had higher math SAT scores than the na-

[5] When we speak of "applicants" we really mean "applications." A number of the applicants to an individual C&B school will also have applied to one or more of the other C&B schools as well as to schools outside this universe. The submission of multiple applications means that the number of applicants will always be less than the number of applications. Later in the chapter we examine overlapping applications in detail and discuss their implications for this analysis.

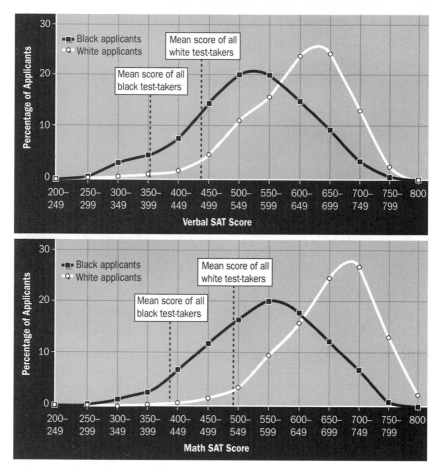

Figure 2.1. Verbal SAT Score and Math SAT Score Distributions of Applicants to Five Selective Institutions, by Race, 1989

Sources: Admissions data provided by five College and Beyond institutions; national data from College Entrance Examination Board 1989, p. 6.

tional average for white test-takers, and 73 percent had higher verbal SAT scores.[6]

Nonetheless, there was a marked disparity in test scores between the black and white applicants (Figure 2.1). If the black candidates for admission to these schools were highly qualified, the white candidates, as a group, must be judged as spectacularly well qualified. More than

[6] At two of these five schools, we also have information on high school rank in class for a large fraction of the applicants. The picture of high qualification remains the same when

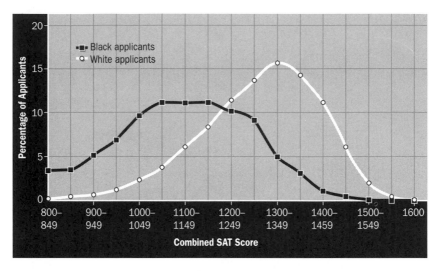

Figure 2.2. Combined SAT Score Distribution of Applicants to Five Selective
Institutions, by Race, 1989

Source: Admissions data provided by five College and Beyond institutions.

95 percent of the white applicants had math and verbal SAT scores above
the averages for all white test-takers. Aggregating the separate verbal and
math scores, we found that the average combined SAT score for white
applicants to these schools (1284) was 186 points higher than the corresponding SAT average for black applicants (1098). While 29 percent of
the black applicants had combined SATs over 1200, nearly three-quarters
of all white applicants exceeded this high benchmark (Figure 2.2). Thus,
it is the exceedingly strong credentials possessed by very large numbers of
white applicants to these schools that present such a challenge to admissions officers concerned with achieving both excellence and diversity.

The difference in test scores between white and black applicants to
these five schools reflects the great disparity in the scores of black and
white test-takers in the United States. Fortunately, this disparity is no
longer as large as it once was. Between 1975–76 (the first year for which
SAT data by race are available) and the late 1980s, the national black-
white gap in SAT scores narrowed fairly steadily; the gap in both verbal

we look through this lens. Over half of all black applicants ranked in the top 10 percent of
their graduating class; over three-quarters of all white applicants were in the top 10 percent.
We focus most of this discussion on test scores rather than high school rank in class because
of data considerations and because high school rank in class is of course affected by the
academic qualifications of the other members of the class.

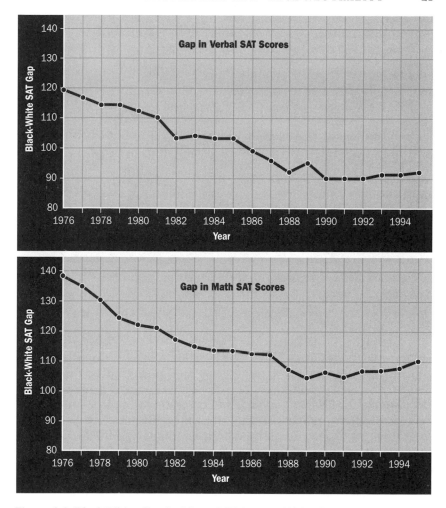

Figure 2.3. Black-White Gap in Mean SAT Scores, 1976–1995

Source: U.S. Department of Education 1996, tab. 126, p. 127.

Note: Data not available for 1977 and 1986. Data points for those years were estimated as the average of adjacent years.

and math scores declined by approximately 25 percent. Since then, however, the gap has held steady and appears even to have widened modestly in the most recent years for which data are available (Figure 2.3). As Figures 2.1 and 2.2 (and Appendix Table D.2.1) demonstrate, the differences continue to be substantial.

There has been a much more pronounced narrowing of the black-white gap in SAT scores among applicants to the most selective colleges. We have comprehensive admissions records for the '76 entering cohorts

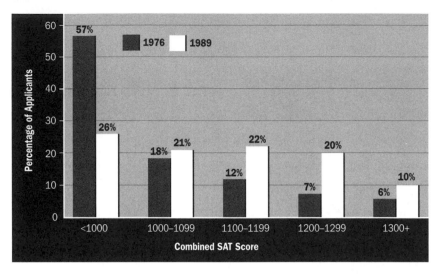

Figure 2.4. SAT Score Distribution of Black Applicants to Two Selective Institutions, 1976 and 1989

Source: Admissions data provided by two College and Beyond institutions.

at two of the five institutions for which we have data for the '89 entering cohorts (one university and one liberal arts college). The comparison between the black applicant pools in these two years is striking (Figure 2.4). The share of black applicants with combined SAT scores below 1000 decreased from 57 percent of those applying for places in the '76 entering cohorts to 26 percent in the '89 pools. More than half of all black candidates in the '89 pools had SAT scores above 1100, as compared with just 25 percent in the '76 pools. The black-white gap in average combined SAT scores of applicants to these two schools fell from 282 points in 1976 to 181 points in 1989.[7]

The marked improvement in the black applicant pools available to these institutions is presumably the result of a combination of factors. More effective recruitment efforts by the schools have helped. So has the growing confidence within the black community of students' ability to compete successfully for places at highly selective institutions and obtain sufficient financial aid. Finally, the number of blacks scoring in the

[7] We lack equally detailed admissions records for the '76 cohorts at the other three schools, but we do have SAT scores for all black and white *matriculants* in 1976 and 1989 at all five of these schools and at the rest of the twenty-eight colleges and universities included in this study; these data (some of which are shown below) suggest strongly that this two-school comparison is not at all atypical.

higher SAT ranges nationwide has increased substantially.[8] Still, progress has been painfully slow, and the remaining gaps are very large. Most troubling of all, a recent study suggests that the black-white gap in test scores among high school seniors may actually widen over the next few years.[9]

There is no reason to suppose that any set of policies is likely to eliminate this gap in pre-collegiate preparation during our lifetimes. Differences between blacks and whites in resources, environments, and inherited intellectual capital (the educational attainment of parents and grandparents) have been long in the making. It would be amazing if they could be eradicated quickly. As a result, it is all but certain that the issue of race-sensitive admissions will continue to be relevant for the foreseeable future.

ADMISSIONS PROCESSES AND PROBABILITIES

Broad Aims of the Admissions Process

What do selective institutions try to accomplish in choosing a class from the large pool of applicants who present themselves for consideration? The most fundamental objective is to be sure that the qualifications of all admitted students are above a high academic threshold. Admissions officers seek to offer places in the class only to those applicants whom they deem intellectually (and otherwise) capable of completing the academic program successfully and benefiting significantly from the experience. The nature of the courses applicants have taken, their secondary school grades, and their standardized test scores are particularly helpful in making these judgments.

After identifying those individuals who seem capable of completing the course of study successfully, most selective colleges and professional schools will still have many more applicants than places available in the entering class. Admissions officers typically give significant weight to four considerations in deciding among the remaining candidates:

- The first consideration is to admit an ample number of students who show particular promise of excelling in their studies. By and large, such students have the greatest likelihood of taking full

---

[8] Alan Krueger (personal communication) has pointed out that if the mean SAT score of blacks were to increase even modestly relative to the mean for whites, the proportion of blacks above some fixed cutoff in the right tail of the distribution would increase substantially (assuming that test scores were normally distributed).

[9] Philips, Crouse, and Ralph (forthcoming); Hedges and Nowell (forthcoming).

advantage of the academic strengths of the institution and contributing to the education of their peers. They play an important
role in setting the academic tenor of the institution.

- The second consideration is the need to assemble a class of students with a wide diversity of backgrounds, experiences, and talents. Graduating students and alumni/ae—of both undergraduate colleges and professional schools—regularly stress that much
of what they gained from their educational experience came from
what they learned from their fellow students. The recruitment of
minority students is one part of the search for diversity, but so
is the admission of students who can participate actively in a
broad array of athletic, artistic, and other extracurricular activities
that will enrich undergraduate life and expose students to new
experiences.

- The third principal consideration is to attract students who seem
especially likely to utilize their education to make valuable or
distinctive contributions to their professions and to the welfare of
society. Colleges and universities receive an exemption from taxa-
tion because they serve a social purpose. Educational institutions
have long made deliberate efforts to attract and educate students
capable of making a difference and contributing something special to society. Before the turn of the century, Jane Stanford
declared that the "chief object" of the new university she had
helped to found was "the instruction of students with a view to
producing leaders in every field of science and industry."[10] Today,
almost every selective college and professional school makes a
similar claim.

- The fourth consideration is to respect the importance of long-
term institutional loyalties and traditions. Almost all selective institutions give some advantage in the admissions process to applicants whose parents or other family members attended the institution (often called "legacies"), and many also pay special attention
to applications from children of faculty and staff. At least one
highly selective institution that seeks to retain strong roots in its
community is said to give greater preference to applicants from
local public high schools than to any other special group.

The purposes just described illuminate the role of test scores and high
school grades in selecting students. There is a widespread misconception
that scores and grades represent the only truly valid considerations in
deciding whom to admit to a selective institution. Thus, one often hears
that students with top scores and the highest grades should be admitted

[10] Quoted in Casper 1995, p. 4.

"on the merits," as if these measures were the sole legitimate basis for admission and that other considerations were somehow insubstantial or even morally suspect. This is patently false. Deciding which students have the most "merit" depends on what one is trying to achieve. In helping selective institutions screen out applicants who seem unlikely to be able to complete the academic work, grades and scores are undoubtedly of critical importance. They also provide the most useful measures available to predict which students will achieve the highest academic record if admitted. Yet even when combined judiciously, test scores and grades still predict academic performance imperfectly, as we will demonstrate in the next chapter. Moreover, such measures play an even smaller role in determining which applicants will contribute to the development of their fellow students or which will go on to be leaders in their chosen fields of endeavor.

Understanding the aims of the institution in choosing its students helps us see why admissions officers in virtually all selective colleges and professional schools look well beyond grades and test scores. Almost invariably, such institutions ask for personal statements, letters of recommendation from teachers or other close acquaintances, evidence of successful participation in extracurricular activities, employment histories, and other experiences that can shed light on the accomplishments and potential of the applicant. All of these factors are weighed in a process that often involves a sequence of decisions made and communicated over an extended period of time.

Professional schools place little emphasis on assembling a diversity of talents for the sake of enriching extracurricular life. Nevertheless, most professional schools value students from a variety of backgrounds and experiences that will enhance the learning experience for all students and expose them to a variety of perspectives. Different professional schools also look for specific traits beyond sheer academic ability that are relevant to successful practice in their fields. Business schools are interested in students who are entrepreneurial and display leadership ability. Medical schools look for students with empathy and understanding. Even in law schools, which place the greatest weight on the traditional measures of academic achievement, other factors matter; a recent study estimates that of the 42,287 whites accepted by accredited schools in 1990–91, 6,321 would have been excluded if admissions officers had looked only at grades and test scores.[11]

In providing this capsule account of the admissions process, we do not mean to suggest that it is flawless or noncontroversial except where race is concerned. Some college alumni/ae believe that too few legacies are

[11] Wightman 1997, p. 16.

admitted, just as some faculty members (and others) think that too much weight is attached to legacy status and to the recruitment of athletes. Some people favor putting more weight on test scores and strictly academic criteria, while others favor giving more emphasis to the enrollment of the proverbial "well-rounded" student. The task for admissions officers is one of judgment in implementing institutional policy rather than of mechanically applying rigid quantitative measures.

Race and the Probability of Admission

Each of the five schools for which we have detailed admissions data has shared with almost all academically selective institutions a commitment to enrolling a diverse student population—and, as one way of achieving this objective, to paying attention to race in the admissions process. This commitment has meant that black applicants have had an appreciably greater chance than whites of being admitted. Overall, approximately 25 percent of all white applicants at these five schools were offered admission for the fall of 1989, as contrasted with 42 percent of all black applicants.

This comparison of the overall percentages of blacks and whites admitted provides, however, an inaccurate picture of the role played by race in the admissions process. Because the distributions of test scores for the two groups differ so markedly, it is necessary to compare blacks and whites with similar SAT scores. When we grouped applicants by SAT interval (using 50-point ranges of combined scores), we found that the advantage enjoyed by the typical black applicant was considerably greater than the 42:25 ratio implies. In the upper-middle ranges of SAT scores, in particular, the admission probability for black applicants was often three times higher than the corresponding probability for white applicants. For example, for applicants who scored in the 1200–1249 range, the probability of being admitted was 19 percent for white candidates, as compared with 60 percent for black candidates (Figure 2.5). Toward the top of the SAT range, the gap narrowed, since both black and white admission probabilities were high.

Examining the relationships between SAT scores and admission probabilities is instructive in two other respects. First, Figure 2.5 shows that SAT scores do affect admissions decisions for black as well as white applicants: the odds of being admitted for both groups clearly rise as test scores increase. Second, and even more important, *we see that SAT scores are by no means the whole story for either group*. Although discussions of the admissions process sometimes make it seem as if true "merit" were a simple function of quantifiable criteria, and especially of test scores, this is

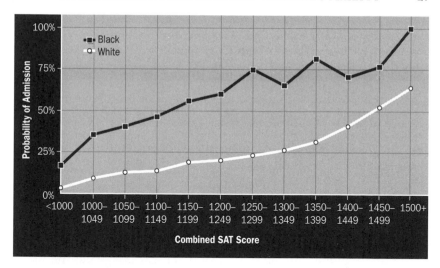

Figure 2.5. Probability of Admission to Five Selective Institutions, by Combined SAT Score and Race, 1989

Source: Admissions data provided by five College and Beyond institutions.

plainly not the case at these schools.[12] Even in the very highest SAT interval (combined SAT score of 1500 or more), less than two-thirds of white applicants were offered admission; in the 1300–1349 range, only 25 percent were admitted. While the odds of being admitted were consistently higher for black applicants, we see that for this group, too, high SAT scores by no means ensured a place in a class. Within each 50-point interval above 1200, the admissions probability for black candidates oscillated between roughly 60 and 75 percent. The same pattern holds when applicants are classified by their high school rank in class. At these highly selective colleges and universities, even being the valedictorian of one's high school class is far from a guarantee of admission; the admission probability for those in the top 5 percent of their high school class was just 31 percent for white applicants and 57 percent for black applicants (at the two schools for which we have high school grades).

It is widely understood that competition for places in highly selective schools is so intense that inevitably many extremely well-qualified white candidates with SAT scores in the highest ranges will fail to gain admission (however hard it may be for individual applicants and their families to accept this fact). For many observers, it may be more surprising to learn that significant numbers of high-scoring black applicants are also

[12] Nor are any of the conclusions stated here altered when we add high school grades as a second numerical criterion. They also matter, but they, too, are far from dispositive.

rejected by these schools. What could be the explanation, given the emphasis placed on diversity and the "scarcity value" of these high-testing minority applicants? Conversations with deans of admissions suggested numerous reasons, almost all of which apply to candidates regardless of race.

In some situations, high SAT scores are offset by other information in the student's file. For example, consider the case of a hypothetical black candidate with a math SAT of 700 and a verbal SAT of 550, for a combined score of 1250. Given the math score, this student could well have been encouraged to be an engineer and could have declared his/her interest in that major. Yet if that student had a low Achievement score (now called SAT II) in a subject such as chemistry and a relatively weak secondary school record in demanding science courses, one dean said categorically that he would reject the applicant—the odds of success in the engineering program at the university in question would just be too low, notwithstanding the high SATs. In other cases, high-scoring black candidates (one dean mentioned a student with SATs over 1300) who earned disappointing grades at excellent secondary schools have been rejected because they were seen as chronic underperformers. In still other cases, judgments about personal qualities were decisive—as they often are for white applicants.

The complexities of the admissions process are also reflected in the special consideration given to "legacies" (children or other relatives of alumni/ae). The overall admission rate for legacies was almost twice that for all other candidates and roughly the same as the overall rate for black candidates.[13] However, legacies who apply to these schools tend to have stronger than average academic credentials, and a different picture is obtained when we take SAT scores into account. In the 1100 to 1199 SAT range, for example, 22 percent of all legacies were accepted, as compared with 18 percent of all other white candidates (and roughly 40 percent of all black candidates). The legacy "advantage" widens in the 1200-to-1299 SAT band (35 percent versus 22 percent for non-legacies and roughly 60 percent for black candidates) and is most pronounced in the 1300-and-over SAT band (where 60 percent of legacies are admitted, as compared with 24 percent of non-legacies and 70 percent of black candidates). To sum up, black candidates are consistently admitted at

---

[13] We have these data for only three of the five schools for which we have detailed admissions records. However, the patterns for these schools are very similar, and we would be surprised if patterns at other schools of equal selectivity differed very much. At these three schools, the overall admission rates (total number of candidates offered admission divided by total applicants of each type) were 39 percent for black candidates, 44 percent for non-black legacies, and 22 percent for non-black, non-legacy candidates.

higher rates than legacies, who in turn are admitted at consistently higher rates than non-legacies, but the "advantage" enjoyed by legacies is concentrated at the upper end of the SAT range. At high SAT levels, the admission probabilities for black candidates and legacies begin to converge.

Identified athletes, who appeared on coaches' recruiting lists, were admitted at still higher rates, up and down the SAT scale. At the school for which we have the most reliable data (a selective school that does not give athletic scholarships), the overall admission rate for athletes who were identified by coaches as promising candidates was 78 percent. Roughly 60 percent of these athletes with SATs below 1150 were offered admission, and the admission rate rises to 84 percent when we consider applicants with SATs of 1150 or higher. This group is hard to compare with others, however, since its members have been pre-selected by the coaches to fill a limited number of slots, and the admissions office feels obliged to admit enough of these applicants to fill the rosters. Nonetheless, the high degree of preference given to this carefully targeted group of recruited athletes is evident.

The overall result is a process that is much more complicated than most public discussions acknowledge. Admissions officers have been "picking and choosing," as we believe they should always do—admitting the candidate who seems to offer something special by way of drive and determination, the individual with a set of skills that matches well the academic requirements of the institution, someone who will bring another dimension of diversity to the student body, or a candidate who helps the institution fulfill a particular aspect of its mission. Talk of basing admissions strictly on test scores and grades assumes a model of admissions radically different from the one that exists today. Such a policy would mandate a fundamental change of direction for institutions that recognize the many dimensions of "qualification": the importance of a good fit between the student and the educational program, the varied paths that individuals follow in developing their abilities, and the pitfalls of basing assessments of talent and potential solely on narrowly defined quantitative measures.

At the five institutions for which we have detailed admissions data, this process resulted in a composite "class" in the fall of 1989 that included 335 black and 3,179 white matriculants—as well as approximately 1,200 Hispanic, Asian, and other matriculants. The average SAT score of the black matriculants was 1157 (compared with an average of 1098 for all black applicants); the average SAT score of the white matriculants was 1331 (compared with an average of 1284 for all white applicants).

These results can be put in historical perspective by comparing them

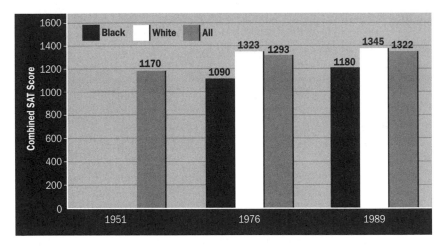

Figure 2.6. Mean SAT Score of Matriculants at Four Selective Institutions, by
Race, 1951, 1976, and 1989

Source: College and Beyond.

Note: Data by race not available for 1951.

with the results of earlier admissions competitions at four of the same five
schools (Figure 2.6).[14] Real progress was made between 1976 and 1989
in reducing the black-white SAT gap. While SAT scores for both white
and black matriculants improved between these years, the improvement
in the scores of the black matriculants was much greater, reflecting the
larger numbers of black applicants with high SAT scores applying to
these schools. As a result, the racial gap in combined SAT scores fell from
233 to 165 points. Equally noteworthy is the overall change in SAT scores
between the early 1950s (when the entering cohorts of '51 were admitted) and the late 1980s. Competition for admission to academically selective schools increased so dramatically during this period that even with
race-sensitive admissions, the average SAT score for black matriculants in
1989 was slightly higher than the average SAT score for all matriculants
in 1951. The alumni/ae of the 1950s should have no reason to question
the qualifications of the black students of today!

   The improvement in the SAT scores of black matriculants emerges
even more clearly when we examine what has happened at the eight most
selective colleges and universities in the C&B universe (defined as those
schools that had average SAT scores for all matriculants in the '89 cohort
of 1300 or higher). The pronounced upward shift in the entire distribution of black SAT scores is evident in Figure 2.7.

---

[14] The fifth school lacked data for the '51 cohort. We show only the average SAT score
for all students for 1951 because there were so few minority students in attendance then
and the identification of students by race/ethnicity on institutional records was very erratic.

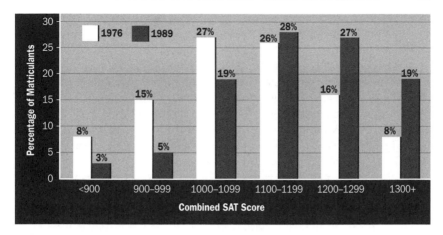

Figure 2.7. SAT Score Distribution of Black Matriculants at SEL-1 Institutions, 1976 and 1989

Source: College and Beyond.

Notes: For 1976, "SEL-1 Institutions" are those for which the mean combined SAT score of matriculants was greater than 1250; for 1989, "SEL-1 Institutions" are those for which the mean combined SAT score of matriculants was 1300 or more.

EFFECTS OF A RACE-NEUTRAL ADMISSIONS POLICY

Within the College and Beyond Universe

How would the imposition of race-neutral admissions policies have changed the composition of the entering classes at the five schools for which we have detailed admissions data? To answer this question, we first have to decide what it means to be "race-neutral" in admissions.[15]

Given the multiplicity of considerations that affect undergraduate admissions decisions, it is hard to imagine that anyone would favor a directive to admit simply "by the numbers" and offer places only to those students with the highest test scores and high school grades. We suggest that one commonsense way of representing (retrospectively) a process in which the race of the applicant was truly unknown to admissions officers is by assuming that black applicants, grouped by SAT ranges, would have the same probability of being admitted as white applicants in those same ranges. Thus, if 25 percent of the white applicants with SAT scores be-

---

[15] It is hard to imagine any admissions policy that, in fact, would be perfectly "race neutral." Race is associated with so many aspects of life in the United States that virtually every other attribute of an applicant—SAT scores, high school attended, parents' occupation and education—has, as it were, a racial component. We use the phrase "race-neutral" in the sense of presumed ignorance of the race of the applicant at the time of application to college, with all other characteristics unchanged.

tween 1300 and 1350 were granted admission, we assume that 25 percent of the black applicants within this same range would be admitted—and so on, up and down the SAT scale.[16]

By combining the data on the distribution of black SAT scores with the data on white admissions probabilities in this way, we can estimate the hypothetical effects of imposing a race-neutral standard on the admissions process. The results of this exercise can be summarized in a single comparison: making these calculations for these five schools reduces the overall probability of admission for black applicants from its actual value of 42 percent in 1989 to a hypothetical value of 13 percent (Figure 2.8). Since the overall probability of admission for white students was 25 percent, the overall black probability under a race-neutral procedure would be roughly half the white probability.[17]

These are hypothetical calculations, to be sure, but they can be compared with one (late-breaking) set of real numbers. As this book was going to press, the University of California at Berkeley reported the results of the first admissions process for a fall entering class after the imposition of a race-neutral standard. Berkeley is not part of the C&B database but it is, of course, a highly selective institution, similar to the schools in our study in many respects (Berkeley's average SAT score in the fall of 1989 of 1176 would put it in our SEL-2 category). The actual effects of the adoption of a race-neutral standard at Berkeley were remarkably similar to the hypothetical effects we estimated for the C&B schools. For the class that entered in the fall of 1997 (when race-sensitive admissions policies were in effect), the admission rate at Berkeley was 48.5 percent for African American candidates and 29.9 percent for white

---

[16] This approach could be elaborated by constructing a logistic regression model predicting admission for white applicants, based on variables such as SAT scores and high school rank in class, and then predicting the admission of black students by using this model. We have experimented with this more complex approach (which has been used, for example, by Wightman [1997] in her study of law school admissions), but other variables, including high school grades, are available only for some part of our sample. In any case, the results of our experiments are qualitatively similar to those obtained by means of the simpler approach outlined here.

[17] This simplified approach does not take account of how altering admission probabilities for any group of applicants would (other things equal) bring about unintended changes in class size. Applying the white probabilities of admission to the black candidates and retaining the same probabilities for the white applicants would cause a reduction in the overall number of matriculants because the white probabilities are lower than the black probabilities. In this instance, correcting for this effect (and maintaining the current class size) would raise the probabilities of admission for both white and black candidates by roughly 5 percent (from 25 to just over 26 percent for whites and from 13 to 13.6 percent for the black applicants).

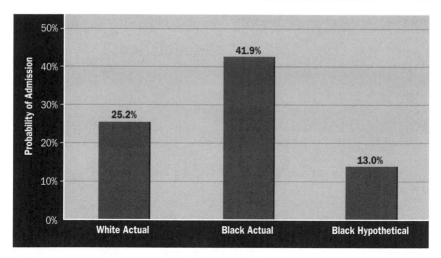

Figure 2.8. Probability of Admission to Five Selective Institutions, by Race, Actual and Hypothetical Probabilities, 1989

Source: Admissions data provided by five College and Beyond institutions.

Note: "Black Hypothetical" is calculated by applying white admission probabilities to the number of black applicants in each 50-point SAT interval.

candidates—as compared with overall admissions rates of 42 and 25 percent for black and white applicants to the C&B schools in 1989. For the class that will enter in the fall of 1998 (with race-neutral policies in effect), the admission rate at Berkeley was 15.6 percent for African Americans and 30.3 percent for white candidates—as compared with hypothetical admissions rates of 13 percent and 26.5 percent for black and white candidates in the C&B schools assuming race-neutrality. Thus in this "real time" case, as in the hypothetical results we obtained for the C&B schools, race-neutrality reduced the overall black probability of admission to almost exactly *half* the white probability.[17a]

How would such a large reduction in the acceptance rate have affected the actual number of black students on the C&B campuses? To answer this question, we need an additional piece of information: the likelihood that a black candidate offered admission will accept the offer—a statistic that admissions officers call "yield." Yield differs between white and black admittees. It tends to be lower for highly qualified black candidates than

[17a] Based on data obtained from the University of California, Berkeley, April 1, 1998 (Public Affairs Office). It is rare that social scientists have an opportunity to compare hypothetical calculations against a true "natural experiment," conducted independently and *after* the hypothetical calculations were made.

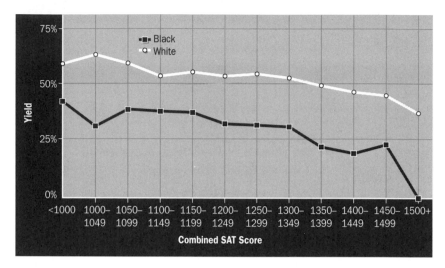

Figure 2.9. Yield by SAT Score and Race at Five Selective Institutions, 1989
Source: Admissions data provided by five College and Beyond institutions.

for comparable white candidates because the black candidates are likely
to be admitted by more schools. It also tends to be lower for all applicants
with high SAT scores because they, too, are likely to have more choices
among schools. We see from Figure 2.9 that the gap between white and
black yields is especially pronounced at the top of the SAT range, which is
not surprising since the very small number of black students with extremely high SAT scores are no doubt accepted by a greater number of
schools and thus have many more options.[18]

If we assume that the yield for black candidates would remain the same
even if far smaller numbers of black students were offered admission (an
extreme assumption, which we relax in the next section), we obtain one
estimate of the ultimate number of black matriculants under this model
of race-neutrality. For these five schools in 1989, the share of the entering
class made up of black matriculants would fall from 7.1 percent (the
actual share) to 2.1 percent (the hypothetical share using the current
black yield).

[18] While we have full admissions records for just five schools, we have data on white-
black yields at seventeen schools. At only one is the black yield as high as the white yield.
Assigning each school a weight of one, we find that the average white-black gap in yield at
the five schools for which we have the most detailed data is 14 points; at the other 12
schools, it is 11 points.

Of course, much depends on whether the imposition of such a policy would affect only a small number of institutions (in, for example, a single state or a single judicial district) or the country at large. If all institutions of higher education were required to adopt race-neutral admission policies, the black yield at all selective schools would almost surely rise, since the typical black candidate who was still accepted by any given school would presumably have fewer options. The potential magnitude of this effect can be estimated by substituting the white yield for the black yield in the calculations. That is, if race were no longer a factor and black applicants in any specified SAT range were to be admitted at the same rate as white applicants in that range, it seems reasonable to assume that their likelihood of accepting would move up toward the white yield.[19]

Making this new assumption increases the projected number of black matriculants, but only modestly. Substituting the white yield for the black yield raises the hypothetical black share in the freshman classes of these institutions from 2.1 percent to 3.6 percent—a level that is still far below the 7.1 percent actual share (Figure 2.10). Under either assumption, the projected reduction in black enrollment at the typical C&B school would be drastic. Here again the admission results announced for the undergraduate class expected to enter Berkeley in the fall of '98, under a race-

[19] As Michael McPherson (personal communication) has observed, the validity of this approach depends on assumptions about black-white application patterns. Using information obtained from the C&B surveys of '89 matriculants, we studied in detail the numbers of applications submitted by white and black matriculants at the C&B schools (see Appendix B for a more detailed explanation of this analysis). While there are some small differences when the data are broken down by SAT scores, socioeconomic status, and the selectivity of the school finally attended, none of these differences is large enough to be consequential. Overall, blacks and whites submitted essentially the same number of applications to schools other than the one the applicant finally attended. Also, the black-white patterns of overlapping applications (and overlapping admission decisions) by type of school proved to be very similar. Would these application patterns persist in a race-neutral environment? Moving to race-neutral admissions might, of course, affect the number of black applicants (as discussed later in the chapter). Reduced odds of gaining admission might discourage some potential black candidates from applying to any of the highly selective schools. Such effects could lead to further reductions in black enrollment.

The white yield is probably best viewed as a ceiling on the likely black yield. In selective, high-cost schools, the white yield seems likely to remain above the black yield for two reasons: (1) the deeper attachments of some white students to particular schools and sets of schools because of longer family histories of attending certain types of schools and the greater likelihood that they will be legacies; and (2) the greater financial resources of the typical white student, who in general has more freedom to accept offers of admission from institutions that are expensive or far from home.

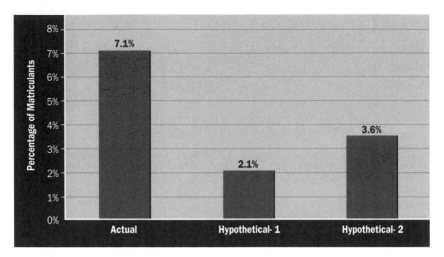

Figure 2.10. Black Matriculants as a Percentage of All Matriculants at Five Selective Institutions, Actual and Hypothetical Percentages, 1989

Source: Admissions data provided by five College and Beyond institutions.

Notes: "Actual" is the percentage of black matriculants in 1989; "Hypothetical-1" is
computed by multiplying the number of black applicants by the white admissions probability and black yield within each SAT interval; "Hypothetical-2" substitutes the white
yield for the black yield.

neutral policy, are entirely consistent: the share of African Americans in
the admitted class is 2.4 percent, as contrasted with 6.8 percent in the fall
of '97, when race-sensitive policies were in effect.[20]

At the same time, the places made available at these five schools by
admitting fewer blacks (assuming overall enrollment levels are fixed)
would result in only a modest increase in the odds of admission for
candidates of other races. We estimate that within this set of schools, even
if white students filled all the places created by reducing black enrollment, the overall white probability of admission would rise by only one
and one-half percentage points: from 25 percent to roughly 26.5 percent.
Thus nearly as many white applicants—including an appreciable number of valedictorians and other highly talented people—would still have
been disappointed. Thomas Kane has used the analogy of handicapped
parking spaces: "Eliminating the reserved space would have only a min-
uscule effect on parking options for non-disabled drivers. But the sight of
the open space will frustrate many passing motorists who are looking for

[20] University of California, Berkeley, April 1, 1998 (Public Affairs Office).

a space. Many are likely to believe that they would now be parked if the space were not reserved."[21]

It is also easy to exaggerate the degree of preference that has been given to black candidates. Looking simply at the aggregate number of black students who would be rejected under a race-neutral standard (compared to the number who would be retained) is by no means the only way to think about the question. As we suggested in the introduction to this chapter, it is on the margins of the admissions process that the degree of preference should be evaluated. The fair comparison is between the qualifications of the group we refer to as the "retrospectively rejected" black students and the other students, presumably mostly white and Asian Americans, who would have taken their places.

While we have no way of knowing which particular white and Asian American applicants were actually displaced, it would be possible to approximate their credentials by examining the test scores and grades of the bottom decile of the white students who were admitted. Linda Wightman has carried out such an analysis for 30 of the most selective law schools. Comparing the scores of the black beneficiaries of race-sensitive admissions with those of the lowest scoring white students produces dramatically different results than those obtained when comparing the average scores for the entire student populations. For example, the

---

[21] Kane (forthcoming). One commentator on this manuscript suggested a provocative analogy with sugar import quotas: the benefit for the limited number of domestic sugar producers is substantial while the cost to each one of the much larger number of consumers, in the form of higher sugar prices, is so tiny as to be essentially invisible. But the diffuse nature of the cost to the many consumers should not, our commentator noted, cause one to favor sugar quotas. That is absolutely right. But in the case of race-sensitive admissions, Kane's reference to handicapped parking spaces takes us in an opposite direction. That is, while the large group of people who are hurt by sugar quotas may not be heard from because the effect on each of them personally is so small, the predominantly white, well-qualified applicants whose chances would be marginally improved by race-neutrality tend to exaggerate, not underestimate, the effects of a race-sensitive policy on them—because each may be confident, even over-confident, that he or she would get "the handicapped parking space" if race-sensitive admissions policies were eliminated. Our point is not that either the targeted beneficiaries or the more diffuse group hurt by the targeting are inherently more deserving. *Rather, we are saying only that it is important to assess the likely consequences of alternative policies accurately.* Whereas the many consumers of sugar may underestimate the likely effects of import quotas on them or ignore such effects altogether, the eager competitors for places in academically selective colleges and universities are, if anything, overly attuned to the effects of race-sensitive admissions policies on their chances of being admitted to the school of their choice. Their high level of awareness is in part an understandable consequence of the fact that admissions decisions are so very important to them.

average LSAT score of all white students was 24 percent higher than the average LSAT score of all black students; this difference shrinks to 10 percent when Wightman compares the LSAT scores of the retrospectively rejected black students with the scores of the lower-ranked white students.[22] This exercise is a good reminder that rather modest differences in the degree of preference given at the margin can lead to large swings in the absolute number of black students enrolled.

In considering the likely consequences of race-neutral admission policies for black enrollment, another possible effect must also be considered. It may be inaccurate to assume, as we have been doing in making these estimates, that black applications and black yields would suffer no ill effects from the imposition of a race-neutral policy. Substituting low odds of gaining admission for favorable odds could well discourage at least some students from applying in the first place. In addition, the prospect of studying and living alongside so few students of one's own race might well reduce yield at these schools by leading black students to attend historically black colleges or other institutions with large black enrollments.[23]

In view of these possibilities, it is hard to predict with precision the ultimate effects of a race-neutral process on total enrollment.[24] But the

---

[22] Data supplied by Linda Wightman in personal correspondence. Focusing on college grades rather than test scores produces very similar results.

[23] In the 1997 entering class, Boalt Hall enrolled one black and fourteen Hispanic students, as contrasted with forty-eight black and Hispanic students the previous year. UCLA's black law school enrollment declined 50 percent (Morris 1997, p. 80). The University of Texas law school enrolled four black students, as contrasted with thirty-one the previous year (Lederman et al. 1997, p. A32). A more recent report in the *New York Times* (Bruni, May 2, 1998, p. A1) suggests that the advent of race-neutral admissions policies at the undergraduate level has led some African American students and staff members at Berkeley to lessen their efforts to recruit outstanding black candidates who were offered places in the '98 entering cohort—and even to suggest that they should consider Stanford. Dana Inman, director of a black recruitment program at Berkeley, is quoted as saying: "We told them [prospective students] that it's a very hostile environment and that we're not welcome here. . . . We weren't pushing them to come to Cal." Only time will tell how much effect such apparent shifts in attitude, justified or unjustified, will have on yield.

[24] Also, admissions processes themselves are changing. There is evidence that early decision and early action programs are becoming increasingly common—and increasingly important, as measured by the percentage of the entering class admitted through them. This is relevant to the question of race and admissions because whites present themselves in disproportionately large numbers in these early admissions programs (in large part because they generally have more information about both particular schools and the application process) and because a candidate's odds of admission are increased by applying for early action or early decision. See Avery, Fairbanks, and Zeckhauser 1997. In short, increased emphasis on these modes of admission favors white candidates and, other things

general implication is clear: imposition of this kind of race-neutral policy would presumably take black enrollments at many of these selective institutions most of the way back to early 1960s levels, before colleges and universities began to make serious efforts to recruit minority students.[25]

In addition to the effects on overall black enrollment at these selective institutions, it is evident that race-neutral policies would have a major impact on the distribution of black students among undergraduate schools. Many now being admitted to the most selective colleges and universities would have to attend schools where the competition for admission is less keen (with some black students at those schools presumably moving to schools further down the academic hierarchy as defined by degree of selectivity, and so on). This pattern is clear even among the five selective colleges and universities for which we have the most detailed admissions records. At the three most selective of these schools, the black share of enrollment would fall from over 7 percent of the entering class to approximately 3 percent. (This assumes that the black yield would rise to the level of the white yield; if the black yield were to stay at its present level, the hypothetical black share would be under 2 percent.) At the other two schools, the hypothetical black share of enrollment would fall from about 7 percent to just under 5 percent (if we use the white yield) or about 3 percent (if we use the black yield).

Simulations Based on National Data

Our confidence in this mode of analysis, and in all of these estimates of the effects of race-neutrality on black enrollment, is bolstered by the results of a simulation in which we combined national data on SAT scores with enrollment patterns for all twenty-eight of the C&B institutions. While all of the C&B schools are academically selective and attract excellent students, the degree of selectivity varies considerably among them. These variations allow us to estimate how mandated race-neutrality in admissions would affect black enrollment at institutions of different

---

being equal, would increase the relative numbers of white candidates who gain admission. This "information advantage" reminds us that it is an oversimplification to think of the admissions process as somehow perfectly "race-neutral" if only no explicitly race-sensitive policies were employed.

[25] Wightman (1997, p. 28) reports a very similar result for law schools. Using essentially the same approach followed here, she estimates that the adoption of a race-neutral policy in law school admissions would have reduced the black share of enrollment to a level approximately equal to the level that prevailed in 1965. Cross and Slater (1997) also discuss systemwide effects of race-blind admissions policies in selective undergraduate colleges, law schools, and medical schools.

degrees of selectivity. For this purpose, we have divided all twenty-eight C&B schools into three "selectivity" groups, based on the average test scores of their matriculants:

- *SEL-1:* C&B colleges and universities for which the average combined SAT score of the entering class in 1989 was at least 1300 (Bryn Mawr, Duke, Princeton, Rice, Stanford, Swarthmore, Williams, Yale)
- *SEL-2:* C&B schools with average SATs between 1151 and 1300 (Barnard, Columbia, Emory, Hamilton, Kenyon, Northwestern, Oberlin, Pennsylvania, Smith, Tufts, Vanderbilt, Washington University, Wellesley, Wesleyan)
- *SEL-3:* C&B schools with average SATs of 1150 or below (Denison, Miami [Ohio], University of Michigan [Ann Arbor], University of North Carolina [Chapel Hill], Penn State, Tulane)

The C&B schools within each of these groupings are representative of a larger number of institutions nationwide with similar academic profiles.[26] Under a race-neutral regime, we assume that white and black students within defined SAT intervals (such as those with verbal SATs between 600 and 700) would apply, be accepted, and attend each set of schools, defined by their selectivity, in the same proportions. The ratio of black to white test-takers within each SAT band is known from national data. Multiplying these ratios by the actual numbers of white matriculants within each of the defined SAT intervals who attended the SEL-1, SEL-2, and SEL-3 C&B schools provides an estimate of the hypothetical number of black matriculants who would attend each grouping of schools under a race-neutral policy.[27] The overall results of the simulation are shown on Figure 2.11. We see, first, that they are entirely consistent with the general tenor of the findings based on examination of the much more detailed admissions records available for five of the C&B schools.

---

[26] See the discussion in the Preface and in Appendix A relating the characteristics of the C&B schools to the larger universe of selective colleges and universities.

[27] In effect, this methodology (explained in detail in Appendix B) examines the combined effects of application, admissions, and enrollment decisions. We can illustrate the method by citing the data for one SAT interval and one category of school. Nationally, there were 59,314 white test-takers and 1,536 black test-takers who scored between 600 and 700 on the verbal SAT (the ratio of blacks to whites was 0.026). At the SEL-1 C&B schools, there were 3,435 white matriculants with verbal SAT scores in this range. Multiplying the ratio of black to white test-takers by the number of actual white matriculants yields an estimate of the number of blacks within this SAT band who would have matriculated at the SEL-1 schools under race-neutral policies: the estimate for the C&B SEL-1 schools is 89. This number can be compared with the actual number of black matriculants in that SAT interval, which was 229.

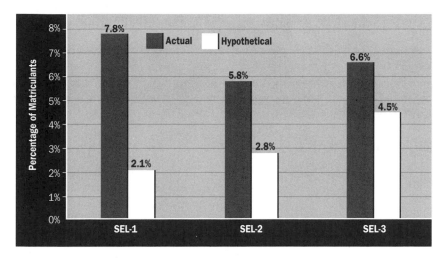

Figure 2.11. Black Matriculants as a Percentage of All College and Beyond Matriculants, by Institutional Selectivity, Actual and Hypothetical Percentages, 1989

Source: College and Beyond.

Notes: "Hypothetical" is the estimated percentage of black applicants who would be admitted under a "race-neutral" admissions policy. See text for further explanation. "SEL-1," "SEL-2," and "SEL-3" indicate institutions for which the mean combined SAT scores were 1300 or more, between 1150 and 1299, and below 1150, respectively.

The simulation also shows clearly (more clearly than the results for the five schools noted earlier) the differential effect of race-neutral policies, depending on the degree of institutional selectivity. Not surprisingly, the greatest impact would occur at those schools where the competition for admission is the most intense. At the SEL-1 schools, the hypothetical black enrollment would be just 2.1 percent of total enrollment, as contrasted with an actual black share of 7.8 percent. At the SEL-2 schools, the hypothetical black share would be just half the size of the current black share. The SEL-3 schools would lose roughly one-third of their black enrollment.[28]

Race-neutral policies would force most of the black students currently attending SEL-1 schools such as Swarthmore and Stanford to attend other institutions. Some would enroll at SEL-2 schools, but because there would not be sufficient places in this tier to accommodate all of those who would have been rejected by the SEL-1 schools, some would move to

[28] These results are based on the simulation using verbal SATs. A companion simulation, using math SATs (shown in Appendix B), produces even more dramatic declines in projected black enrollment. For example, at the SEL-1 schools the hypothetical share would be 1.6 percent rather than 2.1 percent.

SEL-3 schools or attend schools outside the C&B universe entirely.[29] Many of those now enrolled in SEL-2 and SEL-3 schools would also have to attend other schools. There has been a great deal of debate over the effects of such "cascading," with some critics of race-sensitive admissions asserting that black students would actually benefit from precisely this scenario. The argument is that they would be better off studying in less competitive academic environments where their own test scores would match more closely those of their classmates.[30] In subsequent chapters we will present new evidence that bears directly on this important issue.

EFFECTS ON ACADEMIC PROFILES OF
BLACK UNDERGRADUATES

We have shown that race-neutral admissions policies would sharply reduce black enrollment at academically selective colleges and universities. But would we not also expect such policies to improve the academic profile of the much smaller number of black students who would still be admitted to these schools? At least some of those who favor a race-neutral approach believe that it would weed out poorly prepared black students who should not have been admitted in the first place, leaving a smaller but academically superior black cohort. This is not, however, what the evidence from these five schools suggests.

By simulating the effects of a race-neutral policy, using the methods previously described, we can separate black matriculants into two groups—those who would have been retained under a race-neutral system and those who would have been rejected.[31] When we compare the SAT scores of these two groups, we obtain a surprising result: *there is very little difference.*

For the five C&B schools for which we have detailed admissions records, the average combined SAT score of the 170 students who would have been retained is 1181—and the average SAT score of the 165 who would have been rejected is 1145. An important corollary is that the average SAT score for black matriculants after the imposition of a race-neutral admissions policy would remain well below the average SAT score for white matriculants. And this pattern would hold even if admissions were based solely on SAT scores, since there are so many more white

[29] Our analysis of enrollment decisions shows that very high fractions of both black and white students chose to attend the most selective school that admitted them. This was true of 90 percent of white C&B survey respondents and 89 percent of black respondents.

[30] Herrnstein and Murray 1994, p. 476; D'Souza 1991, p. 252; O'Sullivan 1998, p. 41.

[31] Of course, we have no way of knowing which individual applicants within a given SAT interval would have been retained and which rejected; but we can estimate the *numbers* of applicants within each SAT interval who should be assigned to each of these two groups.

applicants than black applicants in the upper reaches of the SAT distribution. As we noted at the start of the chapter, comparing average SAT scores is an unreliable way of judging the degree of racial preference in any admissions process.

To be sure, if admissions were based solely on test scores, the difference in average SATs between the "retained" and the "retrospectively rejected" students would be much greater. But that is not the way admissions processes work. The modest difference in SAT scores that we estimate is a direct result of admissions policies that take many factors into account and that lead to the admission of some number of students with SATs that are lower than the SATs of significant numbers of students who were rejected—a pattern that holds for students from all racial and ethnic groups.

There are, nonetheless, some significant variations among the five schools in the putative effects of race-neutral policies on the academic profiles of black students. At the three schools that are relatively less selective, the introduction of a race-neutral policy would have had the most impact on black matriculants with lower SAT scores. The reason is that lower-scoring black applicants at these schools were much more likely to gain admission than white applicants with comparable SAT scores. At these three schools, the introduction of a race-neutral admissions process would have raised the average SAT scores of black matriculants by 4 percent, 7 percent, and (in the most extreme case) 9 percent.

At the two most selective universities, a race-neutral process would have had a much more limited effect: the projected average SAT score of the black students still enrolled under the race-neutral admissions process would have been only 2 percent higher at one institution and 1 percent higher at the other. In other words, there would have been virtually no difference between the average scores of those who would have been rejected and those who would have been retained.

What explains this puzzling result? In brief, the two most selective universities admitted exceedingly few white or black students with scores below, say, 1100; in this SAT range, the admission probabilities for the two groups were essentially the same (and in some cases actually slightly higher for the low-scoring white applicants, a group that included some recruited athletes). At these relatively low SAT levels, applying the relevant white admission probability to the black candidates leads to no noticeable reduction in the number of black matriculants. In the case of these two universities, the main effects of the introduction of a race-neutral admissions policy would occur within the 1200–1300 SAT range. It is at these higher SAT levels that the white admission probability is very much lower than the black admission probability. As a result, when we applied the white probabilities to black applicants, we found that large numbers of black applicants with SAT scores in these ranges would be retrospectively rejected.[32]

The main point is clear: at all of these selective C&B schools, and especially at the most selective ones, the imposition of a race-neutral admissions policy would have had surprisingly little effect on the overall test-score profile of the remaining black undergraduates.

ADMISSION TO PROFESSIONAL SCHOOLS

Similar kinds of questions about the effects of eliminating race-sensitive admissions apply to professional schools. We have no original research of our own to report in this area, but we can call attention to other studies which come to conclusions very similar to the ones we have reached through our study of undergraduate admissions. The fact that the findings are so similar is not surprising. After all, the leading professional schools in fields such as law, medicine, and business are at least as selective in their admissions as the highly selective undergraduate schools. And, as was pointed out in Chapter 1, they have made similar commitments to increase the diversity of their student populations.

The most comprehensive study at the professional school level has been conducted by Linda Wightman, who examined the credentials of all students who applied in 1990–91 to the 173 U.S. law schools approved by the American Bar Association.[33] Of the total of 90,335 students applying in that year, 57 percent received at least one offer of admission. Included in this total were 42,287 whites, 3,435 blacks, and 2,326 Hispanics. Blacks made up 6.8 percent of all the students admitted, while Hispanics accounted for 4.6 percent.

Wightman then computed how the percentages of minority students accepted would have changed if law schools had admitted students solely on the basis of college grades and standardized test scores, using logistic regressions. As in our studies of undergraduates at academically selective colleges, the results are dramatic. Blacks would have made up only 1.6 percent of the total number of accepted students if all law schools had

[32] Preferences for athletes affect these results, at least in modest ways. At one of the most selective schools in our set, we were able to remove all recruited athletes from the analysis; the effect was to increase modestly the difference in SAT scores for black students before and after the imposition of a race-neutral standard. (This results from removing some number of white students with relatively low SAT scores from the data.) However, the resulting differences in average SAT scores were very small; the recruited-athlete effect does not determine the general pattern of these results.

[33] Wightman 1997.

decided to admit only on the basis of grades and test scores. Hispanics would account for only 2.4 percent.

These computations overstate the system-wide impact on minority applicants, since some who would be denied admission to a particular school under a race-neutral standard could presumably have been admitted to law schools with less demanding entrance requirements. Because Wightman had data for all the ABA-approved law schools, she was able to calculate what would have happened under the optimistic assumption that all minority applicants who could be accepted by any law school would actually enroll in the best institution to which they were admitted (even though this would entail entering an institution of much lower standing in the law school hierarchy, where the financial aid provided would often be less). In this unlikely event, the proportion of blacks among all entering law students in 1991 would have been 3.4 percent, and the proportion of Hispanics would have been approximately the same.

The implications of adopting a race-blind procedure would be particularly severe for the higher-rated law schools. Wightman divided all law schools into six categories according to the average LSAT scores of their entering classes. If all students were admitted solely on the basis of LSAT scores and prior grades, the top tier of schools (i.e., the twenty-five to thirty most selective schools) would have seen their enrollment of blacks decline from 6.5 percent to less than 1 percent. In contrast, 30.4 percent of the entering classes of the sixth, or bottom, tier of schools would have been made up of black students.

A somewhat similar analysis of business school admissions has been carried out by the Battelle Memorial Institute for the Graduate Management Admissions Council.[34] This study found that overall acceptance rates were quite similar among racial groups, with 71 percent of white applicants, 70 percent of blacks, and 78 percent of Hispanics gaining admission to their first- or second-choice school. But the prior grades and test scores of those accepted differed markedly among these groups. The white students who were accepted had a college grade point average of 3.2, compared with 3.0 for blacks and 3.0 for Hispanics. Scores on the GMAT test also varied widely, with white students averaging 544; black students, 465; and Hispanics, 498.

The Battelle investigators conducted a multivariate analysis to determine the likelihood of admission for applicants from different racial groups, holding constant grades, test scores, age, gender, and so on. This analysis revealed that black applicants were 2.7 times as likely to gain admission as whites with comparable records. Hispanic applicants were

[34] Dugan, Baydar, Grady, and Johnson 1996.

2.8 times as likely to be admitted. The greatest advantage was apparently enjoyed by black applicants with GMAT scores below the 50th percentile who applied to highly selective schools (judged by cutoff scores on the GMAT). Although relatively few such applicants of any race were success-ful, black applicants with these characteristics were seven times more likely than whites scoring below the 50th percentile to gain admission to the most selective schools. Unfortunately, the Battelle study does not provide a direct estimate of the effect on black enrollment of the adop-tion of race-blind policies. However, we infer from admissions data that the effects would be considerable.

We have not found comparable studies of the effect of race-sensitive admissions policies in medical schools. Nevertheless, data obtained by Cross and Slater from the American Association of Medical Colleges (AAMC) indicate similar differences in grade point averages. For exam-ple, the median GPA for blacks accepted to medical school in 1996 was 3.1 for college pre-med science courses, as compared with a median GPA for whites of 3.6.[35] As was true of our study of five selective colleges, the median test scores of blacks accepted to medical schools was lower than the median for whites who were rejected. The implication is that race-blind admissions would drastically reduce the number of black students enrolled, especially at the most selective schools.

CAN CLASS-BASED PREFERENCES SUBSTITUTE FOR RACE-BASED PREFERENCES?

Some of those opposed to racial preferences on grounds of principle have advocated substituting what has come to be called "class-based affir-mative action," in which preference in admissions would be granted not on the basis of race, but on the basis of low family income. Because blacks are disproportionately numbered among the poor, proponents believe that class-based policies would achieve racial diversity while restricting preferences to those who have had to overcome genuine economic dis-advantage.[36]

[35] Cross and Slater 1997, p. 16. An analysis of medical school admissions at the Univer-sity of California at Davis (Davidson and Lewis 1997) found that Davis's special admissions program had had "powerful effects on the diversity of the student population" (p. 1153). Minority students accounted for 43 percent of the "special consideration students," and the mean GPA of this category was 3.1, compared with 3.5 for the control population of students admitted under regular standards. The MCAT scores of the "special consider-ation" population were also significantly lower.

[36] The most complete statement of the argument for class-based affirmative action is found in Kahlenberg (1996).

The economist Thomas Kane has looked carefully at the practicality of such an approach and concluded: "No race-blind substitute can substantially cushion the effect of ending racial preferences. The problem is one of numbers."[37] While blacks and other minorities are much more likely than whites to come from poor families, they still make up a minority of all college-age Americans with low incomes. In addition, poor minority applicants are much less likely than poor white applicants to have high test scores. The absolute number of minority students who come from low-income families *and* have high test scores is very small. As a result, according to Kane's analysis, blacks and Hispanics accounted for only 17 percent of all low-income students graduating from high school in 1992 who also scored in the top 10 percent of their class on standardized tests. These high scorers are, of course, the group from which the most academically selective schools draw their candidates for admission. Kane concludes:

> If [a college] wanted its entering class to "look like America" in terms of race and ethnicity, it would have to choose *only* low-income applicants. . . . Favoring low-income applicants with high scores over high-income applicants with similar scores will make its entering class look a little more like the country as a whole, but not much.[38]

The admissions data from the C&B schools do not contain enough reliable information on parents' education or income to permit similar calculations. We do know, however, that these highly selective colleges and universities are even less likely than colleges and universities generally to attract large numbers of truly low-income students who can meet their academic standards. This conclusion is borne out by the experience of the one C&B school for which we do have a partial measure of the socioeconomic status of all applicants in 1989, namely, the educational attainment of parents (a key predictor of income, wealth, and social class). Among the applicants to this school, only 10 percent came from families in which neither parent had a BA, and there were more than twice as many whites as blacks in this group.[39]

While we lack good data on the socioeconomic profile of the C&B applicant pools, we have been able to analyze the socioeconomic status of

[37] Kane (forthcoming).

[38] Ibid. Kane uses data from the National Education Longitudinal Study (NELS). Low-income families are defined as those with incomes of $20,000 or less.

[39] The percentage of black applicants from families in which neither parent had a BA was appreciably higher than the comparable percentage of white applicants, but since the overall number of white applicants was so much larger, the *absolute* number of white applicants from no-BA families was larger. This is the same pattern Kane noted in the national data.

the C&B matriculants. Since the C&B schools seek to enroll individuals from disadvantaged backgrounds, we presume that the applicants they admitted reflect fairly accurately the characteristics of all those with reasonably competitive credentials who sought admission. To describe the overall profile of the entering classes at all twenty-eight of the C&B schools in 1989, we constructed an index of socioeconomic status (SES) tailored to the characteristics of this population.[40] (All such measures are, however, far from perfect. They substantially understate black-white differences in resources because they fail to capture very large black-white gaps in accumulated wealth, and especially in financial assets, that persist after controlling for education and income.[41])

The descriptive results obtained by using this crude measure of socioeconomic status (including comparable figures for the relevant national population) are summarized in Figure 2.12. Three distinct patterns stand out:

- First, as we would have expected, the percentage of black C&B matriculants from a low-SES background is far higher than the corresponding percentage of white matriculants—14 percent versus 2 percent. But what is even more striking, though certainly not surprising, is the small size of both of these groups compared with the relevant national populations (50 percent of all blacks and 22 percent of all whites in the relevant age groups).
- At the other end of the scale, 15 percent of all black matriculants and nearly half of all white matriculants (44 percent) came from high-SES families—as compared with just 3 percent of the national black population and 11 percent of the national white population.

[40] Our low socioeconomic status group consists of matriculants from families in which neither parent had graduated from college *and* family income was less than $22,000; the high socioeconomic status group consists of those from families in which at least one parent was a college graduate and family income was greater than $70,000; the middle socioeconomic status group consists of all others. By pooling data from ETS, CIRP, and C&B survey questionnaires, we were able to assign 84 percent of all '89 C&B matriculants to one of these three categories. We also calculated the percentages of the national population (based on the 1990 Census) in each category, restricting the analysis to those in the same general age group as the parents of the '89 matriculants. As shown in Appendix Table B.2, the percentages of the national population in each of the three SES categories in 1990 were 28 percent (low SES), 64 percent (middle SES), and 9 percent (high SES). We imposed such a restrictive test on membership in the high-SES group so that we could make distinctions among the C&B matriculants. If we had used an "easier" test, so many white matriculants would have met it that the SES variable (which we use elsewhere in the analysis) would have lost its power to discriminate among C&B matriculants.

[41] Oliver and Shapiro 1995.

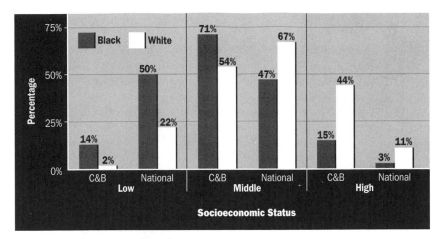

Figure 2.12. Socioeconomic Status Distribution of College and Beyond Matriculants and National College-Age Students, 1989

Source: College and Beyond and 1990 U.S. Census.

Notes: See Appendix B for a definition of socioeconomic status. "National" percentages are based on the education and income of the families of 16–18-year-olds in the 1990 U.S. Census.

- Finally, the middle-SES group contains by far the largest share of the black matriculants (71 percent) and just over half the white matriculants (54 percent). Blacks at the C&B schools are much more likely than blacks in general to come from this middle category, while white matriculants are less likely than whites in general to be found here.

The socioeconomic backgrounds of the C&B matriculants differ so much from the national distribution because of the well-documented correlation between parents' education and income and the academic achievement and preparation of their children.[42] When we sorted the matriculants according to the selectivity of the schools they attended, we found the expected pattern: the SEL-1 schools enroll the highest percentage of high-SES students, both black and white, and the SEL-3 schools are at the other end of the distribution. The differences, however, are surprisingly small. For example, 12 percent of the black matriculants at the SEL-1 schools came from families that meet our definition of low-SES; at the SEL-3 schools, 17 percent meet these criteria. At

[42] As long ago as 1969, Humphrey Doermann (1969), who was director of admissions at Harvard College from 1961 through 1966, called attention to the high correlation between test scores and wealth.

the SEL-1 schools, only 1 percent of the white matriculants came from a low-SES background, as compared with 2 percent at the SEL-3 schools.

These figures demonstrate how unrealistic it is to believe that the C&B schools could achieve diversity—while retaining their high academic qualifications—by focusing even more heavily on the socioeconomic status of their applicants than they do now. Admissions officers continue to be keenly interested in recruiting, admitting, and enrolling well-qualified students from poor backgrounds, whatever their race. This is both one aspect of the search for diversity and a reflection of long-standing commitments to enroll "poor but pious youth," in the language of another day. Although some critics may believe that universities do not try hard enough to find qualified low-income applicants, this charge is probably unjustified. Colleges regularly can and do obtain printouts of every high school student in the United States with grades and test scores above a given level. Thus, the problem is not that poor but qualified candidates go undiscovered, but that there are simply very few of these candidates in the first place.

Financial aid policies are intended to remove economic barriers that might otherwise prevent poor students of any race from attending selective institutions. At present, a number of the C&B schools meet the full need of all admitted students from poor families. This policy is expensive, but has been considered an important institutional priority. A class-based admissions program would of course be even more costly—probably prohibitively expensive.

The C&B schools unquestionably continue to contribute to social mobility. However, they do so today primarily by giving excellent educational opportunities to students from middle-class backgrounds. The academically competitive environment of these schools—both private and public—makes it unrealistic to expect them to serve large numbers of students who come from truly impoverished backgrounds; the fact that 14 percent of the black matriculants at these schools come from families with limited education and low incomes is, in its way, remarkable. At the same time, encouraging larger numbers of students from middle-class backgrounds, both black and white, to attend leading institutions enables those who have worked hard to take the next step. It usually requires more than a single generation to move up to the highest rungs of the socioeconomic ladder.

The findings presented in this chapter lead to five conclusions that stand out as especially important:

First, we estimate that the adoption of a strict race-neutral standard would reduce black enrollment at these academically selective colleges and universities by between 50 and 70 percent. This is the central finding in this chapter. According to these estimates, if blacks had been admitted in the same proportions as whites within each SAT interval (our definition of race-neutrality), black matriculants in 1989 would have constituted no more than 3.6 percent of the entering classes at these schools.

Second, the most selective schools would experience the largest drops in black enrollment. The proportion of black students in these institutions would decrease from about 7 percent to roughly 2 percent of total enrollment.

Third, the need to be sensitive to race in making admissions decisions, if more than small numbers of black students are to be enrolled, stems directly from continuing disparities in pre-collegiate academic achievements of black and white students, coupled with the extraordinary quality of the applicant pools available to the most selective colleges and universities. Racial disparities in test scores and high school grades are substantial and show no signs of disappearing in the foreseeable future. These differences loom especially large in the admissions processes of the C&B schools because of their success in attracting so many applications from exceedingly well-prepared white students.

Fourth, class-based preferences cannot be substituted for race-based policies if the objective is to enroll a class that is both academically excellent and diverse. While it is true that black students are much more likely than white students to come from families of low socioeconomic status, there are almost six times as many white students as black students who both come from low-SES families *and* have test scores that are above the threshold for gaining admission to an academically selective college or university. As a result, even if it were financially possible to admit substantially more low-income applicants, the number of minority students would be affected only marginally. Moreover, substitution of a class-based system would drastically reduce the quality of the eligible pool of black and Hispanic applicants, seriously impeding the goal of preparing the ablest minority leaders for society and the professions.

Fifth, the academic credentials of the black students who would have been rejected if a race-neutral standard had been applied were very good when judged on any absolute scale and were only slightly weaker than those of the black students who would have been retained. Selective schools attract highly talented minority candidates.

Numerical measures of academic qualification (principally SAT scores and high school grades) play an important part in the sorting and sifting of applicants to selective schools, but they are by no means the only factors considered. The myth of pure merit, held and celebrated by many, would have us believe that these institutions want only the "book smart, test smart" students, and that racial preferences are interfering with the precise science such a criterion implies. But the truth is that admitting students is far more an eclectic and interpretive art—with decisions based on judgment, experience, and perhaps even accumulated wisdom—than a series of formulaic calculations.

This overall set of findings can be interpreted as evidence that the efforts made by so many colleges and universities to enroll a diverse group of students have "worked." They can also be interpreted, by critics of these programs, as evidence that taking account of race in admissions is working too well. We would hope, however, that readers would suspend judgment concerning the value of these programs until more information is presented in subsequent chapters concerning the academic performance and subsequent life histories of the black students who were admitted and the broader educational consequences of the presence on campuses of students from diverse backgrounds.

CHAPTER 3

Academic Outcomes

THE ADMISSIONS process—emotionally exhausting as it is for students, their families, and the admissions officers themselves[1]—eventually comes to an end. Students are admitted, rejected, or put on a waiting list; they choose from among the schools that accept them; they collect their belongings; they go off to college—leaving their parents, as one resigned mother put it, "emptying their purses in the cause of higher education." A whole new world of options is available. Some students will focus from the first day on building their resumes for the next application process four years in the future. Some will celebrate the social freedom bestowed upon them by virtue of being on their own for the first time while others will be tormented with homesickness. Some will find themselves momentarily confused, having met their long-standing goal of getting into college and unsure of what to aim for next. Some will lose themselves in their studies, while still others will simply feel lost. The admissions process—with its ultimate "yes or no" conclusion—is quickly seen to have been a beginning rather than an end.

Perhaps the only thing that all will have in common is that each is a student. They will all receive grades. In time, if they stay enrolled, they will all choose a major. Most of them will graduate. Some will leave full of regret ("I was young and stupid," said one College and Beyond respondent), while others will have none ("I just felt that each day of college was better than the last," reported another). No matter what college teaches them about themselves or about life, and no matter what they do after graduating, their experiences as students offer the first testimony about the efficacy of the admissions process.

Some schools have tried to assess the admissions process by looking systematically at how various groups of students have performed in col-

---

[1] The highly intense, demanding nature of the admissions process at many selective colleges and universities—the very antithesis of a mechanical, by-the-numbers approach— is illustrated by the following account of life in the admissions office during the three months prior to the mailing of acceptance and rejection letters: "Illness is not tolerated; personal problems are forbidden; family relationships are put on hold. . . . None of life's emergencies can be accommodated . . . birth and death . . . cannot be allowed to disrupt the reading schedule. The whole day, for eleven or twelve weeks straight, revolves around reading those files" (Fetter 1995, p. 33).

lege, but many have lacked the time or the resources to carry out such studies. Moreover, it is very difficult to obtain reliable results by studying a single institution. The small number of students who enter a college in a given year makes it hazardous to draw conclusions by comparing specific subgroups. Because undergraduates come from an array of backgrounds and choose from such a range of courses of study (including departments with very different grading philosophies), it is hard to know why different students performed as they did. These difficulties are compounded when studying the experiences of minority students, since there are usually too few in any one class to allow more than impressionistic conclusions. While broad patterns may be traced (overall graduation rates are now routinely published), finer-grained analyses are difficult to carry out within such a small population.

Although we could examine the probabilities of admission for subgroups of applicants at only five of the colleges and universities in the C&B database, we were able to analyze the academic performance of more than 32,000 individual students who started at twenty-eight C&B schools in 1989 as well as the paths of another 30,000 who began college in the fall of 1976. These groups include more than 2,300 black students who entered one of these colleges in the fall of 1989, as well as an additional 1,800 from the 1976 entering cohort.

How did these black students perform—including the sizable number who would have been "retrospectively rejected" under a race-neutral standard? What proportion of the black matriculants graduated? How did their graduation rates compare with those of their white classmates, as well as with those of black and white matriculants nationwide? In what subjects did they major? How did they perform academically, both in terms of their grades and in terms of how they might have been predicted to perform on the basis of their test scores and other characteristics? These questions are by no means the only ones we should ask in assessing the value of four years of college. Still, few would disagree that earning a degree, obtaining a depth of knowledge within a field, getting at least reasonably good grades, and (though it is the most difficult to measure) living up to one's potential are the first outcomes by which the admissions policies of selective colleges and universities should be judged.

GRADUATION RATES

The most common admonition parents give to their college-age children is, Graduate! Stories about prominent athletes deciding whether to complete their studies or accept lucrative offers to join professional sports teams before graduating often include poignant comments about promises they made to parents or grandparents that, no matter what, they would finish college. Concern over completing the degree is no doubt at least as strongly felt—though less publicized—among non-athletes and their families. Anyone who has talked with the mothers and fathers of undergraduates thinking about taking time off from their studies knows how anxious such parents often are that their children will never return and receive their diplomas.

Such sentiments are rooted in a commonsense understanding of the advantages associated with being a college graduate. Economists have corroborated the wisdom of these impressions by observing repeatedly that completing a particular stage of education confers added economic value, even to those with very modest academic records. This is sometimes called the "sheepskin effect."[2]

Before going further, we should emphasize a basic point about graduation rates that is sometimes overlooked. Most students who fail to graduate do not drop out because they were incapable of meeting academic requirements. They leave for many other reasons. Inability to do the academic work is often much less important than loss of motivation, dissatisfaction with campus life, changing career interests, family problems, financial difficulties, and poor health. There is a need for much more systematic research on the reasons why students drop out, so that we will understand better what the British call "wastage" (though it is not always that, since some students should not graduate, and perhaps should not have gone to college in the first place). The ordinary kinds of "exit interviews" are unlikely to tell the full story. Some students are reluctant to give their true reasons for leaving school and may not even be entirely certain of their own motives for departing.[3]

Overall Graduation Rates

The overall graduation rate for the '89 black matriculants at the C&B schools was very high by any standard: 75 percent of these students graduated from the college they first entered within six years of matriculation. Using survey data, we estimate that at least an additional

[2] Jaeger and Page (1996, tab. 3) estimate that the net effect on earnings of receiving a BA, independent of years of schooling, is 24.5 percent for white men and 22.3 percent for white women. One of the first references to the "sheepskin effect" appears in Heckman and Polachek (1974). See also Hungerford and Solon 1987.

[3] Tinto (1993) reports that "[l]ess than 25 percent of all institutional departures, nationally, take the form of academic dismissal" (p. 49). In our own work, we attempted to collect data from the C&B schools on the reasons students failed to graduate, hoping to distinguish expulsions from voluntary withdrawals and departures for academic reasons from departures for other reasons, including a desire to transfer. These efforts were largely unsuccessful.

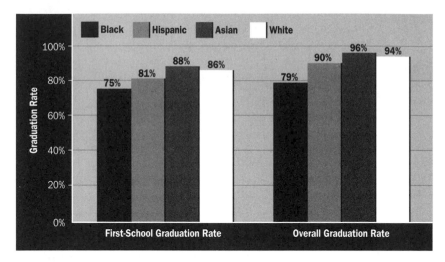

Figure 3.1. First-School and Overall Graduation Rates, by Race, 1989 Entering Cohort

Source: College and Beyond.

Notes: "First-School Graduation Rate" counts as graduates only those students who graduated within six years from the same school at which they matriculated as freshmen. "Overall Graduation Rate" also counts those who transferred from their first school and graduated elsewhere. See Appendix B for a more complete definition.

4 percent transferred and graduated from some other college within this same time frame, bringing the overall 6-year graduation rate to 79 percent (Appendix Table D.3.1). Still more will doubtless graduate in subsequent years.[4] White graduation rates at the C&B schools were higher yet, as were the rates for Asian Americans (who had the highest graduation rate of any group). Hispanic students at the C&B schools had graduation rates that were higher than those for black matriculants but lower than those for whites and Asian Americans (Figure 3.1).

Information about graduation rates in professional schools is more

---

[4] The fact that these are six-year graduation rates must be emphasized. Since some number of matriculants will graduate later on, these figures understate the "final" graduation rate for the cohort, and this understatement could be large. Nationally, 26 percent of all BA recipients and 32 percent of African American BA recipients earn their BAs more than six years after matriculation (Nettles and Perna 1997, p. 277; calculations based on the national Baccalaureate and Beyond Longitudinal Study, First Follow-Up [B&B 1993/1994]). However, students who enroll at the highly selective C&B schools tend to graduate in fewer years than do all students, so the future increase in the graduation rate for the C&B matriculants will be smaller than the corresponding increase for a national student population.

limited, but the patterns seem similar to those we observed for under-graduates in selective colleges. According to information supplied to us by staff members of the Association of American Medical Colleges, 87 percent of "underrepresented" minority students (black, Hispanic, and Native American) entering in 1988 had graduated six years later, compared with 93 percent of their white classmates. Among those entering 163 ABA-approved law schools that agreed to participate in the LSAC Bar Passage Study, 78 percent of black and 88 percent of Hispanic students graduated, compared with 90 percent of white and 89 percent of Asian American students. A separate calculation of graduation rates at 30 of the most selective law schools revealed that 91 percent of blacks and 90 percent of Hispanics graduated.[5]

National benchmarks help us see the C&B graduation rates in context. At these twenty-eight academically selective institutions, the rates for all racial/ethnic groups were exceedingly high when compared with the norm in American higher education. Odd as it may seem, the National Collegiate Athletic Association (NCAA) is the primary source of data on graduation rates for all students. It has published comparable figures showing how many full-time students entering all 305 Division I universities in 1989 received their BA from the same school within six years. The contrast with the C&B graduation rates is dramatic. At Division I schools, 59 percent of all white matriculants and just 40 percent of all black matriculants graduated from the college that they first entered within this time period.[6]

---

[5] Wightman (1997, pp. 4–5, 36) is the source of the data for the 163 ABA-approved law schools. Wightman (personal correspondence) also provided the graduation rates for 30 of the most selective schools.

[6] See National Collegiate Athletic Association 1996. The NCAA only publishes these data for those schools in its "Division I"—a group that is made up of 305 institutions (mostly universities) that compete at the higher levels of athletic competition. Both the NCAA study and the C&B database include only full-time students. One might conjecture that the lower graduation rate of black (and white) matriculants at the NCAA Division I schools is due to the presence of comparatively large numbers of recruited athletes who graduate at below-average rates. This is not the case. NCAA data show that in Division I, the odds of graduating are slightly higher for athletes than for other students, although this result is due in part to the awarding of athletic scholarships and the provision of extensive academic support. Graduation rates vary considerably by gender and sport.

Within a reasonably short time, more national data on the graduation rates of recent entering cohorts, including data on overall ("any-school") graduation rates, will be available through the NELS database. At present, however, few data of this kind appear to exist—which is itself remarkable, given the importance of graduation rates. Data collected in the High School and Beyond survey show the highest level of education attained by 1980 high school seniors in the spring of 1986 (six-year graduation rates). Roughly 56 percent of

Although the gap is smaller at C&B schools than at Division I universities, black students are less likely than whites to graduate from all types of institutions. There are many reasons for these pervasive differences. As the data on test scores indicate, minority students as a group have weaker pre-collegiate academic credentials than do white students. The other factors involved include more limited financial resources, family backgrounds that are less conducive to high educational attainment, and a variety of difficulties in adjusting to predominantly white campuses.[7]

These same forces are at work within the C&B schools. They are, however, present in attenuated form, which presumably helps to explain why black graduation rates are so much higher at the C&B schools and why the black-white gap in graduation rates is so much smaller. Black matriculants at the C&B schools tend to have much higher SAT scores than black college students in general (the scores of black students at the C&B schools are clustered in the far right tail of the national distribution for black test-takers). They are also likely to be self-selected—and to have been selected by admissions offices—on the basis of additional, less measurable criteria that presumably have positive effects on graduation rates. For instance, many may be strongly motivated to compete and to succeed in challenging academic environments. Moreover, while black students in general come from decidedly poorer backgrounds than their white classmates, the black students at the selective schools tend to come from somewhat more affluent and better-educated families than do black students in general. Students from such families, regardless of race, are more likely to graduate than other students.

In addition, institutions that are selective in their admissions policies generally have more financial resources at their disposal than do other colleges and universities. The C&B institutions' relatively generous financial aid programs may be particularly important in enabling black students to stay in school until they graduate. Also, these schools are often able to provide more personal attention, counseling, support, and other resources than less well-funded institutions can afford to make available. Among these "other resources" are large numbers of high-achieving classmates who help to create a climate in which graduation is the "expected thing." A common theme among black matriculants interviewed in the course of this study is that attendance at C&B schools had a

---

the whites and 29 percent of the blacks who enrolled full-time in four-year private colleges had earned a bachelor's degree by 1986 (U.S. Department of Education 1996, p. 317).

[7] For national data bearing on racial differences in "persistence" in higher education, see Nettles and Perna 1997. Nettles and several colleagues at the University of Michigan are embarking on a major study of the reasons why drop-out rates are higher for black matriculants than for other groups of students.

dramatic effect on what they thought they could accomplish and on what they aspired to do.

Whatever the relative importance of these and other factors, one clear conclusion emerges: judged by a national standard, the '89 black matriculants at the C&B colleges and universities graduated in very large numbers.

The Intersection of Student SAT Scores and School Selectivity: The "Fit" Hypothesis

We turn now to a more intensive analysis of factors related to graduation rates within the C&B universe. Because there has been much discussion of the use of SAT scores in the admissions process and a vigorous debate over their predictive power,[8] it is important to know how the SAT scores of the C&B matriculants affected their chances of earning a degree. Do SAT scores correlate with graduation rates within this restricted universe of highly selected individuals?[9] If so, is the relationship the same for black and white matriculants? To provide at least rough answers to such questions, we compared five groups of '89 C&B matriculants, classified by their combined verbal and math SAT scores: below 1000, 1000–1099, 1100–1199, 1200–1299, and 1300 and over.

For both black and white matriculants, the simple association between student SAT scores and graduation rates is at least mildly positive. The higher the student's combined SAT score, the greater the odds that the student graduated from his or her first school (Figure 3.2). The largest increase for both white and black matriculants occurs between the bottom SAT interval and the next higher interval; once we reach the 1100-and-over intervals, the relationship between SAT scores and graduation rates flattens out, especially for black matriculants.

This figure also shows that black graduation rates are lower than white graduation rates within each SAT interval. The obvious inference is that SAT scores are by no means the sole determinant of differences in graduation rates between white and black matriculants. There are clearly other things going on. Some critics of race-sensitive admissions have asserted

[8] Some people favor basing admissions decisions much more heavily on objective data, such as test scores and high school grades, while others believe that the use of test scores, in particular, should be abandoned. For a detailed and useful evaluation of both the issues that have been posed and relevant research, see Jencks and Phillips (forthcoming).

[9] The highly selected character of this population leads to what statisticians call a "restriction on range," which reduces the size of correlations. Thus, the correlations reported below understate the more general predictive power of SAT scores outside the C&B universe.

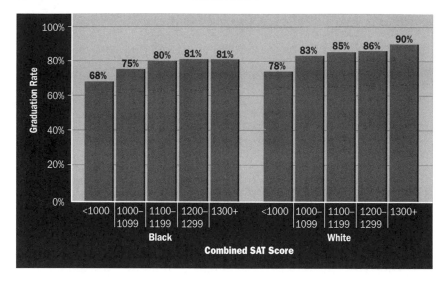

Figure 3.2. Graduation Rates, by Combined SAT Score and Race, 1989 Entering Cohort

Source: College and Beyond.

Note: Graduation rates are six-year first-school graduation rates, as defined in the notes to Figure 3.1.

that the underlying reason for the lower black graduation rates can be found in a mismatch between the black students' preparation and the academic levels of the schools that admitted them. Black students will be more likely to graduate, the argument goes, if they enroll in a school where their own SAT score matches the school's test-score profile than if they "reach too high" and go to a school where most fellow students have higher test scores. The C&B database permits a clear test of this "fit" hypothesis.

While all of the C&B schools are academically selective and attract excellent students, some are more selective than others. To determine how the degree of selectivity of a C&B college affects the graduation rates of its students, we have used three "selectivity" categories, based on the average test scores of each school's matriculants. As noted in the previous chapter, at the SEL-1 schools the average combined SAT score of the '89 entering class was at least 1300; at the SEL-2 schools, it was between 1150 and 1299; and at the SEL-3 schools, it was below 1150.[10]

---

[10] The specific schools assigned to these categories for the '89 entering cohort are as follows: SEL-1: Bryn Mawr, Duke, Princeton, Rice, Stanford, Swarthmore, Williams, Yale; SEL-2: Barnard, Columbia, Emory, Hamilton, Kenyon, Northwestern, Oberlin, Penn-

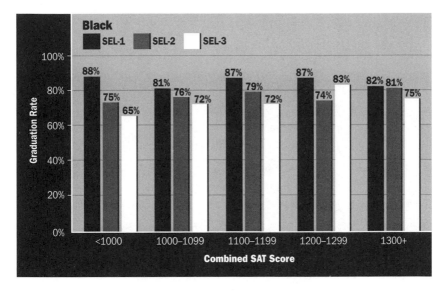

Figure 3.3. Black Graduation Rates, by Combined SAT Score and Institutional Selectivity, 1989 Entering Cohort

Source: College and Beyond.

Notes: Graduation rates are six-year first-school graduation rates, as defined in the notes to Figure 3.1. "SEL-1," "SEL-2," and "SEL-3," indicate institutions for which the mean combined SAT scores were 1300 or more, between 1150 and 1299, and below 1150, respectively.

The data on student test scores, school selectivity, and graduation rates are combined in Figures 3.3 and 3.4 (and presented in more detail in Appendix Table D.3.3). They provide no support for the "fit" hypothesis. In fact, they show that even those black students in the lowest SAT band (those with combined scores under 1000) graduated at *higher* rates, the more selective the school that they attended. The lowest graduation rate for these students occurred at the SEL-3 schools, where there were the largest number of students with SAT scores similar to their own.[11] The

sylvania, Smith, Tufts, Vanderbilt, Washington University, Wellesley, Wesleyan; SEL-3: Denison, Miami (Ohio), University of Michigan (Ann Arbor), University of North Carolina (Chapel Hill), Penn State, Tulane. To repeat a comment made earlier, the SAT scores used throughout this study are before scores were "recentered" by the Educational Testing Service in 1995. The recentering process raised the level of combined scores by approximately 100 points, and the averages cited here would have to be increased by roughly that amount to be compared with scores reported today.

[11] The especially low first-school graduation rate for black matriculants with SATs below 1000 at the SEL-3 universities (65 percent) is due in part to the fact that the open-ended

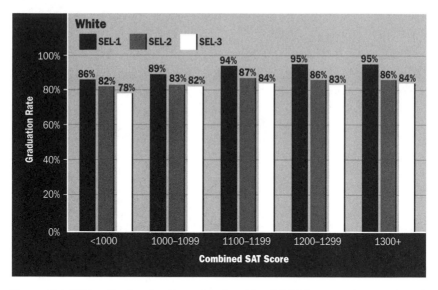

Figure 3.4. White Graduation Rates, by Combined SAT Score and Institutional
Selectivity, 1989 Entering Cohort

Source: College and Beyond.
Notes: See notes to Figure 3.3.

same pattern holds for black students whose SAT scores were in the
1000–1099 and 1100–1199 intervals. These students' test scores matched
most closely the test-score profiles of the SEL-3 schools (where average
SATs for the entire entering class were under 1150). But those black
students in these SAT intervals who attended SEL-1 or SEL-2 schools
(where average test scores were all above 1150, and in most instances far
above 1150) graduated at higher rates than did those black students who
went to schools with test-score profiles that were better statistical "fits"
with their own SATs.

How have the white students with combined SAT scores in these same
SAT ranges fared when they attended schools with higher average SAT
scores than their own? Do their graduation rates conform to the "fit"
hypothesis? The answer, again, is no, though the patterns are less dramatic. In SEL-1 colleges, white students with relatively low SAT scores gradu-

---

below-1000 category at these institutions contains larger numbers of students with quite low
scores than were present in the other C&B institutions. Restricting the comparison to black
students in the 900–999 range raises the black graduation rate to 68 percent and reduces by
a third the gap in graduation rates between black matriculants at these schools and black
matriculants at the SEL-2 colleges and universities. In the under-900 SAT range, the black
graduation rate at the SEL-3 institutions was 62 percent.

ated at higher rates than did students with similar scores who attended SEL-2 or SEL-3 schools (Figure 3.4).

The general conclusion is clear: graduation rates for all C&B students, regardless of SAT score or race, were highest at the SEL-1 schools and next highest at the SEL-2 schools. Black and white matriculants in every SAT interval who attended SEL-1 schools were most likely to earn their degrees. Thus, the higher overall graduation rates achieved by these schools cannot be attributed solely to their success in enrolling students with high SAT scores.

Having looked at the relationship between school selectivity and graduation rates while "controlling" for differences in SAT scores in this simple way (by simultaneously classifying students by both the selectivity of the school they attended and their own SAT score), we now present a somewhat more complex—and more complete—analysis that controls for additional variables. Using a standard multivariate regression approach (explained in detail in Appendix B), we can estimate how graduation rates vary with school selectivity on an "other things equal" basis.

The central finding is that the effect of school selectivity on graduation rates persists after controlling not only for differences in SAT scores, but for other factors as well. In other words, among students of the same gender with similar SAT scores, high school grades, and socioeconomic status, those who attended the most selective schools graduated at higher rates than did those who attended less selective schools. There is very little difference between the actual (unadjusted) graduation rates at each level of school selectivity and the adjusted graduation rates obtained by controlling for these other variables (Figure 3.5).[12]

There are at least three possible explanations for these results. First, the most selective schools have the best opportunity to "pick and choose" among applicants within every SAT category. Hence, the high graduation rates of their matriculants in the lower SAT intervals may reflect the success of these schools in identifying and enrolling students with below-average test scores who had other qualities that gave them excellent prospects of graduating. The second explanation has to do with resources. The schools in the SEL-1 category all tend to be residential, to have relatively small enrollments, and to have sufficient endowments and other financial resources to afford smaller classes and more support services—all factors that one would expect to contribute to high gradua-

---

[12] The adjusted graduation rates can be thought of as estimates of what graduation rates would have been within each group of schools had their students possessed the average characteristics of the entire C&B population. See Appendix Table D.3.4 for the underlying logistic regressions, including the standard errors of the coefficients, and Appendix B for a full discussion of the logistic regressions and the methodology used to derive the adjusted probabilities from them. We use this methodology throughout the study.

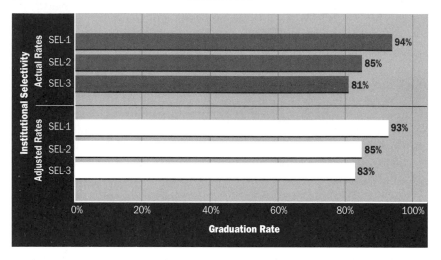

Figure 3.5. Graduation Rates, by Institutional Selectivity, Actual and Adjusted
Rates, 1989 Entering Cohort

Source: College and Beyond.

Notes: Adjusted rates are estimated using a logistic regression model controlling for
student and institutional characteristics (see Appendix Table D.3.4 and Appendix B).
Graduation rates are six-year first-school graduation rates, as defined in the notes to
Figure 3.1. Institutional selectivity categories are as defined in the notes to Figure 3.3.

tion rates. In essence, the same institutional factors that separate the
entire set of C&B schools from the far larger group of NCAA Division I
colleges and universities can be used to distinguish among subgroups of
C&B schools. One long-time college president has also suggested, as a
third possible explanation, that many students at these highly selective
schools are keenly aware of the value of the graduation credential, as
well as of the heavy investment they have made in seeking it, and thus
will make extra efforts to complete their studies, no matter what the
difficulties.

The lower black graduation rate at the SEL-3 schools may be due to a
combination of factors. This category of schools includes the four large
public universities in the C&B universe, and it is possible that the inevitable effects of large enrollments (somewhat less personal attention and
a greater risk that some students will "feel lost") may have especially
severe effects on black students with relatively weak academic preparation who must adjust to a different educational environment.[13] The

---

[13] Together, these four universities enrolled 87 percent of all black students in the '89
cohorts at the SEL-3 schools (and 87 percent of all students, regardless of race). Because

ACADEMIC OUTCOMES

65

relative size of the black student population may also matter: black graduation rates are lower at the two public universities with the smallest percentages of African American students. Finally, need-based financial aid may be less readily available at some of these schools. More research is needed to sort out these interconnected factors.[14]

Meanwhile, it is important to maintain perspective: viewed in a national context, the 68 percent first-school black graduation rate at the SEL-3 schools is a very high rate—not only for blacks, who graduated from NCAA Division I schools at an average rate of 40 percent, but also for whites, whose overall Division I graduation rate was only 59 percent. From a national perspective, it is troubling that so many students—and especially black students—who enter four-year colleges fail to earn a degree. Fortunately, awareness of this problem has increased, and new research (of the kind being conducted by Michael Nettles and his colleagues at the University of Michigan) may suggest new approaches. One large question is the extent to which low national graduation rates are due to the inability of students and their families to meet college costs, rather than to academic difficulties or other factors.

While school selectivity is strongly associated with graduation rates, even after we adjust for the effects of other variables, the same thing cannot be said for SAT scores. The mildly positive association that we saw earlier between SAT scores and graduation rates flattens out dramatically when school selectivity and other factors are taken into account. After controlling for race and gender, high school grades, students' socioeconomic backgrounds, and school selectivity, differences in SAT scores above 1100 provide no clue about the odds of graduating (Figure 3.6). Below 1100, unadjusted differences in graduation rates by SAT interval are diminished substantially when we adjust for the effects of other variables. In short, above a threshold of 1100, SAT scores have a very limited role to play in explaining differences in graduation rates. They help predict at which colleges and universities, within the C&B universe, a student will be admitted and will enroll. But that is almost all they do. The college or university that a student attends is a much better predictor of the odds of graduating than is the student's own SAT score.

---

there are only two private schools in the group with which we can make direct comparisons (one liberal arts college and one relatively small university), we are unable to determine whether the lower black graduation rate for this set of institutions is due to the size and other characteristics of large public universities or to their somewhat lower degree of selectivity. We suspect that the answer is "some of both," but we cannot be sure.

[14] At one point we thought that these lower graduation rates might also be related to in-state versus out-of-state patterns of enrollment or to a concentration of students from low socioeconomic backgrounds; neither of these conjectures stood up to analysis.

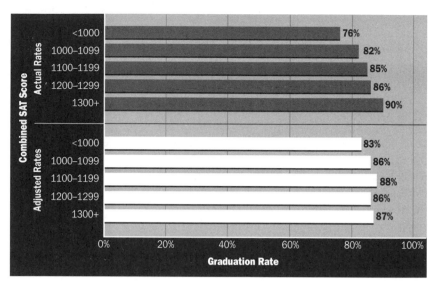

Figure 3.6. Graduation Rates, by Combined SAT Score, Actual and Adjusted
Rates, 1989 Entering Cohort

Source: College and Beyond.

Notes: Adjusted rates are estimated using a logistic regression model controlling for
student and institutional characteristics (see Appendix Table D.3.4 and Appendix B).
Graduation rates are six-year first-school graduation rates, as defined in the notes to Figure 3.1.

Socioeconomic background is another factor bearing on graduation
rates. Within the C&B student population, graduation rates clearly vary
with family circumstances for students from all racial groups (Figure 3.7).
First-school graduation rates range from 88 percent for all students in the
high socioeconomic category to 74 percent for those in the low socioeconomic category.[15] Other variables, including SAT scores and high school
grades, correlate with socioeconomic status (SES), and adjusting for
these interactions weakens but by no means eliminates the clear relation-

[15] It is worth emphasizing that these differences exist in spite of the extensive provision
of financial aid. Need-based aid, which is widely provided at the C&B schools, undoubtedly
helps students from low-income families attend these schools and graduate from them.
However, these data demonstrate that such aid mechanisms cannot be expected to eliminate all of the effects associated with socioeconomic status. Even generous need-based aid
programs generally expect students to borrow and to work to defray some part of their
college costs. Moreover, students with substantial family resources are less likely to be
inclined to drop out of school because of economic pressures at home. Finally, socioeconomic status is associated with many other attributes, such as strong high school preparation and encouragement to do well academically, which are, of course, independent of
financial aid packages.

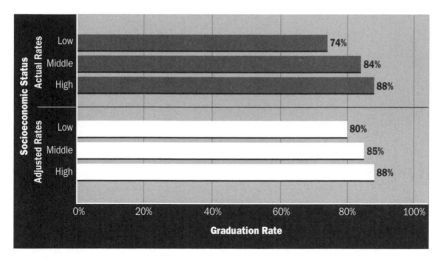

Figure 3.7. Graduation Rates, by Socioeconomic Status, Actual and Adjusted Rates, 1989 Entering Cohort

Source: College and Beyond.

Notes: Adjusted rates are estimated using a logistic regression model controlling for student and institutional characteristics (see Appendix Table D.3.4 and Appendix B). Graduation rates are six-year first-school graduation rates, as defined in the notes to Figure 3.1. See Appendix B for a definition of socioeconomic status (SES).

ship between SES and graduation rates. Whereas the unadjusted gap in graduation rates for all matriculants between the high and the low SES categories is 14 percentage points (88 percent versus 74 percent), the adjusted gap is 8 percentage points. In other words, if those C&B matriculants from low SES backgrounds had been like the "average" matriculant in all other respects, they would still be predicted to graduate at a lower rate than those in the high SES category—but the difference has narrowed from an actual gap of 14 percentage points to an estimated gap of 8 percentage points. Socioeconomic status has a much stronger effect on graduation rates for black students than it does for all students. Among black matriculants, the adjusted gap in graduation rates between students in the high and low socioeconomic status categories is estimated to be 15 percentage points.[16]

We see, then, the respective roles played by socioeconomic status, SAT scores, and school selectivity in determining the graduation rates of the C&B matriculants who entered college in the fall of 1989. Taking account of the effects of these variables shrinks the black-white gap in

[16] See Appendix Table D.3.4 for the underlying logistic regressions, including the standard errors of the coefficients and Appendix B for an explanation of how the adjusted probabilities are calculated.

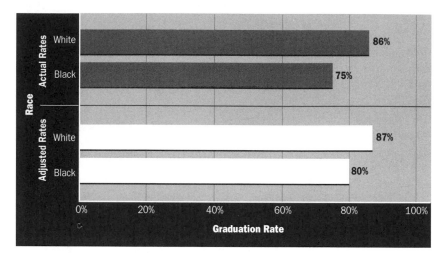

Figure 3.8. Graduation Rates, by Race, Actual and Adjusted Rates, 1989 Entering Cohort

Source: College and Beyond.

Notes: Adjusted rates are estimated using a logistic regression model controlling for student and institutional characteristics (see Appendix Table D.3.4 and Appendix B). Graduation rates are six-year first-school graduation rates, as defined in the notes to Figure 3.1.

graduation rates, but the reduction is less than one might have expected it to be: controlling for other variables reduces the gap from 11 percentage points to an adjusted figure of 7 points (Figure 3.8). We suspect that part of the explanation for the size of the remaining gap is that our treatment of differences in socioeconomic status is insufficient. The measure of socioeconomic status that we use is crude (failing, for example, to capture important differences in accumulated wealth), and a more sophisticated analysis of this and other differences between the black and white populations might make a considerable difference.[17]

Improvements in Graduation Rates

The C&B schools made notable progress in raising their graduation rates for all matriculants between the '76 and '89 entering cohorts. The first-school graduation rate rose from 77 to 85 percent; despite less room for

---

[17] For example, we know that in the black-only regression socioeconomic status has a larger effect on graduation rates. More generally, the black-white gap in graduation rates narrows somewhat when we use the black regression coefficients, but cell sizes are too small to give us great confidence in such results.

improvement, the overall graduation rate (which includes those who transferred and graduated elsewhere) rose almost as dramatically, from 86 to 92 percent. Graduation rates improved for both black and white matriculants, and the black-white gap narrowed somewhat. These improvements are due in part to the general increase in the SAT scores of the C&B matriculants that occurred over these thirteen years, but graduation rates also increased quite consistently within each SAT interval. The greatest progress occurred in the below-1000 SAT interval and in the SEL-3 schools (principally the public universities).[18]

Economists are predisposed to suggest a straightforward economic explanation for the improvement in graduation rates. One of the most striking empirical findings of recent years is the dramatic increase in the wage premium associated with graduation from college as compared with graduation from high school. Between 1979 and 1986, the earnings differential expanded from 32 percent to a record level of roughly 70 percent.[19] Census data for more recent years indicate that this high premium has been sustained and may even have increased somewhat. There is no great mystery as to what has been happening. The U.S. economy is assigning more and more value to higher education as preparation for success in the workplace. As a result, the incentive to finish college is becoming stronger. This is surely one reason why the debate over who gains admission to the most selective schools has become so heated.[20]

There are many other possible explanations. The quality of students enrolled at these colleges may have improved even more than one would think by looking only at SAT scores. On the other hand, it is also possible that there has been some relaxation in grading standards and a somewhat greater willingness to allow "marginal" students to graduate. Another hypothesis that some critics, both inside and outside the academy, have advanced to help explain the rising graduation rates is that the presence of larger numbers of minority students has forced C&B colleges to offer easier courses and majors, which are alleged to be chosen by large numbers of minority students. However, the fact that graduation rates have risen for all races casts doubt on this possible explanation.

[18] See Appendix Tables D.3.1 and D.3.2.

[19] Murphy and Welch 1989, p. 17. For a brief discussion of the correlation between education and earnings, see Card and Krueger (1996). See also Mincer 1974; Levy and Murnane 1992; Card and Krueger 1992a.

[20] See Frank and Cook 1995, pp. 153–56. It is interesting to note the very large increases in graduation rates that occurred between the mid-1950s (exemplified by the C&B '51 entering cohort) and the early 1990s. Over these decades, graduation rates rose by 14 to 20 percentage points within each type of school, and most rapidly (26 percentage points) within the public universities.

Evidence in the next section on the academic majors chosen by minority students makes the hypothesis seem even less plausible.

CHOICE OF MAJOR

Unlike the pursuit of a diploma, the choice of an academic major is an educational "outcome" that resists easy categorization. Whereas it is plainly more desirable to graduate than to fail to graduate, there is no unequivocal benchmark that can be used to evaluate choice of major. Students choose a field of study from a wide array of options and for a wide range of reasons. Some want to follow their current interests, inclinations, or passions; others are more pragmatic and select the major they think will be most relevant to their intended careers.

In the C&B schools, many fields within the liberal arts are seen both as interesting in and of themselves and as training grounds—opportunities to enhance capacities or gain knowledge that can be readily converted into marketable skills. And while there are no "right" or "wrong" choices of major, the choices made often constitute the first step that students take in narrowing their options. Medical schools certainly accept some number of French literature majors (if they have completed the pre-med science requirements), but not that many. Major investment banks and consulting firms are willing to hire classics majors, but usually only if they have demonstrated some facility with quantitative methods. Attendance at a highly selective school may well have a halo effect that provides students who majored in a given field more options than might have been available otherwise—a literate physics major from Columbia, for example, may have as good a chance of getting a job as a Hollywood scriptwriter as a creative writing major from a less well known school—but, by and large, an undergraduate's choice of an academic concentration both influences and constrains subsequent decisions and opportunities. As a result, this decision should be seen—educationally and professionally—as an important bend in the river.

Academic preparation has a definite influence on the choice of a major. The humanities require stronger writing skills, whereas the quantitative social sciences, the physical sciences, and engineering call for stronger training in mathematics.[21] Looking at the fields of concentra-

---

[21] For a detailed analysis of the different ways in which men and women students in a subset of the C&B schools "convert" verbal and math SAT scores into probabilities of majoring in one field or another, see Turner and Bowen (forthcoming). Significant differences related to gender remain after controlling for verbal and math SAT scores.

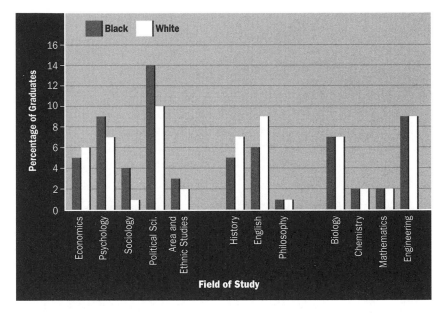

Figure 3.9. Percentage of Graduates Majoring in Selected Fields, by Race, 1989 Entering Cohort

Source: College and Beyond.

Note: Includes first-school graduates only.

tion for the black and white students in the 1989 cohort (Figure 3.9), we see that blacks are noticeably less likely to have majored in English and history, and more likely to have majored in psychology, political science, and sociology. Blacks and whites were equally likely to have majored in philosophy, economics, the natural sciences, and engineering. Contrary to impressions sometimes conveyed,[22] only very small numbers of black students at these schools majored in African American studies or Black

---

Relative to men with the same test scores, women are (for example) more likely to choose psychology instead of economics and biology instead of math or physics.

[22] For example, Graglia (1993, p. 135) has argued: "When the specially admitted students discover, as most soon must, that they cannot compete with their classmates, no matter how hard they try, they will insist, as self-respect requires, that the game be changed. Thus are born demands for black studies and multiculturalism, which perform the twin functions of reducing the need for ordinary academic work and providing support for the view that the academic difficulties of the black students are the result, not of substantially lower qualifications, but of racial antipathy and that the source of the problem is not black but white shortcomings."

studies. In the 1989 cohort, less than 3 percent majored in African American studies, American studies, or area studies of any kind.

Thirteen years earlier, the '76 black matriculants exhibited similar interests in the various fields of study (Appendix Table D.3.5). One of the biggest changes between the '76 and '89 cohorts was in the percentage of black students who majored in engineering. During a period in which there was much debate about the content of the curriculum and academic standards, the number of black students majoring in engineering rose by more than 40 percent (from 6.3 to 8.9 percent of all black graduates).

GRADES AND ACADEMIC "UNDERPERFORMANCE"

While the majors chosen by black students are similar to those chosen by their white peers and provide no cause for concern, their college grades present a more sobering picture. The grades earned by black students at the C&B schools often reflect their struggles to succeed academically in highly competitive academic settings. The average cumulative grade point average (GPA) for the black '89 matriculants was 2.61 on a 4.0 scale—a B-minus. The average for their white classmates was 3.15—somewhere between a B and a B-plus. To some, this 0.52 point difference in average GPAs may seem negligible; in fact it is very large when seen in the context of the overall distribution of grades. The average rank of black matriculants was at the 23d percentile of the class, the average Hispanic student ranked in the 36th percentile, and the average white student ranked in the 53d percentile.[23]

Predicting Rank in Class

When admissions officers analyze an applicant's potential, they often use what they know about the student's test scores, high school grades, and courses taken to predict how that student will perform academically in

[23] We calculated each matriculant's percentile rank, based on cumulative GPA, in his or her entering cohort (a measure which we term "rank in class" for expositional convenience), and we use this measure of academic standing rather than the student's actual GPA. The reason is that "raw" GPAs are scaled somewhat idiosyncratically across schools as a result of differences in grading philosophies, mixes of majors, and other factors, such as the degree of "grade inflation." Imposing a uniform percentile distribution helps to correct for this problem. Because whites compose such a large share of the C&B student population, their average GPA rank has to be close to the 50th percentile.

college. We have the advantage of examining academic performance after the student's college career has been completed, and with full knowledge of how all of the student's classmates fared. With the hindsight provided by college transcripts, we can identify grading patterns within different fields and can control for the effects on rank in class of (for example) having majored in physics rather than in economics. Applying multivariate regression analysis to this rich set of retrospective data allows us to estimate how each factor—a student's gender, race, SAT scores, high school grades, field of study, socioeconomic status—affected his or her grades, with each of the other factors held constant.

This method of analysis allows us to hazard an answer to an important question concerning the development of human capital: did people from various groups perform as well as they were capable of doing? It is commonplace to assert that someone is an "overachiever" or that someone is not living up to his or her potential. The use of multivariate regression analysis permits us to investigate such impressionistic judgments on the basis of the empirical record.

The basic regression used to predict rank in class is presented in Appendix Table D.3.6.[24] We note, first, that the "control" variables perform as expected. For example, women earn higher grades than men (their average rank in class is about 8 percentile points higher than that of equivalent men). Students majoring in engineering earn lower grades than do the humanists, social scientists, and natural scientists; students in the latter fields have an average rank in class 6 to 8 points higher than that of the "equivalent" engineer.

In the context of an effort to predict rank in class, the selectivity of the college attended functions as an additional control variable. A student with a given SAT score, high school grades, and so on, who attends one of the most selective schools, should be expected to have a lower rank in class than a student with the same credentials who attends a school that enrolled a smaller number of top-rated students. This is precisely the pattern we found. Students who attended one of the SEL-1 schools paid, on average, a "penalty" of almost 15 percentile points in class rank, as compared with the class rank earned by students with the same SAT scores and other attributes who went to a SEL-3 school. The comparable "penalty" paid by students who went to SEL-2 schools was 8 points in class rank (as compared with those at the SEL-3 schools). Competing against fellow students with very strong academic credentials naturally affects

[24] This is an ordinary least squares (OLS) regression, so the coefficients have a common-sense interpretation, unlike the coefficients in the logistic regressions which are difficult to interpret unless they are translated into either odds ratios or adjusted probabilities.

one's class rank, even though this disadvantage may well be counter-balanced by other benefits.

SAT Scores

One of the questions in which we are most interested is the predictive power of SAT scores. As we noted in discussing graduation rates, the use of SAT scores in the admissions process has become increasingly controversial. Admissions officers generally view these tests as a useful part of the assessment process because they provide some common ground for evaluating the records of students who come from high schools with very different academic standards. However, there are critics on both sides of this traditional position. Some favor abandoning all use of SATs because, they claim, the tests have little, if any, predictive value; critics on the other side argue that test scores and other "objective" indicators should be the primary criteria for judging candidates.

Looked at in their simplest form, straight tabulations of the C&B data for the '89 matriculants cast serious doubt on the validity of such sweeping pronouncements from either side (Figure 3.10). While there is considerable variation within each SAT interval, the simple association between SAT scores and grades is clear-cut. As one would have expected, class rank varies directly with SAT scores. Among both black and white students, those in the highest SAT interval had an appreciably higher average rank in class than did those who entered with lower SAT scores. (It should also be noted that we are not referring to first-year grades only, but rather to rank in class based on the student's cumulative four-year GPA.)

Moreover, the positive relationship between students' SAT scores and their rank in class portrayed in Figure 3.10 remains after we control for gender, high school grades, socioeconomic status, school selectivity, and major, as well as for race (Appendix Table D.3.6). This relationship easily passes tests of statistical significance, but the magnitude of the effect (the "slope") is modest: for these students, *an additional 100 points of combined SAT score is associated, on average, with an improvement of only 5.9 percentile points in class rank.* No teacher will be surprised to hear that other factors, many of them unmeasurable, affect academic performance—especially in these highly competitive schools where nearly all students have strong academic skills.

The SAT score is a statistically significant predictor of rank in class for black students as well as for all students at the C&B schools (see the separate regression in Appendix Table D.3.6). The relationship between SAT scores and predicted rank in class is, however, even "flatter" for black students than it is for all students: *an additional 100 points of combined SAT*

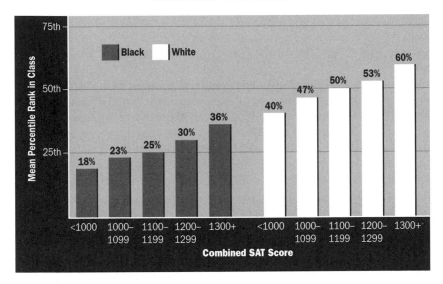

Figure 3.10. Mean Percentile Rank in Class, by Combined SAT Score and Race, 1989 Entering Cohort

Source: College and Beyond.

score is associated with a class rank improvement of only 5.0 points for black students.[25] Still, given what some liberal critics of SAT scores have said about how poorly they predict the academic performance of black students, it is somewhat surprising that the regression equations for the two groups are so similar. Conversely, in view of the importance attached by more conservative critics to differences in SAT scores, it is equally surprising that even a large difference in scores (200 points, say, or the difference between scoring 1100 and scoring 1300) is associated with only a modest difference in predicted class rank (just under 12 percentile points for all students and 10 percentile points for blacks).[26]

[25] We also tested the predictive power of SATs for black students by including an interaction variable (black*SAT) in the basic regression for all students, and found that the coefficient is negative and statistically significant at the 1 percent level. We return later in the chapter to the interpretation of this result.

[26] See, for example, the emphasis placed on the importance of test scores by Murray and Herrnstein (1994). There are two main reasons why differences in test scores have such a modest impact on grades within the C&B institutions. First, these selective institutions are of course choosing carefully those students with relatively low SATs whom they admit. Admissions officers often have other information, such as courses taken, recommendations of teachers, and the like, which persuades them that, lower test scores notwithstanding, the

High School Grades

High school grades, which we measured crudely by asking whether a student was or was not in the top 10 percent of his or her secondary school class, also prove to be a statistically significant predictor of rank in class in college. After controlling for differences in other variables, including SAT scores, we find that matriculants who finished in the top 10 percent of their high school class had a class rank in college 11 points higher than the rank achieved by classmates who had performed less well in high school. For black students only, the college class rank "advantage" associated with having been in the top 10 percent of one's high school class was smaller—6 points. In short, taking account of high school academic standing also helps predict college grades, but this variable, like SAT scores, has only a modest net effect.

Socioeconomic Status

Differences in socioeconomic status (SES) also affect rank in class, even after controlling for SAT scores and high school grades. The measure of SES included in the analysis is based on parental education and income (see Appendix B). Crude as it is, this measure "works" in that students from high SES families had a higher rank in class (on an "other things equal" basis) than did students from middle- and low-SES backgrounds. These differences in predicted class rank are statistically significant, but they too are modest in size: the adjusted percentile rank in class is 51 for high-SES students, 49 for middle-SES students, and 47 for low-SES students.

Measuring Underperformance

The fact that black matriculants entered college with lower test scores, lower high school grades, and lower socioeconomic status than white matriculants explains some part of the black-white gap in rank in class.

---

student in question has demonstrated the potential to handle the academic work. Second, as we noted earlier in discussing graduation rates, essentially all of the students in the C&B population have test scores that are well above a high academic threshold. One of us (Bowen) once studied the highly selective graduate admissions process in an economics department that at that time enrolled only about 15 new students each year. All of those admitted from a large pool of well-qualified candidates had outstanding credentials. Within this select group, it proved impossible to find any set of test scores or other objective indicators that predicted performance very well. As the demographer Ansley Coale was fond of reminding his colleagues, above a (very high) threshold, additional increments in test scores tell us relatively little. Other hard-to-measure factors, such as resilience, creativity, and the ability to benefit from criticism have much more to do with performance.

But even the simple association between SAT scores and rank in class depicted in Figure 3.10 warns us that the full picture is more complex. The average rank in class for black students is appreciably lower than the average rank in class for white students *within each SAT interval.* This unmistakable pattern is found not only in C&B colleges but in professional schools as well.[27] It is one strong indication of a troubling phenomenon often called "underperformance." Black students with the same SAT scores as whites tend to earn lower grades.

This important finding is confirmed when we control for differences in other variables. In the multivariate regression used to predict rank in class, the coefficient associated with being black is both highly significant and large: −16.2. In other words, if the black students in the C&B schools had been equivalent to all C&B students in their SAT scores, high school grades, socioeconomic status, and other characteristics included in the model (gender, selectivity of the school attended, field of study, being an athlete or not), they still would have had a class rank that was, on average, roughly 16 percentile points lower than the class rank of apparently comparable classmates. Of the overall black-white gap in average rank in class of 30 points—obtained by subtracting the average rank in class of black students (23d percentile) from the average rank in class of white students (53d percentile)—only about half of it (14 points) is accounted for by black-white differences in other measurable variables.

This same pattern holds within each group of C&B schools considered separately, whether the schools are classified solely by their degree of selectivity, by their status as a college or university, or as a public or private institution. At the various sets of schools, the adjusted black-white gap in class rank that remains after controlling for other variables ranges from 15 to 21 points. What is important is not these modest differences between types of schools (which in general are too small to pass tests of statistical significance) but the overall consistency of the results.[28]

[27] For an early discussion of underperformance in law and medical schools, see Klitgaard (1985, pp. 162–64).

[28] We performed the same kind of analysis for the '76 C&B cohorts and obtained similar results. We also ran separate regressions for individual schools ('89 cohorts only). For all but three of the twenty-eight schools, the black coefficient is negative and statistically significant. The three schools at which there is no evidence of black underperformance are all liberal arts colleges with small black enrollments (which, of course, makes it harder for the coefficients to pass tests of statistical significance).

Finally, we replicated the multivariate analysis for Hispanic students in the '89 entering cohorts and once again obtained similar, but somewhat muted, results (Appendix Table D.3.6). Hispanic students also have a lower average rank in class than one would predict on the basis of their SAT scores (after controlling for the other variables), but the Hispanic-

The central conclusion is inescapable: black students in the '89 cohorts earned much lower grades than did their white classmates, and the pattern holds even after we control for a number of other factors. This finding is consistent with the results of a considerable amount of other research.[29]

FACTORS LEADING TO GAPS IN PERFORMANCE

There are many possible explanations for the pervasive black-white gaps in graduation rates and grades that persist after controlling for differences in test scores and other variables. Not all of them can be quantified. One basic distinction is between those explanations that stress pre-college factors, such as differences in the quality of high school preparation and in family backgrounds, and those that relate to experiences in college and to the college environments themselves.

Pre-College Influences

The appearance of underperformance may result, at least in part, from unmeasured differences between white and black students who appear to be—but may not actually be—comparable in all relevant respects when they enter college. For example, we know that there are differences in academic preparation that are not captured by SAT scores or high school grades.[30] Some students are simply better prepared than others

---

white gap is only 56 percent as large as the black-white gap—roughly 9 percentile points, as compared with 16 points for black matriculants in the same regression.

[29] For a summary of much of this literature, see Miller (1995); also see Ramist et al. (1994); Jencks and Phillips (forthcoming); and the many studies cited therein, one of which is a paper by Vars and Bowen. That study used more limited parts of the C&B database but discusses at greater length some basic issues of statistical estimation. For example, David Card and Cecilia Rouse (personal correspondence) suggested that there could be more measurement error in SAT scores for blacks than for whites. To test this hypothesis, Vars and Bowen examined the test scores obtained by a subset of black and white matriculants who took the SATs more than once and found that the correlation between the two most recent scores was *higher* for black students than for whites.

[30] Admissions officers have detailed information about applicants for admission, including courses taken, Advanced Placement test scores, and the quality of secondary schools, that goes well beyond the summary measures we could include in our regressions. At one of the C&B schools, we had access to the composite "academic ratings" (based on particular courses taken and grades received, advanced standing, Achievement test scores, and so on) used by the admissions office to assess the academic potential of members of the '89

for the rigors of highly competitive academic settings. In general, black students are more likely than white students to come from educational backgrounds that will not adequately prepare them for the challenges of college.

A comment by a black C&B matriculant from an inner-city school in Detroit who entered the University of Michigan in the fall of 1976 is illustrative:

High school prepared me as well as it could, I guess. What they didn't do was teach me how to study. I was a pretty bright kid and I really didn't have to study a lot. And when I got to college, it was a different thing—you have to study, and I didn't know how. At 18 you don't really know enough about life or yourself. It was enjoyable, but looking back, I would say that I was young and stupid. I didn't work as hard as I should have. . . . I thought I'd be able to skate through, like I did through high school.

We saw in the previous section that ranking in the top 10 percent of one's high school class made less difference to the grades earned by blacks than it did to the grades earned by whites. We suspect, but cannot prove, that the weaker effect of even top high school grades on the academic performance of blacks is another indication that black students with excellent high school records are more likely than white students to have attended high schools that did not prepare them well for college.[31]

---

entering cohort. These ratings predicted academic performance appreciably better than did SATs alone. In addition, their inclusion in the regression equation reduced the black-white gap in grades by about 15 percent. See Vars and Bowen (forthcoming). This analysis, though limited to a single school, reinforces our sense that whites benefit more than blacks from forms of academic preparation not captured by the usual summary measures. At the same time, the modest reduction in the size of the black-white gap in rank in class associated with the introduction of this more sophisticated measure of academic preparation leads us to doubt that any very large part of the black-white gap in performance is due to more careful selection of white candidates than of black candidates within given ranges of SAT scores and high school grades. But it also seems clear that whites benefit more than blacks do from forms of academic preparation not captured by the usual summary measures. (A second set of admissions office ratings, designed to measure personal qualities of applicants, had no predictive power at all as far as grades were concerned.)

[31] We hope that one or more follow-up studies to this research will shed new light on the factors that are particularly important in predicting how well students (and especially black students) from different secondary schools will perform at academically selective colleges.

> *A C&B respondent from Washington University provided a relevant third-person account:*
>
> One of my roommates was asked to leave after the first semester of her sophomore year because she just didn't know how to study; she had come out of the Washington, D.C., public school system and had been an A student. But her idea of studying was to rewrite her notes from class.

At a still deeper level, family background presumably affects directly the pre-college educational preparation that students receive. Place of residence affects the schools children typically attend, and family resources and educational aspirations also influence decisions to send children to academically strong schools (which may not necessarily be close by).[32] High socioeconomic status should also be expected to affect the academic performance of children in a variety of other ways, and we were surprised that the measure of socioeconomic status that we included in the multivariate regression analysis, while statistically significant, had such modest effects on rank in class.[33]

We suspect that our measure of socioeconomic status is a very imperfect proxy for the factors that matter the most. College grades may well be less affected by family income and parental education per se (which together make up our index of socioeconomic status) than they are by the number of books at home, opportunities to travel, better secondary schooling, the nature of the conversation around the dinner table, and, more generally, parental involvement in their children's education. Some students in the high-SES category may receive relatively little in the way of such benefits while others, from more modest family circumstances, may have received an excellent "at home" education—in some instances because of the presence of a "stay-at-home Mom," who has deliberately sacrificed family income. In the main, however, we would expect students from high-SES backgrounds to benefit disproportionately from such influences. Also high-SES families are more likely than other families to help their children anticipate the kinds of academic pressures that they will encounter when they enroll at one of the

[32] However, attempts by Vars and Bowen (forthcoming) to improve the prediction of rank in class by introducing a simple dichotomy between attendance at a public secondary school and attendance at a private one failed to yield statistically significant results.

[33] Moreover, controlling for SES had an imperceptible effect on the predicted black-white difference in class rank. The predicted black-white gap in class rank is reduced by only about 1 percentile point (or 5 percent) when the SES variables are added to the regression. (Regressions without SES are not presented.)

more selective colleges or universities. Finally, students from high-SES families are presumably under less pressure to take jobs during the school year, compared to those from families of more modest means. Just as black-white differences in the usual measures of socioeconomic status fail to reflect at all adequately black-white differences in wealth, we think it likely that our measure of SES understates the special advantages that many students from high-SES families enjoy. This is another instance in which more precisely targeted research is needed.

Experiences in College

A second broad set of hypotheses relates to the college environment. The explanations range from laboratory-tested psychological theories to assertions about discrimination by faculty members, low motivation on the part of black students, special problems of adjusting to predominantly white environments, and poorly conceived institutional policies that at best accept and at worst encourage lower academic aspirations by black students. We will comment on only a few of these possible explanations.

The "stereotype-vulnerability" theory proposed by Claude Steele and his associates at Stanford University holds that highly talented black students are confronted by racial stereotypes that cause them to fear that, despite their previous academic achievements, they will do badly, and that this fear undermines their performance. Such vulnerabilities are sometimes reinforced in stressful situations, particularly in examinations in which individuals are reminded of their group affiliation. The evidence in support of Steele's general hypothesis includes laboratory results for women studying mathematics at Stanford, as well as laboratory results for black students given stressful verbal aptitude tests. When black students were assured that the tests they were taking were *not* used to measure their ability, their performance no longer fell below that of whites.[34] An extension of our research appears to offer further support

---

[34] See Steele and Aronson (forthcoming) and the literature cited therein. In a more popular presentation of Steele's work in the *New York Times Magazine,* Watters (1995) quotes Steele as follows: "Our idea was that whenever black students concentrate on an explicitly scholastic task, they risk confirming their group's negative stereotype. This extra burden, in situations with certain characteristics, can be enough to drag down their performance. We call this burden stereotype vulnerability" (p. 45). The author of the article goes on to describe Steele's experiments: In one experiment, Steele and his colleague, Joshua Aronson, "gave two groups of black and white Stanford undergraduates a test composed of the most difficult verbal-skills questions from the Graduate Record Exam. Before the test, one group was told that the purpose of the exercise was only to research 'psychological factors in-

for Steele's hypothesis, by suggesting that black-white gaps in class rank in highly selective colleges increase as the level of SAT scores rises—but the evidence is not clear-cut.[35]

Mary Patterson McPherson, former president of Bryn Mawr College and a trustee of Amherst College, has emphasized another, simpler, aspect of campus life that may have as much to do with black underperformance as stereotype vulnerability. She observes that, in her experience, the black students who were the most comfortable at whatever college they attended also tended to be the most successful academically. Since students have only a limited amount of time and emotional energy, those able to concentrate on their academic tasks, without constant concern about their place on the campus and their relationships to others, are most likely to do well academically.

Our interviews tended to support this line of reasoning. The academic performance of a number of black students seemed clearly affected by difficulties in adjusting to new environments. Feelings of insecurity are by no means limited to any single group of students. Still, black students may feel them with special intensity (along with other minority students and some low-SES white students).

---

volved in solving verbal problems,' while the other group was told that the test was 'a genuine test of your verbal abilities and limitations.'"

[35] The connection to Steele's work is that stereotype vulnerability might be expected to be most pronounced among the highest of the high achievers at the top of the SAT range, and we find some (but not overwhelming) evidence to this effect. We noted earlier that when we introduce into the analysis a term that captures the interaction between being black and SAT scores, the coefficient is mildly negative but significant (-1.7). The interpretation is that, on average, the gap in class rank between white and black students increases 1.7 points for every 100-point increase in the combined SAT score.

When we examine this pattern at each level of school selectivity, we find that the tendency for the black-white gap in grades to be greatest at high levels of SAT scores is confined to the SEL-1 schools. At these schools, the black-white gap in class rank increases steadily as SAT scores rise. Moreover, the coefficient of the black*SAT interaction term is much larger (-3.4) and highly significant within the SEL-1 schools but insignificant at the SEL-2 and SEL-3 schools. There is, however, more to the story. At the lower SAT levels, black-white gaps are smaller at the SEL-1 schools than at the SEL-2 and SEL-3 schools; at the high SAT ranges, the absolute size of the black-white gap is essentially the same at all three sets of schools. This is simply a slightly more rigorous confirmation of a conclusion stated earlier: contrary to the "fit" hypothesis, black students with modest academic credentials were most successful academically, relative to their white classmates, at the most selective schools. (These results differ slightly from those reported earlier by Vars and Bowen (forthcoming) because less data were available when that paper was written; in effect, Vars and Bowen had data only for a subset of C&B schools very much like the SEL-1 group.)

A comment by one black matriculant—which is similar to many others:

When I arrived at campus for the first time I was a little bit intimidated. I said, "Wow, I wonder if they made a mistake accepting me; am I going to fit in?"—those kinds of feelings. And will I be the dumbest person here?

In other situations, students are reported to have lost their academic focus by devoting too much emotional energy to concerns about what other people were thinking and feeling about them.

A vignette reported in an interview by a 1976 matriculant at the University of Michigan demonstrates how distracting race can be:

I was very well prepared academically, but I think that, being a black student on a largely white campus, the issues I had to deal with weren't always academic. I couldn't always focus 100 percent on academics as I would have wanted to; instead, there were always issues of comfort level in classes, in the dorm situation.

For example, there was one sociology class that I took where we were discussing the perception in this country that if you work hard you *will* do well. Some students of color pointed out that that's not always the case and that sometimes for racial minorities in this country, you work really hard and you don't necessarily achieve a lot. And there was a white student who said that her father worked *really, really* hard and that he earned everything that he got. And basically she didn't appreciate us insinuating that he might not have earned everything that he got. But that wasn't the point. All we were saying was that there were other people who worked just as hard as her father who did not do as well as her father had. And she was so upset, and she started crying. It was just a strange experience.

And then there were people who had never been in a room with a black person in their lives. And because they were uncomfortable, it made you uncomfortable. In sociology classes, people would say, "I've never talked to a black person before." It was probably the sociology classes because of the subject matter; it didn't come up in my engineering classes.

My black friends and I didn't really talk about it too much. I don't think that a black student who does well at a majority white university can afford

> to focus too much on those kinds of things, because you can get consumed by them. And if you allow yourself to become too involved in all of the social issues, you can't achieve well academically. You won't have the energy or the time to put into your studies and do well. It was a conscious effort on my part not to let it get to me. I had friends who I know it affected a lot more. And some of them weren't performing well academically, not necessarily because they didn't have the ability, but because their energy was taken up by so many other things. If you allowed it to happen, it could be a big part of your life.

Of course, many white students had similar difficulties, and some (perhaps even many) black students did not suffer from such problems in the same way. But being a member of a small and visible minority group in an overwhelmingly white community that is known to have excluded black students for generations surely increases the odds of encountering such problems. While it is impossible to quantify their effects, we suspect that such factors account for a not-inconsiderable portion of what we have identified as underperformance among black students.

Still another possible explanation has been offered by anthropologists Signithia Fordham and John Ogbu, who have suggested that black students suffer academically because at least some of them feel peer group pressure to get only mediocre grades:

> One major reason black students do poorly in school is that they experience inordinate ambivalence and affective dissonance in regard to academic effort and success. This problem arose partly because white Americans traditionally refused to acknowledge that black Americans are capable of intellectual achievement, and partly because black Americans subsequently began to doubt their own intellectual ability, began to define academic success as white people's prerogative, and began to discourage their peers, perhaps unconsciously, from emulating white people in academic striving, i.e., from "acting white."[36]

The original ethnographic work by Fordham and Ogbu was conducted at a predominantly black inner city high school, and we are unable to judge its relevance for the high-achieving population of black students in the C&B schools. But there are at least overtones of the same kinds of self-questioning, and questioning of cultural loyalties, in some of the comments volunteered by participants in the C&B surveys. Hugh Price, presi-

[36] Fordham and Ogbu 1986, p. 177.

dent of the National Urban League, has expressed similar concerns, and recently efforts such as the National Urban League's Campaign for African-American Achievment have been launched to instill a stronger sense that, in the words of a recent software commercial, "It's cool to be smart."[37]

Finally, some have argued that black students underperform academically because affirmative action lowers their motivation to do truly outstanding work.[38] The willingness of leading graduate and professional schools to admit black candidates who did not rank at the very top of their classes is alleged to reduce the sense among black undergraduates that they must get absolutely top grades to move up academic and professional ladders. We know of no way to test this hypothesis. It is certainly possible that white students aspiring to gain admission to leading schools of law and medicine feel greater pressure than their black classmates to earn all As. Yet black students surely feel academic pressures too, since they know that many of them who apply to leading schools of law, medicine, and business will fail to gain admission.[39] Also, there is strong evidence, as we show later in the book, that black undergraduates who receive good grades are rewarded handsomely in the marketplace for their accomplishments.

In view of how hard many black matriculants at C&B schools worked to gain admission to these schools, it seems unlikely that many of them would suddenly decide to "coast" academically, though it is certainly possible that some of these students would choose to dedicate much of their time to other activities (which they may never have had an opportunity to pursue before) rather than spend more hours in the library or laboratory. There is, however, an abundance of anecdotal information that many black students feel intense pressure to live up to the standards they and their parents have set for themselves.

---

[37] As part of its Campaign for African American Achievement (Report to the Board of Trustees, August 6, 1997), the National Urban League has counseled: "Pressure from peers not to achieve can undermine the best efforts of teachers and parents. Many have succumbed to the message that achievement is tantamount to 'acting white' and that they will succeed even if they don't do well in school. We must encourage and celebrate youth that do the right thing and we must provide developmental opportunities that enable youth to take charge of their lives and make good decisions."

[38] See Thernstrom and Thernstrom 1997, p. 422.

[39] Wightman (1997, p. 14), reports that only 26 percent of black applications to law schools in 1990–91 were accepted. The overall acceptance rate for underrepresented minorities at medical schools was 39 percent in 1996 (AAMC 1996, p. 8). According to Dugan et al. (1996, p. 12), the acceptance rate of black applicants to their first or second choice business schools was much higher (70 percent).

> *One comment by a black matriculant who has gone on to a highly successful business career is indicative of feelings expressed by many of these students:*
>
> I called home one night, very discouraged, and I got my father on the phone and said, "Dad, I'm working day and night, and I'm busting it. [But] I'm not getting the A's that I've been accustomed to getting. . . . I'm studying six hours a day, and I don't know what else I can do to be successful." And he said, "Boy, let me tell you one thing. When I was your age I was working 10 hours a day, 12 hours a day in a foundry." And that's the last time I ever complained about working hard.

INSTITUTIONAL INITIATIVES

Our school-by-school analysis reveals that there are substantial disparities in academic outcomes among the individual institutions in the C&B database. Such differences can be due either to variations in the effectiveness of initial selection processes or to differing campus environments or to some combination of the two. Careful study of specific situations could lead to a sharper understanding of why better results are being achieved at some schools than at others and of which kinds of initiatives seem to be the most promising. Claude Steele's recent papers contain lengthy commentary on the results achieved by the 21st Century Program at the University of Michigan, to cite one specific case of a successful program at a C&B school.[40]

A somewhat more general indication of the possibilities for improvement can be seen from another program currently operating at several C&B institutions, as well as a number of other colleges and universities. The Mellon Minority Undergraduate Fellowship Program (MMUF) was designed to encourage able minority students (generally chosen during the sophomore year) to consider studying for a doctorate. The program is structured to provide consistent faculty advice and support, as well as practical experience in writing and doing research, and it gives every indication of being highly successful.[41]

Most relevant to the subject of academic outcomes are the undergraduate academic records of the thirty-two MMUF participants who are

[40] Steele (forthcoming).

[41] For a description of the program, see *Report of The Andrew W. Mellon Foundation* (1993); additional information can be obtained from the director of the program, Jacqueline Looney.

also members of the '89 cohorts at ten C&B schools. *All* of the students graduated, as compared with 90 percent of all matriculants at these same schools and 81 percent of all black and Hispanic students. The average SAT score of the MMUF participants was 1168, and their cumulative 4-year GPA was 3.40. At these same schools, the average SAT score of all students in the '89 cohorts was much higher (1304), but their average GPA was lower (3.28). While the care with which these participants were chosen surely helps explain their academic success, the participants also stress the importance of special elements of the program that were designed to provide academic support and increase the sense of being "at home" within these highly competitive institutions.

Outside the C&B universe, mention should be made of other specially designed programs for minority students that have proven effective. At the University of Colorado at Boulder, for example, faculty members responsible for a minority engineering program report that they have fully overcome the prior tendency of minority students to have a GPA averaging one half-point lower than the GPA of white students with similar SAT scores and high school grades.[42]

Successful programs typically combine all or most of several features. They create an aura of high expectations, with the emphasis on meeting intellectual challenges rather than receiving remediation to achieve a minimum standard. They encourage participants to work in groups, where students can help one another and provide mutual support. They offer appropriate advising and counseling. They often assign students to successful minority professionals, who act as mentors. They provide summer internships to broaden student experience. They offer enough financial aid to remove the risk of students having to work excessively to support themselves or even drop out for lack of funds. Some programs involve parents and keep them continuously informed so that they can lend psychological support and encouragement to their children.

The Meyerhoff Program at the University of Maryland, Baltimore County (UMBC) illustrates what a well-designed program for minority students can accomplish. UMBC is a selective, predominantly white public university with an average combined SAT score of 1111. Almost all Meyerhoff students are black and generally have at least a 600 Math SAT score and a 3.0 high school GPA. More than 92 percent of the program's students currently graduate (94 percent in science and engineering). Whereas comparably talented minority students in earlier years achieved a science GPA of 2.5 compared with 3.0–3.1 for comparable white students, Meyerhoff students now obtain a 3.2 average, slightly higher than

---

[42] For a review of other programs, see Cose (1997, pp. 46–47, 52–64); for an example of an apparently successful law school program, see Knaplund and Sander 1995, p. 157.

that of comparably talented white students. Overall GPAs for the program participants average 3.3. More striking still, 75 percent of the 1990–1992 graduating classes of Meyerhoff students are currently attending graduate or professional schools, and approximately 60 percent are seeking a PhD in science or engineering.[43]

The high graduation rates of minority students from the twenty-eight selective colleges in our universe demonstrate how well admissions officers in these institutions have succeeded in fulfilling their first responsibility: to choose students capable of completing their academic work successfully. The fact that graduation rates increase as the selectivity of the college rises and that students of the same academic ability graduate at higher rates when they attend more selective institutions shows that carefully chosen minority students have not suffered from attending colleges heavily populated by white and Asian American classmates with higher standardized test scores. Quite the contrary—they have fared best in such settings. These students certainly do not appear to have been "over-matched" academically by their colleges and universities.

At the same time, the data reveal a pervasive problem. At almost every college in our sample, black students are not only performing less well academically than whites but also performing below the levels predicted by their SAT scores. In fact, this underperformance turns out to be even more important than lower test scores in explaining the gap in class rank between blacks and whites. Although the reasons for underperformance are not entirely clear, successful programs initiated by several colleges suggest that the problem can be addressed effectively. Such efforts underscore the need for all selective colleges to review the performance of their students (minority and non-minority alike) to determine where systemic underperformance exists, and then to take steps to try to eliminate it.

It is troubling that so few selective institutions appear to have made serious efforts of this kind. Most may not even be aware that such a problem exists, at least on such a scale. College and university officials have often tended to focus their efforts on admitting a substantial number of minority students. Most institutions also have special programs for at-risk students to try to make sure that a high percentage of those who

----

[43] Hrabowski, Maton, and Greif 1998, pp. 172–73; supplemented by newer data supplied by Maton (personal correspondence).

enroll graduate.[44] They seem to have been less concerned with finding out whether all of their minority students are performing up to their abilities and what to do about underperformance when it occurs. This is a general problem, not confined to the performance of minority students. The same reasons that cause selective institutions to expend such efforts to attract talented students should lead them to strive with equal fervor to do whatever they can to ensure that all those whom they admit realize their full potential.

At the same time that we encourage efforts to improve academic performance, we should recognize that the great majority of these black students persevered and, as we have seen, graduated. Many of those who had to overcome obstacles feel that they learned a great deal from the process and emerged from it as well-trained, self-confident people. They understand, certainly in retrospect, that the hard days were worth working through. In the colloquial language of one matriculant, "No pain, no gain." Another former student commented, "I felt it was the only period in my life where I really went through a lot of self-doubt in terms of my own abilities to succeed, and by the time I left I didn't feel that way anymore." A third person observed, "There were happy tears and sad tears. Sad because I wasn't living up to my own expectations of what I wanted to write, but there were happy tears because I never had expected that I could do the kind of research that I was doing."

Finally, college grades are by no means the full measure of educational attainment; still less do they determine accomplishment later in life. Performance in college unquestionably influences students' opportunities to attend graduate schools and, eventually, their careers. But how strong have those influences been, and what effect have they had on what

---

[44] For a detailed description and a highly sophisticated evaluation of a variety of programs implemented by the law school of the University of California, Los Angeles, see Knaplund and Sander (1995), pp. 157ff. The authors demonstrate that some but not all of UCLA's programs have significant long and short term positive effects on the academic performance of participants. Unfortunately, it is rare that similar programs at other institutions are evaluated rigorously. Moreover, most academic support programs enroll only students who in some sense are academically at risk; they are unlikely to reach minority students who are in no danger of failing but are still not performing up to their potential. In this regard, it is important to remember that in highly selective colleges and universities, it is the black undergraduates with the highest test scores who tend to perform the furthest below their potential. Even though they are underperforming, these students will tend to have grade point averages above the level that would cause them to qualify for the typical academic support program. Also, their needs are likely to be quite different from those of at-risk students.

minority and non-minority students have achieved in the years following their graduation? The next chapters in this study explore these fundamental questions. To pass an informed judgment, the effectiveness of admissions processes and educational programs needs to be tested beyond the confines of the campus.

CHAPTER 4

Advanced Study:
Graduate and Professional Degrees

AN EXCELLENT undergraduate education is an enormous advantage in life. But we know that a college degree, by itself, is increasingly seen as inadequate preparation for many careers for which it once sufficed. Graduate training has long been necessary for aspiring doctors, lawyers, educators, scholars, research scientists, and clergy; in today's world, advanced degrees are also seen as highly desirable, if not essential, for many other callings, including leadership positions in business, public affairs, and the not-for-profit sector. This marked change is due in large part to the growth of knowledge, the increasingly technical content of many types of work, and greater specialization. There is also a "credentialing" aspect: in a society with much larger numbers of BA recipients, many individuals seek to distinguish themselves from others through further education. Many employers encourage this practice by using graduate degrees as an easy way of choosing among applicants for jobs.

It will surprise no one to learn that individuals with bachelor's degrees from leading colleges or universities enter graduate and professional programs—especially the most highly rated ones—in distinctly above-average numbers. Enhanced access to graduate study has become a major benefit associated with going to a strong undergraduate college—*the* major benefit, some would say. In this chapter, we will examine in detail the success of College and Beyond graduates in earning advanced degrees. We will look particularly carefully at the experiences of black matriculants to determine how these students—many of whom would not have been admitted in the absence of race-sensitive admissions policies—fared after leaving college.

THE IMPORTANCE OF THE PROFESSIONS

Graduate study matters so much because it provides the pathway to the professions—a pathway traversed by larger and larger numbers of college graduates. Despite the never-ending stream of lawyer jokes, horror stories about unnecessary medical procedures, and tales of professors neglecting their classes in favor of abstruse research, careers in "the professions" have increased in desirability.

For the individual who survives the intense competition for a place in the most highly ranked graduate and professional schools and then completes the program of study successfully, the economic rewards can be substantial. Since the 1970s, earnings of highly successful professionals have increased sharply, and more students have been attracted to these callings.[1] But students also pursue graduate study for many other reasons, including deep interest in a particular subject matter, a desire to serve their communities, and an appreciation of the status and opportunities for leadership that are associated with advanced training. The General Social Survey asks Americans to rate the prestige of various occupations, and the resulting rankings (which include every kind of position, from carwash attendant to public opinion pollster to lawyer) serve as testimony to the high esteem that Americans have for professionals. Of the top twenty ranked occupations, only a few (such as mayor of a large city) can conceivably be attained without graduate or professional study.[2]

Competition to enter the professions has increased over the last three decades as schools of law, medicine, and business began to dismantle barriers that had previously discouraged women and members of minority groups, implicitly and often explicitly, from seeking professional training. Monumental shifts have occurred in the size and composition of the applicant pools, as admissions officers have sought to recruit minority students and as many more women have sought places in these programs.[3]

Society has a large and growing stake in graduate and professional education as the need for specialized knowledge and expertise continues to increase.[4] Historian Walter Metzger has argued that we are becoming

---

[1] Bok 1993, pp. 42–64.

[2] In the 1989 survey, the top twenty most prestigious occupations were as follows: (1) surgeon, (2) physician, (3) college or university president, (4) astronaut, (5) obstetrician/gynecologist, (6) professor of mathematics, (7) department head in a state government, (8) mayor of a large city, (9) professor of physics in a college or university, (10) lawyer, (11) professor of biology in a college or university, (12) computer scientist, (13) professor of psychology in a college or university, (14) college professor, (15) physicist, (16) chemist, (17) professor of history, (18) chemical engineer, (19) architect, (20) biologist. See Nakao and Treas 1990, tab. 6. The General Social Survey (GSS) is a personal interview survey of U.S. households conducted since 1972.

[3] While only 39 percent of women nationally aspired to graduate degrees in 1966, by 1996, the figure had risen to 68 percent. Women now are more likely than men to aspire to advanced degrees. See Astin et al. 1997, pp. 78–79, 108–9.

[4] In seeking to identify what distinguishes the professions from other occupations, sociologist William J. Goode (1975, p. 100) stresses the level of trust that certain relationships require—with teachers, doctors, lawyers, psychiatrists, and clergy. This high level of trust has wide ramifications: "The *substance* of the task or problem requires trust between

more and more dependent upon professionals, and that this high degree of dependence puts an added premium not only on professional skills but on the character ("honorableness") of the individuals who serve in these roles:

> As the amount of knowledge increases, so too does the relative amount of ignorance, for each person can know only a decreasing fraction of what can be known; that knowledge, as it becomes more specialized, also tends to become more potent, more capable of being used for good or ill. . . . It is to avert a Hobbesian outcome—a war of each against each in which everyone uses the knowledge he possesses for his own advantage, and pays a terrible price for the knowledge he may lack—that societies urge those occupations that impinge on the vital concerns of human beings to tie their expertise to honorableness.[5]

Society has a strong interest in graduate and professional education for yet another reason: these programs of study have a great deal to do with the preparation of leaders. Yale's president, Richard Levin, has noted that a central mission of the university is the hard-to-define task of selecting and preparing individuals for such roles:

> Academic excellence must remain the most important single criterion for admission to Yale's programs of study, but in our graduate and professional schools as well as in Yale College, we should continue to look for something more—for those elusive qualities of character that give young men and women the potential to have an impact on the world, to make contributions to the larger society through their scholarly, artistic, and professional achievements, and to work and to encourage others to work for the betterment of the human condition.[6]

Such leaders must serve all sectors of society—and be able to work effectively with many different kinds of individuals. It is important that the most promising young people of all races have access to these callings.

ASPIRATIONS

One fact is abundantly clear. Black college students have a remarkably strong interest in advanced training. Nationally, 63 percent of all African

---

client and professional, and thus between professional and society. In more concrete terms, does the solution to the problem require that the professional either symbolically or literally get inside the client, become privy to his or her personal world, able to *harm* the client in some way?" See also Arrow 1974; Schön 1983; and Sullivan 1995.

[5] Metzger 1987, p. 18.

[6] Levin 1996, pp. 7–8.

Americans who entered four-year colleges in 1989–90 aspired to earn an advanced degree of some kind, compared with 61 percent of white students.[7] An even larger share of black matriculants in the '89 cohorts at the C&B schools—87 percent—hoped to earn a master's or other type of advanced degree, compared with 83 percent of white matriculants. Even more noteworthy is the fact that 35 percent of the black C&B matriculants aspired to earn degrees in law or medicine, as compared with 22 percent of their white classmates (bottom panel of Figure 4.1). Nationally, it is also true that more black than white undergraduates aspired to earn degrees in law or medicine, but the black-white difference is much smaller (15 percent versus 13 percent) than it is within the C&B universe. Most surprising of all, almost 25 percent of both black and white C&B matriculants said that they aspired to earn doctorates.[8]

The patterns among the '76 C&B matriculants were very similar, especially for the black matriculants; more blacks than whites in both cohorts hoped to earn advanced degrees (Figure 4.1). While the overall black-white gap in degree aspirations closed modestly between 1976 and 1989, because of higher aspirations for master's degrees (including MBAs)[9] and PhDs by the '89 white matriculants, the black-white gap in aspirations for law and medical degrees increased.

We suspect that a major reason why so many black matriculants desire advanced degrees is that further education is seen as "the way up" by a large part of the black population. Degrees in law and medicine, in particular, have long been regarded as particularly powerful engines of social mobility, and it is no accident that black matriculants are strongly focused on these two fields. The acquisition of impressive professional credentials is one method of countering, at least in part, both stereotyping and discrimination; it can also serve to offset in some measure a relative lack of "connections" and other informal avenues of advancement. Consistent with these impressions, Johnson and Neal have demon-

---

[7] Nettles and Perna 1997, p. 206. The underlying source of data is the Department of Education's Beginning Postsecondary Students Survey, Second Follow-up (1994).

[8] These data are taken from the CIRP surveys of incoming freshmen. In the fall of 1989, these surveys included twenty-four of the twenty-eight C&B schools; missing are Duke, Kenyon, Michigan, Washington, and Yale. In the fall of 1976, the CIRP surveys included twenty-one of the twenty-eight C&B schools; missing are Barnard, Columbia, Denison, Kenyon, Stanford, Tufts, and Yale. These data are for all the matriculants at these schools who completed the CIRP survey form. Some of the other results reported later in the chapter include only the matriculants who answered both the CIRP survey and the C&B survey. National comparisons of aspirations by race were also supplied by CIRP.

[9] The CIRP data do not permit us to separate those who aspired to professional degrees in business from those who may have been contemplating master's degrees in other fields.

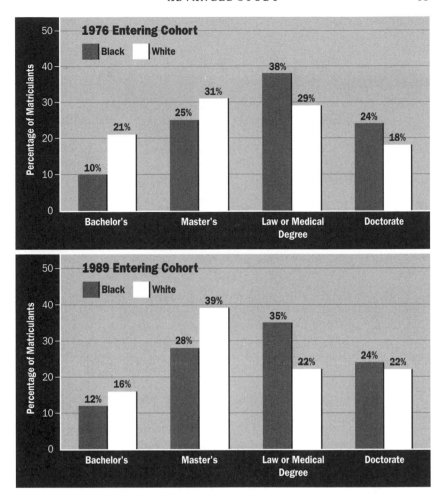

Figure 4.1. Percentage of Matriculants Aspiring to Postsecondary Degrees, by Type of Degree and Race, 1976 and 1989 Entering Cohorts

Source: College and Beyond and the Higher Education Research Institute (see Appendix A).

strated that the male black-white differential in earnings declines with more education and is now smallest among college graduates and largest among high school dropouts.[10]

We also suspect that the general increase between 1976 and 1989 in the degree aspirations of the white matriculants resulted from heightened competition for the more desirable jobs. The rising number of BA recip-

[10] Johnson and Neal (forthcoming).

ients has inevitably reduced the scarcity value of an undergraduate degree. In any case, it is clear that for students in general, the level of academic aspirations is approaching a ceiling. These days, virtually all high-achieving freshmen in college express an interest in earning an advanced degree.

Students who aspire to an advanced degree when they enter college often change their minds in the course of their undergraduate careers. Many were probably naive about what is required to obtain an advanced degree; others may have had exaggerated notions of the "payoffs" from some kinds of graduate study. Still others undoubtedly discovered new interests that they had not anticipated or found that fields that initially seemed inviting were less appealing upon close inspection. All of these changes in direction are entirely natural. College is a time for testing both one's own capacities and one's interests. It is also a time to learn what it really means to become, for instance, a mathematician.

For these reasons, we should expect no more than a rough convergence between what students said about their future plans when they entered college and what they actually ended up doing. Later in the chapter we will see how often the original degree aspirations held by undergraduates when they were freshmen survived various pushes and pulls. But we must first chart the actual record compiled by the C&B matriculants in earning advanced degrees, whatever their intentions when they entered college.

ADVANCED DEGREES EARNED

Overall Patterns

Over half of the '76 matriculants at the C&B schools (51 percent) completed an advanced degree of one kind or another, compared with less than a quarter of the comparable group of matriculants who attended other four-year colleges and universities.[11] Among those C&B students

---

[11] The figure for the comparable group of '76 matriculants is based on the responses of a national control group of individuals of the same age who enrolled at four-year colleges and universities (see Appendix A). It may seem strange to begin this analysis by treating all matriculants as the base for such percentages, since it is (with rare exceptions) only those who earn undergraduate degrees who pursue advanced degrees. However, since this study is particularly concerned with the outcomes of race-sensitive admissions processes, it is desirable to trace the paths followed by all those who enrolled as freshmen, not just those who earned BAs. In much of the chapter, however, we will focus on the subsequent educational histories of those who graduated, in part because this approach allows us to study reasonably precisely the effects on advanced degree attainment of undergraduate major,

who graduated (including those who transferred and graduated from another institution), 56 percent earned graduate or professional degrees.

The patterns for black and white graduates of the '76 cohorts at C&B schools are remarkably similar (left side of Figure 4.2 and Appendix Table D.4.1). Both groups had the same very high propensity to earn advanced degrees. Especially striking are the large fractions receiving professional or doctoral degrees—40 percent of all black graduates and 37 percent of all white graduates. ("Professional" degrees are defined here as degrees in law, medicine, or business; "doctoral" degrees include both PhDs and most other doctorates but for purposes of this analysis do not include JDs or MDs, which are treated as part of the professional category.)[12]

The record of C&B graduates contrasts vividly with that of all holders of BAs nationwide (Figure 4.2).[13] Only 38 percent of the latter earned advanced degrees of any kind, compared with 56 percent of the C&B graduates. The differences are even more pronounced with respect to

---

the selectivity of the school attended, and cumulative rank in class. It is possible to envision a two-stage approach in which we would first analyze the factors related to graduation—as we did in the previous chapter—and then connect this analysis to an examination of the probability of earning an advanced degree, conditional on graduation. However, since C&B matriculants graduate in such large numbers (and hence dominate the results for all matriculants), this more complex analysis seems unnecessary here. Reporting patterns of advanced degree attainment for graduates rather than for all matriculants might seem to some to be "stacking the deck" in favor of the C&B population since we are looking only at those C&B matriculants who surmounted the graduation hurdle (the "winners," as one commentator put it). In fact, when comparing the results for C&B students with national benchmarks, the bias goes in the other direction. Since such an unusually high proportion of C&B matriculants graduate, the true advantage they achieve over matriculants nationwide in earning advanced degrees is understated when we treat graduates as the base for the calculation.

[12] Results for the '89 C&B matriculants were very similar to those just described for the '76 matriculants. A number of the members of this cohort are still in graduate school, and we can only project ultimate completion rates. However, we can report that when the C&B survey was conducted (1997), 58 percent of black graduates had either received advanced degrees or were enrolled in advanced degree programs, as contrasted with 55 percent of white graduates. The corresponding figures for professional and doctoral programs are 35 percent (black graduates) and 32 percent (white graduates). These figures make no allowance for attrition from graduate study, which is plainly unrealistic. An offsetting bias is that some members of this cohort who were not enrolled in graduate school at the time of the survey will enroll subsequently. For all of these reasons, the '89 data can be regarded only as indicative of likely trends.

[13] These national data are taken from the decennial Census. Our other source of national data, the national control group study had cell sizes too small to permit detailed comparisons based on race.

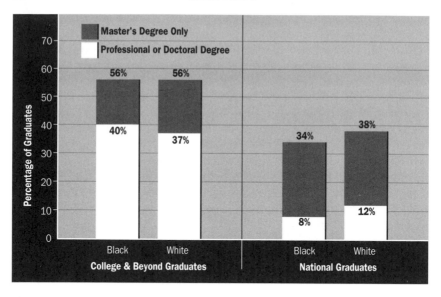

Figure 4.2. Percentage of Graduates Attaining Advanced Degrees, by Type of Degree and Race, College and Beyond Graduates and National Graduates, 1976 Entering Cohort

Source: College and Beyond and 1990 U.S. Census.

Notes: The "Professional or Doctoral Degree" category includes law, medical, business, and other professional and doctoral degrees; the "Master's Degree Only" category includes those students whose highest degree was a master's degree other than the MBA. "National" percentages are based on 1990 U.S. Census tabulations of advanced degrees attained by persons who were age 37 to 39 in 1990.

degrees in professional and doctoral programs. White C&B students were more than three times as likely as all white BA recipients to receive degrees of these kinds; black C&B graduates were five times more likely to obtain professional or doctoral degrees than were black BA recipients nationwide.

What accounts for the success of C&B students in earning advanced degrees, compared with college graduates in general? One possible explanation is that the C&B schools, as a general rule, do not offer professional training to their undergraduates. A few of the C&B institutions have undergraduate programs in business, more have programs in engineering, and there are a scattering of other programs that might be considered "professional"; in the main, however, these schools confer undergraduate degrees in the arts and sciences. In much of the rest of higher education, because undergraduate professional programs are more common, students outside the C&B universe may feel less need for professional training at the graduate level.

However, other explanations seem more compelling. As we saw in Chapter 2, matriculants at the C&B schools have decidedly above-average SAT scores, which means that they are likely to score well on the standardized tests required of applicants for graduate study. Matriculants at C&B schools also tend to come from more affluent families than do college students in general, and from families that are likely to encourage graduate study. Plainly, much self-selection occurs, with secondary school students who think they may want to be doctors, lawyers, or professors much more likely than other secondary school students to enter one of the C&B colleges. All these factors would lead us to expect matriculants at selective institutions to attend graduate and professional schools in disproportionately large numbers. Nonetheless, the magnitude of the differences in educational attainment is surprising.

Types of Professional and Doctoral Degrees

A finer-grained picture is obtained when we examine the types of professional and doctoral degrees that were earned by the '76 C&B cohort (Figure 4.3). Despite their lower grades and test scores, black C&B graduates were slightly more likely than white C&B graduates to earn degrees in law and medicine, and equally likely to earn degrees in business. They were far more likely to earn advanced degrees in these fields than white graduates in the general college-going population—about seven times more likely in law and five times more likely in medicine.[14] Evidence from the survey of the '89 C&B cohort indicates that the black "advantage" in earning professional degrees has been maintained over the last ten to fifteen years.

The situation is somewhat different in the case of doctoral programs. Even at the highly selective C&B schools, black graduates in the 1976 cohort were less likely than their white classmates to pursue PhDs. Some of these students may have felt that professional degrees offered more direct ways of serving their communities. Another factor may have been different choices of majors by black and white students, with white students more inclined to major in fields, such as physics, that are especially likely to lead to doctoral study. Whatever the reasons, the situation may be changing. By the time the 1989 cohort was surveyed, the black-white

[14] These ratios are based on comparisons of the black percentages at the C&B schools with the white percentages within the sample of college attendees in the national control group study. (As noted earlier, the cell sizes in the control group are too small to permit calculation of similar percentages for black college attendees. Unfortunately, Census data do not permit comparisons by type of professional degree.)

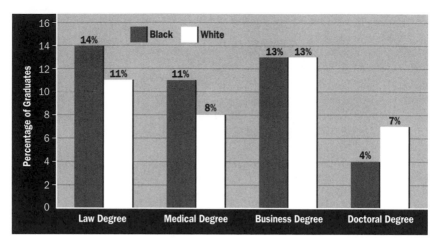

Figure 4.3. Percentage of Graduates Attaining Professional or Doctoral
Degrees, by Type of Degree and Race, 1976 Entering Cohort
    Source: College and Beyond.

enrollment gap in PhD programs had closed to 1 percentage point
(8 percent of white graduates, as compared with 7 percent of black
graduates).

Attendance at Top-Rated Professional Schools

Just as the selective C&B institutions attract well-prepared undergraduates and also have the intellectual and financial resources to provide
"added value," the top tier of graduate and professional schools functions in the same ways. These schools serve as a screening mechanism
through which high-achieving undergraduates pass on their way to
careers in the professions, including places in the leading corporations,
law firms, and hospitals. Major law firms in New York, for example, often
recruit almost exclusively from ten or fifteen (or fewer) law schools;
similarly, leading corporations tend to recruit more heavily from leading
business schools.[15] For this reason, and others, competition for admission to the best graduate and professional schools is keen, and one of

[15] These observations are based on comments by practitioners. There is a straightforward economic rationale for this practice. Searching for job candidates is expensive, and
even though there may be an absolutely extraordinary candidate at a less well known law or
business school, the odds of finding and attracting the candidate (and then the odds of the
candidate's succeeding) may not be high enough to justify the resources required to
extend the search process.

the many advantages of attending an excellent undergraduate college is that the odds of gaining admission to a top-tier graduate program are enhanced.

Attending a highly rated undergraduate school is helpful, first of all, because of the quality of the education made possible by well-regarded faculty, well-equipped libraries and laboratories, and the presence of other high-achieving students. In addition, there is a "credentialing" effect.[16] Graduate and professional schools are likely to prefer candidates who they know have already undergone a competitive screening process and who are thought to have had a solid academic grounding, including practice in writing and research. As the long-time dean of admissions at Yale Law School, James Thomas, noted:

> Seeing where someone has been battle tested and survived means a great deal to us. Someone who has played—and succeeded—on a tough field lets us take a little more risk and admit someone who strikes our faculty as having that something that's going to make a difference in the world. Does this mean that we don't take someone from an off-the-beaten-track school? No, but that person has to have every single thing in line—there's no margin for error. (Personal correspondence)

From the perspective of the graduate school, accepting students from well-regarded undergraduate colleges is a way of reducing the inevitable risks involved in deciding which applicants are most likely to succeed.

We would expect, then, that the academically selective schools in the C&B universe would send disproportionate numbers of their graduates to the most highly ranked professional schools. And so they do. To quantify this pattern, we used published rankings to designate a set of "quality tiers," and then to isolate a "top tier." The drawing of lines between tiers is inevitably arbitrary, and we attach no importance to the categorization of any particular professional school; all we would claim is that the rankings used are generally consistent with one another and with what one would have expected to find. The top tiers were defined quite narrowly to include only twelve medical schools, eight law schools, and six business schools. In a recent year, these small sets of top-tier schools awarded 8.6 percent of all medical degrees, 6.6 percent of all law degrees, and 5.7 percent of all business degrees.[17]

---

[16] Some use the phrase "credentialing effect" to connote only the symbolic benefit of having gone to college, especially, one assumes, to a prestigious college or university (Collins 1979); we use the phrase in the broader sense of both the symbolic and the substantive benefits associated with having attended a very good undergraduate school.

[17] See Appendix B for an explanation of the methodology used to arrive at these rough rankings. We have been deliberately restrictive in defining these tiers, but we do not think that more inclusive definitions would change the tenor of the results.

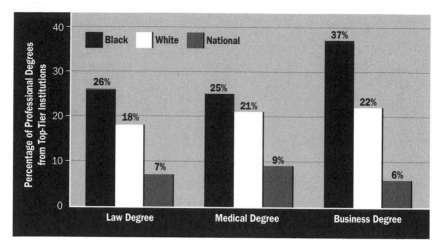

Figure 4.4. Percentage of Professional Degrees Received from Top-Tier Institutions, by Type of Degree and Race, College and Beyond and National Degree Holders, 1976 Entering Cohort

Source: National Science Foundation–National Institute of Health Survey of Graduate Students and Postdoctorates in Science and Engineering, and College and Beyond.

Notes: See Appendix B for definition of "Top-Tier Institutions." "Black" and "White" refer to College and Beyond cohort only. "National" refers to percentage of all professional degrees that were conferred by top-tier institutions in 1985.

The concentration of both black and white graduates of the C&B schools in these top-tier professional schools is demonstrated in Figure 4.4 (which shows the numbers of C&B graduates who obtained degrees from the top-tier schools as percentages of all C&B graduates who obtained each type of advanced degree). In all three professional fields, black C&B students were even more heavily represented than white C&B students at the top-tier schools. For example, 26 percent of the black law school graduates from the C&B undergraduate institutions received degrees from one of the eight most highly ranked law schools, as compared with 18 percent of the white law school graduates from the C&B schools and 7 percent of law school graduates from all undergraduate institutions. The same general pattern is seen in medicine, although the black-white difference is considerably smaller.[18] The concentration of black C&B graduates in the leading business schools is exceptionally pronounced—37 percent of these black recipients of MBA degrees at-

[18] The differential between black and white attendance at the top-tier medical schools is somewhat wider in the '89 cohort: 22 percent of blacks from the C&B schools who went on in medicine attended a top-tier school, as compared with 17 percent of their white counterparts.

tended one of the six top-ranked business schools. The odds that a black C&B student with an MBA would have graduated from a top-tier business school were *six* times higher than the odds for the typical business school graduate nationwide.

FACTORS PREDICTING ADVANCED STUDY

The success of recent classes of black students in obtaining advanced degrees—including disproportionate numbers of degrees from the country's best professional schools—answers some questions and raises others. The presence in the leading graduate and professional schools of unusually large numbers of black students from the C&B schools can be interpreted—properly—as an indication of the effects of race-sensitive admissions policies within the graduate and professional schools. But this pattern reflects as well the strong desire of so many of these students to attain advanced degrees and the success they have enjoyed as undergraduates in some of the country's most selective undergraduate programs. In a very real sense, the increased numbers of black and Hispanic holders of law degrees, medical degrees, business degrees, and PhDs can be credited to the joint efforts of students of high ambition, strong undergraduate programs, and graduate institutions that have worked hard to enroll larger numbers of talented minority students.

In this section, our main objective is to examine in detail the factors that have operated at the undergraduate level to help or hinder this process. How important have SAT scores been in determining which students have and have not attained advanced degrees? Have the patterns of advanced degree attainment differed according to the selectivity of the undergraduate school that students attended and the grades they earned? We also want to know to what extent progression through programs of advanced study can be attributed primarily to students' own degree aspirations. Since these factors are interrelated, we show their net effects on the attainment of professional and doctoral degrees by using the same kind of multivariate regression analysis employed in the previous chapter.

Aspirations and Attainment

As we saw earlier in the chapter, many C&B matriculants enter college fully intending to go on to graduate study in a field that they have already identified. We also know that many of these expectations change, for reasons of every kind. An obvious question, then, is: to what extent did

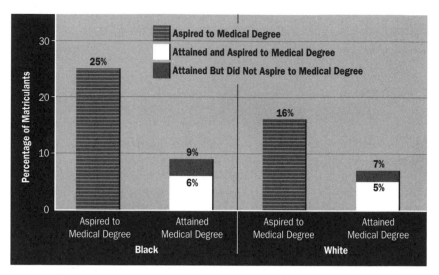

Figure 4.5. Percentages of Matriculants Aspiring to and Attaining Medical Degrees, by Race, 1976 Entering Cohort

Source: College and Beyond and CIRP data provided by the Higher Education Research Institute (see Appendix A).

the '76 C&B matriculants, black and white, convert their aspirations into the receipt of advanced degrees in the fields that they specified when they began their undergraduate studies?

Focusing on medicine helps to illustrate how pre-college aspirations bear on eventual patterns of graduate study. In Figure 4.5 we see that an extraordinarily large percentage of all black matriculants at the C&B schools originally aspired to a medical degree—25 percent. These aspirants contributed a large share of the 9 percent of black matriculants who eventually earned medical degrees (6 of the 9 percent came from this population). The remaining 3 percent of black matriculants with medical degrees came from the much larger population of black matriculants who did *not* aspire to a medical degree when they entered college. Put another way, about 25 percent of those who aspired to earn a medical degree did so, as contrasted with roughly 4 percent of those who had no such aspirations. It is abundantly clear, therefore, that pre-college aspirations were important in leading students to medical school.[19]

[19] There are data stretching back to the 1950s showing that early aspirations are more characteristic of doctors than of lawyers and members of other professions. See Merton, Reader, and Kendall 1957.

The same general patterns hold for white graduates (see right-hand side of Figure 4.5). In fact, in the end, nearly the same percentage of white graduates earned medical degrees (7 percent vs. 9 percent of the blacks). Moreover, the white doctors were drawn in approximately the same relative numbers from the white pools of aspirants and non-aspirants as was the case with the black doctors.

These facts are the fundamental ones. It is also true that there was more "slippage" between aspirations for medical degrees and attainment among blacks than among whites. Many students of all races lose the struggle with organic chemistry. But the appreciably higher percentages of black matriculants who aspired to become doctors also tells a crucial, and often unrecognized, part of this story. Clearly, an unrealistically large number of black high school students arrived at college thinking that medicine would be the right career for them. As a group, white matriculants probably had more relevant information when they arrived at college, since they are more likely than black students to receive good counseling in high school and hence to abandon unrealistic plans to become doctors at an earlier stage. High-achieving black students may have been more strongly encouraged than their white high school classmates to contemplate medicine as a career—and may have known less about other possible vocations.[20] In the end, though more black students who started down this path ended up pursuing other goals, it is essential to remember that an even higher percentage of black graduates than of white graduates earned medical degrees.

We found the same pattern for law. More blacks than whites entered college intending to earn a JD (in both 1976 and 1989), equal numbers received JDs, and higher percentages of black aspirants also ended up not receiving them.[21] The pursuit of the PhD is marked by strangely

[20] To illustrate this point even more dramatically, it is worth examining the black and white populations at just the SEL-1 institutions. At these schools in 1976, 30 percent of the entering black students started out intending to go to medical school (as opposed to 15 percent of the whites). Looked at in one way, the fact that two-thirds of this group (19 percent of the black student population) either failed to attain this goal or chose another path can be read as a confirmation of the theory that being "overmatched" academically is detrimental to the progress of black students. But the other fact—that 11 percent of all black matriculants at SEL-1 institutions aspired to and received medical degrees (as opposed to 7 percent of the whites) makes clear that it is the inflated denominator (i.e., the unusually high number of black medical degree aspirants) that needs to be emphasized.

[21] The importance of pre-college advanced degree aspirations, for students of all races, is evident in the simple tabulations and confirmed when we adjust these tabulations to control for other variables (see Appendix Table D.4.2). Among all C&B graduates who

unrealistic aspirations. As noted above, in 1989, 24 percent of all blacks and 22 percent of all whites said that they intended to get a PhD. Of course, very few of these students—black and white—will actually do so. Interestingly, twice as many black students who did *not* aspire to a PhD as those who did (4 percent versus 2 percent of the total sample) are now in PhD programs. This is a further indication that while many African Americans lack information about some kinds of advanced study and related career options when they enter college, they are, nonetheless, converting the opportunities offered by a high quality undergraduate education into large numbers of graduate and professional degrees.

SAT Scores

To what degree is the likelihood of later advanced study discernible at a young age, before students even enter college? How much can we learn about future patterns of graduate study from the SAT scores of aspiring undergraduates? Such questions are of obvious relevance to the debate over race-sensitive admissions, since the predictive power of SAT scores figures so prominently in it.

Among both white and black graduates from the '76 cohort, the percentage earning advanced degrees increases as SAT scores rise (Figure 4.6). The relationships are quite similar for blacks and whites. We see that 34 percent of whites with combined SAT scores under 1000 earned advanced degrees of one kind or another, compared with 71 percent of white graduates in the 1300 or more SAT interval; the corresponding increase in the case of black graduates is from 52 percent to 85 percent. Similarly, the bottom panel of the figure shows how the percentage of students who went on to earn professional or doctoral degrees increases as SAT scores rise.

But how much of the apparent "credit" for predicting who will go on to advanced study do SAT scores themselves deserve? In Figure 4.7, we compare the actual relationship between SAT scores and the attainment of advanced degrees (this time for all '76 C&B matriculants, black and white) with the adjusted figures that are obtained when we take account of the interrelationships among SAT scores, high school grades, socioeconomic status, and the selectivity of the undergraduate schools that students attended. A comparison of the top and bottom panels of the figure shows that adjusting for these variables reduces the sizes of the

aspired to earn an advanced degree, 56 percent did so; among those who did not have advanced degree aspirations, only 30 percent earned more than a BA. The adjusted percentages (estimated by assuming that the aspirants and non-aspirants were similar in all other respects) are 60 percent and 44 percent, respectively.

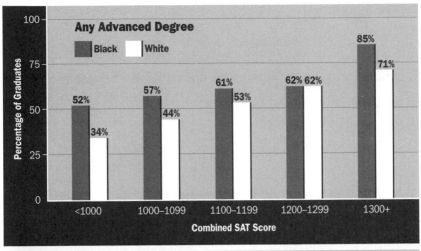

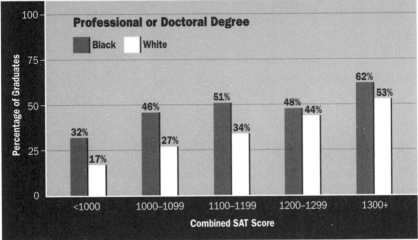

Figure 4.6. Percentage of Graduates Attaining Advanced Degrees, by Combined SAT Score and Race, 1976 Entering Cohort

Source: College and Beyond. *Note*: The "Professional or Doctoral Degree" category is as defined in the notes to Figure 4.2.

step-like increases in advanced degree attainment associated with rising SAT scores by about one-third. In other words, the academic skills measured by SAT scores continue to play a substantial role in predicting which undergraduates go on to attain higher degrees even after we take account of interrelationships with high school grades, socioeconomic status, and school selectivity.

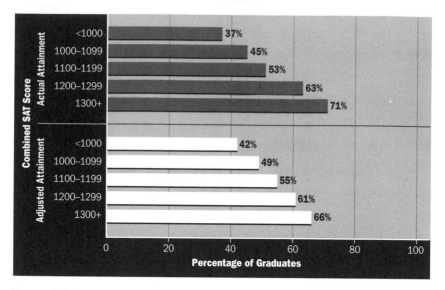

Figure 4.7. Percentage of Graduates Attaining Advanced Degrees, by Combined SAT Score, Actual and Adjusted Percentages, 1976 Entering Cohort

Source: College and Beyond.

Note: Adjusted rates are estimated using a logistic regression model controlling for student and institutional characteristics (see Appendix Table D.4.2, Model 2, and Appendix B).

A large part of the long-term effect of pre-collegiate academic achievement on the likelihood that students will earn advanced degrees of course makes itself felt through the effects of the abilities and preparations measured by SAT scores on college rank in class and field of study. But we find that SAT scores continue to have some independent impact on advanced degree attainment even after allowing for these modes of impact.[22] The explanation may be that admission to graduate and profes-

---

[22] As we would expect, when college grades and academic major are added to the regression equation, the differences in advanced degrees attained across the SAT intervals decline substantially (see Model 3, Appendix Table D.4.2). But we do not believe this is the model to use in measuring the "true" impact of SAT scores. As explained at greater length in Chapter 5 (when we examine the relation between SAT scores and earnings), it is important not to overcontrol by including variables such as college rank in class that are central parts of the mechanism of impact. The more appropriate measure of the impact of SAT scores on advanced degree attainment, "other things equal," is shown by the set of adjusted figures presented in the bottom panel of Figure 4.7, where the control variables are limited to high school grades, socioeconomic status, and school selectivity (Model 2). See Chapter 5 and Appendix B for a fuller discussion of the reasons why we use this sequential series of models.

sional school is also at least partially dependent upon analogous tests (LSATs, MCATS, GMATs, and GREs), and that those who did well when they took the SATs are also likely to succeed later when confronted with similarly constructed problem solving exercises. (In subsequent research, we hope to test this hypothesis directly.) The fact that SAT scores are helpful in predicting advanced degree attainment, as well as graduation rates and rank in class, is one reason why we believe that they should continue to be used in the admissions process.

However, while SAT scores serve as a useful predictor of advanced degree attainment, two other points should be stressed. First, SAT scores are better predictors of advanced degree attainment for white graduates than for black graduates (see Appendix Table D.4.3). Second, distinctions based on level of SAT score should not be overplayed within the extraordinarily high achieving C&B universe. In many ways, the most remarkable figures shown in the top panel of Figure 4.6 are the high percentages of those in the lower SAT intervals who nonetheless attained advanced degrees (both black and white graduates). In view of the generally high academic standing of the entire '76 C&B student population, we should not be too surprised to discover that a substantial number of those at the lower end of these SAT distributions went on to earn MDs, JDs, MBAs, and PhDs (as well as other advanced degrees). Nevertheless, the results, classified by SAT range, are still noteworthy. Even in the lowest SAT interval (combined SAT scores below 1000), 32 percent of black graduates earned professional degrees or PhDs, along with 17 percent of their white classmates.[23] Clearly, race-sensitive admissions and recruiting efforts on the part of professional and graduate schools helped to make this possible. But these data are indicative of more than merely having gained admission to graduate programs, since they are based on success in completing the degree requirements.[24]

We are also reminded again of how high the threshold for admission to these schools is—and of how well those students have done who were not that far over it. Having relatively modest SAT scores within this highly selective student population certainly has not disqualified students with drive and ambition from pursuing advanced study. The high numbers of

---

[23] The corresponding percentages earning an advanced degree of any kind (which includes MAs) were 52 percent for blacks with SATs under 1000 and 34 percent for whites with SATs under 1000 (Figure 4.6).

[24] Of course, graduate and professional study represents an opportunity, not an end in and of itself. The C&B students (both black and white) who attained advanced degrees should be examined on the basis of what they have done with the opportunities offered to them. In subsequent chapters we will examine how their advanced training has affected their job opportunities, civic involvement, and satisfaction with life.

students from the lower SAT intervals who not only earned BAs but went on to complete graduate study (including professional and PhD programs) is testimony that the C&B admissions offices have been making capable judgments in managing the sorting function.

The major implication of this part of the analysis for race-sensitive admissions is that many black matriculants who would have been rejected under a strict race-neutral admission policy went on to earn advanced degrees, including professional and doctoral degrees. Focusing just on the black graduates in the '76 cohort who entered college with SATs in the 1100–1199 interval, we see that half of them received a professional or doctoral degree and that another 10 percent earned a master's degree of some other kind—for a total of 61 percent with advanced degrees (Figure 4.6). According to the estimates of retrospective rejections presented in Chapter 2, roughly two-thirds of these graduates would not have been admitted to their undergraduate schools under a race-neutral standard.

School Selectivity and Grades

While pre-collegiate academic records and aspirations affect the chances that an undergraduate will go on and attain an advanced degree, the experiences and grades of students in college have a much stronger impact on patterns of graduate study. Graduate and professional schools rely heavily on such data in selecting students, and the aspirations and plans of college graduates are, of course, affected by their undergraduate experiences.

We saw in the previous chapter that school selectivity had a powerful independent effect on graduation rates, and especially on the graduation rates of black students. By and large, the same pattern holds in predicting attainment of graduate degrees. Both black and white graduates of the most selective colleges and universities (the SEL-1 schools) earned professional and doctoral degrees at especially high rates: 51 percent of white graduates and 48 percent of black graduates. Graduates of SEL-2 schools had slightly lower rates. A sharper drop-off occurred among students graduating from the SEL-3 institutions, with 31 percent of black and 27 percent of white graduates earning professional or doctoral degrees (Figure 4.8).

The most selective of the C&B colleges and universities were especially important "feeders" to doctoral programs. Of all graduates from the '76 cohort at the SEL-1 schools, 12 percent subsequently earned a doctorate, and 96 percent of these degrees were PhDs in the arts and sciences or in engineering (the remaining 4 percent were in education, divinity, and other fields). Black graduates were less likely to earn doctorates than

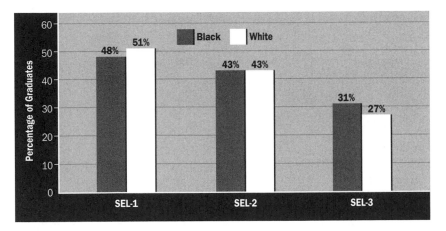

Figure 4.8. Percentage of Graduates Attaining Professional or Doctoral Degrees, by Institutional Selectivity and Race, 1976 Entering Cohort

Source: College and Beyond.

Notes: The "Professional and Doctoral Degree" category is as defined in the notes to Figure 4.2. "SEL-1," "SEL-2," and "SEL-3," indicate institutions for which the mean combined SAT scores were 1250 or more, between 1125 and 1249, and below 1125, respectively.

their white classmates; even so, 6 percent of all 1976 black matriculants who graduated from the SEL-1 schools earned doctorates. As the SEL-1 colleges and universities became ever more academically selective in the 1980s, they attracted students who were even more likely to enroll in doctoral programs. In the '89 cohort, 14 percent of all graduates from these schools (and 11 percent of black graduates) subsequently enrolled in PhD programs. It is also noteworthy that there have been perceptible shifts in interest among black graduates toward doctorates in the humanities and engineering (though the social sciences continue to rank first in popularity).

For all graduates, controlling for other variables reduces appreciably the strength of the relationship between school selectivity and receipt of a professional or doctoral degree: the gap in degree attainment between members of the '76 cohort at the SEL-1 schools and those at the SEL-3 schools is cut in half, from 24 to 13 points. In contrast, making the same kinds of adjustments for black graduates only reduces the corresponding gap in degree attainment from 12 points to 11 points. Once again, the selectivity of the school appears to have had more of a lasting effect on black matriculants than on matriculants in general.[25]

[25] See Appendix Table D.4.4. This proposition holds with even greater force for matriculants than for graduates because of the compounding of advantages. Black ma-

One would expect college grades to be at least as important a predictor of advanced degree attainment as school selectivity. To examine this relationship, we divided the entering cohort at each school into thirds, based on percentile rank in class, and compared those matriculants who ranked in the top third of the class with those in the middle third and those in the bottom third.

Rank in class does indeed help to explain which students eventually earned advanced degrees (Figure 4.9). These tabulations show that the proportions of students, black and white, earning advanced degrees vary directly with rank in class. They also show that, within each third of the class, blacks are more likely than whites to earn advanced degrees. All of these relationships persist when we examine them on an "other things equal" basis. The adjusted percentages of students earning professional and doctoral degrees (and advanced degrees in general) turn out to be indistinguishable from the actual values. We find that, no matter what we control for, college grades have a powerful independent effect on whether or not students later earn advanced degrees.[26] It makes sense that a law school admissions committee or an academic department selecting from among PhD applicants will care a great deal about a student's demonstrated academic achievement. These results should give comfort to those who believe that academic achievement matters and hard work pays off.

But at these highly selective colleges, it is by no means only the students with the highest grades who went on to graduate and professional schools. Perhaps the most important substantive finding revealed by Figure 4.9 is that very large numbers of black graduates who were in the middle third of the class at the C&B schools subsequently obtained advanced degrees (68 percent, with 50 percent acquiring professional or doctoral degrees). Indeed, a surprisingly large fraction of black graduates in the bottom third of the class also earned advanced degrees (49 percent, with 34 percent earning professional or doctoral degrees).

The differences between black and white graduates appear to be even more pronounced when we focus on the top-tier schools of law, medicine, and business. Since cell sizes become so small when we attempt to cross-classify individuals within particular fields, we report only summary figures for law, business, and medicine combined (Figure 4.10). Black C&B students are clearly more heavily concentrated than white C&B students in the top-tier professional schools.

---

triculants are more likely to graduate from the most selective schools, and those who graduate are more likely to earn professional or doctoral degrees.

[26] See Appendix Tables D.4.2 and D.4.3.

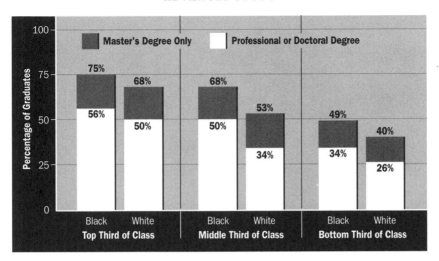

Figure 4.9. Percentage of Graduates Attaining Advanced Degrees, by Type of Degree, Class Rank, and Race, 1976 Entering Cohort

Source: College and Beyond.

Note: Degree categories are as defined in the notes to Figure 4.2.

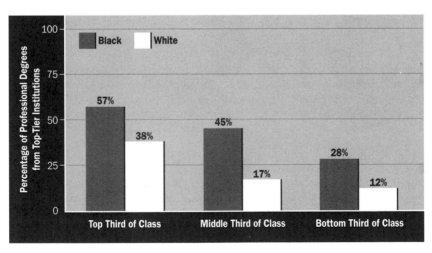

Figure 4.10. Percentage of Professional Degrees Received from Top-Tier Institutions, by Class Rank and Race, 1976 Entering Cohort

Source: College and Beyond.

Note: See Appendix B for definition of "Top-Tier Institutions."

One can interpret these data as a further indication that graduate and professional schools gave preference to black candidates from the C&B schools, and they undoubtedly did. But what is equally striking about these findings is that large numbers of *white* students who had ranked in the middle or bottom third of the class at these highly selective undergraduate schools were also admitted to such programs and earned advanced degrees. Indeed, 40 percent of all white students in the bottom third of the class later earned an advanced degree of some kind and more than a quarter earned a professional or doctoral degree—with no benefit, obviously, from racial preference.

The "Fit" Hypothesis

A recurring question is whether black students who went to one of the most competitive colleges or universities, and perhaps ended up in the middle or bottom third of the class, were later penalized for their "venturesomeness." Would such students have been more successful in pursuing advanced degrees if they had attended a less selective institution, where they might have received better grades? The answer to this important question appears to be no, at least in most cases. The multivariate regressions provide the most compelling evidence. For all students, as well as for black students considered separately, going to a SEL-1 or a SEL-2 school increased appreciably the odds that a student would earn a professional or doctoral degree—after holding constant SAT scores and other pre-collegiate variables such as high school grades, socioeconomic status, and advanced degree aspirations.[27] Students with equivalent SAT scores were more likely to earn advanced degrees, the more selective the school they attended, even if they had to accept a lower GPA at a more selective school. For example, among black '76 matriculants who ranked

[27] Appendix Table D.4.3 (Model 3) shows that attending a SEL-1 or SEL-2 school increased the odds of earning a professional or doctoral degree after controlling for rank in class as well as for SAT scores and other measures of pre-collegiate academic achievement. But the Model 3 regressions "over-control" for the effects we want to observe here, since the proper comparison is not between students attending schools of different degrees of selectivity who had the same SAT scores *and* the same rank in class. It is more appropriate to compare students who had the same SAT scores but different grades, because of the effects of school selectivity on rank in class. When we drop the rank-in-class variable from the analysis (Model 2) the SEL-1 and SEL-2 variables continue to be positively and significantly associated with the odds of earning a professional or doctoral degree. In fact, while the parameters are, as we would have expected, somewhat smaller in the regressions that do not contain rank in class (Model 2) the differences between the two sets of parameters are modest (Appendix Table D.4.3).

in the bottom third of the class at a SEL-1 school, 42 percent went on to earn professional or doctoral degrees. The price these students paid for attending a SEL-1 school (approximately 15 points in class rank, as compared with others who attended a SEL-3 school) was more than outweighed by other factors that cause graduates of highly selective schools to earn advanced degrees in exceptionally large numbers.

THE BLACK-WHITE GAP IN DEGREE ATTAINMENT

In the previous chapter, we analyzed "net" differences by race in graduation rates and grades and found that blacks did less well than whites on an "other things equal" basis. But we now observe the opposite pattern when we examine the first post-college outcome: successful completion of programs of graduate study. The actual proportions of white and black graduates earning graduate and professional degrees were about the same, but the adjusted proportions—obtained by correcting for the effects of other variables—are quite different (Figure 4.11).

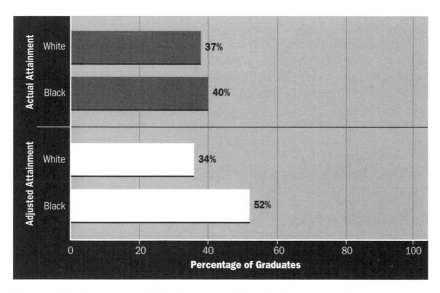

Figure 4.11. Percentage of Graduates Attaining Professional or Doctoral Degrees, by Race, Actual and Adjusted Percentages, 1976 Entering Cohort

Source: College and Beyond.

Notes: Adjusted rates are estimated using a logistic regression model controlling for student and institutional characteristics (see Appendix Table D.4.3 and Appendix B).

Black graduates of the C&B schools earned advanced degrees in very large numbers in spite of having lower SAT scores, lower socioeconomic status, and lower grades than most other students. Had the black students had the same characteristics as their classmates, we estimate that more than half of them would have earned professional or doctoral degrees, as compared with 34 percent of white graduates. We believe that this projected difference reflects the greater desire of black students to earn such degrees, combined with the opportunities for advanced study that race-sensitive admissions at the graduate and professional school level have made available to them. These results are consistent with the view that such training, and the attendant credentials, matter most to those who feel that they still have barriers to overcome.

The significance of the figures and statistics presented in this chapter goes far beyond the accumulation of degrees. The C&B minority graduates with advanced degrees are the backbone of the emergent black and Hispanic middle class. Their presence has brought greater diversity to the emergency clinics and surgery rooms of leading hospitals, to government offices and law firms, to corporate hierarchies, and to the practice of entrepreneurship. They have also gained the training that will allow them to offer medical services to traditionally underserved communities and give political leadership to struggling urban constituencies.

Whatever careers they choose, African American graduates with advanced degrees have exceptional opportunities to contribute. With all the controversy over race-sensitive admissions and all the minority students who have been admitted to graduate and professional schools, minority professionals remain in relatively short supply. Their influence extends well beyond the workplace, important as it is there. Successful black and Hispanic professionals serve as role models for nephews and nieces and are available to advise a neighbor or a family friend on medical, legal, or financial matters. In doing so, they provide "networks" similar to those that have benefited the majority white community for many generations. In other words, they can serve as strong threads in a fabric that binds their own communities together and binds those communities into the larger social fabric as well.[28]

[28] See Gates and West 1996, especially pp. 31–38.

The respect conferred by the black community on black professionals is illustrated by the following comment by a black woman physician who attended Bryn Mawr:

I have to say I'm surprised at times at how much respect other people give me. I tend not to introduce myself as "Doctor." But even at church, if people find out that I am a doctor, they may call me "Doc" or whatever. I mean it's not on my checks, not on my credit cards. But when people find out, I say, "You can call me by my first name," and African Americans say, "No, no, no, we *will* give you your props; you've earned them." It's kind of nice—and that's a kind of racial thing—that other black people I've met are very respectful even when I'm not asking for it. I guess it means a lot that somebody's done it.

A major purpose of higher education is to build intellectual capital. Academic "tests" of various kinds are at work at all stages of this process. At the undergraduate level, students have to persist and satisfy the requirements for the BA. Graduate and professional schools then make their own decisions as to which of these former undergraduates to admit, and their faculties in turn decide which individuals qualify for advanced degrees.

But an even stronger set of "market tests" operates after students complete their formal education, and continues throughout life. Would a major consulting firm subject its clients to associates recruited from a business school that had enrolled students who lacked the ability to produce a well-thought-out business plan? Would law firms that demand hundred-hour work weeks hire graduates incapable of producing under pressure? Would teaching hospitals accept interns and residents if they had doubts that these people could cope in traumatic situations?

These questions remind us that access to further education offers only an opportunity, not a guarantee, of becoming one of the society's next generation of leaders. In this spirit, we turn now to a detailed examination of the uses to which these students have put the intellectual capital in which they, their families, their colleges and universities, and society at large have invested so heavily.

CHAPTER 5

Employment, Earnings, and Job Satisfaction

WHENEVER ECONOMISTS discuss how individuals have fared, they think first of wages or earned income—the dollar valuation that the market has put on a person's activities in the workplace. For all its evident limitations—its failure to value leisure, civic contributions, family satisfactions, or even the prestige, power, and other psychic benefits (or penalties) associated with different types of work—this summary statistic serves as one useful way of measuring success in one's career.

Many studies have demonstrated that the human capital built by education generates substantial economic returns.[1] As we noted in discussing graduation rates, these returns have risen dramatically in recent years. There is much evidence from longitudinal studies (discussed later in the chapter) that economic returns on investments in education are enhanced by attendance at institutions of high quality. More impressionistic surveys of the graduates of universities such as Stanford and a plethora of anecdotes concerning the highly successful graduates of other College and Beyond schools also suggest that studying at these schools has been amply rewarded in the marketplace.[2] Such mundane financial considerations are one obvious reason why aspiring African Americans seek admission to the best undergraduate (and professional) schools, and why their competitors for the limited number of places in the entering classes are equally eager to attend these institutions.

The C&B database provides a rich opportunity to document in detail how the '76 matriculants at twenty-eight academically selective colleges and universities have fared in the marketplace. Moreover, the large number of black students in the survey population enables us to compare their occupational choices and earnings with those of their white classmates as well as with the earnings of black (and white) graduates of other four-year institutions.

Because this material is somewhat complex, it may be helpful to begin with a brief "reader's guide." In the first section of the chapter, we examine patterns of labor force participation for men and women to deter-

---

[1] The classic reference is Becker (1993).

[2] See, e.g., *Cream of the Crop* by Katchadourian and Boli (1994), a study of a sample of the Stanford class of 1981; the tongue-in-cheek title speaks for itself. See also the sources cited ibid. and in Pascarella and Terenzini (1991, pp. 508ff.).

mine how many work, and how many work full-time. In the second section, we report the earned income of all those who matriculated at the C&B institutions, and then (separately) the income of those who did and did not graduate; we also compare the incomes of the C&B graduates with those of all holders of BAs nationwide. We next consider, in the third section, the pathways whereby C&B students have transformed undergraduate educational opportunities into earnings opportunities.[3] In the fourth setion, we explore the effects on the earned income of white and black matriculants of factors such as SAT scores, the socioeconomic status of the student's family, the selectivity of the college attended, the major field of study, and rank in class, all on an "other things equal" basis. In the last section of the chapter, we move beyond earnings and consider how much satisfaction these former students feel they are receiving from the jobs they have chosen.

LABOR FORCE PARTICIPATION AND WORK STATUS

Nearly all male graduates of the '76 C&B cohorts worked in April 1995 (the reference period for the C&B survey). Only about 3 percent said that they did not work during the month in question, and 93 percent worked full-time. The figures for white male C&B graduates are nearly identical to those for white holders of BAs nationwide. In contrast, the percentage of black male C&B graduates not working was lower than the percentage of black male college graduates nationwide (3 percent versus 6 percent). Similarly, the percentage of black male C&B graduates who were working full-time was higher than the corresponding percentage for black male graduates nationwide (93 percent versus 87 percent).[4]

---

[3] In Appendix C, we present a fuller treatment of the ways in which earned income varies depending on advanced degrees earned, sector of employment, and occupation.

[4] When we want to provide direct comparisons with national benchmarks, we contrast the figures for C&B graduates (including those who transferred and graduated from a school other than the one they entered initially) with those for the graduates of all four-year colleges and universities. It would have been better to compare matriculants, since we want to know what has happened to all those who started out at particular types of institutions, not just those who graduated. Unfortunately, there are no Census data for matriculants. (Census data do exist for individuals with "some college," but it is impossible to know how many of these people entered four-year colleges, as contrasted with other kinds of educational institutions.) Comparing C&B graduates with all graduates does not, however, solve fully the problem of comparability. The reason is that graduation rates have been higher among the C&B population than among all matriculants at four-year institutions, and graduates do better in the labor market than do non-graduates. Thus, comparisons restricted to graduates understate the differences in labor market performance between those who enrolled at C&B schools and all others.

It is the women who are most interesting from the standpoint of work status. There are pronounced dissimilarities between black women and white women, both within the C&B cohorts and nationally (Figure 5.1). Over 20 percent of the white women graduates in the C&B population did not work during the survey month, and less than 60 percent worked full-time. The contrast with the black women who graduated from the same C&B schools is striking: only 5 percent of the black women were not working, and 85 percent worked full-time. The same kinds of black-white differences are present in the national data, but the gaps are smaller (more white women were working, and more were working full-time, while fewer black women were working, and fewer were working full-time).

In part at least, these patterns reflect differences in marital status and in family income. The black women were more likely to be single; those who were married typically had less family income at their disposal than did white married women. More of the white women were married and affluent (especially in the C&B population), and some number of these women appear to have chosen to "spend" some part of the family's re-sources on non–labor market pursuits, presumably devoting extra time to child care or to volunteer activities. Fewer of the black women had such options.

Adjusting for differences in marital status, family income, and other factors between white and black women reduces but by no means elimi-nates what one commentator has called the "leisure gap." Whereas white women who do not work outnumber black women who do not work by a ratio of nearly 4 to 1 (21 percent to 5 percent), the adjusted ratio shrinks to roughly 2 to 1.[5] As one would expect, women with advanced degrees were, other things equal, more likely than other women to be working. This was particularly true of women who had invested the most in their education, in time or in money: those with medical degrees and those

---

Since such very high fractions of the C&B matriculants graduate, the C&B data for matriculants and graduates are very similar. Nonetheless, we will focus our basic analysis (when not making national comparisons) on matriculants, since we do not want to exclude the small number of C&B students who never received degrees from any institution.

[5] This result uses the same methodology employed in Chapters 3 and 4 and explained in detail in Appendix B. It is based on a logistic regression that predicts labor force participa-tion for women and includes controls for SAT scores, high school grades, socioeconomic status, college selectivity, major, class rank, attainment of advanced degrees, a rough esti-mate for spouse's income, marital status, and children (Appendix Table D.5.1). Most of the coefficients associated with these control variables, excepting those discussed below in the text, fail to pass tests of statistical significance.

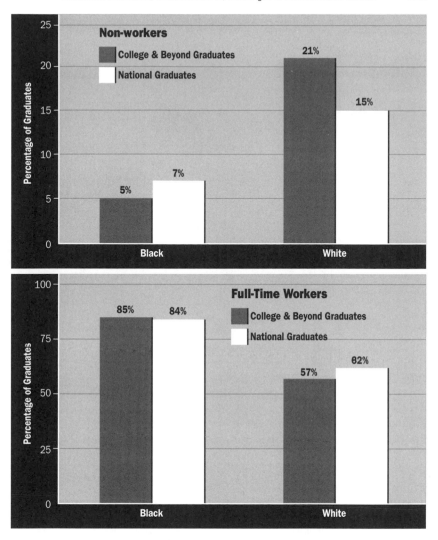

Figure 5.1. Labor Force Participation of Women in 1995, by Race, College and Beyond Graduates and National Graduates, 1976 Entering Cohort

Sources: College and Beyond and 1990 U.S. Census.

Note: "National" percentages are based on 1990 U.S. Census tabulations of women age 37 to 39 with a bachelor's or higher degree.

with PhDs. Especially important in influencing decisions not to work were the presence of children and the financial resources contributed by a spouse's high income. The strong attachment to the labor market of black women persists even after these other factors have been taken into account.[6]

The differences in work status between black and white women graduates are, however, much smaller now than they were in earlier years. The reason is obvious. While the percentage of white women from the '76 C&B cohort who were not working (20 percent) seems—and is—high in comparison with the comparable figure for black women, it is exceedingly low in relation to the corresponding percentage for all women twenty-five years earlier. At the time of the 1960 Census, more than 60 percent of all married women 35–44 years old (roughly the age range of the members of the '76 cohort when they were surveyed) were neither working nor looking for work.[7] Thus, the "leisure gap" appears to be closing because of broad social and economic forces that have encouraged much larger fractions of women in every demographic group to enter the labor force.

EARNED INCOME

Annual Earnings of Full-Time Workers

We turn now to the annual earnings of those graduates of the '76 cohort who were working full-time when they were surveyed.[8] One point is immediately clear: graduation from a C&B institution did not erase the familiar differences in compensation associated with gender and race. Black graduates earned less than their white classmates, and women

---

[6] The C&B surveys also contain information about work histories, which make it possible to carry out a more careful analysis of time in and out of the labor force and consequently the amount of work experience that has been accumulated. Experience obviously needs to be taken into account in interpreting earnings differentials. For a fuller discussion of such relationships, see Goldin (1990). Since the focus of this study is on race, rather than gender, we have not explored this dimension of the C&B database; in the future, we expect that others will pursue such questions, as well as the links between pre-collegiate preparation, choice of major, choice of occupation, and labor market commitments.

[7] Stated the other way around, the labor force participation rate for all married women 35–44 years of age was 37 percent in 1960 and 76 percent in 1995 (U.S. Bureau of the Census 1997, p. 403, tab. 629).

[8] Only 4 percent of all C&B male graduates and 22 percent of all C&B women graduates worked part-time. We restrict this analysis to full-time workers because comparisons with Census data are much more problematic when part-time workers are included; also, what we want to approximate is a kind of "wage rate," with hours of work held constant.

earned less than men (Figure 5.2).[9] We note, however, that the average annual earnings of the black women C&B graduates fell short of the average earnings of the white women C&B graduates by less than $2,000 ($64,700 versus $66,000). In contrast, the black male graduates of the C&B schools earned, on average, roughly $17,000 less than their white male classmates ($85,000 versus $101,900). If we compare all matriculants, not just those who earned BA degrees, the black-white differences become larger: the gap for male matriculants rises to $22,000, and the gap for female matriculants becomes $3,200.[10]

Even more revealing are comparisons with national benchmarks, which we can provide only for graduates.[11] As the comparisons for full-time workers shown in Figure 5.2 demonstrate, the graduates of the '76 C&B cohort have been exceedingly successful in the marketplace. On average, black women from the C&B schools earned 73 percent more ($27,200 more) than did all black women with BAs. The C&B earnings advantage was even greater for black men, whose average earnings were 82 percent greater ($38,200 more) than the average earnings of all black holders of BA degrees.[12] White graduates of the C&B schools also earned

[9] The figures for C&B graduates shown in Figure 5.2 are estimated mean annual earnings in 1995, when most of these graduates were about thirty-eight years old. As explained earlier, we focus on C&B graduates to permit comparisons with Census data; we include C&B matriculants who transferred and graduated from other schools. See Appendix B for a description of the income intervals included on the survey questionnaire and the method used to estimate means.

[10] This widening of the black-white earnings gap when we include all matriculants in the calculations is due mainly to black-white differences in graduation rates, combined with the tendency for all C&B non-graduates, black and white, male and female, to earn appreciably less than the corresponding groups of graduates (39 percent less for black male non-graduates, 39 percent less for white male non-graduates, 41 percent less for black female non-graduates, and 34 percent less for white female non-graduates.) The "transfer" graduates—those who graduated from a school other than the one that they entered first—consistently earned less than the first-school graduates but more than the non-graduates. (These are, of course, all raw, or unadjusted, differences; later in the chapter we present adjusted means for matriculants, which take account of the effects of other explanatory variables.)

[11] The most reliable national benchmarks are data derived from the 5 percent sample of the 1990 Census. As explained in Appendix B, we extracted the records of those BA recipients who matched the C&B age groups and definition of full-time workers.

[12] These already large C&B premiums for black graduates are larger yet when we compare the earnings of all graduates, not just those who worked full-time. In the case of black men, the premium rises from 84 percent to more than 100 percent; that is, the average earnings of all black graduates of C&B institutions were more than *twice* the average earnings of all black holders of BAs ($82,000 versus $41,000). For black women, the C&B premium rises from 73 percent to 82 percent.

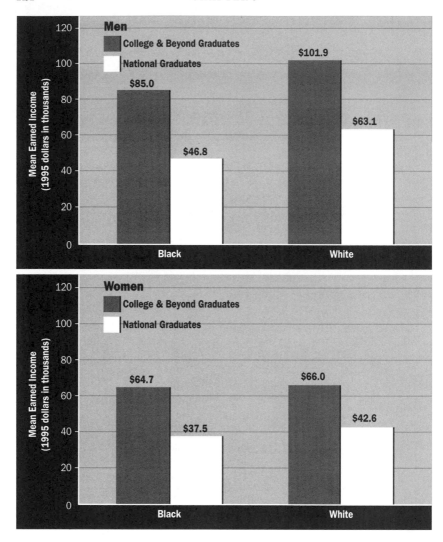

Figure 5.2. Mean Earned Income in 1995, by Race and Gender, College and Beyond Graduates and National Graduates, 1976 Entering Cohort

Sources: College and Beyond and 1990 U.S. Census.

Notes: For College and Beyond graduates, mean earned income is derived from income ranges reported by full-time, full-year workers. For National graduates, the 1989 income of full-time, full-year workers aged 37 to 39 is converted to 1995 dollars. See Appendix B.

much more than did all white holders of BAs, but their earnings advantage was "only" 55 percent for the women and 61 percent for the men.

These data make clear that the earnings disadvantage for blacks vis-à-vis whites was appreciably smaller for C&B graduates than it was nationally. The average black female graduate of the C&B schools earned 2 percent less than her white classmate, whereas the average black female BA in the national population earned 14 percent less than her white counterpart. The corresponding earnings disadvantage for the black men was 17 percent for the C&B graduates versus 35 percent for all black male BAs.[13]

Averages tell only part of the story, and in Figure 5.3 we "go behind the averages" and show the cumulative percentages of BA recipients (grouped by race and gender) who earned more than $10,000, more than $50,000, and so on, up to more than $200,000. One of the most striking impressions conveyed by these data is the large number of '76 C&B graduates, both black and white, who had extremely high earnings at young ages.

As might be expected, the white men from these schools have done especially well—nearly 20 percent were earning over $150,000 when they were still in their thirties. Approximately 10 percent of the black male C&B graduates earned more than $150,000, almost 25 percent earned $100,000 or more, and roughly 70 percent of them earned $50,000 or more. One-quarter of the white women C&B graduates, and nearly as high a percentage of the black women, earned more than $75,000. Fully 50 percent of both the black and the white women earned more than $50,000. These percentages are at least double the comparable percentages for all holders of BAs nationwide. It is in these high-middle income ranges that the earnings gaps between graduates of C&B schools and graduates of all colleges nationwide are most pronounced.

Selection Bias

Such comparisons suggest that attending a C&B school improves an individual's economic prospects dramatically. But the fact that these schools are so selective implies that some part of these substantial earnings differentials must be due to the high quality of the students admitted in the first place ("selection bias"). Since the Census does not collect SAT scores, we cannot correct for selection bias by making direct comparisons

---

[13] These differences could be due in part to a college quality effect in the national data. That is, white students outside the C&B universe might be more likely than black students outside this universe to have attended other academically strong institutions (flagship state universities, for example).

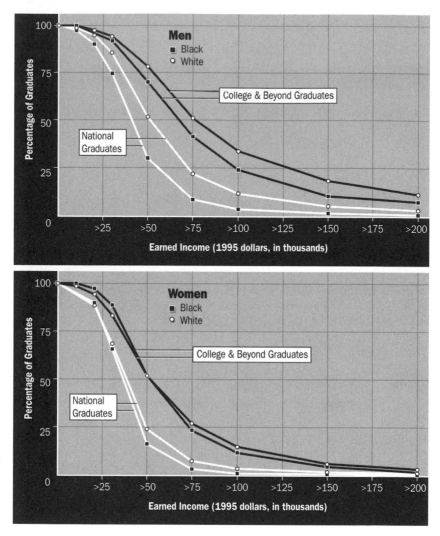

Figure 5.3. Cumulative Earned Income Distribution in 1995, by Race and Gender, College and Beyond Graduates and National Graduates, 1976 Entering Cohort

Sources: College and Beyond and 1990 U.S. Census.
Notes: See notes to Figure 5.2.

between individuals in a given SAT range who did and did not go to C&B schools. There are, however, two ways in which we can assess the meaning of the observed earnings differentials between C&B graduates and all holders of BAs.

First, we can compare the average earnings of C&B matriculants with the average earnings of similarly talented matriculants from the control group survey conducted by the National Opinion Research Center (NORC).[14] We lack test scores for the control group respondents, since we had no way of obtaining admissions data or institutional records for them; still, we can identify a high-talent, high-achieving "tail" of the control group population by using information we collected on their college grades. Of all white males in the sample who attended four-year institutions, 11 percent reported that they had received "mostly As" in college. Let us make the admittedly rough assumption that this top decile of the control group sample of college matriculants is roughly comparable in academic "quality" to *all* C&B matriculants and compare the average earnings of the two groups. The control group matriculants who earned "As" in college had average earnings of $71,400, which is appreciably higher than the figure for all white male matriculants in the control group ($61,500), but far below the C&B average for white male matriculants ($98,200). Thus, this very crude attempt to correct for differences in student quality eliminates just over one-quarter of the "raw" wage premium enjoyed by the white male C&B matriculants; the remaining premium is $26,800 ($98,200 minus $71,400), as compared with an initial premium of $36,600 ($98,200 minus $61,500).[15]

[14] The control group survey is described in Appendix A. We are using here the responses of those white members of the '76 control group who graduated from a four-year college or university and worked full-time. The control group cell sizes are not large enough to permit separate comparisons for black graduates.

[15] We made similar calculations for white women graduates in the control group sample. The appropriate adjustment for student ability in the case of the women appears to be essentially the same as the adjustment for men. The A students among the women NORC matriculants earned more than the non-A students ($39,500 versus $30,400), which implies a 27 percent adjustment.

Of course, some of the high-achieving students from this national sample may also have gone to selective schools, and for that reason, our method of correction may understate the true premium attributable to attendance at a C&B school. The crude method of adjustment used here may understate the true earnings premium associated with attendance at a C&B school for a second reason; response bias appears to have had a much larger effect on the estimates of average earnings obtained from the control group survey than on the estimates obtained from the C&B survey (see Appendix A). We believe that correcting both estimates for response bias would increase rather substantially the earnings differential between the C&B matriculants and the control group population.

A very different approach is to review the findings of national longitudinal studies of the economic returns to college quality that have tried to control for pre-college differences in student ability. These studies confirm that there is a large earnings premium associated with attendance at highly selective institutions. They also indicate that anywhere from 10 percent to 50 percent of the observed premium can be attributed to the higher test scores of the students who enroll in the most selective schools. The consensus is that, even after controlling for ability as best one can, highly significant economic returns are gained by attending a more selective college or university.[16]

Have these returns to college quality been enjoyed by minority students as well as by white students? The evidence suggests that the strictly economic payoff from attending a selective college has been even greater for minorities than for whites. Both Behrman et al. and Daniel, Black, and Smith have found that the return on college quality for black men is several times the return on college quality for white men. While not all studies have reported such large relative returns for minorities, none has contradicted the qualitative conclusion that providing opportunities for minority students at high-quality institutions has been a good investment.[17]

While hardly definitive, the combination of the control group comparisons and the review of longitudinal studies persuades us that:

- There is, indeed, a real wage premium associated with enrollment at an academically selective institution;
- This premium is substantial (even at a fairly early stage in one's career); and
- The premium is at least as high, and probably higher, for black students than for white students.

PATHWAYS TO CAREER ADVANCEMENT

Why have graduates of selective colleges achieved so much economic success in their chosen careers? Advocates for these institutions naturally believe that part of the reason that their graduates do well is the superior

---

[16] See Loury and Garman 1995; Daniel, Black, and Smith 1997; Brewer, Eide, and Ehrenberg 1996; Behrman et al. 1996.

[17] The literature does, however, contain one counterclaim. Loury and Garman (1995) found that blacks earn more by attending a selective school, but that this gain is more than offset for blacks whose SAT scores are substantially below the median SAT of the college attended. However, Kane (forthcoming) points out that this result derives entirely from the fact that Loury and Garman do not distinguish attendance at a historically black college or

quality of the education they receive. This is not a proposition that can be tested rigorously. It is fair to say, however, that compared to other undergraduate institutions, selective colleges tend to have more resources, better facilities, more generous financial aid, and more faculty members who have strong reputations in their fields. In addition, students are surrounded by classmates of exceptional ability, who set high standards of intellectual excellence and offer challenging examples to emulate. In view of these advantages, there is reason to believe that the quality of education at selective institutions does contribute something to the premiums subsequently earned by their graduates, although it is impossible to determine exactly how much.

Attending a selective college may also contribute to later-life success by raising the career ambitions of students who attend. Most young people are quite uncertain about their future when they arrive as freshmen. Attending an institution with exceptionally able students and alumni/ae who have traditionally enjoyed successful careers no doubt raises the expectations of many undergraduates as to what they can and should accomplish in their later lives.

As we saw in the previous chapter, selective colleges help their students gain admission to graduate and professional schools (and often to top-tier programs), which in turn assist them in moving ahead in their careers. Admissions officers at professional schools often give more weight to academic records from colleges that are familiar to them and which are known to have high standards and students of exceptional quality. Thus, a law school applicant who has done well academically at a highly selective college may be forgiven a modest LSAT score more readily than someone from a college that is less well known.

As a result, larger numbers of C&B graduates entered highly regarded professional programs and went on to earn substantial financial returns on these further investments in their education. The data in Appendix C (see especially Figures C.1a and C.1b) demonstrate that these enhanced career opportunities have powerful effects on earning power.

Our data also indicate that graduates of the C&B institutions— especially the black graduates—are much more likely than their counterparts who attended other four-year colleges to gravitate into the higher-paying, for-profit sector (see Appendix C, especially Figures C.2 and C.3). This is not to say that large numbers of black graduates of C&B

---

university from attendance at an institution that enrolls mostly white students. When this distinction is taken into account, national data sources, such as High School and Beyond, do not support Loury and Garman's conclusion.

schools do not also choose to work in the not-for-profit and governmental sectors; they do.[18] Government employment often provides more security and better benefits than jobs in the private sector, and job security may be an especially important consideration for many black graduates (who are likely to have less financial capital and less access to other family resources than the typical white graduate).[19] Nonetheless, we have seen that larger numbers of the black C&B matriculants elected to pursue careers in the private sector.

The occupations that C&B graduates choose represent another part of the pathway to higher earnings. Within sectors, C&B graduates chose particular occupations that are relatively high paying, and only relatively small numbers held clerical and other types of jobs that provide only modest compensation (see Appendix C, Figures C.4a and C.4b). We also find that within specified occupational categories, both black men and black women graduates of the C&B schools earn more than their national counterparts.[20]

In short, inside each niche—defined by advanced degree earned, sector of employment, and occupation—the typical black C&B graduate (in common with his/her white classmates) earns more than do most holders of BA degrees in the United States. This is presumably due to a combination of above-average pre-collegiate skills, a good undergraduate education, demonstrated capacity to "get it done" in competitive environments, the continuing importance of institutional reputations, and, yes, "connections"—the same kinds of advantages that have benefited generations of white graduates of these highly selective schools.

While graduation from a selective college hardly guarantees a successful career, it may open doors, help black matriculants overcome any negative stereotypes that may still be held by some employers, and create opportunities not otherwise available. One black '76 matriculant makes the point particularly clearly:

> I wanted to take a job that would give me preparation for law school. Based on my association with some people at Yale, I got a job as a paralegal at a law firm in New York. Well, I got there, and these guys at the law firm said, "No,

[18] The percentage of all black holders of BAs nationwide who work for local, state, or the federal government continues to be very high: 46 percent for the women and 37 percent for the men; among the black C&B graduates the corresponding percentages are 31 percent for the women and 21 percent for the men (Figure C.2).

[19] As Richard Freeman (1976) has noted: "Public employers, particularly the federal government, offered qualified blacks better job opportunities than the private sector in the new market" (p. 151).

[20] This pattern holds for all of the gender/occupational groupings shown in Appendix Table D.C.1b.

no, no, you don't want to be here. We're going to call over to 'X' corporation and get you a job over there." So I worked in the corporate auditor's office through some Yale connection and got to see the workings of a corporation from an inside—and interesting—position as opposed to doing some sort of scut work. I got to talk to senior executives about how their departments work and even make recommendations about efficiencies.

It wasn't that any of these people knew me. They knew the association I belonged to at Yale—one of the secret societies. They took my resume and then they met me. I earned my way and got the job. But, it was these connections that got me the introduction. . . . Obviously, I had to have some talent, but if I'd gone elsewhere, that talent wouldn't have been exposed to these community leaders who took an interest in the young people and the young talent coming out of Yale and then helped to funnel it toward the right places, be it law school or the right business.

It bears repeating that success requires much more than old school ties and graduation from a well-known institution. Achievement requires ability and dedication. Beyond that, minority graduates, in particular, may have to surmount special obstacles independent of the college or professional school they attended. In the words of two recent black graduates of Princeton (who participated in a panel to describe business careers to undergraduates), "Minorities must work harder and be smarter" and expect "to be judged at a higher standard." As one of the panelists put it, "If anything goes wrong, there's a stereotypical reaction that 'We knew this would happen.'"[21] Still, however complex the feelings of individual alumni/ae may be and whatever difficulties they may have experienced, graduation from a selective college—with a national reputation, a talented faculty, good facilities, and constant challenge from academically gifted classmates—appears to create career opportunities for minority students that they would not otherwise have had.

FACTORS AFFECTING EARNINGS OF C&B MATRICULANTS

The earnings of each C&B matriculant depend not only on a host of personal qualities and perhaps even "accidents of life," but also on factors that can be studied more systematically.[22] These factors are not, however,

---

[21] Similarly, law professors David Wilkins and Mitu Gulati (1996) have written about the subtle factors, especially differences in the amount of mentoring, that affect the chances that black and white associates will become partners in large law firms.

[22] In this section and in the rest of the chapter, we report on the C&B population alone,

independent of one another, which complicates the analytical task of disentangling their individual effects. For example, SAT scores help determine the type of school attended, the field of study chosen, and the grades earned by the matriculant. As we saw in the previous chapter, these factors in turn affect the odds that a student will earn an advanced degree, and hence help to determine whether the individual can pursue a professional career of one kind or another.[23]

In an effort to parse out the effects of key variables on the earnings of white and black matriculants, we developed a series of five models, which we present in full in Appendix Tables D.5.2 through D.5.5. (Separate sets of regressions are presented for men and women, and for black men and black women.) Since these models are so important to the analysis that follows, we need to explain briefly the characteristics of each:

- Model 1 includes only those variables known at the time a student applied for admission to college: race, gender, SAT scores, high school grades, and the family's socioeconomic status.
- Model 2 adds only the selectivity of the school attended (SEL-1, SEL-2, SEL-3).
- Model 3 adds two important "in-college" measures: the student's major field of study and cumulative rank in class.
- Model 4 adds information on the highest degree attained: bachelor's, master's, law, medicine, business, or doctorate.
- Model 5 adds information on sector of employment (private, self-employed, nonprofit, government).

The purpose of these models is to help determine how certain key variables (such as SAT scores or grades) gain or lose power to predict earnings as we add more control variables. Sometimes, therefore, we will refer to several of the models listed above and other times we will discuss only the most inclusive model. The additional tables in Appendix D

---

since Census earnings data cannot be linked to measures of aptitude, type of four-year school attended, rank in class, or major field of study. We focus on factors affecting the earnings of all C&B matriculants, not just those who earned BA degrees, since it is the success of the entire entering cohort that is the best indicator of the effectiveness of the admissions process and the subsequent educational programs of the schools.

[23] The series of regression models described below, in which variables are added sequentially, is intended to address these complexities, at least in some measure. These are ordinary least squares (OLS) models, similar to those used in Chapter 3 to predict rank in class; the dependent variable is earned income. (We also estimated the same models using earnings expressed in natural logarithms and found the results to be qualitatively similar.) For a more detailed discussion of our methodology, see Appendix B.

contain details that will be of interest to some readers but not others; in the text we highlight what we believe to be the most important findings.

SAT Scores

We begin by examining to what degree the earnings of C&B matriculants, and of black matriculants considered separately, can be predicted by the SAT scores that students brought with them to college. This question is of obvious relevance to the debate over the long-term consequences of admitting students with scores below those of many of their classmates.

In general, higher SAT scores were quite consistently associated with higher average earnings for both men and women matriculants in the '76 C&B cohort (see the actual, or "unadjusted," bars in the top of each panel of Figure 5.4). For the men, the two largest increments in earnings occur below the middle of the SAT range. Matriculants with SAT scores below 1000 had average earnings that were $6,100 (or about 7 percent) lower than those of matriculants in the 1000–1099 SAT interval, who in turn had average earnings that were $9,000 (or roughly 9 percent) lower than the average for those with SAT scores in the 1099–1100 interval. However, the relationship between SAT scores and earnings flattens out when we move to higher SAT levels. The average earnings of those C&B men with SATs of 1100–1199 were only about 6 percent lower than the average earnings of those in the 1200–1299 interval, and the average earnings of those in this category were only 1 to 2 percent below the earnings of those in the highest SAT range, with scores of 1300 and higher. Among the women, there are larger earnings increments at the high SAT levels (and a much smaller increment between the 1000–1099 and 1100–1199 intervals); as in the case of the men, the women with SAT scores below 1000 had noticeably lower average earnings than those with higher SAT scores.

For both men and women, these differences in earnings, seen in relation to SAT scores, are reduced somewhat when we add controls for high school rank in class and socioeconomic status. They narrow much more when we also control for school selectivity (bottom panels of Figure 5.4, which are based on Model 2 in Appendix Tables D.5.2 and D.5.3). That is, one of the main ways in which high SAT scores influence earnings is by increasing the chances that a student will attend a highly selective school; as we will see later in the chapter, students who went to the most selective schools tended to earn more than students who attended less selective schools. However, once we hold school selectivity constant, and examine the SAT-earnings relationship among those matriculants who, in effect,

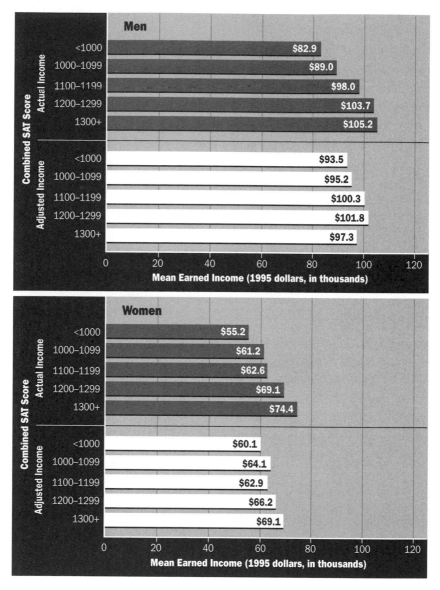

Figure 5.4. Mean Earned Income in 1995, by Combined SAT Score and Gender, Actual and Adjusted Income, 1976 Entering Cohort

Source: College and Beyond.

Notes: Actual mean earned income is derived from income ranges reported by full-time, full-year workers. Adjusted means are estimated using an ordinary least squares regression model controlling for student and institutional characteristics (see Appendix Tables D.5.2 and D.5.3, Model 2, and Appendix B).

enrolled at "the same schools," SAT scores lose much of their power to predict earnings.[24]

The relationships between SAT scores and earnings for black men and women are rather similar in their general configuration to the results for all C&B matriculants (see Appendix Tables D.5.4 and D.5.5). The main difference is that the overall relationship between SAT scores and earnings is more erratic for black men and women than it is for their white classmates. For example, black men in the 1000–1099 SAT interval have average earnings that are $10,000 *higher* than the average earnings of black men in the 1100–1199 SAT interval. There remains, however, clear evidence of a "threshold effect." Black students in the lowest SAT category paid a considerable "penalty," in that their average earnings were quite a bit lower than the average earnings of their black classmates in the next higher SAT interval (1000–1099); this "penalty" is erased partially, but by no means entirely, when we control for school selectivity.[25]

---

[24] The independent (statistically significant) relationship between SAT scores and earnings disappears almost entirely when we add additional controls for field of study and grades (Model 3 in Appendix Tables D.5.2 and D.5.3). But adding these additional controls for in-college outcomes is not, in our view, the most appropriate way to isolate the effects on earnings of the pre-collegiate qualifications that SAT scores represent. We would expect the aptitudes and preparation for college captured by test scores to exert much of their long-term impact on earnings via the route of improved academic performance. Thus, we do not want to deprive SAT scores of "credit" for enhancing earnings by affecting the ability of students to choose "hard" majors, to graduate, and to earn good grades. It is true that SAT scores also affect the odds that a student will be admitted to a highly selective school, and that SAT scores affect life-time earnings prospects through this channel as well as by affecting performance in college. This last avenue of impact is clearly relevant from the standpoint of the individual student deciding how important it is to do well on the SATs. From a broader perspective, however, "credit" for the enhanced earnings opportunities that are associated with attendance at a highly selective school (after controlling for the SAT scores of entering students and other pre-collegiate variables) should go to the *school*, not to the factors that helped the student gain admission. It is the relationship between SAT scores and earnings that remains after we have controlled for this "choice-of-school" effect that is most relevant to assessments of the admissions process. We want to know how reliably SAT scores predict how well students will do within particular school environments and then—compared with others who had the same educational opportunities—later in life.

[25] See Appendix Tables D.5.4 and D.5.5. For black men, the actual difference in average earnings between these two SAT intervals was $22,200 and the adjusted difference, after controlling for the interrelationship with school selectivity and other variables, was $15,500. For black women, the actual difference was $10,200 and the adjusted difference was $2,900. We attribute the more erratic relationship between SAT scores and earnings for black matriculants in part to the fact that there are fewer of them (which poses a more serious

Socioeconomic Status

Male and female C&B matriculants from high-SES backgrounds consistently had much higher average earnings than students from the middle-SES categories, who in turn earned more than students from low-SES backgrounds.[26] The unadjusted differences are large, especially for those at the top of the SES scale. High-SES matriculants earned, on average, at least 20 percent more than classmates from middle-SES backgrounds (see Figure 5.5). The unadjusted earnings advantage enjoyed by black matriculants from high-SES backgrounds was even greater than the advantage enjoyed by all matriculants—black men from high-SES backgrounds (a small number, to be sure) averaged $35,000 more in annual earnings than did black matriculants from middle-SES families.

Broadly speaking, about half of the unadjusted differences in earnings are eliminated when all of the controls in Model 5 are introduced (compare the bottom half of each panel of Figure 5.5 with the top half). Almost all of this compression is due to the presence in Models 4 and 5 of variables for advanced degrees attained. Apparently the high socioeconomic status of a family exerts a large part of its effect on the future earnings of children by increasing the chances that they will earn advanced degrees in fields such as law, medicine, and business.[27]

---

problem here than in other parts of the analysis because we are looking separately at men and women and also restricting the population to those who were full-time workers). In addition, as we saw earlier when we examined the relationship between SAT scores and grades in Chapter 3, there is a general tendency for SAT scores to tell us less about the future performance of black matriculants than about the future performance of their white classmates.

[26] We are using the same specially constructed measure of socioeconomic status, based on parents' education and income, explained in Chapter 2 and Appendix B.

[27] The earnings premiums associated with highest advanced degree attained are shown in Appendix Tables D.5.2 and D.5.3, Model 4 especially. On an "other things equal" basis, men whose highest degree is in law earned $20,000 more, on average, than men with BAs only; men with medical degrees, $69,000 more; men with business degrees, $29,000 more. The corresponding earnings premiums for women were $29,000 in law, $52,000 in medicine, and $33,000 in business. For both men and women, earnings penalties are associated with not earning a BA, with earning a master's, and with earning a doctorate (compared to a BA only). The patterns for black men and black women, considered separately, are very much the same. Also, adding controls for sector of employment (Model 5) has little effect on these results. See Appendix C for a fuller discussion of the relationship between advanced degrees and earnings.

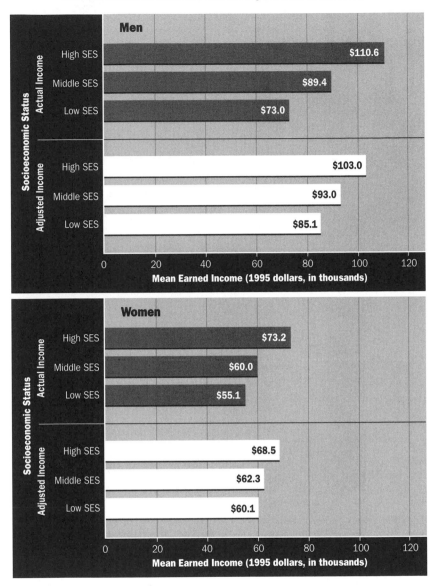

Figure 5.5. Mean Earned Income in 1995, by Socioeconomic Status and Gender, Actual and Adjusted Income, 1976 Entering Cohort

Source: College and Beyond.

Notes: Actual mean earned income is derived from income ranges reported by full-time, full-year workers. Adjusted means are estimated using an ordinary least squares regression model controlling for student and institutional characteristics (see Appendix Tables D.5.2 and D.5.3, Model 5, and Appendix B). See Appendix B for definition of socioeconomic status (SES).

Still such adjustments by no means make the underlying differences in earnings disappear. Gaps remain of roughly $10,000 between those from high-SES backgrounds and those from middle-SES backgrounds in the case of the men and approximately $6,000 in the case of the women, or about 10 percent for both groups. Whether these differences seem large or small depends on one's assumptions and expectations. In the absence of broad access to the leading colleges and universities, differences in economic circumstances related to class would surely be much greater than they are today. Nevertheless, it has to be said that the "leveling" that results from being educated at a C&B college or university (even when accompanied by the attainment of advanced degrees) by no means eradicates the beneficial effects of high socioeconomic status on *earned* income. One would expect high-SES origins to have a long-term effect on total *household* income as a result of inherited wealth; we see here that high-SES also has an independent long-term effect on the earnings capacity of individuals. For men (though not for women), the earnings penalty associated with low socioeconomic origins also persists.[28]

The results for black students are roughly similar to those for all students, but there are two differences. First, controlling for the effects of advanced degree attainment removes less of the unadjusted difference in earnings for high-SES blacks than for high-SES whites. Second, while high socioeconomic status is, if anything, even more of an advantage for black C&B matriculants than for white matriculants, low socioeconomic status has no statistically significant effect on their earnings.

School Selectivity

Average earnings correlate very strongly with the selectivity of the school attended. Classifying the C&B schools by their degree of academic selectivity, as we did in previous chapters, yields very regular patterns (Figure 5.6). For women and men, blacks and whites, average earnings were highest for those who attended the most selective schools (the SEL-1 group, where the average test scores of incoming students in the fall of 1976 were 1250 or above), next highest at the middle level of selectivity (the SEL-2 schools, where average test scores were between 1125 and 1249), and lowest at the remaining schools, which, while still highly selective, were less selective than the others in the C&B database (the SEL-3 schools, where average test scores were below 1125). The differ

[28] This finding contradicts that of Michael Hout (1988), who reported that graduation from college removes virtually all effects of socioeconomic status.

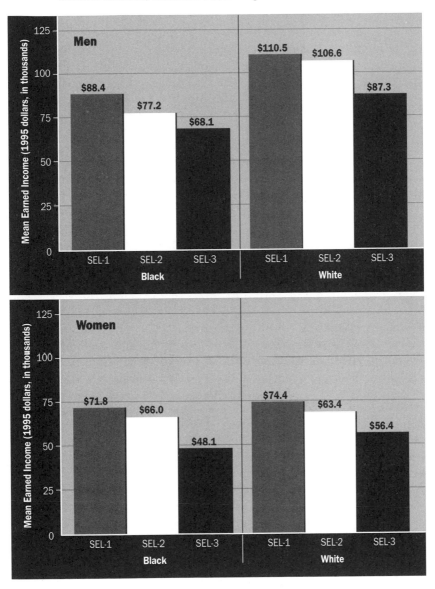

Figure 5.6. Mean Earned Income in 1995, by Institutional Selectivity, Gender, and Race, 1976 Entering Cohort

Source: College and Beyond.

Notes: Earned income is derived from income ranges reported by full-time, full-year workers. "SEL-1," "SEL-2," and "SEL-3," indicate institutions for which the mean combined SAT scores were 1250 or more, between 1125 and 1249, and below 1125, respectively. See Appendix B.

ences are substantial. Those who went to a SEL-1 school earned, on average, approximately $20,000 per year more than those who went to the SEL-3 schools, and from $5,000 to $10,000 more than those who attended SEL-2 schools. As can be seen from Figure 5.6, these patterns are consistent for men and women, blacks and whites.

These simple, unadjusted, relationships between school selectivity and earnings are essentially unaffected when controls of all kinds are introduced. In this case, the apparent, "surface" relationships are real; they are not merely a reflection of hidden associations with other factors, such as SAT scores or advanced degree attainment. Whatever the underlying reasons are—genuine differences in the quality of the education offered or merely "prestige" or credentialing effects—attending more selective schools is associated with a clear earnings advantage for matriculants.[29]

Grades

There is much folk wisdom to the effect that students who receive the highest grades end up in cerebral but modestly compensated jobs, while classmates with less impressive academic records earn much higher incomes. There are abundant examples, no doubt, that seem to confirm this impression. As a result, it may come as something of a surprise to find that grades (measured here by rank in class to standardize for differences in scales across schools) correlate quite strongly—and positively—with levels of compensation (Figure 5.7). For both black and white graduates of the C&B schools, and for women as well as men, the average earnings of those who ranked in the middle third of the class were higher than the average earnings of those in the bottom third, and the average earnings of those in the top third were higher yet. Of course, even the bottom third of the class from the C&B schools did well financially by any normal standard, earning much more, for example, than the national averages for all graduates of four-year colleges.

The large premium associated with doing well academically, like the premium associated with attendance at the more selective schools, is unaffected by the introduction of controls for SAT scores, socioeconomic

---

[29] See Appendix Tables D.5.2–D.5.5. Since the adjustment process makes so little difference here, we present only the actual (unadjusted) differences in the text. Some part of the earnings differential associated with attendance at a more selective institution may also reflect unobservable differences in the students themselves not captured by SAT scores, high school grades, or socioeconomic status (see the earlier discussion of selection bias).

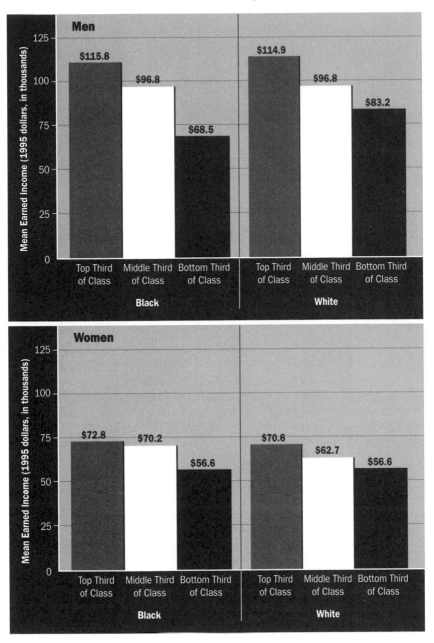

Figure 5.7. Mean Earned Income in 1995, by Class Rank, Gender, and Race, 1976 Entering Cohort

Source: College and Beyond.

Note: Earned income is derived from income ranges reported by full-time, full-year workers. See Appendix B.

status, type of school attended, field of study,[30] advanced degrees held, and sector of employment. We expected that grades would lose much of their predictive power after the hurdle of admission to graduate or professional school was cleared, but this was not the case. Grades have a powerful independent effect on earnings. On an "other things equal" basis, the typical male C&B matriculant who ranked in the top third of his class earned $21,000 more than a man in the bottom third; the corresponding premium for women was $8,000 (over a lower base). We presume that achieving high grades reflects a range of qualities, including perseverance and the ability to apply one's skills to the task at hand, as well as brainpower, that are rewarded in the marketplace as well as in the classroom.

Interestingly, the financial penalty for receiving low grades in college appears to be somewhat greater for black students (men and women) than for white students. This is an important finding, especially when taken in conjunction with the earlier evidence that black students with given SAT scores tend to earn lower grades than their white classmates with the same test scores. It reinforces the urgency of understanding better why the academic performance of black students tends to be below predicted levels. It also serves as a reminder that the market offers definite incentives for black matriculants to do well academically.

The "Fit" Hypothesis Once Again

Some writers have claimed that black students who benefited from race-sensitive admissions would have fared better had they attended schools in which their academic credentials were more exactly matched to those of

---

[30] Average earnings vary appreciably by field of study, in part because of the relationships among major, advanced degrees attained, and occupation. For example, a male natural science major earned, on average, $24,000 more than a humanities major who had the same pre-college and in-college characteristics; similarly, the estimated average earnings of male social science majors and male engineering majors exceeded those of men in the humanities by $22,800 and $8,700, respectively (see Model 3 in Appendix Table D.5.2). Among women C&B graduates, we estimate that those who majored in engineering earned $27,300 more than women who majored in the humanities, and that those in the natural sciences and the social sciences earned, respectively, $17,700 and $16,300 more than the humanities majors (Model 3 in Appendix Table D.5.3). The earnings advantages associated with majoring in the natural sciences, as contrasted with all other fields, are much greater for black men and women (Appendix Tables D.5.4 and D.5.5). We do not use Models 4 and 5 in the appendix tables to compare earnings across fields of study because they also control for attainment of advanced degrees and sector of employment, which are of course principal channels through which field of study affects earnings, and which thereby mute the predictive power of field of study.

their white classmates. In Chapter 3 we examined this "fit" hypothesis in the context of graduation rates and grades and found that it did not stand up to scrutiny. Black students in the C&B universe with modest SAT scores graduated in larger numbers from the most selective schools than did those who attended schools in which their classmates were more like them in terms of SAT scores. It is possible to perform the same test using average earnings, rather than graduation rates, as the criterion of "success."

The results are summarized in Table 5.1. These grids show student SAT scores across the top, school selectivity down the side, and average earn-

TABLE 5.1

Mean Earned Income in 1995, by Institutional Selectivity, Race, Gender, and Combined SAT Score, 1976 Entering Cohort (thousands of 1995 dollars)

	Combined SAT Score				
	< 1000	1000–1099	1100–1199	1200–1299	1300+
Black men					
SEL-1	86.7	83.6	87.7	—	—
SEL-2	71.0	91.8	67.7	—	—
SEL-3	60.5	90.0	—	—	—
All	66.9	89.1	79.7	103.5	70.0
White men					
SEL-1	132.7	104.5	118.0	108.3	110.0
SEL-2	109.7	105.2	106.2	100.7	102.5
SEL-3	81.7	83.6	90.3	90.5	98.6
All	86.2	89.0	97.8	102.9	105.0
Black women					
SEL-1	75.3	78.1	73.5	—	—
SEL-2	61.9	61.2	83.6	—	—
SEL-3	47.1	—	—	—	—
All	55.5	65.7	75.3	51.5	—
White women					
SEL-1	54.3	83.8	74.4	77.0	73.3
SEL-2	62.0	66.1	64.2	70.1	77.9
SEL-3	53.5	56.8	56.2	61.8	64.1
All	54.8	60.2	61.4	69.1	73.6

Source: College and Beyond.

Notes: Earned income is derived from income ranges reported by full-time, full-year workers. "SEL-1" indicates institutions with mean combined SAT scores of 1250 or more; "SEL-2" indicates institutions with mean combined SAT scores between 1125 and 1249; "SEL-3" indicates institutions with mean combined SAT scores below 1125. Dashes represent cells with fewer than 20 observations.

ings in the cells defined by the intersection of student SATs and school selectivity.[31] For present purposes, the most relevant columns are those that show the earnings of black matriculants with SAT scores in the lower ranges. We see that those black women with SAT scores in the below-1000 range who attended the SEL-1 schools earned much more than those who attended the SEL-2 schools, and that those who attended the SEL-2 schools earned appreciably more than those who attended the SEL-3 schools. The same pattern holds in the 1000 to 1099 range (except that there are too few observations in the SEL-3 category to permit showing a number in that cell). The results for the black men are similar,[32] as are the results for white women and white men. These findings are consistent with the regression analysis, which demonstrated that, after holding SATs constant, black students who attended the more selective schools gained an earnings advantage.

The general conclusion seems straightforward. While there may well have been other differences between students with similar test scores— differences that affected both their educational opportunities and their varying degrees of success in the marketplace after college—the admissions processes seem to have gauged these differences well. Black students admitted to the most selective of the C&B schools did not pay a penalty in life after college for having attended such competitive institutions. On the contrary, the black (and white) matriculants with academic credentials that were modest by the standards of these schools appear to have been well advised to go to the most selective schools to which they were admitted.

THE REMAINING BLACK-WHITE EARNINGS GAP AMONG MEN: A PHENOMENON IN SEARCH OF AN EXPLANATION

The selectivity of the schools that students attend, the majors that they choose, and the grades they earn continue to have clear effects on earnings (as does the family's socioeconomic status) even when interactions

---

[31] Cell sizes become something of a problem when we limit the group being studied to those who were working full-time, and then cross-classify the individuals who remain by race, gender, SAT interval, and school selectivity. Average earnings in cells that had fewer than 20 observations are not shown.

[32] There is one aberration. For black men in the 1000–1099 SAT range, average earnings were higher at the SEL-2 schools (and at the SEL-3 schools) than they were at SEL-1. As the lower panel of Table 5.1 indicates, this same "bump" is present, but to a lesser degree, among the white men.

among these variables are taken into account.[33] At the same time, the color of one's skin also continues to matter, at least for men. This is the final conclusion to be drawn from our analysis of the earnings data for C&B matriculants.

In the case of women, the black-white gap in actual earnings, which is modest to begin with ($3,200), disappears entirely when we control for the effects of other variables. The adjusted averages for black and white women are nearly identical (Figure 5.8).[34] Adjusting for the effects of other variables diminishes the size of the black-white earnings gap for men as well, reducing it by slightly more than half its original size. But the remaining gap of $8,500 is hardly inconsequential. One might have thought that adjusting for the effects of lower SATs and grade point averages, differences in the fields of study chosen, lower socioeconomic background, and differences in the selectivity of the school attended, advanced degrees attained, and sector of employment would have made the black-white difference in earnings for men disappear entirely. But that is not the case. Such adjustments eliminate only about 60 percent of the unadjusted gap for men.[35]

This highly significant differential is important enough to merit further exploration. Possible explanations can be grouped into several categories:

- It is, of course, possible that shortcomings in our measures of some variables (such as socioeconomic status) account for at least

[33] These same basic relationships hold for women and for men, for black and white matriculants; indeed, the similarity of the patterns is quite striking, as can be seen by comparing the separate regressions (Appendix Tables D.5.2–D.5.5). In a further effort to see if any of the independent variables behaved appreciably differently for black graduates than for white graduates, we introduced interaction terms that were intended to show the joint effect of being black and, say, graduating in the top third of one's class. In general, the coefficients were not significant.

[34] The complete lack of any "net" effect of race on the earnings of women can also be seen by examining the coefficient for the black variable in Model 5, Appendix Table D.5.3. It is one-third the size of its standard error. The earnings figures reported in Figure 5.8 are slightly different from those presented in Figure 5.2 because these are for all matriculants, rather than just graduates. Both sets of data include only full-time workers because of the difficulties involved in calibrating and comparing part-time earnings.

[35] Also, as one commentator on an earlier draft of this book has suggested, it is possible to go too far in adjusting for differences between black and white students in estimating the black-white earnings gap. For example, black-white differences in the distribution of employment by sector may reflect in part patterns of discrimination or racial preference; to the extent this is true, adjusting for differences in sector of employment may lead to an understatement of the "true" size of the black-white earnings gap.

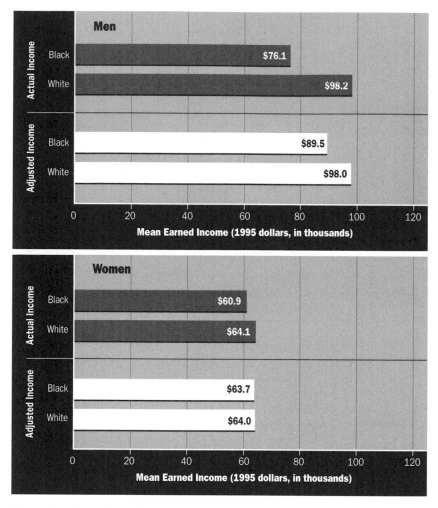

Figure 5.8. Mean Earned Income in 1995, by Race and Gender, Actual and Adjusted Income, 1976 Entering Cohort

Source: College and Beyond.

Notes: Actual mean earned income is derived from income ranges reported by full-time, full-year workers. Adjusted means are estimated using an ordinary least squares regression model controlling for student and institutional characteristics (See Appendix Tables D.5.2 and D.5.3, Model 5, and Appendix B).

part of the remaining gap, but we have no way of evaluating this possibility.

- We thought that considering occupational categories might help to explain the gap, on the grounds that further information about particular jobs might paint a more accurate picture of why people earned what they did than we obtained by looking only at advanced degrees and sector of employment; however, including detailed job variables did not reduce the gap at all.

- We suspected from inspection of the earnings distribution curve for men (see Figure 5.3) that the relatively large number of white men with extremely high earnings might be responsible for much of this gap, and in fact the size of the gap is reduced when we truncate the earnings distribution at a lower level. But even this approach, which leaves open the question of why there are such differences at the highest levels of compensation, yields an adjusted gap in average earnings of $6,400.[36]

- We made elaborate efforts to test the effects of pre-college goals reported by these matriculants when they were freshmen (such as "be well off financially"), thinking that differences in motivations or ambitions might be relevant. Some of these seventeen measures of pre-collegiate aspirations, gathered via CIRP surveys, did turn out to have predictive power, but none, considered individually or collectively, changed the black-white earnings gap.

- Finally, in an effort to test as best we could whether other affective characteristics (related to self-confidence) not captured in measures of academic performance might influence earnings, we added a set of twenty-two self-ratings (from leadership skills to stubbornness to physical attractiveness) that appear on the Cooperative Institutional Research Program questionnaire that is administered when students enter college. But including these variables also failed to reduce the black-white earnings gap.

This relentlessly persistent earnings gap for men raises important issues. One question, raised by several people who commented on a draft of this book, is whether this gap is a measure of the effects of discrimination in the marketplace. Other commentators asked whether

---

[36] We assigned all individuals who reported earning $200,000 or more to the next-lower earnings category ($150,000 to $199,000) and kept the same point estimate of earnings in that range ($175,000). This amounts to refusing to count any earnings above $175,000.

it might be evidence of the same kind of "underperformance" that we observed when examining rank in class, and, if so, what would explain such patterns. In either case, whether we believe the gap results from unfair treatment or underperformance, why does it persist for black men and not for black women? We have no basis for hazarding answers to such thorny questions, and we certainly do not want to exaggerate the size of the gap, which is modest when viewed in relation to national earnings differentials reported in Census data. Nevertheless, this finding does compel us to wonder whether even the black male students who graduated from selective C&B schools have found the fabled "level playing field" that so many agree should be our nation's objective.

JOB SATISFACTION

Money is by no means the only thing that matters in a job. The career choices that C&B graduates make have definite economic consequences, as we have demonstrated, but they surely have other consequences, too. How have these graduates felt about the occupational choices they have made? What have they sought from their careers, and what have they found? Are black C&B matriculants more or less satisfied with their jobs than their white classmates?

The first observation to be made is that overall satisfaction with jobs is very high for the entire cohort: 89 percent of all C&B matriculants who worked full-time reported being very or somewhat satisfied with their current jobs, and 52 percent said they were very satisfied.[37] The proportion expressing any degree of dissatisfaction ranged from 9 to 11 percent. Men and women reported very similar levels of overall satisfaction. Black C&B respondents expressed somewhat lower levels of job satisfaction than did white respondents (as discussed in detail below).

There have always been those who believe that "the poor man in the sun is happier than the rich man in his castle." (To which the economist Jacob Viner used to retort, "I believe it when the poor man tells me.") Not surprisingly, we have found that, for both blacks and whites, job satisfaction rises steadily with income and that income is by far the strongest determinant of job satisfaction. Across all sectors of employment, and within each, respondents in the higher income brackets were much more

---

[37] By way of comparison, a 1996 Inc./Gallup survey found that 71 percent of the U.S. workforce reported being "satisfied" with their jobs. See Seglin (1996).

likely than those in the lower income brackets to say that they were very or somewhat satisfied with their jobs. Over two-thirds of both women and men with earnings of $150,000 or more said they were very satisfied with their jobs; this percentage then falls steadily as earnings decline (Figure 5.9). This finding is consistent with the literature, and with common sense.[38]

Occupation and sector of employment also matter. Some people appear to have been willing to trade off some amount of income for other rewards associated with certain kinds of careers. For example, many C&B graduates with PhDs chose careers in academia or in research that were less remunerative than other jobs in the for-profit sector but presumably more satisfying.[39]

In general, we found that those in the not-for-profit sector and governmental sector were significantly more inclined than those in the for-profit sector to be very satisfied with their jobs (Figure 5.10). These differences remained qualitatively the same when we adjusted the results to take account of differences in other variables. Those in the for-profit sector were less satisfied with their jobs than others, their higher earnings notwithstanding, and, as one would expect, introducing earnings as a control variable widened these gaps appreciably. The most satisfied C&B graduates, however, belonged to a different group altogether. In keeping with the "American dream," both blacks and whites who were self-

---

[38] See Diener 1984. These results stay essentially the same when we use multivariate regression analysis to adjust for the effects of other variables (Appendix Table D.5.6). In short, the strong association between earnings and job satisfaction holds after controlling for other factors, such as selectivity of the school attended, advanced degrees held, or sector of employment (which does, however, as we show immediately below, have an independent effect on job satisfaction). The fact that C&B men with middle and low incomes are less likely to be satisfied with their jobs than women in these earnings brackets probably reflects differences in earnings expectations.

[39] A distinguished professor of English literature, Alvin Kernan, explains his choice of a career as follows: "I fully understood that choosing an academic life was to give up the rewards of power and money that law or business could bring, but it seemed worth it to live life against the background of the Himalayas of language, the great works that revealed essential human experience. Chaucer's knight defined duty and service, Othello jealousy, Pope's dunces stupidity, Wordsworth nature, Dickens the city and goodness of heart, Eliot alienation and modern angst. A literary education was as broad as it was deep, forcing familiarity with chivalry and revolution, with gods and devils. And always you learned about, or better still, internalized these matters not through the abstractions of sociology or the large-scale events of history but as they were experienced personally, under intense pressure, by human beings, fictional, of course, but still human and much like yourself" (forthcoming).

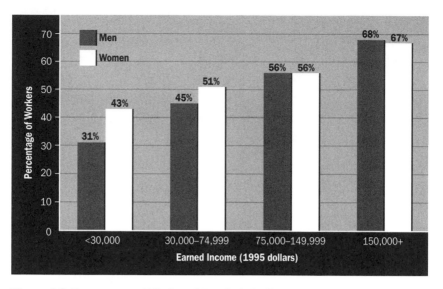

Figure 5.9. Percentage of Workers "Very Satisfied" with Job, by Earned Income and Gender, 1976 Entering Cohort

Source: College and Beyond.

Note: Only full-time, full-year workers are included.

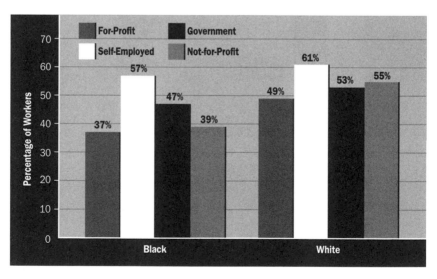

Figure 5.10. Percentage of Workers "Very Satisfied" with Job, by Employment Sector and Race, 1976 Entering Cohort

Source: College and Beyond.

Note: Only full-time, full-year workers are included. Adjusted percentages are estimated using a logistic regression model controlling for student and institutional characteristics (See Appendix Table D.5.6 and Appendix B).

employed reported the highest degree of job satisfaction (before and after adjusting for the effects of other factors).[40]

There were significant dissimilarities in what black and white respondents to the C&B surveys said they were seeking from a job—and in what they were finding. While nearly the same percentages of white and black matriculants rated intellectual challenge as a very important job criterion,[41] a higher percentage of black respondents than of whites rated almost all other criteria as very important. As Table 5.2 (left side) indicates, these job attributes ranged from one that we would expect to elicit a large difference (fair treatment of women and minorities) to a host of other considerations related to employment opportunities, job security, and comfort on the job. For one reason or another, black graduates of the C&B schools seem to want more from their work than do their white classmates.

On the other hand, the gaps between whites and blacks in the degree of satisfaction they reported deriving from their jobs were smaller than the gaps in what they were seeking. In four areas (flexibility of schedule, low stress, good benefits, and job security) the percentages of whites and blacks reporting that they were very satisfied were within 3 percentage points of each other (Table 5.2, right side). In other areas—including intellectual challenge, independence, high level of responsibility, child care, high income, service to society, and good promotion opportunities—more whites were satisfied, but most of the differences were relatively modest, ranging from 4 to 10 points. However, in the area of fair treatment of women and minorities, the gap in the percentages saying they were very satisfied was 15 points (31 percent of blacks were very satisfied, as compared with 46 percent of whites).

---

[40] As we know, both undergraduate majors and advanced degrees are related to earnings and sector of employment. We were surprised to learn that the fields in which students majored had no discernible effect on the likelihood of their being very satisfied with their jobs. The actual (unadjusted) measures of job satisfaction show that those with medical degrees are very satisfied with their jobs; however, when controls for income are introduced, the adjusted probability of being very satisfied with one's job is lower for those with medical degrees than for those with BAs only. Those with law degrees are less likely than any other category of advanced degree holders to report high levels of satisfaction. At the other end of the spectrum, those with MAs and PhDs are most likely to be very satisfied with their jobs—after adjusting for other factors, especially differences in income. (See Appendix Table D.5.6.)

[41] The precise wording on the survey questionnaire was: "When thinking about a job, how important is each of the following to you?" Choices were: "Very important," "Somewhat important," and "Not important." See Appendix A for the entire survey instrument.

TABLE 5.2
Workers' Views of Selected Job Attributes, by Race, 1976 Entering Cohort

Job Attribute	Percentage Rating Job Attribute "Very Important"		Percentage "Very Satisfied" with Attribute	
	Black	White	Black	White
Intellectual challenge	82	83	53	83
Independence/autonomy	76	74	61	75
Flexible schedule	60	49	55	49
High level of responsibility	61	65	56	65
Low stress	29	13	17	13
Pleasant work environment	69	53	38	53
Job security	63	46	42	46
Child care	17	8	18	8
Treatment of women/minorities	92	54	31	54
High income	58	48	24	48
Good benefits	78	56	50	56
Good promotion opportunities	69	48	23	48
Service to society	49	34	46	34

Source: College and Beyond.
Note: Only full-time, full-year workers are included.

Overall, white respondents were appreciably more likely than black respondents to be very satisfied with their jobs (Figure 5.11).[42] Adjusting for other factors, including family circumstances and sector of employment, reduced this gap, but only very modestly: from 10 percentage points to 8. Differences in earnings and in other factors are relevant, but they do not account fully for this difference in job satisfaction between whites and blacks.

———————

To the extent that earnings measure success, race-sensitive admissions policies have accomplished much. Compared with college graduates of every race, black graduates of C&B schools are not only more likely to be

[42] These results do not change when we examine the responses of men and women separately. One reason black women may be much less satisfied with their jobs than white women is that a much higher proportion of black women are employed. If the distribution of tastes for work is the same for black and white women but a higher proportion of black women work for other reasons (such as lower spousal income), one would expect black women, on average, to have lower job satisfaction.

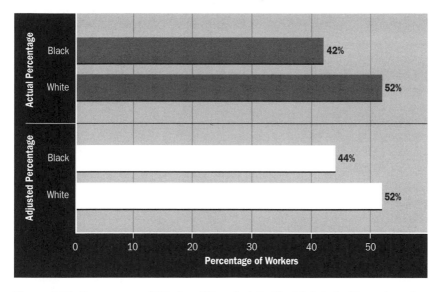

Figure 5.11. Percentage of Workers "Very Satisfied" with Job, by Race, Actual and Adjusted Percentages, 1976 Entering Cohort

Source: College and Beyond.

Notes: Only full-time, full-year workers are included. Adjusted percentages are estimated using a logistic regression model controlling for student and institutional characteristics (see Appendix Table D.5.6 and Appendix B).

employed, they are much more highly represented in professions such as law and medicine; they are also earning more within whatever sector of employment or occupation they have chosen. The earnings premiums enjoyed by C&B black graduates, relative to black college graduates nationwide, are very substantial—even larger than the premiums enjoyed by their white classmates.

Having started out with comparatively lower test scores and less family affluence, the black students who entered the C&B schools in 1976 have successfully converted the "capital" provided by academically selective schools into high-paying and satisfying careers—and at young ages. This finding stands out even though we also recognize that there are surprisingly persistent black-white earnings gaps among men, for which we have no convincing explanation.

Within the universe of C&B colleges and universities, we also found noteworthy differences in the earnings of black matriculants. While, as a group, they do very well financially, those who attended the more selective schools or earned better grades were more successful financially than others. While SAT scores have a modest effect on earnings, school selectivity and rank in class have a more lasting impact.

For the high-achieving people who attend selective colleges and universities—as for everyone else—work often ends up being a large part of life. But there is more to living than work alone, just as there are other ways of measuring success apart from the amount of money one earns. It is to these aspects of life that we turn in the next chapter.

CHAPTER 6

Civic Participation and Satisfaction with Life

WE HAVE seen in the previous chapter that African Americans who attended the College and Beyond schools have had very considerable success in the workplace. Without question, these schools have contributed to the building of human capital as conventionally defined. But a college education should do more more than simply prepare students for careers. What contributions have C&B matriculants made to civic and community endeavors? What are their family circumstances, and how satisfied are they with their lives?

CIVIC PARTICIPATION

Writing one hundred and fifty years ago, Alexis de Tocqueville noted the distinctive tendency of Americans to address societal needs of every imaginable kind through participation in voluntary associations:

> Americans of all ages, all conditions, and all dispositions constantly form associations. They have not only commercial and manufacturing companies, in which all take part, but associations of a thousand other kinds, religious, moral, serious, futile, general or restricted, enormous or diminutive. The American makes associations to give entertainments, to found seminaries, to build inns, to construct churches, to diffuse books, to send missionaries to the antipodes; in this manner they found hospitals, prisons, and schools. If it is proposed to inculcate some truth or to foster some feeling by the encouragement of a great example, they form a society. Wherever at the head of some new undertaking you see the government in France, or a man of rank in England, in the United States you will be sure to find an association.[1]

Americans continue to volunteer and join associations in large numbers. By most accounts, they are more inclined to do so than citizens of any other advanced democracy.[2] In keeping with this tradition, American colleges and universities have long prided themselves on educating indi-

[1] Tocqueville [1840] 1990, p. 106.
[2] Bok 1996, pp. 326–327.

viduals who will be good citizens—effective participants and respected leaders in civic as well as commercial activities. They have sought to educate students who will go on to live lives that are not only personally satisfying and rewarding, but socially productive. Schools noted for their emphasis on the liberal arts, such as those included in the C&B universe, have been especially likely to emphasize public service as a goal.[3]

It is only in recent years, however, that most colleges have associated such a broad objective with the racial composition of the student body.[4] The active recruitment of minority students that began in the 1960s was motivated by more than a conviction that the enrollment of a diverse student body would improve the educational process for everyone. It was also inspired by a recognition that the country had a pressing need for well-educated black and Hispanic men and women who could assume leadership roles in their communities and in every facet of national life. How well have these colleges and universities succeeded in selecting public-spirited students and encouraging them to contribute beyond the workplace?

Participation of C&B Matriculants in Civic Activities

The '76 respondents to the C&B surveys participated in civic activities in *very* large numbers—*nearly 90 percent of the cohort participated in one or more such activitity in 1995.*[5] This high propensity to engage in volunteer efforts is not unique to those who attended C&B schools. A Gallup survey conducted for the Independent Sector, which used somewhat different questions, found that about half of all Americans, and 70 percent of all

---

[3] One example is Woodrow Wilson's famous phrase, "Princeton in the Nation's Service" (coined when he was president of that institution).

[4] Oberlin is a notable exception, in that it has a long tradition of preparing black students for leadership roles.

[5] Respondents were asked whether during the previous year (1994–95) they had been participants or leaders in one or more of thirteen defined types of activities. The categories included youth organizations (scouting, Little League, etc.); professional/trade associations; political clubs or political organizations; religious activities; community/neighborhood improvement and civil rights organizations; social service or social welfare work, such as volunteering in a hospital; sports clubs; cultural organizations, such as museums; school boards or other educational organizations at the elementary or secondary level; alumni or alumnae activities at the college level; and environmental or conservation groups (see section C of the questionnaire, reproduced in Appendix A, for a complete list). Respondents were also asked if they had been participants or leaders in any prior year. In most of our analysis, we concentrate on involvement in 1995, since we are more confident in the reliability of responses tied to a specific (recent) year.

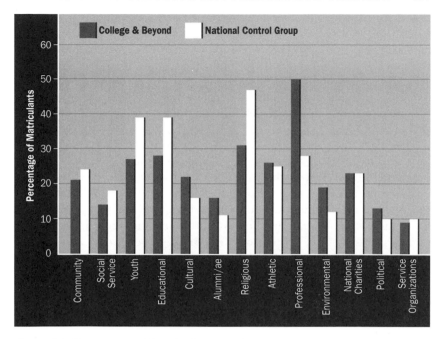

Figure 6.1. Percentage of Matriculants Participating in Civic Activities in 1995, by Type of Activity, 1976 Entering Cohort

Sources: College and Beyond and National Control Group Study (see Appendix A).

college graduates, volunteered for some form of civic activity in 1995.[6] According to the national control group study, which used the same questions as the C&B survey, the overall civic participation rate for the control group matriculants at four-year colleges was nearly as high as the participation rate for the C&B matriculants (87 percent). Those respondents who did not go to a four-year college had a participation rate of 75 percent.

C&B matriculants were, however, noticeably more likely than the control group to participate in professional and trade associations, college-related functions such as fund-raising and student recruitment, cultural and arts activities, and environmental and conservation programs. The control group matriculants, on the other hand, were more likely to participate in community and social service activities, youth organizations such as scouting and Little League, religious activities, and groups such as the PTA that operate within elementary and secondary schools (Figure 6.1).

---

[6] Independent Sector 1996. Figures in the text are for the 35–44 age bracket. We should note, however, that one type of activity on our list (sports and sports clubs) is unlikely to meet the Gallup definition of "doing volunteer work."

A distinctive and noteworthy finding from the C&B data is that the black C&B matriculants were even more active than their white classmates. In contrast, the Gallup survey of civic involvement found that white and black college graduates nationwide participated at exactly the same rate. A national longitudinal study that followed a large sample of high school seniors over time also shows very similar participation by college-educated whites and blacks in the volunteer activities covered by our survey.[7]

The black men from the C&B schools were especially likely to be involved. In seven of the ten types of activity shown in Figure 6.2, the percentage of black men who participated is higher than the corresponding percentage of white men (top panel). The bars in the left and center sections are most telling. Black men were appreciably more likely than white men to participate in the clusters of activities that include community, social service, youth, and elementary or secondary educational organizations. One-third of all black men from the C&B schools participated in community or neighborhood improvement groups. About one-third participated in the work of youth and religious organizations, and 24 percent participated on school boards or other activities related to elementary and secondary schools. Black men were also more likely than their white classmates to contribute their efforts to cultural/arts organizations and to the work of college and university alumni/ae associations. Over one-quarter were involved in activities such as student interviewing and fund-raising, and 21 percent were engaged in cultural activities, including volunteering for museums and arts organizations.

A graduate of the University of Pennsylvania relates his current engagement in alumni activities to help he received when he was an undergraduate:

At Penn, things changed a lot once I found the Society of Black Engineers. They were always handing you off to different people who could help you, people who had been through the classes. Everybody else seemed to have some sort of group—fraternities who had study tests from older groups or whatever. So I was fortunate that the Society ended up doing this for me.

---

[7] Data collected in the third follow-up on *High School and Beyond, Senior Cohort, 1986,* show essentially no black-white differences in participation in political clubs, organized volunteer work, literary/art groups, educational organizations, and service organizations. Blacks were more involved than whites in youth organizations, church-related activity, and community groups. Whites were more involved in professional organizations and sports teams or clubs.

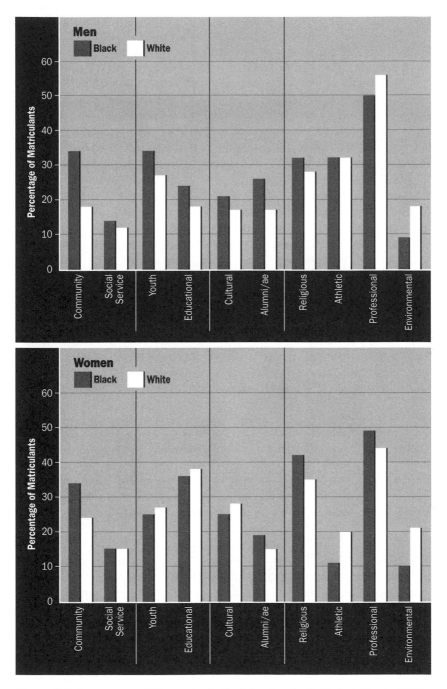

Figure 6.2. Percentage of Matriculants Participating in Civic Activities in 1995, by Type of Activity, Race, and Gender, 1976 Entering Cohort

Source: College and Beyond.

> One of my former classmates is working at Penn now, and he's soliciting alumni mentors for the new students. So we're doing an alumni network over e-mail to keep in contact with new students and help them along and answer questions as they go through the process.

The patterns for black women in the '76 cohort are roughly similar (bottom panel of Figure 6.2), but they exhibit some differences. White women from the C&B schools were even more likely than black women to participate in youth and education programs. However, when we confine the analysis to women who worked full-time, this pattern disappears— and is replaced by the "male pattern," showing greater participation by black women. Women who work part-time or not at all are more likely than other women to participate in such activities, and, as we saw earlier, significantly more white women than black women do not work.[8]

Leadership

Colleges and universities have long stressed the importance of preparing their students to do more than just participate; they have sought to educate graduates who would assume leadership roles outside the workplace as well as within it. The C&B surveys provide compelling evidence of their success in this regard. The number of black men serving as leaders is particularly impressive—especially in the community, social service, youth, and schools arenas (left side of the top panel of Figure 6.3). More generally, *in every type of civic activity shown in these figures, the ratio of black male leaders to white male leaders is even higher than the ratio of black male participants to white male participants.*

The high percentage of black women from the C&B schools who held leadership positions is also noteworthy (bottom panel of Figure 6.3). Only in environmental, sports, and school groups were white women more likely than black women to serve as leaders. Although much higher proportions of black women held full-time jobs, they were more likely than white women to assume leadership positions in community, social service, alumni/ae, religious, and professional groups.

[8] The difference in labor force participation rates affects the figures for female participation in professional and trade associations in the same way. When we restrict the comparison to women who worked full-time, the "male pattern" of slightly higher participation for whites than for blacks reappears.

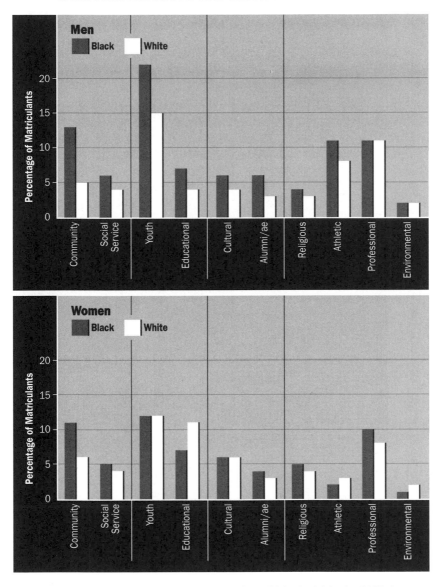

Figure 6.3. Percentage of Matriculants Leading Civic Activities in 1995, by Type of Activity, Race, and Gender, 1976 Entering Cohort

Source: College and Beyond.

We also found that black matriculants (both women and men) were more likely than white matriculants to be leaders in more than a single civic arena. Of the black matriculants with multiple leadership responsibilities, 25 percent were leaders in three or more areas; the corresponding percentage for whites is 19 percent.

The '89 matriculants exhibit patterns similar to those of the '76 cohort(Figures 6.4 and 6.5). The degree of involvement is quite remarkable, given how young these people are, how many are still in graduate school, and how few have yet to reach a stage in their lives at which they are settled in a community. More than 40 percent of the black men participated in the category of "community service," which includes "community centers, neighborhood improvement, social action associations, or civil rights groups," and 12 percent served in leadership roles—three times as high a percentage as we find among the white male respondents. The percentages for the black women are equally impressive.

In all likelihood, these findings reflect a demand for leadership skills that must be understood in relation to the relatively scarce supply of black men and women with comparable records of accomplishment. However, while the market demand for blacks to assume leadership roles is part of the explanation for their high level of involvement, it is not the full explanation. The high overall participation rate of black men and women as rank-and-file volunteers, not only as leaders, testifies to their desire to contribute. While service on boards and in other leadership positions may be thought to confer visible benefits, such as prestige, such rewards cannot be the motivation for "helping out"—merely as a participant—with a civic improvement project or a tutoring program.

Factors That Predict Leadership

These broad patterns of participation conceal many variations. The reasons why one person would assume the leadership of an alumni/ae fundraising organization are often quite different from those that cause another person to become the president of a PTA. In order to understand the influence of such factors as household income and family circumstances, we chose to focus on three clusters of activities: (1) community and social service; (2) youth groups and elementary or secondary education; and (3) cultural and alumni/ae affairs.[9]

[9] Separate logistic regressions for each of these three clusters, predicting that an individual will serve in a leadership role, are shown in Appendix Table D.6.1.

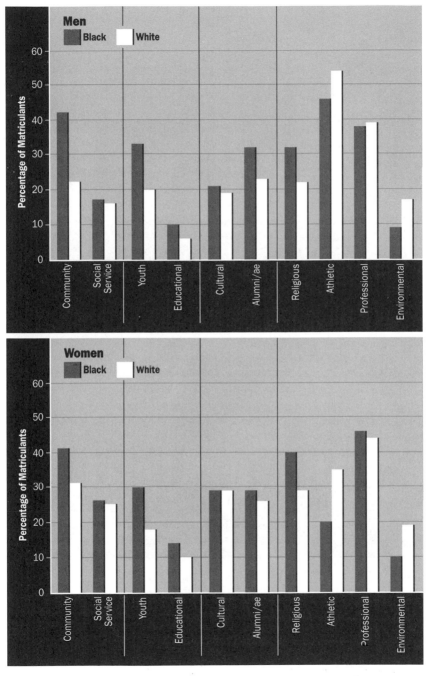

Figure 6.4. Percentage of Matriculants Participating in Civic Activities since College, by Type of Activity, Race, and Gender, 1989 Entering Cohort

Source: College and Beyond.

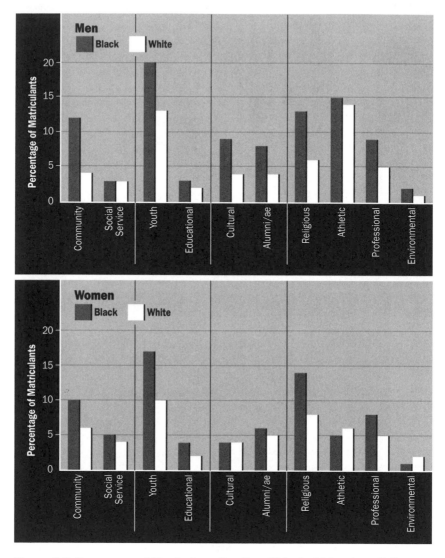

Figure 6.5. Percentage of Matriculants Leading Civic Activities since College, by Type of Activity, Race, and Gender, 1989 Entering Cohort

Source: College and Beyond.

SAT Scores and Grades

We begin with the same kinds of questions raised in other chapters about the role played by SAT scores and academic performance in predicting outcomes such as advanced degree attainment. In this case, test scores and college grades make very little difference. Among C&B matriculants, civic participation rates do not correlate with SAT scores or rank in class. The distinguished public servant Adlai Stevenson once remarked in his self-deprecating way that he had "never been threatened by Phi Beta Kappa." In this same spirit, many of the more recent graduates of these schools, up and down the academic scale, have clearly found ways to make their own contributions to civic and public life.[10]

Family Circumstances

Family circumstances influenced the types of civic activities in which those who attended C&B schools, black and white, chose to provide leadership. As one might expect, raising children increased dramatically the likelihood that people would take a strong interest in activities that are child-related: 23 percent of all parents had taken on leadership responsibilities in the youth-education cluster of activities, as contrasted with 6 percent of those without children. Moreover, there is no evidence that affluence drives the graduates of C&B institutions away from leadership of those organizations most concerned with the disadvantaged. In fact, individuals with high family income were somewhat *more* likely to be leaders in community and social service work (and in the youth-education cluster) than were individuals with lower family incomes. Very high family income correlates even more strongly with the assumption of leadership roles in cultural and alumni/ae circles—which is hardly surprising, since having money is both one indication of accomplishment and an intimation that the person in question may be able to contribute dollars as well as (one hopes) effective leadership.[11]

School Selectivity

Within the C&B universe, how has attending a more selective school affected the likelihood that an individual will be a leader in one or another of these three areas of civic activity? In the case of youth and educa-

---

[10] The same statement can be made about differences in socioeconomic status, which have little to do with subsequent patterns of civic leadership (Appendix Table D.6.1).

[11] All of these relationships hold up when we control for other variables. Sector of employment also correlates with leadership activities, even after controlling for income and educational attainment. In general, those who were self-employed and those who worked for not-for-profit entities were more likely than those in the for-profit or governmental sectors to serve as leaders of civic organizations. (See Appendix Table D.6.1 for the underlying regressions.)

tion programs, leadership patterns are dominated, as we have just seen, by family considerations and especially the presence of children; school selectivity has a relatively modest independent effect, and, in general, SEL-3 matriculants are more likely to be leaders in this area than either SEL-1 or SEL-2 matriculants.[12] In sharp contrast, attendance at a more selective school raised the odds that an individual would serve as a leader of an alumni/ae or arts organizations, such as the board of a museum. Over 10 percent of those who matriculated at SEL-1 and SEL-2 schools later held leadership positions in these areas, as contrasted with 6 percent of those at the SEL-3 schools; an even higher percentage of the black men from the SEL-1 schools led cultural or alumni/ae groups (17 percent versus 7 percent at SEL-3 institutions). Black matriculants at the most selective schools were also more likely to be leaders in community and social service organizations. These differences, however, are associated with the fact that these matriculants were even more likely than the matriculants at SEL-2 and SEL-3 schools to have obtained advanced degrees.[13]

Selective colleges have long encouraged their students to become involved in both alumni/ae affairs and in community service. Also, in making their admissions decisions, they typically give some weight to evidence that particular applicants have already demonstrated the energy, initiative, and leadership qualities associated with helping others. Since the 1970s, many of these colleges and universities have intensified their efforts to encourage undergraduates to engage in community service, both on their own campuses and acting in concert with other schools. It is possible that the extra resources devoted to outreach programs by some of these schools, which often are targeted at community service projects, have had an effect on subsequent patterns of civic involvement.

A black woman from the 1989 cohort at Yale explained how her undergraduate experience encouraged her to continue volunteering:

I had gone to Appalachia with a group from Fairfield University during my spring break to build low-income housing. Within a day I realized that I

---

[12] Those who attended SEL-3 schools were more likely to have children than those who attended SEL-1 and SEL-2 schools; moreover, they were more inclined than those who went to SEL-1 or SEL-2 schools to lead activities in this area on an "other things equal" basis (see the multivariate regression results in Appendix Table D.6.1A).

[13] The actual (unadjusted) percentages of leaders of community and social service organizations among black men are 20 percent for the SEL-1 schools, 17 percent for the SEL-2 schools, and 14 percent for the SEL-3 schools. In the most relevant multivariate regression (Appendix Table D.6.1A, Model 2), attendance at the SEL-1 and SEL-2 institutions (as contrasted with attendance at the SEL-3 institutions) is highly correlated with providing leadership in the community and social service cluster.

wanted to bring this back to Yale and have the people there experience what I'd experienced—the different culture, the people, very low income. It kind of amazed me that in 1990 there were still latrines in people's yards rather than indoor plumbing. I volunteered in middle school and in high school, but that trip really changed me, and I started volunteering for real. I was involved in this program for four years—I went down twice after I graduated.

What I liked about Yale was that Yale had a lot of resources. Dwight Hall—the volunteer umbrella organization—supported us with some money, even though most of their money goes to organizations in the New Haven area.

Advanced Degrees

Advanced degrees earned by C&B matriculants were, if anything, even more highly correlated with civic leadership than either school selectivity or family circumstances. Moreover, there are notable black-white differences that were not found when we considered other variables. Particularly striking is the high degree of commitment to community and social service organizations by those African Americans with advanced degrees. Whereas 15 percent of the white C&B lawyers were leaders of community or social service entities, an even higher percentage of black lawyers (21 percent) held such leadership positions. The black-white gap is higher still in the other advanced degree categories (Figure 6.6). Twice as many black MDs occupied such leadership roles (18 percent, versus 9 percent of whites).[14] Of the black C&B respondents with doctorates, one-third (33 percent) were leaders of organizations such as community centers, neighborhood improvement associations, civil rights groups, and hospital planning boards; in contrast, only 6 percent of white holders of doctorates served in such capacities.[15]

[14] This finding is an important addition to Davidson and Lewis's (1997) study of students who had attended the University of California, Davis, medical school. That study asked about the practice characteristics of minority doctors but did not inquire into their civic participation. While the authors found no major differences in the types of practices pursued by the "regular" and "special-consideration" students, our findings indicate that it would be a mistake to conclude that there are no differences between racial groups in civic contributions. Also, an earlier AAMC study found that minority physicians were more likely than other physicians to care for underserved populations. See Association of American Medical Colleges (1996), p. 36.

[15] Higher percentages of blacks with advanced degrees also held leadership positions in the arts-alumni/ae and the youth-education clusters.

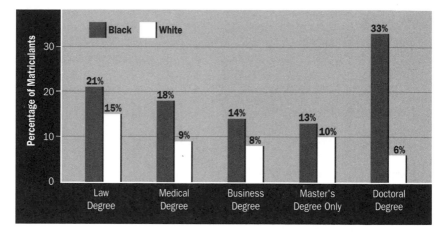

Figure 6.6. Percentage of Matriculants Leading Community or Social Service
Activities since College, by Type of Advanced Degree and Race, 1976 Entering
Cohort

Source: College and Beyond.

Notes: "Master's Degree Only" includes those students whose highest degree was a
master's degree (other than an MBA).

> *A black woman lawyer describes her civic activities and her motivation as follows:*
>
> My main involvement has been with the Oregon Association of Black Law-
> yers. We do things like mentoring law students to get through that first year.
> And we're involved in the community, helping small start-up community
> businesses. There's a community bank that opened up recently that we're
> doing our best to help. Even though being a lawyer doesn't mean that
> much to me, I do realize my importance as a role model, showing kids who
> might have a lot of motivation, and perhaps less academic preparation than
> I did, that it can be done.

Black Leadership

Other things equal, black '76 C&B matriculants were much more likely
than their white classmates to have taken on leadership positions in
virtually every type of civic endeavor. This clear pattern, so evident in the
simple tabulations, is confirmed by statistically significant findings in
multivariate regressions used to predict leadership roles within the
various clusters of volunteer activity (Appendix Tables D.6.1A and

D.6.1B). This black-white gap is just as persistent as the other black-white gaps that we discussed in earlier chapters. How are we to interpret the presence of so many black C&B respondents in leadership positions? What are the implications of this pattern for the black community and for the society at large?

The willingness of black C&B graduates to assume leadership roles is particularly significant in light of the role of civic participation in building a stable community structure. Recently, a debate has taken place over whether fewer Americans are participating in civic organizations than in the past, sparked by political scientist Robert Putnam's article "Bowling Alone." In this article, Putnam argued that "American social capital in the form of civic associations has significantly eroded over the last generation."[16] While his findings have been criticized,[17] Putnam's basic premise—that "civic engagement and social connectedness" make a critical difference in forming a more stable society—is both supported by other research and consistent with common sense. The idea that social capital either accumulates or erodes within a community gives greater significance to the ways in which highly talented black men and women choose to spend their non-working time. It underscores the fact that this group of well-educated individuals is charged, in effect, with twin responsibilities: not only to help build a more integrated American society, but to strengthen the social fabric of the black community.

There has also been much debate about the effects, some of them unintended, that the success of the civil rights movement has had on the black community. Perhaps the most dramatic warning was voiced more than ten years ago by sociologist William Julius Wilson, who noted that new opportunities for advancement have led to an "exodus of middle-class blacks," whose presence had "provided stability to inner-city neighborhoods and reinforced and perpetuated mainstream patterns of norms and behavior."[18] In response to this problem, economist Glenn Loury has written of the need for successful blacks to help in the revitalization of the black community by providing much needed "moral leadership":

---

[16] Putnam 1995, p. 73. Putnam argues that "[b]roken down by type of group, the downward trend is most marked for church-related groups, for labor unions, for fraternal and veterans' organizations, and for school-service groups" (p. 72). He speculates that this decline in civic engagement may result from persistent forces, such as the high rate of geographic mobility and consequent need for much "re-potting," demographic transformations, and the effects of technology, especially television, on how people spend leisure time.

[17] Ladd 1996.

[18] Wilson 1987, p. 7.

We can demand that a consumer franchise company give dealerships to black entrepreneurs, but not that the high school valedictorian be black. This, to my mind, is a solid basis for the moral argument that ways must be sought to enlist those blacks who have achieved a modicum of security and success in the decades-long task of eradicating the worst aspects of black poverty. The nature of the problems besetting inner-city communities, the character of political advocacy by blacks in the post-civil-rights era, and the drift of politics in contemporary America seem to require that any morally defensible and realistic program of action for the black community must attend first to the fostering of a sense of self-confidence and hope for the future among members of the black underclass. Certainly the federal government can play a critical role in this process. Yet it is equally clear that the black business, academic, and political elites must press for improvement in their own peoples' lives through the building of constructive internal institutions, whether government participates or not.[19]

Can black elites supply the kind of leadership that Loury describes? Henry Louis Gates, Jr., director of the W.E.B. Du Bois Institute at Harvard, recalls his days as a Yale freshman in 1968, and expresses the concern that more recently the black community has become split between the "haves" and the "have nots":

> We were "a people" and we couldn't be free until all of us were free. . . . Above all else, it meant that we [the black students at Yale and other elite institutions in the late 1960s] were at one with "the revolution," standing tall in defense of "the people.". . . For many of us, our solidarity with the Panthers [during the Bobby Seale trial in New Haven] was the Talented Tenth's finest moment; its war tales our opium as middle age approached. Soon, however, graduation inevitably came, calling us to the newly-expanded opportunities in graduate and professional schools, and then on to similarly expanded opportunities in the broader professional and academic world. . . .
>
> What happened next is one of the most curious social transformations in class structure in recent American history. Two tributaries began to flow, running steadily into two distinct rivers of aspiration and achievement. By 1990, the black middle-class, perilous though it might feel itself to be, had never been larger, more prosperous, nor more relatively secure. Simultaneously, the pathological behavior that results from extended impoverishment engulfed a large part of a black underclass that seemed unable to benefit from a certain opening up of American society that the Civil Rights movement had long envisioned and had finally made possible.[20]

[19] Loury [1985] 1995, pp. 48–49.
[20] Gates 1998.

The admissions policies of selective colleges and universities have clearly helped to bring to the "talented tenth" the "newly expanded opportunities in the broader professional and academic world," which was, as Orlando Patterson has pointed out, their purpose.[21] But these policies cannot be of much direct benefit to "the truly disadvantaged."[22] The crucial question is whether those members of the black community who have had the opportunity to advance economically have done so without looking back.

Gates expresses the concern that the success of the black elite (as contrasted with the circumstances of "the people") may make it impossible to recapture the unity that was felt in the 1960s. Evidence of the activities of the black men and women from the C&B schools offers hope, however, that an ever-larger cadre of black men and women may provide the leadership that Loury envisages. It is still too soon to be certain whether this will occur. Possibly, black graduates of selective colleges and universities will gradually come to mimic the behavior of the majority and replicate the so-called "white flight" to suburbia, allowing the lure of personal gain and affluent lifestyles to remove them from feeling an obligation to social service. At this point, however, the C&B data documenting the contributions of black C&B members of both the 1976 and 1989 entering cohorts (and especially of those with advanced professional degrees) suggest that many of the most advantaged black men and women *are* giving back and maintaining ties to their communities, while also forging links with the broader American society.

It is, as Gates notes, "an awesome burden of leadership" that pulls these black graduates both toward their roots and simultaneously away from them. Some may argue that they could, or should, be doing even more. Such a judgment is not ours to make. But the fact that this group is consistently providing more civic leadership than its white peers indicates that social commitment and community concerns have not been thrown aside at the first sign of personal success.

[21] "Affirmative action . . . is, by its very nature, a top-down strategy, meant to level the field for those middle- and working-class persons who are capable of taking advantage of opportunities denied them because of their gender or ethnic status." Patterson 1997, p. 155.

[22] William Julius Wilson (1987) coined this term and defined it as follows: "Included in this group are individuals who lack training and skills and either experience long-term underemployment or are not members of the labor force, individuals who are engaged in street crime and other forms of aberrant behavior, and families that experience long-term spells of poverty and/or welfare dependency" (p. 8).

> *A black graduate of the University of North Carolina who now teaches explains his motivation for community involvement:*
>
> We have a mentoring program in our church. We spend a lot of time with the kids in the choir that I direct. I also volunteer as the musical director for an after-school musical drama program.
>
> I spoke recently with one of my classmates who is a lawyer in Raleigh about why we're involved with all of these things. And what we realized is that we tried to do all the right things—all the "white" things at the right "white" schools—and took all the usual steps up the ladder. And what we found when we got there—when we got all the way up the ladder—is that there isn't a lot of difference. People still see you first of all as black.
>
> Because you get that rude awakening, I think you end up feeling that you better hold on to those things that you knew before. And some part of that is what leads us back, to make sure that we keep roots in the community and keep this thing going. Like the people who helped us.

How many of the individuals from the C&B schools would have risen to the same leadership positions had they gone to other colleges and universities? No doubt many would have felt—and found ways to express—the same kinds of social commitments. But we believe that attendance at the C&B schools also made a difference. As we will see later, many black graduates of C&B colleges and universities credit their undergraduate experiences with helping to develop an active interest in community service. Also relevant is the finding that black matriculants who attended the most selective C&B schools were, on an "other things equal" basis, even more actively involved in certain kinds of leadership roles than were other black C&B matriculants. By extension, attendance at academically selective colleges and universities may have provided more encouragement and opportunity to lead civic activities than the same students would have experienced had they gone elsewhere.

This interpretation is supported by evidence showing that blacks who attended C&B colleges assumed civic leadership roles more often than black matriculants at all four-year colleges. Data from the nationwide control group survey indicate that black C&B matriculants were more likely than all black matriculants in the national sample to serve as leaders of civic organizations not only within the cultural and alumni/ae category, but also within the community and social service cluster.[23]

---

[23] The number of black respondents in the control group is too small to permit reliable comparisons by specific type of civic activity. However, combining men and women

While it is impossible to measure the nature and quality of the leadership provided, it is also likely that attendance at C&B schools provided a strong platform from which to contribute to civic life. Graduates of well-known and highly selective colleges, universities, and professional schools are aggressively sought after by organizations as board members and volunteer leaders. The education received by these individuals, especially those who went on to earn professional degrees, presumably equipped many of them to be extremely useful contributors. In the business world, the exceptionally high dollar rewards received by C&B graduates reflect, in some measure, how much their contributions are valued. The non-profit world lacks an equivalent "currency" but it seems quite likely that the simple counting of instances of leadership understates the true value of the civic contributions made by these individuals.

Our findings call into question Cornel West's observation: "The present-day black middle class is not simply different than its predecessors—it is more deficient and, to put it strongly, more decadent."[24] The patterns of civic involvement present in our data suggest that the two tributaries of which Gates speaks have not yet shifted their course to become entirely separate from one another.

Participation in Political Life

Since political involvement is in some respects a domain of its own, we have separated it out from other types of civic activity. But the basic pattern is very much the same. When asked if they had participated in 1995 in "political clubs or organizations or local government activities," 19 percent of the black men in the '76 cohort responded in the affirmative, as contrasted with 14 percent of their white classmates. And the percentage of black men serving in leadership positions (5 percent) was slightly higher than the corresponding percentage for white men (4 percent). Women were less inclined than men to be involved in political life, but here, too, the percentage for black women was some-

---

and using the clusters described above allow us to make meaningful comparisons. The patterns are clear in the two clusters described in the text: black C&B matriculants were more likely to be leaders than both white C&B matriculants and the national sample of black matriculants. In the third cluster (youth and education), the percentage of black C&B leaders is slightly higher than the percentage of black leaders in the control group sample.

[24] West 1993, p. 54.

what higher than the percentage for white women (15 percent versus 12 percent).[25] The same patterns are found when we ask individuals if they "*ever* participated" in a political organization or local government activity—in fact, the gap between the percentages of black and white men from the C&B schools who served in leadership roles widens.[26]

The percentage of white C&B respondents who said that they voted in 1992 was slightly higher than the percentage of black respondents (94 percent versus 90 percent). As one would expect, these percentages are higher than those for Americans in the same age range who did not go to college (78 percent of the non-matriculants in the control group). They are not appreciably higher, however, than the percentage of voters among the matriculants in the control group survey (91 percent of whom said that they voted).[27]

The vast literature on the political beliefs of college graduates indicates that going to college tends to encourage the adoption of more liberal political views.[28] What sorts of views do the C&B matriculants express, and how do their views differ by race and gender? In the 1976 cohort, the responses of the black C&B matriculants to questions asking them to rate themselves on a liberal-conservative scale indicate that both men and women are more conservative on economic issues than on social issues, while the men are somewhat more conservative than the women. Overall, the white '76 C&B matriculants are modestly more conservative than their black classmates. On economic issues, in particular, the white men are more conservative than any other group, with a mean score of 3.5 on a scale of 1 to 5, where 1 = "very liberal" and 5 = "very conservative"; the black men register a mean score of exactly 3.0—which is surely as "middle of the road" as one can be! Of course, all of these averages conceal the presence of both the flaming radical and the arch-conservative.[29]

---

[25] These percentages are all higher than those (of all races) in the national control group survey.

[26] Of all black male C&B matriculants, 9 percent ever served in leadership roles, as compared with 6 percent of all white male C&B matriculants. See Appendix Table D.6.2 for documentation of all findings cited in this section.

[27] See Appendix Table D.6.2. Census data report lower percentages of voters in the 35–44 age range—64 percent of all Americans and 81 percent of college graduates are said to have voted in 1992 (U.S. Bureau of the Census 1997, p. 288, tab. 462).

[28] Pascarella and Terenzini 1991, p. 277–8.

[29] The '89 cohorts are slightly less conservative on both economic and social issues than the '76 cohorts, which we interpret mainly as a life-cycle phenomenon.

FAMILY LIFE

Marital Status

It has become uncommon for undergraduates to be married while in college, to leave college in order to marry, or, for that matter, to marry within a short time after graduating.[30] The growth in labor force participation among women has had much to do with these tendencies. Nevertheless, many marriages still emerge from friendships made in college.

The '76 C&B graduates have several clear characteristics as far as marital status is concerned (Figure 6.7). In many respects, graduates of these academically selective schools, roughly twenty years after they entered college, followed the same patterns as other college graduates of the same ages: black women were less likely to be married, and more likely to be separated or divorced, than were any other race-gender grouping; at the other end of the spectrum, white women and white men were most likely to be married and least likely to be divorced or separated; black men are the intermediate group, with marriage percentages that were higher than those for black women, but lower than those for white women and white men.

There is, however, a more interesting pattern. C&B graduates were *much* less likely to be divorced or separated than were other college graduates of the same ages (bottom panel of Figure 6.7).[31] These propositions hold for women and men, and for both black and white C&B graduates. What explains the consistency of this pattern? There is no

---

[30] Higher levels of education are associated with lower age-specific birth rates, and fertility among highly educated women has declined for at least three decades. Also, there is a well-documented trend toward later childbearing, which is most pronounced among better-educated women. See Rindfuss, Morgan, and Offutt 1996.

[31] There were also some differences between the C&B groups and the national groups in the percentages who were never married, but these differences were much smaller and in many cases were not significantly different from zero. We compare the C&B results with the national data reported in the Census rather than with the figures obtained from the survey of our national control group principally because the Census data permit black-white comparisons while the control group data do not (also, the Census data are much less subject to response bias). It should be noted, however, that the divorce-separation rate reported for all graduates in the control group survey (5 percent) was lower than the rate reported in the Census. This result may be due in part to the size and direction of the response bias in the control group data discussed in Appendix A. Differences in the precise formulations of the questions used on the C&B and control group surveys, as contrasted with the formulations used by the Census, could also help explain these patterns.

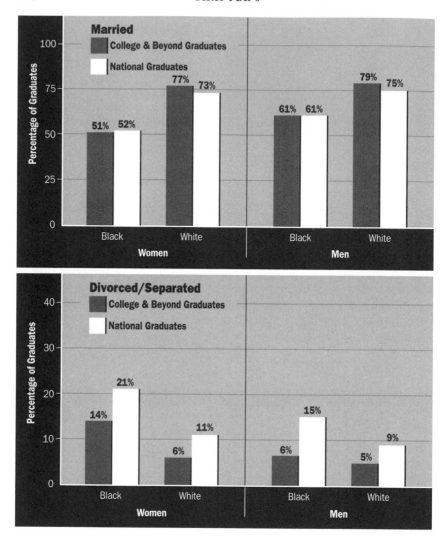

Figure 6.7. Percentage of Graduates Whose Marital Status in 1995 Was Married or Divorced/Separated, by Race and Gender, College and Beyond Graduates and National Graduates, 1976 Entering Cohort

Sources: College and Beyond and 1990 U.S. Census.

Note: "Married" data excludes five schools surveyed in Wave 1 (see Appendix A).

certain answer. We also suspect that C&B matriculants marry later (but we lack sufficient data to be sure), and we know that later age at first marriage lowers the probability of divorce. Some have speculated that C&B graduates may be too busy to get divorced, while still others have made the tongue-in-cheek suggestion that they make too much money to be able to afford divorce!

Family Income

Family (or household) income is often considered one of the most important indicators of well-being, and for good reason. As we will show in the last section of this chapter, it is strongly correlated with how satisfied people say they are with their lives. The earned income figures for full-time workers cited in the previous chapter would suggest that C&B graduates have unusually high family incomes, and that is indeed the case. Average household income was over $100,000 for white men, white women, and black men; only the black women graduates, with an average household income of $93,000, were below this level.[32] These family incomes are especially impressive given the fact that almost all of the C&B respondents were still in their late thirties when our surveys were conducted. The family income "premiums" enjoyed by the C&B graduates, when compared with holders of BAs nationwide, are substantial by any definition of the word. They range from nearly $32,600 for black women graduates of the C&B schools to $37,500 for the white women, $42,700 for white men, and $44,400 for black men (Figure 6.8).

These differentials and premiums are best understood by examining the two main components of household income: the average earned income of individual C&B graduates (shown as the bottom part of each bar in Figure 6.8) and "other income" (shown on the bars as the difference between earned income and total household income). "Other income" is a combination of spousal earnings and earnings on assets, including inherited wealth.[33]

---

[32] We do not show the detailed distributions of household income, analogous to the curves showing cumulative earned income presented in Chapter 5, because the shapes of the two sets of curves are so similar. Relatively large numbers of both black and white C&B graduates from the '76 cohorts reported an average household income over $150,000 (Appendix Table D.6.3).

[33] We are unable to distinguish between these two sources of additional household income because the C&B surveys did not ask explicitly about either spouse's income or income from assets (see Appendix A). It should be emphasized that the measure of average

If we look first at the men, we see that differences in earned income are quite good predictors of differences in household income; the average amounts of "other income" are roughly comparable for black and white men, for C&B graduates, and for the national sample of BA recipients. There are, however, some interesting, if modest, differences. The C&B male graduates (black and white) had larger amounts of "other income" than did all male graduates. This result holds even though spousal earnings are the major source of "other income," and a relatively large number of the spouses of the male C&B graduates were "not working" (34 percent for white men; 25 percent for black men). Apparently, spouses who did work earned high enough incomes to more than compensate for the lack of labor force participation on the part of the others. Clearly, these women could choose not to work more readily than other spouses precisely because of their high household income.[34]

The patterns for women, unlike those for men, differ markedly by race (bottom panel of Figure 6.8). Black C&B women graduates had larger amounts of "other income" than all black women graduates ($34,300 versus $28,200). As a result, the considerable earnings premium enjoyed by black C&B women is enlarged when we compare their household incomes with the household incomes of all black women with BAs. The more striking comparison is with the white women C&B graduates. These women had, on average, over *twice* the other income of their black female classmates ($69,900 versus $34,300) and thus enjoyed much higher household incomes even though they had less earned income.[35] The other income of all white women graduates is also high, but not nearly as high as that of the white women from the C&B schools ($49,700 versus $69,900). Thus, the premium enjoyed by white women graduates who attended C&B schools is enlarged considerably when we focus on household income rather than just their own earned income.

---

earned income shown here is the average earnings of all graduates, whatever their work force status, which is the relevant measure to compare with average household income of all graduates; the figures for average earnings used in Chapter 5 were restricted to the earnings of full-time workers.

[34] In fact, the average household income of white married women in the C&B population who did not work at all is larger than the average household income of the married women (white and black) who worked either part-time or full-time (Appendix Table D.6.4).

[35] If we restrict the comparisons within the C&B population to married women, the differences in household income between the black women and the white women are greatly diminished. The overall differences by race are influenced markedly by differences in marital status (Appendix Table D.6.4).

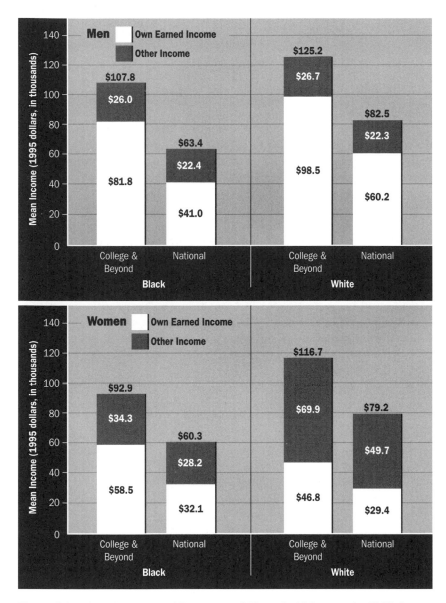

Figure 6.8. Mean Own Earned Income and Household Income in 1995, by Race and Gender, College and Beyond Graduates and National Graduates, 1976 Entering Cohort

Sources: College and Beyond and 1990 U.S. Census.

Notes: "Other Income" includes spouse's income and other non-earned income. Household income is the sum of own earned income and other income (sum may not add up to total due to rounding).

SATISFACTION WITH LIFE

Objective measures of civic participation, family life, and household income have been the bedrock of this chapter. These indices can be complemented, however, by subjective measures that tell us how satisfied C&B respondents are with their lives. The general level of satisfaction is high. Among those who matriculated in '76, only 1 percent reported being "very dissatisfied," and only 6 percent checked "somewhat dissatisfied." Nearly 90 percent said that they were either "very satisfied" or "somewhat satisfied with life."[36]

While very few black or white matriculants are dissatisfied (or even neutral on the question), the level of satisfaction is noticeably higher for whites than for blacks, especially at the top of the satisfaction scale (Figure 6.9). Nearly half of the white women (46 percent) say that they are "*very* satisfied," as compared with less than a third of the black women (27 percent). There is also an appreciable difference in the percentages of white and black men reporting that they are "very satisfied" with life (41 percent versus 30 percent). The gaps for both men and women are reduced when we examine the percentages who say that they are either "satisfied or very satisfied" (Figure 6.9).[37]

Satisfaction in Specific Domains

We can gain greater insight into what drives these self-ratings of overall satisfaction by looking at the answers given to an additional set of questions that probed satisfaction in specific domains (friendships, nonworking activities, health and physical condition, family life, and place of residence). Although the overwhelming majority of respondents

---

[36] The exact question on the C&B survey instrument was: "In general, how satisfied would you say you are with your life right now? Would you say you are . . . 1) Very satisfied; 2) Somewhat satisfied; 3) Neither satisfied nor dissatisfied; 4) Somewhat dissatisfied; 5) Very dissatisfied." The overall results for the '89 C&B matriculants are essentially the same as those for the '76 matriculants.

[37] These patterns are consistent with the findings of research conducted in the 1970s. In their pathbreaking study, Campbell, Converse, and Rodgers (1976) found that "[b]lack women were . . . much less satisfied than black men or whites" (p. 465). They also found generational differences (younger blacks were less satisfied than older blacks). Most basic of all was their finding that "[a]ll educational levels of blacks scored lower on the life satisfaction index than whites" (p. 467). Campbell (1981) subsequently published a more popular version of the same study.

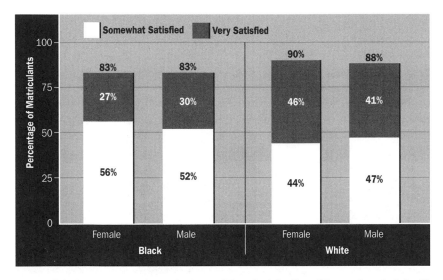

Figure 6.9. Percentage of Matriculants "Very Satisfied" or "Somewhat Satisfied" with Life, by Race and Gender, 1976 Entering Cohort

Source: College and Beyond.

checked one of the top categories, there are some revealing differences (Figure 6.10).[38]

The patterns of black-white differences vary according to gender. When asked about the three domains to the left of the line on the figure (friendships, non-working activities, and health/physical condition), black women were somewhat less likely than white women to indicate that they gained "a great deal" or even a "very great deal" of satisfaction from them. The pattern is reversed for men. In these domains, black men expressed somewhat higher levels of satisfaction than did white men. In the two domains to the right of the line (family life and place of residence), both black women and black men were less satisfied than white women and white men. The contrasts between men and women are even more pronounced among '89 graduates. In this younger group, black men are as satisfied as white men, or even more so, in four of five do-

---

[38] Survey respondents were asked: "How much satisfaction do you get from your friendships [non-working activities, health, etc.]? 1) A very great deal; 2) A great deal; 3) Quite a bit; 4) A fair amount; 5) Some; 6) A little; or 7) None." The different wording of the questions, and the different scales, reflect our interest in phrasing these questions in ways that would permit comparisons with the General Social Survey (GSS) described below. Responses by both the '76 and '89 cohorts are summarized in Appendix Table D.6.5.

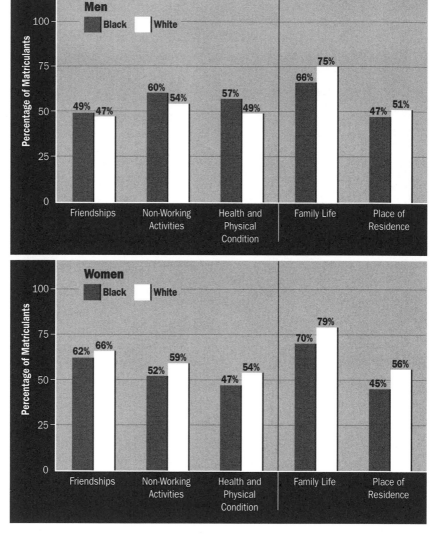

Figure 6.10. Percentage of Matriculants Deriving a "Great Deal" of Satisfaction from Selected Aspects of Life, by Race and Gender, 1976 Entering Cohort

Sources: College and Beyond and 1990 U.S. Census.

mains; black women remain less satisfied than white women within each category (Appendix Table D.6.5).[39]

Comparisons with the General Social Survey (GSS) reveal that black members of the '76 C&B cohort were much more satisfied with both their place of residence and their non-work activities than were all black holders of BAs. The greater affluence of the C&B population probably explains why they are more satisfied with where they live. Quite possibly, the greater satisfaction among C&B black graduates with non-work activities reflects their extremely active civic involvements, documented earlier in the chapter. On the other hand, the black C&B graduates derived somewhat less satisfaction from family life than did black respondents to the national GSS survey—though the absolute levels of satisfaction with family life were high for both groups.[40]

Factors That Predict Satisfaction

In considering more systematically the factors that predict being "very satisfied" with life, we begin with one important non-finding. For the '76 C&B matriculants, satisfaction with life did not correspond at all with their SAT scores of long ago; the proportions who said that they were "very satisfied" varied from 42 percent to 45 percent, with the higher percentages in the lower part of the SAT range (Appendix Table D.6.6). This "pattern"—such as it is—is the same for black and white matriculants (Figure 6.11).[41]

The clearest set of differences in satisfaction is between those in the bottom third and those in the middle third of the class. This difference was especially pronounced among the black matriculants: in the '76 cohort, 33 percent of those in the middle third of the class were very satisfied as

[39] There is a clear difference between these domain-specific results for the '89 men and the results for overall satisfaction. The black men from the '89 cohort were much less likely to be very satisfied with their lives as a whole than the white men (32 percent versus 39 percent), the similar responses to the questions about satisfaction in specific domains notwithstanding. We suspect that at least part of the explanation is that job satisfaction is not included within these domains, and we saw in Chapter 5 that blacks were generally less satisfied than whites with their jobs.

[40] The most peculiar aspect of these results is that in the national sample, blacks were appreciably more satisfied with their health than the black members of the C&B cohort. This pattern was also found among the whites surveyed, but it was less pronounced. We have no explanation.

[41] The same conclusion holds for the more recent matriculants. For members of the '89 cohort, there is no consistent relationship between SAT scores and overall degree of life satisfaction expressed by black or white C&B matriculants (Appendix Table D.6.6).

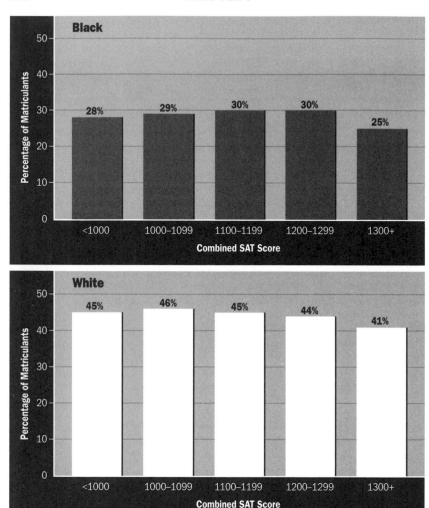

Figure 6.11. Percentage of Matriculants "Very Satisfied" with Life, by SAT Score and Race, 1976 Entering Cohort

Sources: College and Beyond and 1990 U.S. Census.

contrasted with just 27 percent of those in the bottom third. The corresponding percentages for the white matriculants were 45 percent and 41 percent. The pattern is similar in the '89 cohort, and the black-white difference was larger. We see again that black students who ranked in the bottom third of the class seem to have paid a greater price for their academic performance (with "price" measured here in terms of satisfaction with life) than did white students who also ranked in the bottom third.[42]

The relationship between life satisfaction and the selectivity of the C&B school that an individual attended is clear-cut for white matriculants—there is no apparent relationship. Precisely the same percentages of white matriculants at SEL-1, SEL-2, and SEL-3 colleges and universities reported that they are "very satisfied" with life (43 percent in each case). Among the black matriculants, however, we find that those who attended the SEL-3 schools were slightly more inclined to be very satisfied than those who attended either the SEL-1 or SEL-2 schools (30 percent versus 27 percent at both SEL-1 and SEL-2). The gap between the SEL-3 group and all other C&B matriculants widens, and is statistically significant, when we control for other variables, and especially for differences in household income (Appendix Table D.6.8).[43]

Household income is a powerful predictor of life satisfaction. Over half of both whites and blacks with *very* high household incomes ($150,000 or more) are very satisfied with life. The percentages of C&B matriculants who are very satisfied drop steadily as we move to successively lower levels of household income (Figure 6.12). Yes, money matters.[44]

In another regression (not shown), we included a variable for civic

[42] See Appendix Table D.6.7. Differences in satisfaction between those who ranked in the top third and the middle third of the class also appear to vary somewhat by race, but the differences are erratic. Black matriculants in the middle third were as likely to be very satisfied with life as black matriculants in the top third, whereas white matriculants in the middle third in the '89 cohort were less likely to be "very satisfied" than white matriculants in the top third.

[43] This pattern does not hold, however, for the '89 matriculants. In this cohort, the black students who attended the SEL-3 schools were significantly less satisfied with life than those who attended the SEL-1 and SEL-2 schools.

[44] Holders of advanced degrees are also more likely to be very satisfied with life than those who have only BAs, who in turn are more satisfied than those who did not finish college. This pattern is analogous to the finding some years ago that college dropouts were less satisfied with life than either high school or college graduates (Campbell, Converse, and Rodgers 1976, p. 137). Among those with advanced degrees, those with medical degrees are the most likely to be in the "very satisfied with life" category, followed by those with professional degrees in business and law. Holders of MAs appear more likely to be very satisfied with life than recipients of doctorates. White and black C&B matriculants exhibit very similar patterns in these respects. Controlling for differences in other variables, especially household income, reduces these differences, but does not eliminate them altogether. In particular, both blacks and whites who earned medical degrees and MAs remain significantly more satisfied with life than other C&B matriculants, even after we take account of associated differences in income and other variables (Appendix Table D.6.8).

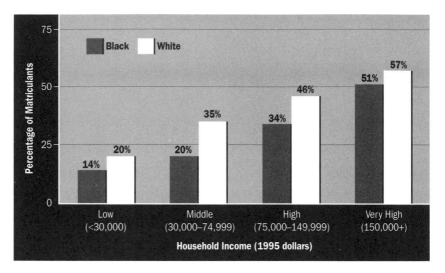

Figure 6.12. Percentage of Matriculants "Very Satisfied" with Life, by Household Income and Race, 1976 Entering Cohort

Source: College and Beyond.

leadership and found that those who had led civic organizations were significantly more likely to be very satisfied with life than those who had not—a relationship that holds for all C&B matriculants, but even more strongly for blacks than for whites. It is hard to interpret this finding. It could mean that those who contribute outside the workplace, and are recognized by their peers as leaders, take real satisfaction from such contributions and accomplishments. But it could also mean that those who are most satisfied with life in all its dimensions are most likely to be civic leaders. In either case, the proclivity of C&B alumni/ae—and especially black C&B alumni/ae—to be involved in community and other activities is associated with a high level of life satisfaction. Doing "good" and doing "well" should go together, and they do—at least for these former students from academically selective institutions.

Race and Life Satisfaction

We conclude this discussion by returning to a recurring theme: the consistently lower degree of satisfaction with life expressed by black members of the C&B cohorts compared with that expressed by their white classmates. In the '76 cohort, the actual (unadjusted) difference is 15 percentage points (29 percent versus 44 percent). Adjusting for the effects

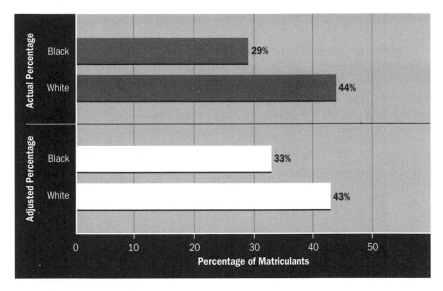

Figure 6.13. Percentage of Matriculants "Very Satisfied" with Life, by Race, Actual and Adjusted Percentages, 1976 Entering Cohort

Source: College and Beyond.

Note: Adjusted percentages are estimated by using a logistic regression model controlling for student and institutional characteristics (see Appendix Table D.6.8, all matriculants, and Appendix B).

of other variables reduces this difference to 10 points (see Figure 6.13).[45] In other words, only about one-third of the reported difference between blacks and whites in life satisfaction can be attributed to differences between the groups in factors such as household income; the other two-thirds remains to be explained.

Until the last decade or so, many might have been surprised by this gap. After all, these black men and women obviously had the good fortune to attend an excellent college or university, and we have seen that exceptionally large numbers of them graduated, went on to earn advanced degrees from leading institutions, to secure important positions in the workforce, to earn far more money than college graduates generally, and to be active on behalf of a wide variety of good causes. Recently, however, a series of studies have explained in great detail that "making it" into the middle class is far from a guarantee that a black person will lead a

---

[45] In the '89 cohort, the actual black-white difference is 12 percentage points (28 percent versus 40 percent). The adjusted difference is 10 percentage points (30 percent versus 40 percent). For underlying logistic regression see Appendix Table D.6.8.

life free of concerns about discrimination or humiliating treatment of one kind or another.

The very title of Ellis Cose's 1993 book, *The Rage of a Privileged Class,* was a wake-up call for many who had been unaware of the feelings of significant numbers of the black middle class. In his next book, Cose reported that soon after the publication of *The Rage,* he was invited to speak at a symposium organized by *Forbes* magazine that was attended by many members of the business establishment. Cose recalls:

> What stood out for me from that symposium, however, was not the crowd or the quasi-academic conversation, but a chance encounter in a corridor with a sales executive and his wife. The wife was a homemaker and the executive was a corporate functionary of no obvious distinction. In the course of the conversation, it became clear that they were tickled to be rubbing shoulders with the important people *Forbes* had assembled; they apparently took their own presence there as a sign that they had arrived socially. At one point, the wife, beaming brightly, told me she had enjoyed my comments and then added, "It must really be unusual for you to be among the elite."
>
> I found the statement both amusing and appalling. . . . [L]ong after they had gone, I found myself reflecting on that woman's view of society, on the way she automatically assumed that being black meant that one spent little time in what she imagined to be the elite world.[46]

Empirical support for the existence of an "educated black malaise" comes from survey research work done by Howard Schuman, Charlotte Steeh, Lawrence Bobo, and Maria Krysan. They observe that "given the existence of some continuing real discrimination, middle-class blacks have no way of knowing whether what seems to be unfair treatment (the taxi that speeds by, the poor seating in a restaurant) is, in fact, due to deliberate discrimination or to something more innocuous."[47] From this perspective, it is hardly surprising that in survey after survey, blacks attach much more importance than whites to racial discrimination, and that "[higher levels of] education are associated with more, rather than less, belief in the continued prevalence and importance of racial discrimination."[48]

The personal testimony of successful black graduates of C&B institutions offers some of the most compelling explanations of why a black person who has "made it" might still be less satisfied with life.

---

[46] Cose 1997, p. 209.

[47] Schuman et al. 1997, p. 277. See also Bobo and Suh 1995.

[48] Schuman et al. 1997, pp. 276–77; see also their summary of survey data. In addition, see Feagin and Sikes (1994), Hochschild (1995), Bobo and Suh (1995), and the sources cited in these studies and Cose (1997).

A black doctor tells of her experiences in the hospital:

I've actually seen events where I felt black people were treated differently in the ER. A black woman with right lower quadrant abdominal pain is assumed to have a sexually transmitted disease whereas a white woman is presumed to have appendicitis until proven otherwise. I've seen it. And I know that if I were rolled in there, nobody knows I'm a Bryn Mawr graduate, a Case Western graduate; I'm a young black woman and they're going to assume that I have a sexually transmitted disease. So that makes me angry at times. . . . Or I've been in medical records and people ask me to pull their charts even though I'm wearing a white coat and a beeper and a stethoscope. But all they see is a black female face and they just assume that I'm a clerk.

A black lawyer explains why she has not worked in private practice:

I found that academic training and good grades and being fairly articulate are not what sold one to private firms. They were looking for someone who reminded them of themselves. And I do not remind the typical private practitioner of himself in any way. I think that being black had a great deal to do with it. Being a woman, I think, meant less. A white hiring partner may not have gone to law school with women, may not have partners who are women. But he had a mother and he has a wife. Women are a part of his life and if they move into another dimension of his life—co-worker—at least they're familiar to him. It is amazing how color—a black face—can totally overwhelm them.

I've found that even working for the government, people are uncomfortable on a certain level, even though they don't really understand it. They wait for me to make them comfortable. But I've always been a quiet, withdrawn, introspective person. I'm not going to be able to make anyone else feel comfortable. I think that they could handle that if I were white and they would realize that I'm just shy. But because I'm black and they're automatically uncomfortable and then I don't do anything to make them more comfortable, I'm seen as deliberately isolating myself.

A 1993 graduate describes her experiences teaching in a number of prep schools:

My first job after Williams was at one of those schools that really wanted people of color, but they hadn't been able to keep one for very long. I was prepared for them, but they weren't prepared for me. They hadn't really given much thought to what to do when, say, the parents of a kid confused you with the nanny of another student or what happens when a parent questions your qualifications because they've never had contact with anyone who looks like me.

I was looking for a place where my skills would be appreciated. I'm really at the point where I say that straight out in interviews: "Look, if you want me because I'm a woman and because I'm African American and because I'm trotting along this series of degrees, don't bother. Don't think about how many diversity committees I can head up or how many admission fairs I can go to or how many times you can stick me in your yearbook to make yourself look diverse. But think about what I can really offer your community and your school and your students."

Jennifer Hochschild describes this phenomenon as the paradox of "succeeding more and enjoying it less."[49] She suggests that until about 1970, blacks were reasonably optimistic that things would get better, but that attitudes then began to shift. Since then, middle-class blacks have become more pessimistic. Once the most obvious barriers have either come down or been overcome, and problems still persist, blacks find it more difficult to maintain the view that if only one does everything "right," all will work out for the best.

One of our findings seems consistent with these observations. When we control for the effects of other variables, we find that '76 black matriculants at the SEL-1 and SEL-2 schools are significantly less satisfied with their lives than those who attended SEL-3 schools. The (adjusted) percentage of black matriculants in the "very satisfied" category is 12 points lower at the most competitive of the C&B schools than at the SEL-3 schools (33 percent versus 21 percent). The same adjustment process results in a difference of only 2 points for all matriculants.[50]

We presume that black students who attend the most selective colleges and universities are especially likely to move on into life believing that they are prepared to do well and to be accepted. As one black ma-

[49] Hochschild 1995, p. 72.

[50] The adjusted proportions are calculated from the regressions presented in Appendix Table D.6.8 by means of the methods described in Appendix B. We noted earlier that the actual (unadjusted) differences in satisfaction by school selectivity are much smaller for black matriculants and non-existent for all matriculants; the main reason is the set of associations that link school selectivity, household income, and satisfaction with life. As can be seen from Appendix Table D.6.8, the coefficients for the school selectivity variables are much larger for black matriculants than for all matriculants.

triculant who earned good grades at one of the most selective schools put it, "What more could I have done?" When such individuals experience real or even imagined problems, they are probably more inclined than white graduates of the same schools, or black graduates of slightly less selective schools, to wonder if something is seriously wrong—either with the society or with themselves—and to feel some degree of dissatisfaction with their lives.[51]

While frustrating experiences (and perhaps other stresses as yet un-identified) contribute to lower levels of satisfaction among even the most accomplished African Americans, another of our findings is that excep-tionally high earnings "trump" all other variables. For those with *very* high household incomes, over $150,000, there is no discernible difference in life satisfaction between black and white matriculants. (The adjusted percentages of matriculants who are very satisfied with life is 53 percent for all matriculants and 51 percent for blacks alone.) But below this top level, the degree of satisfaction begins to diverge substantially. Even at the "high" income level, between $75,000 and $149,999, many more whites than blacks are very satisfied (43 percent versus 32 percent), and the gaps continue to widen at the mid- and low-income levels (derived from the regression results in Appendix Table D.6.8). Apparently, only the small number of black households that are at the very top of the income distribution feel largely free of the stresses and strains associated with being black in America.

The success of the black 1976 matriculants in earning advanced degrees and finding good jobs offers a partial response to the question of whether these students deserved to be admitted to the C&B schools in the first place. Their contributions outside the workplace provide additional con-firmation. With all of their success economically, however, and all of their contributions to the community, these black graduates still have modestly lower family incomes than comparable white graduates. They are also less satisfied with important domains of their lives. These gaps are neither surprising nor necessarily permanent. One could hardly expect that the legacy of racial inequities would disappear entirely, even for the tal-

---

[51] As we reported earlier (note 43), the relationship between school selectivity and satisfaction with life runs in the opposite direction for '89 black matriculants. There are two possible interpretations. One is that blacks who attended the most selective schools in more recent years are encountering fewer frustrations than did their predecessors. The other is that the '89 matriculants have not been out of school (including graduate and professional schools) long enough to have had experiences comparable to those of the '76 matriculants.

ented individuals in this study, only three decades after the Civil Rights movement.

From a broader societal perspective, it is encouraging to see how many of these individuals—while still in their thirties—have already led civic endeavors of many kinds, including activities related both to the needs of local communities and to the colleges and universities from which they graduated. Moreover, their younger "cousins"—the '89 matriculants— give every indication of at least matching this record of civic contribution. The black alumni/ae of these schools have already demonstrated a marked tendency to "give something back" through participation and leadership outside the workplace as well as within it. This civic spirit, revealed through actions taken rather than good intentions expressed, and demonstrated over time through volunteering in schools, neighborhoods, museums, and civic associations of every kind, is surely one important indicator of "merit."

CHAPTER 7

Looking Back: Views of College

A NUMBER of critics of race-sensitive admissions argue—as Dinesh D'Souza has done in *Illiberal Education*—that "American universities are quite willing to sacrifice the future happiness of many young blacks and Hispanics to achieve diversity, proportional representation, and what they consider to be multicultural progress." As we have stressed throughout this book, the experiences of black students admitted to the College and Beyond schools in 1976 and 1989 suggest another point of view. Their graduation rates and (in the case of the '76 matriculants) subsequent life histories speak for themselves. But have these students borne other costs? Has the diversity of viewpoints that they brought to campus come at the expense of their own educational experience? "Would not these students be much better off," as D'Souza asked, ". . . where they might settle in more easily [and] compete against evenly-matched peers?"[1]

Although the advanced degrees that individuals have received, the amount of money that they earn, and the civic activities in which they are involved reveal particular facts about their life stories, people's perceptions of their experiences constitute a different "reality" that is also important. Some, in looking back at a childhood that had all the external trappings of a traditionally happy time—birthday parties, loving parents, and a nice house—may still not remember it as a happy time; in such cases, all of the externally verifiable facts are in one sense irrelevant. When we set out to assess how people who attended the C&B colleges and universities fared in life, we wanted to discover not only the objective facts of their histories but also the impact that college had on their subjective evaluations of their own lives. In considering the value of educational experiences—and especially those of minority students—we wanted to know how these former students themselves assess what they learned and whether they believe, looking back, that they made the right choice in attending a selective college.

We begin by examining how satisfied the C&B students were with their undergraduate education some twenty years after they matriculated. Were African Americans less satisfied than whites? Were the '89 matriculants more or less satisfied than those who entered college thirteen

---

[1] D'Souza 1991, pp. 40, 43.

years earlier? How strongly were SAT scores and rank in class correlated with students' satisfaction?

We are also interested in the "regrets" expressed by these former students. How many would have chosen a different school if they were able to make the choice again? Would they have selected a different major? Would they have spent more or less time studying, socializing, or participating in various extracurricular activities? Finally, we want to know what types of skills these former students regard as important in life and how much they feel that their college experience developed these capacities. By linking recent responses to information volunteered by the same individuals when they took their SAT tests, we can compare what students said they needed to learn when they entered college in 1976 and what they believe—twenty years later—they did learn.

SATISFACTION WITH COLLEGE

Overall Measures

The '76 C&B matriculants overwhelmingly expressed satisfaction with their undergraduate education. Over 60 percent were "very satisfied," nearly 90 percent were either very satisfied or somewhat satisfied, and only 6 percent were dissatisfied (Appendix Table D.7.1). These figures are especially striking since they refer to the school at which the student first enrolled and include not only those who graduated from this school, but also those who transferred to other schools from which they subsequently graduated, as well as those who never received a BA from any school. Predictably, students who finished at the C&B schools they entered originally were more positive in their evaluations than students who left prior to graduation. Two-thirds of the matriculants who graduated from their first school were "very satisfied," as contrasted with 40 percent of those who transferred and graduated from other schools and 32 percent of those who dropped out and did not graduate from any school.

This is the pattern that one would expect to find, since decisions to transfer or drop out were presumably often motivated by disappointment with some aspect of the school that the student first entered.[2] What is surprising is that three-quarters of the transfer graduates were either "very satisfied" or "somewhat satisfied" with their *first* school; similarly, of

---

[2] In most instances, it is difficult to identify with precision the reasons why students left their first schools. As noted in Chapter 3, our own attempts to determine how many matriculants failed to meet course requirements, or were asked by the first school to leave for disciplinary reasons, were not very successful.

the drop-outs who did not graduate elsewhere, 71 percent said that they were either very satisfied or somewhat satisfied (Appendix Table D.7.1). Many decisions to transfer or drop out were probably precipitated by financial, educational, health, or other personal problems that did not reflect adversely on the school. The point to emphasize is that the degree of satisfaction expressed by students who graduated from the school they first entered (the group on which we focus throughout much of the chapter), differs only in small measure from the degree of satisfaction expressed by all matriculants.

While there are some differences, responses do not vary markedly by race or gender. Both black and white matriculants, women and men, expressed high degrees of satisfaction with their undergraduate education. In the '76 cohort, slightly higher percentages of white than black matriculants were either "very satisfied" or "somewhat satisfied," but the differences are negligible (Figure 7.1, top panel). Of all black matriculants—including those who transferred and those who never received a BA—only 6 percent expressed any degree of dissatisfaction, and only 1 to 2 percent were "very dissatisfied." The corresponding percentages for white matriculants are almost identical.

The '89 C&B matriculants express, if anything, even more satisfaction with their education than their predecessors in the '76 cohort. In all four subgroups—black men and black women, white men and white women—the percentages of matriculants responding "very satisfied" or "somewhat satisfied" are higher in the '89 cohort than in the '76 cohort (Figure 7.1, bottom panel, and Appendix Table D.7.1). In general, levels of satisfaction increased by 2 to 7 percentage points between the two cohorts; the gains are larger among black males than they are among any other group.

This increase in reported satisfaction with college from the '76 to the '89 cohort is somewhat surprising, since it might seem that those away from college longer (who have been, overall, very successful in life) would be more inclined to look back favorably on their college experiences than those who left school more recently and may be less certain what the future holds. Of course, external factors may have been responsible. Over time, student populations, schools, and the society around them change (immediate post-college job opportunities, for example, may be better for '89 matriculants than they were for '76 matriculants). Since we have no way of distinguishing among these many factors, we are not inclined to put great weight on the small differences in the results for the '76 and '89 cohorts. Perhaps the main value of the '89 figures is to confirm the broad patterns evident in the '76 data and to suggest that there has been no fall off in satisfaction among the more recent entering cohorts.

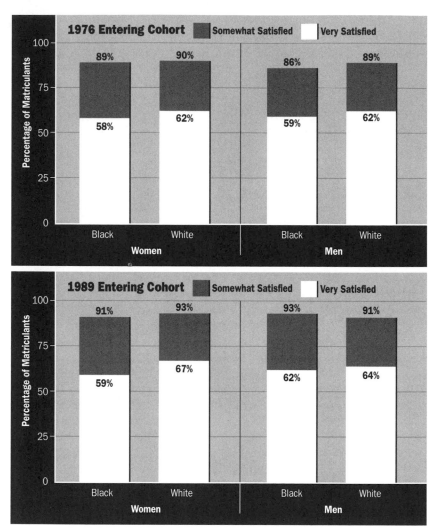

Figure 7.1. Percentage of Matriculants "Somewhat Satisfied" or "Very Satisfied" with College, by Race and Gender, 1976 and 1989 Entering Cohorts
Source: College and Beyond.

Black-White Comparisons

The small black-white differences that we found when we considered the responses of all matriculants disappear almost entirely when we focus on what is in some ways a group better positioned to assess their overall educational experience—those who stayed at the schools they first entered, chose majors, and graduated.[3] Roughly two-thirds (65 percent) of all black graduates in the '76 C&B cohorts were "very satisfied" with the colleges they attended; 67 percent of the white graduates felt the same way. This difference of 2 percentage points is cut to 1 percentage point after we control for differences in grades and other "in-college" variables and later life outcomes, such as household income. There is no statistically significant relationship between race and satisfaction with college among the members of this cohort—or among the members of the '89 cohort.[4]

As we reported in the last chapter, the black men and women who entered the selective C&B schools in 1976 were, on average, appreciably less satisfied with their lives than were their white classmates; the resonance of this finding was amplified by the fact that most of this gap in life satisfaction remained even when the marks of accomplishment (advanced degrees and differences in earnings) were taken into account. We now see that no such gap exists when the same people are asked about their satisfaction with college. The black men and women who graduated from the C&B institutions apparently feel very differently about their college experiences than they do about their lives in general. This disjunction between satisfaction with college and satisfaction with life is even more pronounced when we classify black students by the selectivity of the schools they attended. Those who attended the SEL-1 schools, who were least satisfied with their lives, were most satisfied with their college

[3] This approach has the advantage, among others, of allowing us to compare the responses given by students who majored in different fields, earned different grades, and were at the schools they were asked to evaluate long enough to be in a position to comment on mentoring relationships, the amount of time they spent studying, and other questions of interest. We lack key pieces of information about those who dropped out. Nonetheless, we wanted to begin this analysis by being as inclusive as possible and asking about the views of those who transferred or dropped out altogether, as well as the views of those who finished the course of study. In the C&B student population, the graduates are, of course, the dominant group in terms of relative numbers, and, as we have seen, there is surprisingly little overall difference in the degree of satisfaction expressed by the graduates and by all matriculants: the overall percentage very satisfied rises by roughly 5 to 6 percentage points, from about 62 percent to 67 percent, when we consider graduates only.

[4] In both sets of regressions, the coefficients for the black variable were smaller than their standard errors (Appendix Tables D.7.2 and D.7.3). In the model 5 regressions, we include advanced degrees; we also include sector of employment and household earnings as control variables for the 1976 cohort, but not the 1989 cohort. The reason for including these post-college measures is that how individuals feel about their college experiences may be affected by whether they think that college helped them attain advanced degrees, work in the sector of their choice, or be well off financially. In any case, the results are essentially the same with or without these controls.

experience; conversely, those who attended the SEL-3 schools were more content with their post-college lives but less enthusiastic about their college experiences.[5]

SAT Scores and School Selectivity

For all students in both the '76 and '89 cohorts, there is a very slight positive relationship between SAT scores and satisfaction with college. This correlation, which is weak for all students, is non-existent for black students considered separately. Moreover, the overall pattern disappears even among whites when we control for school selectivity and other variables (Appendix Tables D.7.2 and D.7.3).

It is instructive to explore further the relationship between the SAT scores of individual black students, the selectivity of the schools that they attended, and how satisfied these students were with their college experience. In this way, we can test directly another variant of the "fit" hypothesis—the assertion that black students with academic credentials less impressive than those of their white classmates are likely to end up as "victims" of affirmative action policies. This question can be posed, in effect, to the black students themselves. Were students with SAT scores distinctly lower than the norm at their schools less satisfied with their educational experience than students who went to colleges or universities where there were larger numbers of other students with similar scores—where they might be presumed to have found a better "fit" from the standpoint of academic preparation?

As we can see from the data presented in Figure 7.2 (and Appendix Table D.7.4), there is no support for the "fit" hypothesis. More specifically:

- Within the C&B universe, the percentage of black graduates with SATs below 1000 who report that they are "very satisfied" with their undergraduate education is far higher among those who attended the more academically selective colleges and universities than it is among those who attended the SEL-3 institutions.
- More generally, we see that within *every* SAT interval, black students in the '89 cohort were more likely to express a high level of satisfaction with their undergraduate education if they attended one of the most selective colleges or universities. The pattern is more mixed in the '76 cohort, but there is certainly no evidence that black students at the most selective schools were less satisfied

---

[5] See Appendix Tables D.6.8 and D.7.4.

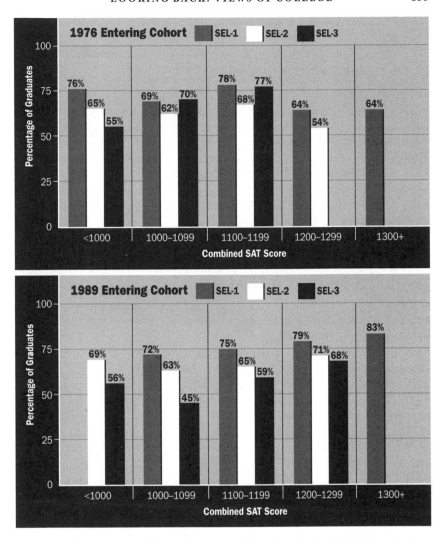

Figure 7.2. Percentage of Black Graduates "Very Satisfied" with College, by Institutional Selectivity and SAT Score, 1976 and 1989 Entering Cohorts

Source: College and Beyond.

Notes: "Graduates" refers to first-school graduates. For 1976, "SEL-1," "SEL-2," and "SEL-3" indicate institutions for which the mean combined SAT scores were 1250 or more, between 1125 and 1249, and below 1125, respectively. For 1989, "SEL-1," "SEL-2," and "SEL-3" indicate institutions for which the mean combined SAT scores were 1300 or more, between 1150 and 1299, and below 1150, respectively. Some bars are omitted because the category contained fewer than 20 observations.

than those at the less selective schools. If the black graduates, especially those with relatively low test scores, suffered by dint of having been admitted to the most academically demanding colleges and universities, they certainly don't seem to know it![6]

For white students as well as black students, the more selective the college, the more satisfied the graduates. We do not suggest, however, that the degree of selectivity per se is the main explanation. Schools with high average SAT scores tend to have more financial resources and to be able to afford faculty, facilities, and other amenities of distinctly above-average quality. Whatever the underlying forces at work, the percentage of "very satisfied" responses for the '76 cohort reaches 73 percent at SEL-1 schools, declines to 68 percent at SEL-2 schools, and drops again to 63 percent at SEL-3 schools. The differences in degree of satisfaction associated with school selectivity are at least as pronounced among black graduates as they are among white graduates, and the patterns for the '89 cohort are very similar (Appendix Table D.7.5).

These patterns do not pertain only to those who graduated from these schools. When we looked separately at matriculants who graduated neither from their first schools nor from any other school, we found that the black dropouts from both the SEL-1 and SEL-2 schools were more satisfied with their college experience than were the white dropouts from these schools; at the SEL-3 schools, the percentages were the same. In short, there is no evidence that black students who did not attain a BA felt "victimized" in a way that white students did not; if anything, the black students look back more favorably on their college experience.

The central conclusion is clear: a highly competitive academic environment was certainly not a problem for the overwhelming majority of matriculants, black and white, at the C&B schools. On the contrary, judging by their own expressions of satisfaction, it is those students who attended

---

[6] We also observe that black graduates were most likely to be "very satisfied" with their undergraduate education if they went to a C&B school that was either highly selective or relatively small in size. There are exceptions to this generalization, but there are not many. There are eight colleges and universities in the C&B universe where the percentage of black graduates in the '76 cohort classifying themselves as "very satisfied" was at least 5 percentage points *higher* than the comparable percentage for white graduates: of these, 6 are liberal arts colleges and 2 are private universities. In both the most selective universities and the colleges, it is the black *men* who are most satisfied. It is possible that institutions with large student bodies may have seemed more impersonal, and that this attribute could have been especially problematic for some minority students. Results of logistic regressions support this interpretation. When we added size-of-school variables, we found negative correlations between these variables and degree of satisfaction.

the most academically competitive institutions who were the most satisfied with their undergraduate educational experience. This finding, evident in the simple tabulations, is confirmed when we control for other variables (Appendix Tables D.7.2 and D.7.3).

Rank in Class

The relationship between being "very satisfied with college" and grades earned in college is also revealing (see the lower portion of the bars in Figure 7.3). For white and black students, in both the '76 and '89 cohorts, satisfaction with college is consistently highest for those with the best grades, and so on down the scale.[7] The members of what some used to refer to as the "contented bottom third," with their "Gentlemen's Cs," may indeed be content (with slightly over half of them "very satisfied"), but they are less content than their classmates with better grades. For black students, there is an even larger gap in satisfaction between those who ranked in the middle third of the class (80 percent "very satisfied" in the '76 cohort and 75 percent in the '89 cohort) and those who were in the bottom third (57 percent "very satisfied" in '76 and 61 percent in '89). This differential is further evidence that academic achievement not only matters for all students, it seems to matter especially for black students.[8]

As was the case with school selectivity, the simple relationship between satisfaction and rank in class is clear and does not change when we control for other variables. However, the direction of causation is less obvious. Does modest academic performance lead to feelings of relative dissatisfaction with college, even after the passage of some years, or does relative dissatisfaction with some aspect of college affect a student's grades? We leave to others, and to another day, the parsing out of such

[7] The only "blip" occurs for black graduates in the '76 cohort who ranked in the top third of the class; these students were less satisfied than black graduates from their cohort who ranked in the middle third, but this apparent anomaly disappears in the '89 cohort, where the same regular relationship between grades and satisfaction with college holds over all grade intervals for both black and white graduates.

[8] We should be careful, however, not to exaggerate the magnitude of this effect: 91 percent of all black graduates in the '76 cohort who finished in the bottom third of the class were either "very satisfied" or "somewhat satisfied" with their undergraduate education, as compared with 90 percent of all white graduates in the bottom third of the class. The corresponding percentages in the '89 cohort are even higher: 93 percent for black graduates in the bottom third of the class and 90 percent for white graduates with comparable rank in class (see Figure 7.3).

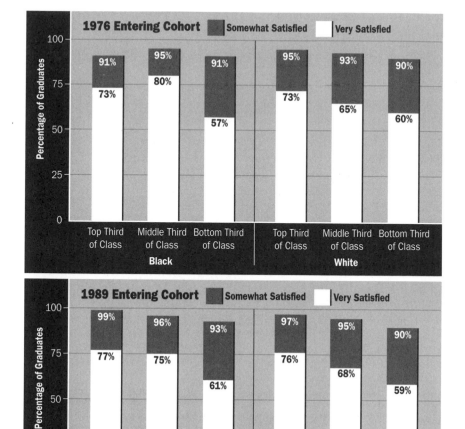

Figure 7.3. Percentage of Graduates "Very Satisfied" with College, by Class
Rank and Race, 1976 and 1989 Entering Cohorts

Source: College and Beyond.

Note: "Graduates" refers to first-school graduates.

interactions. What can be said with confidence is that academic performance, in these avowedly academic institutions, is an important predictor of satisfaction with college, over both the short-term and the long-term.

Mentoring

Another factor that might be expected to affect satisfaction with college is the help and attention students received from "mentors." The percentage of graduates of C&B schools in the '76 cohort who said that there was someone who took a special interest in them, and to whom they could turn for advice or support, was higher for blacks than it was for whites: 55 percent versus 47 percent.[9] In the '89 cohort, even higher percentages of both black and white graduates reported having mentors: 70 percent of black graduates and 59 percent of their white classmates (Appendix Table D.7.6).

The types of people who served as mentors are also of interest. When asked who served in this capacity, 84 percent of white students with mentors in the '76 cohort cited faculty members, as compared with only 66 percent of black students. On the other hand, 39 percent of black students with mentors cited college deans or other administrators, as compared with 15 percent of white students. This finding offers strong support for the proposition that efforts to help black matriculants make the transition to academically demanding colleges and succeed there have been "top down" in some measure, with deans and other administrators devoting relatively more time and attention to this process than many faculty members.[10] Athletic coaches were also more commonly cited by black men than by white men (16 percent of those with mentors

[9] The precise wording of the question was: "While you were an undergraduate, did anyone associated with your school, other than fellow students, take a special interest in you or your work—that is, was there someone you could turn to for advice or for general support or encouragement?" See Appendix Table D.7.6 for a summary of responses to this question and to the follow-up question asking about the types of individuals who provided such assistance. The difference in overall percentages between black and white graduates is statistically significant at the 1 percent level of confidence.

[10] Lowe (forthcoming). There are relatively more black deans and other administrators than black faculty, and this could also be part of the explanation for the black/white disparity in mentoring percentages. Some black deans were, of course, recruited precisely because of the relative lack of black faculty and the desirability of having some number of black adults in the academic community.

versus 9 percent)—a pattern that is reversed among the women.[11] Finally, black graduates were almost twice as likely as white graduates to cite alumni/ae as sources of advice and support, a result that we believe reflects the special efforts of alumni/ae recruiters at many of these colleges to identify promising black candidates and then to follow their progress. The fact that alumni/ae bodies at all of these colleges remain predominantly white suggests that this pattern cannot be explained primarily in terms of the efforts of black graduates.

The difference a faculty mentor can make is illustrated by this recollection of a black woman in the '89 cohort at Princeton who is now in medical school:

I had a religion professor . . . who was a huge influence on me. We disagreed a lot. So in disagreeing, we basically forged a medium through which we could really carry out our conversation and fight it out. We always ended up agreeing to disagree but it was good for me, because it allowed me to understand that it's okay to believe something other than what the professor is saying. In [my] Haitian culture, if you disagree with your elders, you're not supposed to say anything. It was difficult to start in this mode. In class one day early on, he [the religion professor] saw that I wasn't saying anything and he asked me—in French—"What do you think?" So I told him that he knew that I couldn't say anything because I disagreed—he clearly knew about my culture. And he said, "No, this is different. You should say what you believe." Throughout college, he would check on me and say, "Are you remembering to say what you think?" He's the one who ultimately made me realize that at Princeton, you have to talk. Otherwise people won't know that you understand the issue at hand or that you have your own opinion. I'm glad—if I hadn't had his class during the first year, then I probably would have been more quiet in the subsequent years than I actually was at the end.

The likelihood of having a mentor depended on the type of school attended. Within the '76 cohort, 62 percent of all graduates and 64 percent of black graduates from liberal arts colleges reported that there was someone who took a special interest in them. At the large public universities, a considerable amount of mentoring also occurred, with 40 percent of all graduates, and 52 percent of black graduates, identifying one

---

[11] The main difference between the '76 and '89 cohorts in types of mentors is that the relative number of faculty mentors apparently declined for white graduates (Appendix Table D.7.6).

or more individuals to whom they could turn for advice and support. The private universities are intermediate in this regard, but closer to the public universities than to the liberal arts colleges. These data show that liberal arts colleges, with their relatively small enrollments, offer personal support to especially large numbers of their students. It is particularly noteworthy that of those liberal arts college graduates who had mentors, 90 percent had faculty mentors. We regard all these percentages as encouraging, in light of what is sometimes said about the allegedly impersonal nature of much of higher education.

As one would predict, students who had mentors were definitely more likely to be "very satisfied with college" than those who did not. This pattern holds for the '76 and '89 cohorts, for all gender/race subgroups, and after controlling for other variables (Appendix Tables D.7.2 and D.7.3). Of course it is possible that students who were destined to end up being very satisfied with college were more inclined than their classmates to seek out and find mentors. But it also seems likely that attentive advising, counseling, and the simple provision of encouragement and support made some difference in the lives of many of these students. There is much anecdotal evidence to support this commonsense observation.

REGRETS

We also asked the members of the '76 and '89 cohorts more specific questions about what they would have done differently if they had known earlier what they know now and had their lives to live over again. Specifically, they were asked if they would change their choice of college, choice of major, or allocation of time while in college. For reasons explained in the previous section, we focus on the responses of graduates in presenting results. We did, however, tabulate the responses for matriculants as well, and when we also include those who either transferred or dropped out, the frequency of "regrets" naturally goes up, but generally only by about 3 or 4 percentage points.

Choice of School

As one would expect, there is a strong association between the degree of satisfaction students feel toward their college experience and their likelihood of choosing the same college again. There are, however, some differences in patterns between the '76 and '89 cohorts.

Within the '76 cohort, 57 percent of the black graduates of the C&B schools say that they would be very likely to enroll at the same college again, and only 14 percent say that they would be unlikely ("not at all likely") to do so. For white C&B graduates, the corresponding percentages of those very likely to enroll again and those unlikely to do so are 64 percent and 10 percent. The members of the '89 cohort were even more inclined to reaffirm their original choice of school: 72 percent of black graduates and 74 percent of white graduates said that they would be very likely to choose the same school again; only 6 to 7 percent say that they would be unlikely to make the same choice again (Appendix Table D.7.7).

Responses vary according to the selectivity and the type of school attended. In general, graduates of the most selective institutions (SEL-1 schools) would be most strongly inclined to go back to the same school. Otherwise, much depends not just on the selectivity of the school but on its type (college or university, private or public). Two findings stand out:

- First, whereas a somewhat higher percentage of graduates of liberal arts colleges than of private universities said that they were "very satisfied" with college (73 percent versus 67 percent), a higher percentage of the private university graduates said that they would be "very likely" to choose the same college again (63 percent versus 59 percent for the liberal arts colleges). These patterns apply to white and black graduates alike (see Appendix Tables D.7.5 and D.7.7). Apparently some number of the liberal arts college graduates, while very satisfied with their undergraduate education, would now prefer to have gone to a different kind of institution, perhaps one with a wider range of curricular offerings.[12]

- Second, the public universities received relatively higher scores on "very likely to choose the same college" than they did on "very satisfied with the undergraduate education." We interpret this relationship as testimony to the bargain that first-rate public universities, of the kind included in the C&B universe, offer to their matriculants. These schools provide very strong academic programs at tuition levels far below those at more or less comparable private institutions.[13]

---

[12] A member of the '76 cohort at one college commented in an interview, "I can say in hindsight that if I had it to do over again, I don't know if I'd go to a liberal arts college. The way that the market is today you really have to have skills. I see people who majored in computer science and financially they're doing much better than I am. If I send my daughter to [the same college], I'd want her to do something where she'd be very marketable—science, health, fields where there will be good jobs. It's so hard these days—there's no such thing as job security anymore. One day you have a job and the next day you're told that the company is downsizing."

[13] The difference in responses to the combination of satisfaction and choice-of-college questions is evident primarily among the white graduates of the public universities. It

How are regrets about choice of school related to SAT scores? In particular, is there any evidence that appreciable numbers of black graduates of the most selective schools, who entered with modest SAT scores, have had second thoughts about their choice of school? The answer is a flat no. At the most selective institutions, only 10 percent of black graduates from the '76 cohort with SAT scores between 1000 and 1099 would be "not at all likely" to go to the same college again—and the percentage is even lower among the '89 matriculants (5 percent). The percentage of black graduates with 1000–1099 SAT scores who expressed regrets about choice of college is highest (17 percent) at the SEL-3 schools and at the liberal arts colleges (both 18 percent). These schools may have admitted some black students who were not happy there, and who, in retrospect, regretted their choices—but the numbers are small. And the same patterns exist for white graduates.

In contrast to SAT scores, class rank is clearly related to regrets about choice of college. As one would expect, black students in the bottom third of the class were more likely than other students to regret their choice of college. Once again, doubts about choice of college among low-ranking students were greater among those who attended the schools in the SEL-3 category. Even here, however, the percentage expressing "regrets" (respondents who would be not at all likely to go back to the same college) never rises above 19 percent among the black graduates of the '76 cohort—or above roughly the 11 percent level among black graduates of the '89 cohort. And, again, the same patterns emerge when we look at the views that white students express concerning their choice of school.

Choice of Major

Many more alumni/ae have regrets about their choice of major than about their choice of school. In the '76 cohort, 29 percent of all black graduates and 21 percent of all white graduates say that they would be "not at all likely" to choose the same major again, and only 36 percent of the black graduates and 41 percent of the white graduates say that they would be "very likely" to choose the same major. In the '89 cohort, smaller

---

probably reflects the fact that white matriculants were less likely than black matriculants to qualify for need-based financial aid at the expensive private institutions (because of their generally higher levels of household income) and therefore were more likely to have to pay full tuition, or something close to it, at those schools. In answering the question about "choosing the same college again," respondents might well give some weight to tuition levels, whereas they would be less likely to do so in answering the "satisfaction" question.

percentages of the graduates, both black and white, expressed dissatisfaction with their choice of major; 19 percent of black graduates and 16 percent of whites said that they would be unlikely to choose the same major again (Appendix Table D.7.8.)

Regrets differ significantly by broad field of study, but we will not report these figures in any detail in the text because the patterns are erratic over time. Suffice it to say that in the '76 cohort, serious second thoughts were most common among graduates who majored in the social sciences. By the time of the '89 cohort, attitudes toward broad fields had changed in several respects. Most notably, those '89 matriculants (both black and white) who majored in the humanities are much more positive about this choice of major than were their predecessors (see Appendix Table D.7.8 for more detail).

Allocation of Time

More than half (57 percent) of all black graduates in the '76 cohort felt that they didn't study enough while in college; 40 percent of their white classmates expressed the same regret. There are only slight differences in the responses to questions about time spent in other ways, such as on social life and extracurricular activities (Figure 7.4).[14] The relationships between "wishing I had studied more" and rank in class are relentlessly consistent for both white and black graduates, and for members of both the '76 and '89 cohorts. Overall, less than 20 percent of all those who graduated in the top third of the class now wish that they had studied more, whereas nearly half of those in the middle third and slightly more than two-thirds of those in the bottom third regretted not having spent more time "hitting the books" (Appendix Table D.7.9).

The greater (relative) number of black graduates who regret not having studied more is in large part related to their lower overall rank in class. But even when we limit the comparison to those who graduated in the top third of the class, we find that a higher percentage of black graduates than white graduates in the '89 cohort wish that they had studied more (25 percent versus 16 percent). These retrospective expressions of regret by African American respondents need to be thought about in the context of the debate over factors affecting their academic performance discussed in Chapter 3, and especially the suggestion that peer group pressures discourage studying.

[14] The members of the '89 cohort expressed essentially the same set of views; an even higher fraction of black graduates wished that they had studied more (65 percent). See Figure 7.4.

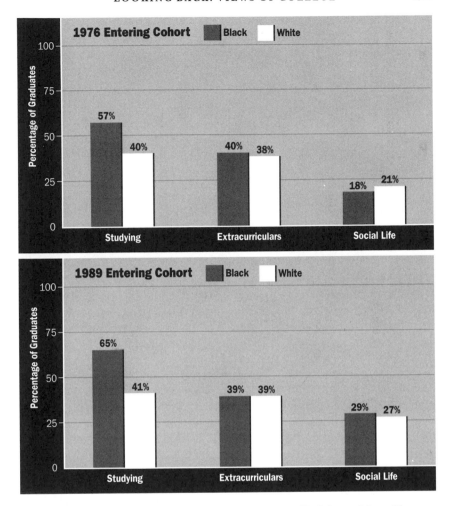

Figure 7.4. Percentage of Graduates Who Wish They Had Spent More Time on Selected Activities, by Race, 1976 and 1989 Entering Cohorts

Source: College and Beyond.

Note: "Graduates" refers to first-school graduates.

WHAT WAS LEARNED?

Undergraduate education at all of the C&B schools is intended both to build intellectual capital and to encourage personal growth. Which capacities do graduates consider most important, and to what degree do they credit their colleges with helping them develop these skills? To answer these questions, respondents to the C&B survey were given a list of skills or capacities (including categories such as "analytical and problem-solving skills," "ability to write clearly," "ability to work independently," "ability to form and retain friendships," and "ability to have a good rapport with people holding different beliefs"). They were then asked, first, to indicate how important each has been in their life since college, and second, how much their undergraduate experience helped them develop in these areas. Responses were on a scale of 1 to 5 with 5 being the highest rating.

There was substantial agreement among black and white graduates, in both the '76 and '89 cohorts, as to which of these skills had proved to be "very important" in their lives after college (Table 7.1). Analytical skills, the ability to write clearly, to communicate well orally, to work independently, and to adapt to change, were assigned especially high rankings by all graduates. More than 60 percent of black and white respondents in the '76 and '89 cohorts stated that each of these was "very important." One of the noteworthy features of the results reported in Table 7.1 is that more black graduates than white graduates felt that almost all of these skills/capacities were "very important" in their lives. We are not sure how to interpret this pattern, but it could simply mean that, after reflecting on their lives in a society in which race continues to matter, black graduates were more inclined than whites to think that they needed all the powers that they could command.

Of greater moment for this study are the responses to the second set of questions, which sought to ascertain how much students felt their undergraduate experience had contributed to their intellectual and personal development. Overall, black graduates rated their undergraduate experience more highly than did their white classmates (Table 7.2).[15] Only in "ability to form and retain friendships" and (for the '89 cohort only) "ability to relax and enjoy leisure" did white graduates rate the contribution of college more highly than black graduates. The differences in responses were especially large in the percentages who reported that college contributed "a great deal" to their "ability to communicate well orally," "ability to adapt to change," and "competitiveness."[16] Among the members of both the '76 and the '89 cohorts, black graduates were twice

---

[15] These ratings varied by type of school, but the black-white differences are quite consistent within each category. In general, the more selective schools and the liberal arts colleges as a group received the highest ratings—particularly in contributions to analytical skills, writing ability, and ability to work independently.

[16] These positive responses were not confined to graduates. The black matriculants who never received a BA consistently reported that their colleges contributed more in almost all of these dimensions than did the whites who never finished college.

TABLE 7.1
Percentage of Graduates Who Consider Selected Skills "Very Important" in
Their Lives, by Race, 1976 and 1989 Entering Cohorts

| | *Percentage Rating Skill "Very Important"* | | | |
| | 1976 Entering Cohort | | 1989 Entering Cohort | |
	Black	*White*	*Black*	*White*
Academic skills				
Analytical skills	87	85	83	83
Ability to communicate well orally	79	68	78	69
Ability to write clearly and effectively	71	65	68	62
Knowledge of particular field/discipline	46	43	45	43
Professional skills				
Ability to work independently	74	67	73	68
Ability to adapt to change	72	61	70	66
Leadership abilities	61	47	56	47
Ability to work cooperatively	56	50	61	58
Rapport with people holding different beliefs	53	45	60	56
Competitiveness	25	20	30	22
Personal/social skills				
Ability to form and retain friendships	41	44	53	57
Religious values	41	21	36	18
Ability to relax and enjoy leisure	40	33	47	45
Active interest in community service	24	15	29	14

Source: College and Beyond.
Note: "Graduates" refers to first-school graduates.

as likely as white graduates to emphasize the contribution of the college
to developing an "active interest in community service." This finding
supports our earlier conjecture that experiences in college contributed
to the strong proclivity of black matriculants to participate in civic activities after college.

"Leadership skills" were also valued especially highly by black graduates in both cohorts, and anecdotal accounts make clear that access to
these highly selective institutions helped them learn how to function—
and how to lead—in multi-racial settings.

> *A black graduate of Northwestern who went on to earn an MD:*
>
> I was a leader of a number of organizations on campus. Most of that had to do with film—and I'm in medicine now, so that was going pretty far afield. Because I was the head of an organization that promoted films across campus, we had a large organization that was a money-making machine, and I was the head of it. I think I developed leadership qualities from doing that sort of thing, and that has served me well in college, in medical school, and beyond.

TABLE 7.2
Percentage of Graduates Who Believe College Contributed "a Great Deal" to the Development of Selected Skills, by Race, 1976 and 1989 Entering Cohorts

	Percentage Who Believe College Contributed a "Great Deal"			
	1976 Entering Cohort		*1989 Entering Cohort*	
	Black	*White*	*Black*	*White*
Academic skills				
Analytical skills	45	41	50	47
Ability to communicate well orally	27	17	33	25
Ability to write clearly and effectively	39	33	48	40
Knowledge of particular field/discipline	29	29	41	37
Professional skills				
Ability to work independently	42	36	42	40
Ability to adapt to change	26	17	38	30
Leadership abilities	19	12	27	23
Ability to work cooperatively	19	13	28	26
Rapport with people holding different beliefs	28	23	43	42
Competitiveness	28	20	29	24
Personal/social skills				
Ability to form and retain friendships	24	27	37	46
Religious values	8	4	11	7
Ability to relax and enjoy leisure	11	12	23	26
Active interest in community service	10	4	24	13

Source: College and Beyond.
Note: "Graduates" refers to first-school graduates.

There is a striking congruence between the rankings of skills that the graduates now regard as most important and the rankings of skills that college helped them develop in the fullest measure. In the main, these graduates appear to have taken from college the things that they now regard as most important in their lives.

A black man from the '89 entering class at Yale who now works as a talent agent:

I remember one literary criticism course where one of the main things we did was look at paragraphs and chapters as a stand-in for the whole text—so how does this sentence, this paragraph, represent the whole work? And that's something that I've done as I've looked at scripts here in Hollywood. It's a good way into the script, but I also have found that doing this sets me apart from other people who are talking in generalities and not in specifics. Who would have known that would have played a role in my career? But it has.

A black graduate of the University of Pennsylvania talked about perseverance, learned by studying math:

Mostly people were saying I couldn't do it. I had a hard time with math, even though I wanted to be an engineer. I didn't make it through because I was any kind of math whiz. I made it through because I basically said that I wasn't going to fail. And I just kept pushing. When I got into the first engineering class, the professor asked how many of us—and there were hundreds of us in the class—hadn't taken calculus. It was me and maybe a dozen other people that raised our hands. That was pretty intimidating, to say the least. But, it didn't stop me from giving it a shot. . . . I just always took math. Three years were required, and I ended up taking three and a half or four. The thing that I learned most was perseverance. Sticking with a problem until you solve it—that's about the most important thing that any engineer can learn.

Our findings take on even more meaning when considered in the context of how these C&B graduates rated themselves before they entered college as freshmen. Thanks to the cooperation of the College Entrance Examination Board and the Educational Testing Service (ETS), we were able to go back in time and examine how C&B graduates in the '76 cohort graded themselves in a number of academic and non-

academic categories when they took the SAT test in 1975 or 1976.[17] Not
surprisingly, we found that the C&B graduates as a group were much
more likely than all test-takers to rank their abilities in the top 1 percent
or the top 10 percent of their age group. We also found that the black
graduates of the C&B schools assigned themselves higher ratings in essentially every category than did all SAT test-takers (Appendix Table
D.7.10),[18] but that the black C&B graduates were less inclined than their
white classmates to rate themselves at the very top of these scales.

The College Board's Student Descriptive Questionnaire included
questions about three important skills—written expression, spoken expression, and leadership abilities—that were also part of the C&B survey.
This linkage permits us to ask whether students who entered college
feeling they were not among those at the top of their peer group in these
key areas now feel, looking back, that college contributed to their growth
in these areas. Thus, we separated students into two groups: those who
felt, when they took the SAT, that they were already in the top 10 percent
in each of these categories, and all others. The second group we regarded collectively as having expressed, de facto, some "room to improve" in their writing, speaking, and leadership skills. Roughly 50 percent of the black graduates and 45 percent of the white graduates were in
the "Below Top 10% (Room to Improve)" category when they completed
the pre-college survey.[19]

Among the black students who classified themselves as having room to
improve in writing skills, 33 percent felt that college contributed "a great
deal" in this respect, as compared with 23 percent of their white classmates. When we add the next level of responses (also including those
who ranked the contribution of college "4" on a scale of 1 to 5), the gap

[17] All prospective test-takers filled out a Student Descriptive Questionnaire prior to
taking the SAT. These questionnaires garnered information about students' backgrounds,
interests, aspirations, and self-ratings (see Appendix A and Appendix Table D.7.10). Working with the College Board and ETS, we were able to link the data collected by ETS to our
database. Fortunately, some of the ETS categories—writing clearly, spoken expression,
leadership skills—match our categories almost perfectly.

[18] There are two categories that are exceptions to this generalization: test-takers in
general assigned themselves a slightly higher average rating in "mechanical ability" and
"artistic ability" than did black C&B graduates. It can also be noted that in three categories,
"getting along with others," "acting ability," and "leadership ability" black C&B graduates,
on entering college in '76, rated themselves more highly than did their white classmates.

[19] These percentages vary by skill category, but not by much. The percentages who rated
themselves "below top 10%" are, by category: written expression—49 percent of black
graduates, 44 percent of white graduates; oral expression—52 percent of black graduates,
51 percent of white graduates; leadership abilities—43 percent of black graduates, 43 percent of white graduates.

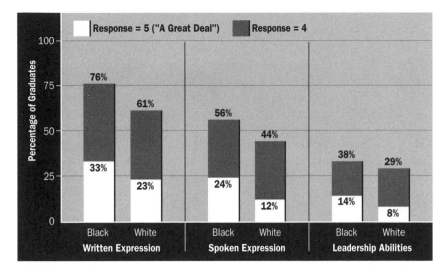

Figure 7.5. Percentage of Graduates with Low Self-Ratings Who Benefited from College in Selected Areas, by Race, 1976 Entering Cohort

Sources: College and Beyond and College Entrance Examination Board.

Notes: Graduates with "low self-ratings" in a selected area are those who rated their ability below the top 10 percent of their peers on a pre-college questionnaire administered by the College Entrance Examination Board. "Graduates" refers to first-school graduates.

between black and white students widens: 76 percent of black graduates as compared with 61 percent of white graduates. Similar gaps exist with respect to the other two skill categories common to both surveys, oral communication and leadership skills (Figure 7.5).

It is undoubtedly true that those graduates—black and white—who entered college with well-developed skills gained further strength in areas in which they already excelled. Those who had ranked themselves in the top 10 percent on entry to college reported even higher gains than those who gave themselves lower rankings (with black members of this top group even more likely than white members to credit college with having made a great deal of difference). There is everything to be said for enhancing talents already identified. But in some ways even more compelling is the evidence of the progress made by those who entered college with a lower level of confidence—conscious of their limits and lacking the conviction that they were already in the top 1 percent or top 10 percent of their age group. The black students who felt that they had room for improvement were much more likely than white students to rate the college contribution highly.

The twenty years between the time they entered college and the time of the C&B survey surely brought many changes in the lives of members of the '76 cohort that affected their self-images and colored their recollections of college. Nonetheless, the ETS pre-college data support the interpretation that more black graduates than white graduates have concluded—somehow, at some point—that college helped them develop critically important skills. How does one judge the worth of an increased capacity to exercise leadership or a greater degree of confidence in making a speech or presenting ideas in a meeting? No one can give precise answers to such questions. But what can be said on the basis of these data is that substantial numbers of C&B graduates—and relatively more black graduates than white graduates—felt that college made a difference.

This is the chapter of the study in which the former students speak for themselves. Because of the doubts some have expressed about the wisdom of enrolling black students in the competitive environment of selective colleges, what is most impressive about these retrospective evaluations is the high degree of satisfaction with college that these students reported. They felt much more positive about their educational experiences than they did about their lives in general.

Clearly, the black matriculants (and graduates) from the most selective institutions—even if they may at times have felt hard pressed academically—did not let such challenges defeat them. It is time, therefore, to abandon the idea that well-intentioned college and university admissions officers have somehow sacrificed the interests of the black students whom they have admitted. That is not the conclusion suggested by measures of graduation rates, advanced degrees, or subsequent earnings, and it is certainly not the view of the vast majority of the black students who were admitted. There are—and always will be—individual students, black and white, who feel underprepared for college and overmatched by their new academic environments; but anecdotal accounts of frustration and disappointment should not be allowed to substitute for the overwhelming weight of evidence based on the positive experiences of so many C&B matriculants.

At the same time, we find—and it is a reassuring finding for those who have been teachers and graded papers—that academic performance matters for all students, especially black students. Not surprisingly, students tend to be more satisfied with the quality of their undergraduate academic experience if they ranked higher than the lower third of the class—and those students who ranked in the top third were most satisfied of all. This finding applies to all students, regardless of race. It should remind everyone concerned with teaching and academic advising that even more effort has to be devoted to encouraging all students, whatever their background or circumstances, to take full advantage of their educational opportunities.

Finally, it is especially heartening to learn from the data presented in the last part of this chapter that black students with specific educational needs believe that they have benefited at least as much as their white classmates, and probably more, from what these colleges seek to give their students. "Value added" is no doubt impossible to measure in any precise way, but the responses of the black graduates of the C&B institutions certainly encourage us to think that they have gained substantially from the time they spent in selective colleges and universities.

CHAPTER 8

Diversity: Perceptions and Realities

IN REFLECTING on his time at Harvard in the 1850s, Henry Adams wrote that "chance insisted on enlarging [Adams's] education by tossing a trio of Virginians" into a class composed overwhelmingly of students from New England. As Adams recalled, both he and the Virginians (one of whom was "Roony" Lee, son of Robert E. Lee)

> knew well how thin an edge of friendship separated them in 1856 from mortal enmity. . . . For the first time Adams's education brought him in contact with new types and taught him their values. He saw the New England type measure itself with another, and he was part of the process.[1]

After quoting this passage, Harvard president Neil Rudenstine observed that this particular experiment in education may not have been a full success since "neither Adams nor Lee was able to reach across the gap between them. . . . Both [were] constrained by differences in heritage, history, temperament, and culture that were in the end too vast to overcome." And yet, Adams at least recognized his own limitations when he concluded that he was "little more fit than the Virginians to deal with a future America." In any event, as Rudenstine emphasizes, this

> lesson in education . . . produced an awareness of what might, under different circumstances, have proved possible. It also altered Adams' consciousness, and forced him to confront and assess a type of person he had never before known. It drove him to reach new conclusions about himself and his own limitations, and even led to some understanding (vastly over-simplified) of representative southerners and the South. Chance had "enlarged" his education, almost in spite of himself.[2]

We are reminded that the concept of diversity is far from new in American higher education. For more than 150 years, educators have stressed its educational value. Originally, diversity was thought of mainly in terms of differences in ideas or points of view, but these were rarely seen as disembodied abstractions. Direct association with dissimilar individuals was deemed essential to learning. The dimensions of diversity

---

[1] *The Education of Henry Adams* (1907), quoted in Rudenstine 1996, p. 6. In this classic autobiography, Adams refers to himself in the third person.

[2] Rudenstine 1996, p. 7

subsequently expanded to include geography, religion, nation of birth, upbringing, wealth, gender, and race.

Eloquent statements attesting to the educational value of diversity abound, as do anecdotal accounts of its effects on the outlook and even the lives of numerous individuals. It is more difficult to find systematic evidence of its effects, in part because definition, measurement, and analysis are very difficult in this area. We have by no means resolved the problems involved in explaining precisely how, in what circumstances, and to what degree diversity on campuses has enriched education. Circular processes are everywhere evident, and disentangling cause and effect is extremely difficult: students most predisposed to benefit from diversity are most likely to report its beneficial effects, and positive attitudes toward diversity may well color perceptions of what was gained from the college experience. Nonetheless, the College and Beyond surveys permit a more careful quantitative analysis than has been possible heretofore of (1) the importance attached to race relations by those who attended academically selective colleges and universities; (2) their perceptions of the contribution their undergraduate education made in this area; (3) the reported extent of interactions among individuals of different races, beliefs, and circumstances; and (4) matriculants' views of the efforts C&B institutions are making to educate a diverse population of students.

Although we are concerned primarily with racial diversity in this book, it bears repeating that diversity extends well beyond race and encompasses differences in background, socioeconomic status, country or region of birth, point of view, and religion.[3] We focus on racial diversity because that is the subject of this study and because the efforts of colleges and universities to achieve such diversity have proved to be highly controversial. Other kinds of diversity—such as coming from a rural background or being from a distant area of the country—are rarely questioned as appropriate considerations in the admissions process. Of course, it would be an oversimplification to assume that all African Americans, any more than all midwesterners or all Lutherans, represent anything resembling one point of view. The scope of our study, however, is too broad to allow us to investigate such finer grained levels of diversity.

---

[3] For an extended discussion of why the college years represent an unusual opportunity to grow through meeting and learning to understand others, see Axtell (forthcoming). College, Axtell notes, is a time when "students are thrown together in close quarters with several thousand self-selected and usually friendly 'others' in a relatively safe environment where speech and thought are ideally free, and intellectual stretching is encouraged by parents, faculty, and society at large." For the classic explanation of "the contact hypothesis" (i.e., the idea that interpersonal contact breaks down stereotypes and therefore reduces prejudice) see Allport 1979.

"WORKING WITH," AND "GETTING ALONG WITH," PEOPLE OF DIFFERENT RACES AND CULTURES

We begin our exploration of this complex subject by looking first at how C&B matriculants gauge the importance, in their own lives, of being able to relate well to individuals of different races and cultures. We then examine their assessments of what their colleges contributed in this regard.

Importance in Life

If people attached little importance to the ability to "work effectively" and "get along well" with people from different races and cultures, it might not matter much whether colleges help individuals to develop this capacity. In point of fact, however, nearly half of the '76 respondents to the C&B survey (44 percent) said that the ability to "get along" was "very important." (A five-point rating scale was used, with 1 representing "not at all important," and 5 representing "very important.") Over three-quarters of the respondents (77 percent) assigned one of the top two ratings (4 or 5) to the capacity to work effectively and relate to other people across racial or cultural divides. Almost no one said (or, the cynic might suggest, admitted to believing) that this ability was "not at all important."[4]

The importance attached to the ability to function across racial lines—high as it is for white C&B matriculants—is higher yet for black matriculants (Figure 8.1). Fully 74 percent of '76 black matriculants rated the ability to "work effectively" and "get along" with people from different races/cultures as "very important;" 94 percent assigned one of the top two ratings to this capacity. To grasp the full significance that black respondents attached to being able to work and interact across racial and cultural divides, it is instructive to compare the emphasis whites and blacks place on two related but different kinds of "diversity"—the one,

[4] See question A13 on the questionnaire administered to the '76 matriculants (Appendix A) for the exact wording of the question. We combined "race/culture" because of the common tendency in colloquial speech to use this "joint" terminology. However, as Anthony Appiah (1997) explains so well, this linkage can be the source of much confusion. Racial identity is regarded as important by many middle-class African Americans, Appiah argues, in part because there are so few true cultural differences between them and comparable white Americans, even though the two groups are often viewed (and sometimes treated) quite differently.

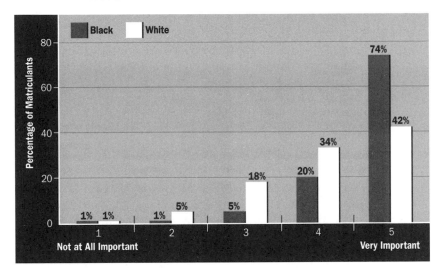

Figure 8.1. Perceived Importance in Life of "Ability to Work Effectively and Get Along Well with People from Different Races/Cultures," by Race, 1976 Entering Cohort

Source: College and Beyond.

discussed above based on differences in race/culture, and the other associated with differences in beliefs. When asked to rate the importance of the "ability to have a good rapport with people holding different beliefs," 45 percent of whites and 52 percent of blacks checked "very important." When asked about "the ability to get along well with people of different races," 42 percent of whites and 74 percent of blacks checked "very important." As Anthony Appiah explains, race is much more central in the lives of black Americans than in the lives of white Americans.[5]

The large differences by race are hardly surprising. Because of their minority status, it has to be much harder for black Americans, at least for those who regard themselves as upwardly mobile, to contemplate "doing

[5] Appiah 1997, p. 31. There are also large differences between women and men in attitudes toward diversity, with women more likely than men to emphasize the importance of race relations. Among the '76 matriculants, 52 percent of all women rated the ability to "get along with people from different races and cultures" as very important, as compared with 36 percent of all men. These gender differences are found among blacks as well as whites, but they are larger within the white population. Occupation matters, too. For example, doctors (both white and black) attach a higher value to the ability to "get along" than do lawyers and, for that matter, individuals in general.

well" in life if they are unable to work effectively with members of the white majority. They have no choice but to take seriously the importance of "getting along." For this simple reason, the educational value of learning to cope with diversity may well be even greater for black students than for white students—in spite of the fact that much of the discussion of diversity focuses on ways in which white students are presumed to learn from black classmates. The classic statement of this position was provided by Sir Arthur Lewis, a Nobel Prize–winning economist, in a 1969 article:

> Blacks in America are inevitably and perpetually a minority. This means that in all administrative and leadership positions we are going to be outnumbered by white folks, and we will have to compete with them not on our terms but on theirs. The only way to win this game is to know them so thoroughly that we can outpace them. For us to turn our back on this opportunity, by insisting on mingling only with other black students in college, is folly of the highest order.[6]

The next question is whether there is evidence of any shift over time in the importance attached to "getting along." Even though the methodology is far from perfect, we can compare the responses given by '76 matriculants (white and black) with the responses to the same question given by C&B matriculants in the '89 entering cohort.[7] There are pronounced differences. Both the white and black members of the latter cohort were more inclined than their predecessors to regard getting along well with individuals of other races and cultures as "very important" in life. Among white matriculants, the percentage checking "very important" rises from 42 to 55 percent as we move from the '76 to the '89 cohort; among black matriculants, the percentage checking "very important" rises from 74 to 76 percent.

In deciding what significance to attach to this apparent attitudinal shift from one college generation to the next, we should ask if larger numbers of the '89 respondents were inclined to assign "very important" ratings to *all* types of abilities. Are we observing only a kind of "grade inflation," with the more recent graduates tending to be more positive in all of their assessments? This does not seem to be the case. For example, the ratings assigned by the two cohorts to the importance of various academic capacities were almost precisely the same, and religious values

---

[6] Lewis 1969, p. 52.

[7] A major problem with such intergenerational comparisons, based on surveys conducted at the same point in time, is that the respondents from the two cohorts differ in the amount of post-college life they have lived as well as in the historical period when they went to college; ideally, it would be desirable to distinguish among "maturation or age effects," "period effects," and "cohort effects." See Riley, Foner, and Waring 1988.

were regarded as *less* important by the '89 matriculants than by the '76 matriculants (see Table 8.1). In short, while some part of these differences may be age related, the incremental importance attached to racial understanding appears to be meaningful in and of itself.

Particularly noteworthy is the relative importance assigned by the '76 and '89 matriculants to the two separate dimensions of diversity distinguished earlier: getting along with people of different races/cultures and having good rapport with individuals holding different beliefs (the two shaded rows in Table 8.1).[8] While blacks in both cohorts assigned even more importance than whites to relating well to individuals of different races, the black-white gap in assessments is modestly narrower among the '89 matriculants than among the '76 matriculants. There appears to have been even more of a change in outlook among whites than among blacks when it comes to race, but not when it comes to beliefs.

Moreover, within the white population, there was a particularly large increase in the importance attached to race relations among those individuals who occupied leadership positions in civic organizations. Of the sizable number of white members of the '89 cohort who report that they are already serving in some civic leadership capacity, 59 percent said that getting along well with individuals of different races and cultures was "very important," compared to only 43 percent of the white civic leaders in the '76 cohort. It is not surprising that those most active in one public arena or another have become increasingly sensitive to the need to relate well to individuals of other races and cultures.

While it is impossible to be sure what is behind these shifts, they may reflect important changes in the realities that confront everyone in the United States. The increased importance attached to being able to work with, and get along with, people of different racial and cultural groups makes very good sense in light of known demographic trends: the country in which the '89 matriculants will live and work will have a more diverse racial makeup than the one that earlier cohorts encountered. As the population of the country becomes ever more racially diverse, and as white Americans see their dominant majority status erode, the need to work effectively with individuals of other races will become an increasingly inescapable reality to members of *every* racial group. In the business and professional worlds and in much of civic and public life, white enclaves will be less and less imaginable.

---

[8] Note, too, that between the '76 and '89 cohorts, increased importance is associated with the ability to "work cooperatively" and to "form and retain friendships"—which are still other ways of describing the importance of "getting along."

TABLE 8.1
Percentage of Matriculants Who Rated Selected Skills "Very Important"
in Life, by Race, 1976 and 1989 Entering Cohorts

	Black			White		
	1976	*1989*	*Difference*	*1976*	*1989*	*Difference*
Academic skills						
Ability to communicate well orally	77	78	1	67	69	2
Knowledge of a particular field/discipline	45	44	−1	43	43	0
Analytical and problem-solving skills	85	82	−3	84	82	−2
Ability to write clearly and effectively	70	68	−2	64	62	−2
Professional skills						
Ability to work effectively and get along well with people of different races/cultures	74	76	2	42	55	13
Ability to have a good rapport with people holding different beliefs	52	60	8	45	56	11
Ability to work cooperatively	57	62	5	50	58	8
Ability to adapt to change	71	71	0	62	66	4
Competitiveness	24	30	6	19	22	3
Ability to work independently	72	72	0	67	68	1
Leadership abilities	60	56	−4	47	47	0
Personal/social skills						
Ability to form and retain friendships	39	52	13	44	57	13
Ability to relax and enjoy leisure	39	46	7	33	44	11
Active interest in community services	25	29	4	15	14	−1
Religious values	42	36	−6	22	18	−4

Source: College and Beyond.

Note: Respondents were asked to rate the importance of selected skills on a scale of 1 ("not at all important") to 5 ("very important").

The Contribution of College

What difference did college make in developing the ability to work with, and get along with, people of different races and cultures? This companion question is, if anything, even more relevant to the debate over the role to be played by race in the admissions process.

Almost half of the white respondents from the '76 C&B cohort believe that their undergraduate experience was of considerable value in this regard: 46 percent gave college a rating of 4 or 5 on a five-point scale (where 5 = "a great deal"), and 18 percent said it helped "a great deal." An appreciably higher percentage of black matriculants gave college credit for helping them develop these "getting along" skills (57 percent gave their college experience either a 4 or a 5 rating, and 30 percent gave it the highest rating).

These percentages increased substantially between the '76 and '89 cohorts (Figure 8.2). The percentage of white matriculants who said that college contributed "a great deal" was nearly twice as high in the '89 cohort as in the '76 cohort (34 percent as compared with 18 percent), and the percentage of black matriculants assigning the highest rating to

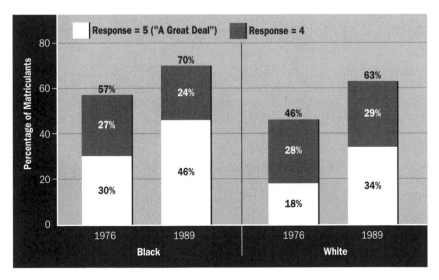

Figure 8.2. Perceived Contribution of College to "Ability to Work Effectively and Get Along Well with People from Different Races/Cultures," by Race, 1976 and 1989 Entering Cohorts

Source: College and Beyond.

Note: Respondents were asked to rate the contribution of their undergraduate experience on a scale of 1 ("none at all") to 5 ("a great deal").

the contribution of college in this area also went up sharply (from 30 percent to 46 percent).

To be sure, some part of these reported increases may be due simply to the fact that the '89 matriculants are temporally closer to their undergraduate days than are the '76 matriculants. College experiences inevitably loom larger in the lives of the more recent matriculants, who have also had less opportunity to learn some of these same skills through workplace experiences and civic participation. Thus there appears to have been an increase of roughly 10 percentage points in the frequency with which respondents assign the top rating to other abilities. (For example, the percentage saying that college contributed "a great deal" to the development of analytical skills increased from 38 percent of white '76 matriculants to 45 percent of white '89 matriculants [Table 8.2].) But the increases between the '76 and '89 cohorts in the percentages of respondents assigning a top rating to the ability to "get along with people of different races and cultures" are *much* larger in both absolute and relative terms: 16 percentage points for both white and black matriculants. There were also distinctly above-average increases in the frequency with which both black and white respondents gave their colleges a great deal of credit for helping them develop rapport with people holding different beliefs—the second dimension of diversity (see the two highlighted rows in Table 8.2).

We conclude that a real shift in actual experiences occurred between the years when the '76 matriculants attended the C&B schools and the years when the '89 matriculants attended these same schools. Students in '89 may have been more aware than their predecessors of the importance of learning to "get along" (as suggested by their answers to the question of how important that is in life), and therefore may have taken more advantage of the opportunities that their college experience offered them in this regard. At the same time, colleges and universities may have become more adept at creating an environment in which students could learn from classmates who were different from themselves. When colleges first began to enroll much larger numbers of minority students, they sometimes assumed that the right kinds of interactions and educational experiences would occur more or less automatically. Subsequently, college administrators learned that creating a productive learning environment required much thought. Those who have worked to improve the quality of the undergraduate educational experience should be encouraged by the evidence that progress has been made.

It is beyond the scope of this study to examine which institutional approaches have been more or less effective in achieving the educational benefits of diversity. However, we can report that smaller size and residential living appear to make a positive difference. While all types of educa-

TABLE 8.2
Percentage of Matriculants Who Rated College as Contributing "a Great Deal" to Development of Selected Skills, by Race, 1976 and 1989 Entering Cohorts

	Black			White		
	1976	1989	Difference	1976	1989	Difference
Academic skills						
Ability to communicate well orally	27	33	6	16	24	8
Knowledge of a particular field/discipline	27	40	13	26	36	10
Analytical and problem-solving skills	41	48	7	38	45	7
Ability to write clearly and effectively	36	46	10	31	38	7
Professional skills						
Ability to work effectively and get along well with people of different races/cultures	30	46	16	18	34	16
Ability to have a good rapport with people holding different beliefs	28	43	15	22	40	18
Ability to work cooperatively	18	27	9	12	25	13
Ability to adapt to change	27	39	12	17	29	12
Competitiveness	26	30	4	19	23	4
Ability to work independently	39	41	2	34	39	5
Leadership abilities	17	27	10	11	22	11
Personal/social skills						
Ability to form and retain friendships	22	37	15	25	44	19
Ability to relax and enjoy leisure	12	23	11	11	26	15
Active interest in community service	9	22	13	4	12	8
Religious values	8	11	3	4	7	3

Source: College and Beyond.
Note: Respondents were asked to rate the contribution of college to the development of selected skills on a scale of 1 ("none at all") to 5 ("a great deal").

tional institutions included in the C&B universe received "high marks" from their '89 matriculants for the contribution that college made to "getting along," the liberal arts colleges received the highest grades. This was true for ratings assigned by both black and white matriculants. Among the '89 matriculants at the liberal arts colleges in the C&B universe, 43 percent of the whites and 50 percent of the blacks gave their schools the highest rating.

Other studies have also found that college can contribute to the development of values conducive to better race relations. Linda Sax and Alexander Astin, in their analysis of the effects of college on the development of various aspects of citizenship, conclude that racially diverse college environments and involvement by students in activities that cut across racial lines contribute to what they term greater "cultural awareness" and stronger commitments to improving racial understanding.[9]

In focusing on relations between racial groups—and especially between blacks and whites—one can quickly lose sight of the importance of diversity within, as well as between, all of these groups. Recent interview studies by Richard Light at Harvard provide a wealth of examples of how minority students can learn a great deal at college from and about other minority students. It is also easy to forget the importance of differences in religion as well as race and culture.

A Cuban woman at Harvard:

My roommates are all Asian but they're all of different nationalities. The more I get to know my Vietnamese roommate, the more I learn. Our cultures have the same emphasis on family, but her culture has much more reverence for tradition. She has thousands of years of tradition to respect. If you're Cuban and in the United States, you left your history behind and even the culture is not as old.

A white woman in the '89 cohort at the University of North Carolina (Chapel Hill):

When I was a resident advisor, a student who was Muslim came to see me. He came in to see me privately because he wanted to find a place to say his

---

[9] Sax and Astin 1997. The study compares the views of over 27,000 students at 388 four-year colleges when they were freshmen in 1985 with their views four years later. The authors control, at least roughly, for a large number of characteristics of entering students that might be expected to affect outcomes.

prayers every morning and he had to face a certain direction to say them. I remember being struck by just how radically different it was from the way that I was raised. And I came away realizing that he was just as committed to his faith as I was to mine and that I had to respect him for that.

INTERACTIONS AMONG DIVERSE GROUPS

The four years spent at a residential college have long offered a time and a place for extensive interaction around the clock. When one considers the natural tendency on the part of students to associate with (and especially to live with) individuals like oneself, it is likely that many students encounter a wider range of people in college than they will ever see again on such an intimate, day-by-day basis. After mixing together in classrooms and dormitories, on playing fields and in extracurricular activities, and at parties and other campus events, they clearly appreciate the value of interacting with a diverse group of peers.

No one doubts that having intelligent fellow students in classes, in study groups, and as roommates is a crucial part of the educational process. But in bringing together people of different races and backgrounds, educators have recognized that much can be learned from one's peers beyond learning how to solve differential equations and how to interpret a Michelangelo sculpture; it can also mean learning what it is like to grow up in a home with divorced parents, or to be looked at with suspicion because of the color of your skin. Implicit in the idea of traveling—"going away to college"—is the notion that there is something to be learned from being in new surroundings, with new people, some of whom may be quite different from those you knew before.

A white woman in the '89 cohort at Wellesley:

My three suitemates were a third-generation Chinese American woman from LA, an African American from Arizona, and a Saudi woman. And so I met their friends, too. Being in college government was another way to jump over initial gaps, when you can say, "Were you at the meeting last night? I missed it, what did you hear?" And from that point you just became friends.

I came from a large regional high school in northern Wisconsin. It's not that I didn't have friends from other racial groups—it was just a demographic impossibility.

A white man in the '76 cohort at Columbia:

It was substantially more racially diverse than Salt Lake City. On my floor freshman year, there were Latinos, Blacks, Asians, and among the "white" people there were orthodox Jews, a guy who had been to Eton, a guy whose family were refugees from the junta in Greece. Coming from an environment where a Catholic person was a big deal, here I was going to movies with people from Tokyo and the South Bronx. I remember being really surprised meeting guys named Hector and Tyrone, who would look down over Morningside Heights and say, "I live right over there." There was a good will because basically you're all in gym class; you're all 18 years old.

Personal accounts such as the ones in the boxes abound, and there is much to be learned from them. But how much interaction in fact occurs? How often do students of one race truly become acquainted with students of other races? Is the idea of interaction more mythical than real, given the recognizable (and understandable) tendency of people to want to be with individuals like themselves, with whom they feel comfortable?

Knowing that it is difficult for individuals to recall past states of mind with any accuracy, we framed a series of questions that approached this topic in as fact-based a manner as possible by asking what people did rather than what they felt. We asked respondents whether, when in college, they had known individuals who were different from themselves—who were from other regions or other countries, from much wealthier or much poorer families, who were much more liberal or much more conservative in their political views. We also asked whether the respondents had known students of other races. In an effort to prod memories and also to learn in which campus settings students met one another, we asked the respondents to mark whether they had met other students in dormitories and residences, in classes, by playing sports and participating in other extracurricular activities, or by socializing. Finally, in an effort to "raise the bar" and allow for a finer-grained analysis, we asked the respondents if they had "known *well* two or more students" in the indicated categories. We did not attempt to define what knowing someone "well" meant, but rather hoped that our wording would encourage those being surveyed to ponder their answer, rather than merely give what might have been an easy and expected response.

The Overall Extent of Interaction

We found, first, that the overall level of reported interaction is extremely high at the C&B schools. While some '89 matriculants no doubt spent disproportionate amounts of time with classmates who were like themselves (hockey players rooming with hockey players, black students eating at predominantly black tables, conservative students enjoying the camaraderie of a conservative political club, and so on), the large majority of students of all kinds "knew *well*" two or more individuals in many different categories. This high degree of interaction was found among black and white students alike (top panel of Figure 8.3).

We see, for example, that nine out of ten of these former students knew well two or more individuals who were from different regions of the United States; that roughly half knew well two or more students from a different country (interestingly, more blacks than whites came to know foreign students); that roughly 70 percent of both blacks and whites knew well two or more students from a much wealthier family—a finding that reflects the presence in these schools of distinctly above-average numbers of students from wealthy families—and that over half of both blacks and whites knew well two or more individuals who were from a much poorer family, two or more who were politically much more conservative, and two or more who were politically much more liberal.

The bottom panel of Figure 8.3 charts the interactions of black and white matriculants across racial groups. In spite of the fact that black students constituted less than 10 percent of all '89 matriculants at each of the C&B schools (with a single exception, where black students made up 12 percent of the entering cohort), 56 percent of white respondents knew well two or more black students. Moreover, less than one in ten knew no black students or did not answer the question. Nearly nine out of ten black students (88 percent) knew well two or more white students. So, if there was self-segregation on these campuses—as there surely was in some instances and during "some part of the day"—the walls between subgroups were highly porous.

We are reminded of a black student at Princeton in the early 1970s who asked plaintively why some people had trouble understanding his decision to serve *both* as head of the Black Student Association on campus and

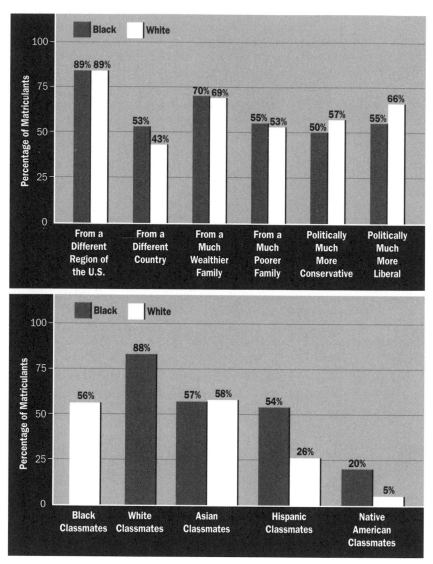

Figure 8.3. Percentage of Matriculants Who Knew Well Two or More People with Selected Characteristics, by Race, 1989 Entering Cohort

Source: College and Beyond.

as head of the predominantly white undergraduate student government (and to have a white roommate). He didn't see why anyone would expect him to have to choose between spending a substantial amount of time with his fellow black students and spending an equally substantial amount of time with white friends. From his perspective, the two kinds of activities (and the two sets of friends) were highly complementary.

The bottom of Figure 8.3 also shows interactions by black and white students with other racial groups. The degree of interaction with Asian students was about the same for white and black matriculants, and white matriculants were about as likely to know well two or more Asian students as they were to know well two or more black students—a result that is somewhat surprising in light of the fact that Asian students were much more numerous on these campuses than black students. Interactions with Hispanic and Native American students were more common among black matriculants than among white matriculants, which may reflect some sense of a common bond. The full matrix of interracial interactions is shown in Table 8.3. The smaller number of Hispanic students on these campuses, and the very small number of Native American students, may explain why the degree of interaction with them tends to be somewhat lower.

Before examining factors that influence the degree of interaction, we can report on where students of various races most commonly met each other. "Class or study groups" and "same dorm or roommate" were mentioned most frequently by those who knew well two or more individuals from another race, with roughly 93 percent of blacks and 80 percent of whites citing each of these two venues. Approximately two-thirds of both blacks and whites met individuals of the other racial group at "parties or other social activities" and through "extracurricular activities" (including

TABLE 8.3

Percentage of Matriculants Who Knew Well Two or More Students of Another Race by Respondent's Race, 1989 Entering Cohort

| Respondent's race | *Percentage who knew well two or more students who were:* | | | | |
	Black	Hispanic	Asian	Native American	White
Black		54	57	20	88
Hispanic	68		69	15	93
Asian	57	38		8	92
Native American	62	30	45		73
White	56	26	58	5	

Source: College and Beyond.

athletics). Residential colleges and universities presume that each of these activities can lead to educationally beneficial interactions, and these simple tabulations suggest that they are correct.[10]

Factors Influencing the Extent of Interaction

If one thing is clear from the evidence presented in Chapter 2, it is that adopting a strict race-neutral standard in admissions would reduce dramatically the enrollment of black students at the C&B schools. One obvious question (among many others) is what effect a large reduction in numbers of black matriculants would have on interactions among the diverse racial groups on these campuses.

We are able to examine empirically the relation between the share of the student body that was black and the fraction of the white student body that came to know well two or more black students (Figure 8.4). While many other variables are at work, there is an unmistakable association between the relative size of the black student population and the degree of interaction between white and black students. As one would expect on the basis of simple numerical probabilities, the degree of interaction varies directly with the black share of enrollment.[11]

If we arbitrarily divide the schools into those above and below a 5 percent level of black enrollment (in the fall of 1989), we find that 60 percent of whites at schools above the 5 percent cutoff knew well two or more black students, whereas 49 percent of white students at schools with less than 5 percent black enrollment had this same degree of interaction. Because of the small number of institutional observations (and the presence of outliers), it is risky to put too much weight on the slope of a simple linear regression line of the kind shown in the figure. Still, the regression line has the advantage of using all the data that we have, and it implies that a drop in the share of black enrollment from, say, 8 percent to 4 percent could be expected to reduce the percentage of white ma-

[10] All of these statistics are for students who reported that they had known well two or more individuals who were black (or white, in the case of black respondents). The patterns are the same for students who reported that they knew well only one student from other racial groups.

[11] The relative size of the black student population also correlates positively with white perceptions of the contribution that college made to their ability to get along across racial lines and with the degree of emphasis that white students believe their colleges should place on enrolling a racially/ethnically diverse student population—though not with the importance attached to getting along (see Appendix Table D.8.1).

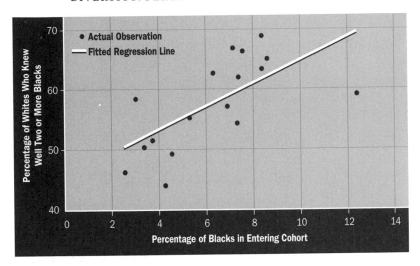

Figure 8.4. Percentage of Blacks in Entering Cohort by Percentage of White Matriculants Who Knew Well Two or More Blacks in College, 1989 Entering Cohort

Source: College and Beyond.

triculants who knew well two or more black students from 61 percent to 53 percent.[12]

These data do not permit us to estimate directly the likely effects of the even greater drop in black enrollment that would probably result from race-neutral admissions, but there is another way to think about the possible effects of such a policy. We can look at the extent of the interaction that occurs now between white students and the much smaller number of Native American students on these campuses and in the most selective professional schools. And, as we saw in Table 8.3, the interaction between whites and Native American students at the undergraduate level was very limited, presumably because their numbers were so small. We do not mean to suggest that even large reductions in the number of black students would drive the degree of interaction to zero (there were interracial contacts, after all, in earlier days, when there were very, very few

[12] This estimate of the relationship between the percentage of black students on a campus and the frequency of interaction between black and white students is consistent with the results obtained from a logistic regression used to predict the likelihood that a white student would know well two or more black students. The percentage of black students in the cohort was a highly significant predictor in a multivariate regression that also included SAT scores, socioeconomic status, school selectivity, and gender.

black students on these campuses). But the drop in interactions would certainly be substantial.

There are obvious reasons for expecting the proportion of black students in the class to affect the degree of interaction with white students. A larger number of black students of course provides a more significant presence in the dorms and in the classrooms. But there are also considerations that take us beyond the pure statistical likelihood of chance meetings. A greater number of black students almost certainly ensures more variety within the black student population; there will be more individuals with their own special interests, personal histories, hobbies, and so on—all the factors that send people of all kinds off on their own trajectories and that often bring people together regardless of race or culture. For this reason, greater diversity within the minority community tends to create a greater number of potential avenues of interaction. A second effect brought about by the presence of larger numbers of an outnumbered population is a decreased tendency to "close ranks." As the number of black students on campus increases, there is likely to be less of a sense of strong "outsider" group affiliation that inhibits movements into the mainstream.[13]

Other factors beyond the size of the minority group affect interactions. A number of the points above the regression line shown in Figure 8.4 (which identify schools at which the actual degree of interaction was higher than one would have predicted on the basis simply of the black share of enrollment) represent schools with exceptionally high average SAT scores. If we divide the C&B schools into strata defined by average SAT scores, we find that 64 percent of white matriculants at the SEL-1 schools (where average SATs were 1300 or more) knew well two or more black students, as compared with 54 percent at the SEL-2 schools (which had average SATs between 1150 and 1299), and 53 percent at the SEL-3 schools (which had average SATs below 1150).[14]

If we turn the question around, and ask about the percentage of black matriculants who knew well two or more white students, the pattern is perfectly congruous: 92 percent of black students at the SEL-1 schools

---

[13] There may also be more interaction—out of necessity—at the bottom end of the numerical scale. When there are very few black students, those who are enrolled have no option but to interact with white classmates. Thus, we suspect that the relationship between relative numbers of black students and interactions with white classmates may be U-shaped.

[14] Students at SEL-1 schools also reported higher levels of interaction along *every* dimension of diversity listed on the questionnaire (geographical origin, political views, wealth, and so on). Most of the factors suggested below as possible explanations for the higher levels of racial interaction (excepting the racial composition of the student body) are probably relevant in explaining all of these kinds of interactions.

reported knowing well two or more white students, as compared with 87 percent at the SEL-2 schools and 87 percent at the SEL-3 schools. In short, those campuses that are the most highly selective in their admissions, and that attract students with the highest SAT scores, are also the schools in which there is the most black-white interaction. These are also the schools that would lose the largest numbers of black matriculants if a strict race-neutral admissions policy were adopted.

The positive correlation between school selectivity and the degree of interracial interaction is confirmed when we use a multivariate regression to control for the influence of other variables. There were relatively more black students at the SEL-1 schools (6.7 percent of all matriculants as compared with 6.2 percent at the SEL-2 schools and 6.0 percent at the SEL-3 schools), but the higher level of interaction at the SEL-1 schools is not explained by these modest differences. When we control for the relative number of black students, SAT scores, and socioeconomic status, the differences in levels of interaction by school selectivity are increased, not reduced. The adjusted estimates of the percentages of white students knowing well two or more black students are 66 percent at the SEL-1 schools, 58 percent at the SEL-2 schools, and 53 percent at the SEL-3 schools. These differences are highly significant.

What accounts for the distinctly above-average levels of interracial interaction at the most selective schools? According to our data this pattern is *not* a function of discernible pre-collegiate differences in either the personality traits of the students who enrolled in each set of schools or the racial make-up of the secondary schools from which the students came.[15]

When we link the self-ratings obtained from the CIRP pre-collegiate surveys with the C&B data on the same students' in-college interactions, we obtain findings that seem at first glance to offer an explanation. Specifically, high pre-collegiate self-ratings on certain personal traits are positively associated with a greater likelihood of white students' knowing well two or more blacks in college. Those who rated themselves highest on leadership, popularity, and social self-confidence were most likely to have extensive interaction with blacks (Appendix Table D.8.2). This finding makes eminently good sense, since individuals who are outgoing and confident are more likely to interact with people in general as well as more likely to be willing to step outside their usual circle of friends. But are these personal skills—which predispose some students to high levels

---

[15] In this section we are considering only the interactions of whites with blacks. Since virtually all of the black respondents reported knowing two or more whites well, it is difficult statistically to isolate factors that lead to a greater or lesser degree of interaction with their white classmates.

of interaction—the reason why the white students at the most selective institutions have the most extensive interactions with black students? The answer appears to be no. While the predictive power of these personality traits holds within each set of C&B schools grouped by selectivity, these types of students are *not* present in appreciably larger numbers at the most selective schools.[16]

The next question we asked was whether students who had gone to a racially diverse high school were more or less inclined to get to know people of other races—the assumption being that earlier experience of going to school with people of different races might make it easier to cross racial divides in college. Using ETS data, we were able to identify the racial mix of each respondent's high school and determine whether students from more racially mixed secondary schools were more likely to interact with students of other races in college. Once again, there is a clear non-finding: for the 1989 matriculants, the racial mix of the high school played no role in predicting their college interactions. Whether their secondary school had no black students or was over 10 percent black, the patterns of subsequent interaction were the same.[17]

While other characteristics of the students themselves, that we have failed to measure, may be part of the explanation, we think that the higher level of interaction at the most selective schools is mainly attributable to attributes of campus life at these institutions. The most selective institutions have more financial resources and lower enrollments in relation to resources than do the other schools. These attributes mean that classes tend to be smaller and that more institutionally provided support is available for residential life and extracurricular activities. These institutional investments are intended, at least in part, to encourage the very kinds of interactions we are discussing.

Presumed Effects of College Interactions

It is impossible to separate the effects of interactions in college from the effects of a multitude of other forces that also shape subsequent attitudes, events, and experiences. At the most basic level, however, we

[16] See Appendix Table D.8.3; the mean self-ratings are remarkably similar across the SEL-1, SEL-2, and SEL-3 groupings.

[17] Specifically, the percentage of white students who got to know well two or more black students was 55 percent for students who attended secondary schools with less than 1 percent blacks in attendance, 56 percent for students from secondary schools with 1–3 percent blacks, 57 percent for students from secondary schools with 4–10 percent blacks, and 54 percent for students from secondary schools with more than 10 percent blacks.

would expect white students who had extensive interactions with black students in college to have the most extensive interactions across racial lines after college. And that is precisely what we find. Of white '89 matriculants who knew well two or more black students in college, 72 percent reported that they had also gotten to know well two or more blacks after leaving college; in contrast, less than half of white C&B matriculants who knew fewer than 2 blacks in college had a similar level of interaction after leaving college. It is possible—even likely—that the same attitudes and predilections that led to extensive interactions in college carried over and influenced the kinds of friendships and associations formed after college. But it is also possible—and also likely—that more frequent interactions in college made it easier to get along with people of other races after college.

A black member of the '76 cohort at the University of Michigan:

I grew up in Detroit, and I really had no contact with any white people at all. My first roommate as a freshman was a white guy and we became very good friends, which was a surprise to me. . . . He was just a decent guy. Now, I'm the only black guy in this office, and I don't have any problem with that. But that goes back to my having had this guy as a roommate. A lot of [black] people wouldn't be able to function in this situation, just like a lot of white people wouldn't be able to function in an all black company. But if you get exposed to [people of different races] at a younger age, then I think a lot of the problems could be alleviated. I don't want my children to be constantly worried about race. I think they've got better things to do.

Experiences in graduate and professional schools also appear to have shaped later patterns of interaction. Those white graduates who went on to earn professional degrees in law, medicine, and business were appreciably more likely than the other '89 matriculants to report extensive interactions with members of other races after college: 66 percent of the holders of professional degrees reported that they knew well two or more blacks, as compared with 59 percent of the rest of the cohort. And of those matriculants with professional degrees who knew well two or more blacks, 81 percent said that they had met at least one of these people in graduate school. This latter statistic is, we believe, a direct reflection of the diversity of student bodies in professional schools. Efforts to increase diversity were important, these data suggest, in encouraging interactions across racial lines at a time when important professional skills were being acquired.

The extent of post-college interaction in the workplace is also impressive. Of those '89 white matriculants who earned BAs and then took jobs, 61 percent reported having gotten to know well two or more blacks. While this percentage is lower than the corresponding percentage among those who earned advanced degrees, we regard the 61 percent figure as evidence that recent graduates are moving into positions that permit—and probably require—far more interaction across racial lines than anyone would have imagined twenty-five years earlier.

In light of these patterns, it is not surprising that those white matriculants who knew well two or more black students in college attach considerably more importance to getting along well with members of other races than do their classmates who had fewer interactions. Sixty percent of those who had the most interactions with black students in college rated getting along with others of different races as "very important," compared with 51 percent of those who knew one black student well and 40 percent of those who did not feel that they knew any black students well. Causation surely flows in both directions (since those students who see value in interaction are most likely to get to know a variety of classmates). Still, it seems reasonable to believe that experiences with black students enhanced to at least some degree the appreciation of white students for the importance of "getting along" with people of different races and cultures.

As a final possible indicator of the value attached to interactions, we can report that the white matriculants who knew well two or more black students were much more satisfied with the whole of their college experience than were those with fewer interactions. Roughly 70 percent of the white matriculants with the most extensive interactions across racial lines reported that they were "very satisfied" with their undergraduate education, compared with 62 percent of those having some interactions and 55 percent of those with no substantial interactions with individuals of other races. No doubt this pattern is due in substantial part to the tendency of outgoing students, who like to meet lots of different people, to enjoy all of their experiences more. But testimony by individual students suggests that the presence of a diverse student population was certainly a "plus" factor in how they felt about their undergraduate education.

Taken together, these findings suggest strongly that large numbers of the C&B matriculants have taken advantage of the learning opportunities offered by the more diverse student populations present on these campuses in recent years.[18]

---

[18] In reading an early draft of this chapter, Richard Light of Harvard was struck by the consistency of the overall pattern, and he reminded us (in personal correspondence) that it is this "accumulation of evidence" across many subgroups and many campuses that is

ASSESSMENTS OF INSTITUTIONAL POLICIES AND PRIORITIES

By the '76 White Respondents

The '76 C&B matriculants had been out of college roughly fifteen years when they were asked to complete the C&B survey. Many of them had gone on to graduate and professional schools before working in a wide variety of occupations and participating in an equally wide variety of civic and public arenas. Their experiences after college give them useful perspectives—not only on the kinds of skills and capacities that they learned in college (which we reported in the previous chapter), but also on the policies and priorities of the colleges and universities that they attended.

To elicit their views on these questions, we asked, first, how much emphasis they believe their undergraduate school *currently* places on

- faculty research
- teaching undergraduates
- a broad liberal arts education
- intercollegiate athletics
- other extracurricular activities
- a commitment to intellectual freedom
- residential life
- alumni/ae concerns
- a racially/ethnically diverse student body

As a companion question, we then asked, "How much emphasis do you think your undergraduate school *should* place on each of these areas?"[19]

The views of the white '76 matriculants on the current emphases of their undergraduate institutions are summarized in Figure 8.5 (top panel). There is wide agreement that these colleges currently place the most emphasis on the strictly academic/intellectual pursuits (the cluster of four bars on the left side of the figure), with faculty research leading the way with an average score of 4.3 on a five-point scale (where 5 indicates "a great deal" of emphasis and 1 indicates "very little or none"). All of the other academic/intellectual aspects of college life also received ratings of at least 4.0, the score assigned to "teaching undergraduates." The other areas of activity—residential life, extracurricular activities, alumni/ae concerns, and intercollegiate athletics—received ratings that

---

particularly convincing—more convincing than any one result looked at in isolation.

[19] See Appendix A, questions A14 and A14a, for the exact format of this part of the questionnaire.

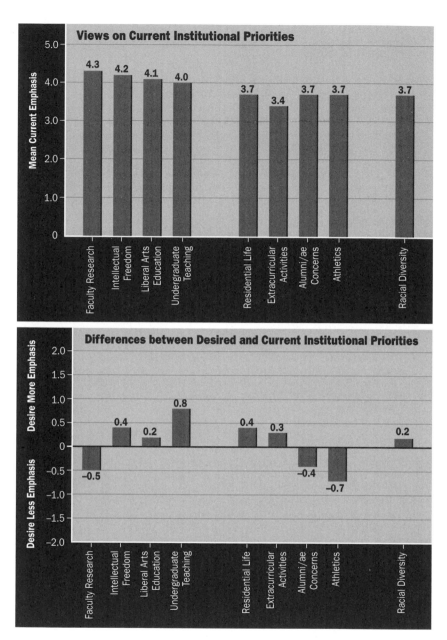

Figure 8.5. White Matriculants' Views on Institutional Priorities, 1976 Entering Cohort

Source: College and Beyond.

Notes: Respondents were asked to rate both the current emphasis they believed their undergraduate schools placed on each priority and how much emphasis they thought their schools *should* place on each priority. The responses to both questions were on a scale of 1 ("very little/none") to 5 ("a great deal"). The upper panel of the figure shows the mean ratings of current emphasis, and the lower panel shows the mean differences between responses to the two questions.

ranged from 3.4 to 3.7. Enrolling "a racially/ethnically diverse student body" received essentially this same degree of emphasis, as reflected in its score of 3.7.

Comparing the perceptions of *current* emphasis with what these respondents thought their colleges *should* emphasize is especially revealing (Figure 8.5, bottom panel). In general, there is a considerable degree of satisfaction with current emphases, which is what we would expect given the high degree of satisfaction with college reported in the previous chapter. Nonetheless, there are notable differences among the areas. The '76 matriculants favor reducing the emphasis on faculty research and increasing—markedly—the emphasis on undergraduate teaching, which they perceive to be high already, but not high enough.[20] No one who has talked extensively with undergraduate students or alumni/ae will be at all surprised by either of those results!

The matriculants also favor increasing somewhat the emphasis given to the quality of residential life and to extracurricular activities other than athletics. On the other hand, they think that too much emphasis is placed on alumni/ae concerns. They would like to reduce appreciably the emphasis that these colleges and universities give to intercollegiate athletics, and it seems mildly ironic that the magnitude of this difference between "current emphasis" and what the emphasis "should be" is similar to the corresponding difference for faculty research.[21]

This is the context in which to place the views expressed concerning racial and ethnic diversity. White '76 matriculants favor giving somewhat more emphasis, not less, to racial and ethnic diversity. The score of 3.7 for "current emphasis" should be compared with a score of 3.9 for what the "emphasis should be," and the difference of 0.2 points (Figure 8.5, bot-

[20] We estimate the degree to which respondents wanted their colleges to give more or less emphasis to each item by noting the *difference* between the average scores given when they were asked for their perceptions of current emphasis and the average scores given when they were asked what the emphasis should be. For example, "teaching undergraduates" received an average score of 4.0 for "current emphasis" and an average score of 4.8 for "emphasis should be"—which results in a difference of +0.8 and the conclusion that the respondents would like to have more emphasis placed in that area.

[21] There are some predictable differences in responses to these questions between those who attended universities and those who attended liberal arts colleges. For example, respondents who went to universities believe that their schools place more emphasis on research and less on teaching than do respondents who attended liberal arts colleges. While there are also some differences between the two groups of respondents in that degree of emphasis they think *should* be given to these activities, these differences are smaller. In general, there is a somewhat closer congruence between perceptions of "current" and "desired" emphasis among those who went to liberal arts colleges than among those who were undergraduates at research universities.

tom panel), is more or less in line with (for example) views expressed concerning the emphasis that should be given to a broad liberal arts education.

It is possible to pinpoint more precisely the degree to which the white '76 matriculants believe that their schools should be putting more emphasis on racial/ethnic diversity. The respondents can be divided into three groups. The first group consists of those whose estimates of the current emphasis given to diversity match precisely the degree of emphasis that they feel should be given to diversity. (That is, these are the individuals who assigned, say, a 3 to the "current-emphasis-is" question and a 3 to the "emphasis-should-be" question—or a 1 or 2, or 4 or 5, to both questions.) This is the group that believes that the "right amount" of emphasis is now being given to diversity; it includes those who think little emphasis is being given and who favor giving little emphasis, those who think a lot of emphasis is being given and should be given, and those who are in the middle on both counts. The percentages of responses in this "right amount" category are shown in the shaded cells in Table 8.4. The second group consists of those who think that "too little emphasis is being given to diversity," and it includes, for example, people who checked a 3 on the scale indicating the degree of emphasis they believe is being given now and either a 4 or a 5 on the scale indicating

TABLE 8.4

White Matriculants' Views on Institutional Emphasis on Racial Diversity, 1976 Entering Cohort

	Desired Emphasis (percent)					
	None				Great Deal	
View on Current Emphasis	1	2	3	4	5	Total
1 (none)	0.2	0.2	0.6	0.9	1.1	3.0
2	0.3	0.8	3.2	3.3	2.8	10.5
3	0.5	1.2	6.9	9.3	6.1	23.9
4	0.6	1.5	6.9	14.7	11.2	34.8
5 (great deal)	0.8	1.1	3.5	5.6	16.8	27.8
Total	2.4	4.8	21.0	33.8	38.0	100.0

Too little emphasis (sum of cells to right of diagonal)	38.8
Right amount of emphasis (sum of shaded diagonal cells)	39.4
Too much emphasis (sum of cells to the left of diagonal)	21.9

Source: College and Beyond. Totals may not equal sums of rows or columns due to rounding.

how much emphasis they think should be given to diversity. These responses are shown in the cells to the right of the shaded cells in Table 8.4. Finally, the third group consists of those who think that "too much emphasis" is being given to diversity, and their responses are shown in the cells to the left of the shaded ones.

When we add up the responses in each of the three broad categories, we find that 39 percent of all white '76 matriculants think that their colleges are giving the "right amount" of emphasis to racial/ethnic diversity, 39 percent think that "too little emphasis" is being given, and 22 percent think that there is "too much emphasis" on diversity. These findings reveal widespread support by white matriculants for institutional efforts to enroll a diverse student body—support that comes from those who "were there" and thus are able to base judgments on first-hand experience, as well as on their broader sense of what constitutes sound policy.

By the '76 Black Respondents

In every respect but one, the views of the black '76 matriculants on institutional priorities are extraordinarily similar to the views of their white classmates (compare Figures 8.5 and 8.6). The orderings of activities and priorities by the black matriculants—both their estimates of current emphasis and their desires for shifts in emphasis—are so close to the orderings by the white matriculants that the two sets of figures are almost indistinguishable. In company with their white classmates, the black matriculants want less emphasis to be placed on faculty research, more emphasis on undergraduate teaching, more emphasis on residential life and on extracurricular activities, and less emphasis on athletics and alumni/ae concerns (though the black respondents are more sympathetic to paying attention to alumni/ae concerns than their white classmates). Black matriculants attach the same value to a broad liberal arts education as their white classmates. One clear conclusion is that these two groups of matriculants give every indication of having attended very much the same institutions, and of having taken away with them very similar priorities and educational values.

But there is one marked exception to these generalizations. The black matriculants think that their colleges and universities currently give appreciably less emphasis to racial/ethnic diversity in the student body than do their white classmates—the respective scores assigned to "current emphasis" on diversity are 3.7 among the white '76 matriculants and 3.0 among the black matriculants. While 3.0 is not a low score in any absolute sense—it is, after all, roughly the midpoint of the 1–5 range—it is the

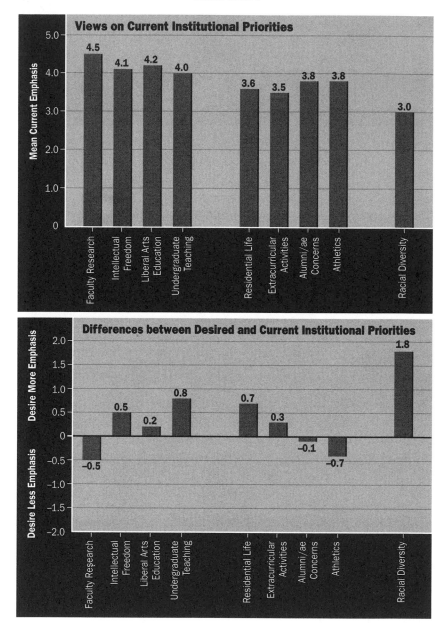

Figure 8.6. Black Matriculants' Views on Institutional Priorities, 1976 Entering
Cohort

Source: College and Beyond.
Notes: See notes to Figure 8.5.

lowest score given to any area. The difference between the white and black matriculants in these assessments can be seen even more clearly if we move beyond average scores and look at the distributions: at the top of the scale, 11 percent of all blacks and 28 percent of all whites believe that their schools attach a "great deal" of emphasis to racial/ethnic diversity; conversely, at the bottom of the scale, 34 percent of black matriculants and 14 percent of whites believe that their schools attach relatively little emphasis to diversity (as measured by the assignment of scores of 1 or 2 on the five-point scale).

Differences are even greater when we consider the answers given to the question of "what-the-emphasis-should-be." While both whites and blacks are in favor of increasing the emphasis on diversity, the black matriculants assign this objective a far greater importance than their white classmates, ranking it just below "teaching undergraduates" in overall importance. For black respondents, the difference between what they perceive to be the current emphasis and what they think the emphasis should be is so large (1.8 points, using the average scores) that it dwarfs all other differences.

It is hardly surprising that a group for so long discouraged from attending these institutions should feel strongly that considerable effort should now be devoted to including more people like them. In interpreting this result, one should take care to place it in the context of other findings from the survey. We saw earlier that the black matriculants are very pleased with the education they received at these schools and are more persuaded than their white matriculants that their undergraduate experience made important contributions to their ability to get along across racial lines. The strong interest of the black respondents in encouraging their schools to make greater efforts to attract talented minority students may not only reflect the importance they attach to race-sensitive admissions but also, in part, their sense of how important their undergraduate education was to them.

By All '89 Respondents—With a Look Back at the '51 Cohort

The '89 matriculants were asked to answer these same questions about current and desired emphases on various aspects of college life, and the overall pattern of their responses was so similar to the pattern for the '76 matriculants that it is unnecessary to comment in any detail on the results. (The data are summarized in full in Appendix Table D.8.4.) The main point to stress is the "sameness" of these two sets of survey results— for both black and white matriculants.

There is, however, a difference between the responses of the '76 and '89 matriculants in their assessments of the emphasis given to racial/

ethnic diversity. While both white and black '89 matriculants think that their schools give more "current emphasis" to diversity than did their '76 counterparts, the '89 black matriculants assign an *appreciably* higher score to current emphasis on diversity than do the '76 black matriculants: 3.4 versus 3.0 (the white score, in contrast, goes up only from 3.7 to 3.8). We interpret this change as indicating that, with the passage of time, more black matriculants have come to believe that their schools are serious about increasing the diversity of their student bodies. As in the case of the '76 matriculants, both white and black '89 matriculants think that their schools should put even more emphasis on diversity than they believe is placed there at present.

If we look back in time and compare the responses to these same questions of white matriculants who entered the C&B schools in the fall of 1951, we learn, first, that these people, who are now in their mid-sixties, have a rather different sense of the degree of emphasis that their colleges place on diversity today. Nearly half (45 percent) of them think that these schools currently place "a very great deal" of emphasis on racial and ethnic diversity, as compared with 28 percent in the '76 cohort and 36 percent in the '89 cohort. In the early 1950s, there were, of course, *very* few minority students on these campuses, and the contrast between "then and now" may account in part for this difference in perceptions. The views of the '51 cohort on what emphasis *should* be given to diversity are of even greater interest. Fewer members of this generation might be expected to favor placing a great deal of emphasis on diversity, and that expectation is borne out by the data. But what is surprising is how small the differences are: 41 percent of the white members of the '51 cohort believe that a great deal of emphasis should be placed on enrolling a racially and ethnically diverse student body, as compared with 37 percent in the '76 cohort and 48 percent in the '89 cohort. While roughly a third of the members of this earlier cohort believe that the C&B schools currently place too much emphasis on diversity, almost half feel that the current emphasis is about right, and 17 percent would prefer even more emphasis.[22]

In Relation to Type of School, Student SAT Scores, and School of Choice

Examination of these same responses by type of school attended shows mainly the relentless consistency of the patterns described above: they hold for both '76 and '89 cohorts at every type of school in the C&B

---

[22] These percentages are based on the same kind of analysis that is reported in Table D.8.4 for the '76 cohort.

universe, whether the schools are classified by degree of selectivity, as liberal arts colleges or universities, or as public or private institutions. The matriculants who attended liberal arts colleges are inclined to give slightly more emphasis to diversity than those who attended universities, and the black and white students at the most selective private institutions are most inclined to think that their schools are placing considerable emphasis on diversity—and to approve of such efforts. But these distinctions are relatively modest. It is the close congruence of the broad set of findings across institutional types that deserves to be highlighted (Appendix Table D.8.5).

Another question concerns the relationship between attitudes toward diversity and the student's own SAT score on entering college. White students with relatively modest SAT scores might be expected to be both more conscious of efforts to promote racial/ethnic diversity and more concerned about them, since they could conceivably see themselves (and others like them) as "at risk" if greater efforts are made to enroll minority students.

The data tell an entirely different story (Figure 8.7). Across the broad middle range of test scores, there is absolutely no difference by SAT level in the percentage of white students who believe that "a great deal" of emphasis should be given to diversity. The desired emphasis on diversity is slightly lower among the highest-testing white matriculants. And the desired emphasis on racial/ethnic diversity is higher, not lower, among the '76 white matriculants with the lowest SAT scores. These students came from somewhat more modest socioeconomic backgrounds, and for that and other reasons, they may be more inclined to identify with minority students than are white students with the very strongest academic preparations. (This interpretation is supported by the logistic regression used to predict the likelihood that white students will know well two or more black classmates. The likelihood of interracial interaction was negatively correlated with high SAT scores and positively correlated with lower socioeconomic status.) There is certainly *no* evidence that the white students with modest academic credentials have felt threatened by diversity. Again the desired emphasis on the part of the '89 cohort on diversity is remarkably similar to the views of the '76 cohort.

Among the '76 black matriculants, there is a clear relationship between an individual's SAT scores and the desired degree of emphasis on diversity: the lower the person's SAT score, the more likely the student is to want the school to place "a great deal" of emphasis on diversity. This is exactly as expected, since it is, of course, those minority students with modest test scores who have presumably benefited most from efforts to increase diversity. This same general pattern holds for the black '89 matriculants, but the desired emphasis on diversity is essentially constant below the 1300 level of SAT scores.

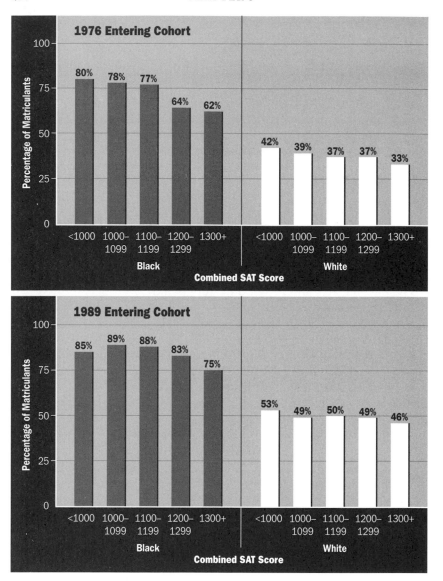

Figure 8.7. Percentage of Matriculants Favoring "a Great Deal" of Emphasis on Racial Diversity, by SAT Score and Race, 1976 and 1989 Entering Cohorts

Source: College and Beyond.

If there is a group of matriculants whom one might expect, a priori, to be most likely to resent efforts to increase racial/ethnic diversity, it is presumably those white matriculants who were not admitted to their first-choice schools and might, justly or unjustly, blame this disappointment on the admission of minority students. We are able to test this proposition directly, since we know from the survey which of the white respon-

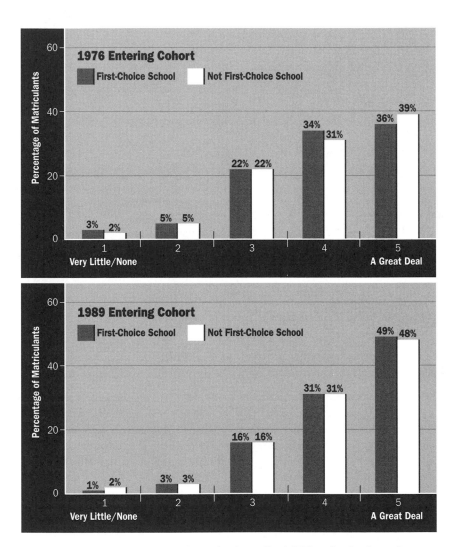

Figure 8.8. Desired Institutional Emphasis on Racial Diversity, by Attendance at First-Choice School, 1976 and 1989 Entering Cohorts

Source: College and Beyond.

dents did, or did not, attend their first-choice schools. Among the '76 matriculants, the attitudes of the two sets of respondents toward racial/ethnic diversity on campus are as nearly identical as one could possibly imagine them to be (top panel of Figure 8.8). Those who did not attend their first-choice schools are as supportive of efforts to enroll a racially/ethnically diverse student body as are those who were more successful in the admissions process.

The '89 white matriculants might have been expected to be more sensitive on this score, since they have had less time to get over whatever hurt they felt when rejected by their first choice schools; also, the issues surrounding race-sensitive admissions have been more widely discussed in recent years. These considerations notwithstanding, the same conclusion holds true for the '89 white matriculants as for the '76 matriculants: there is absolutely no difference in attitudes toward diversity between those who attended their first-choice schools and those who did not (lower panel of Figure 8.8).

Many educators and knowledgeable observers—from Thomas Jefferson and Henry Adams to present-day college presidents—have emphasized how much students can learn from going to college with a diverse group of classmates. Students seem to agree. Surveys of college seniors regularly reveal that they feel they learn almost as much from their fellow undergraduates as they do from their textbooks and professors.

For more than one-third of a century, virtually every selective college and professional school has affirmed the value of race as an important aspect of diversity in broadening the education of students. Most recently, the presidents of the sixty-two member institutions of the Association of American Universities issued a unanimous statement declaring:

> We believe that our students benefit significantly from education that takes place within a diverse setting. In the course of their university education, our students encounter and learn from others who have backgrounds and characteristics very different from their own. As we seek to prepare students for life in the twenty-first century, the educational value of such encounters will become more important, not less, than in the past.

Beyond periodic statements of this kind, however, there has been very little effort to determine systematically whether the educational effects of racial diversity actually fulfill the expectations of university leaders.

In the absence of hard evidence, public impressions of the impact of racial diversity have been largely dependent on reports published in the news media. Since harmonious relations among human beings are rarely newsworthy, it is not surprising that most media stories about race on campus have emphasized racial demonstrations, confrontations with university administrators, and tensions erupting between black and white undergraduates. Student demands and inflated rhetoric have drowned out the more humdrum daily interactions that take place among students of all races and backgrounds.

In this environment, it is not surprising that critics have begun to question just how positive racial diversity has been for the education of students. Some skeptics have expressed doubts about the existence of any benefits and have appropriately asked, Where's the evidence? Others have gone further, suggesting that racial incidents on campus reveal that diversity achieved through race-sensitive admissions can actually lead to tension and misunderstanding of a harmful sort. Thus, in their recent book, *America in Black and White,* Stephan and Abigail Thernstrom observe:

> The university had wanted to make minority students feel at home. But with the dramatic increase in minority numbers and with the creation of ethnic theme houses, the level of minority student discomfort actually rose. With more minority students in this environment came more interracial tension—especially tension between whites and blacks. . . . A widely reported incident in September 1988 made that abundantly clear. In the wake of an argument over black lineage, two intoxicated white students defaced a Beethoven poster in such a way as to make the composer look black. The action took place in Ujamaa, the African-American residential house, and subsequently provoked a number of racially ugly meetings and a flyer on which the word "niggers" was scrawled by unknown actors. The scrawl was unfairly attributed to the students who had altered the Beethoven drawing, and thus they quickly became victims themselves—blamed for acts they didn't commit. Anti-white leaflets began to appear, most of them urging an all-black dorm, and pins were jammed into the photographed faces of white students on a picture board.[23]

In the course of this study, we have heard many comments and personal accounts from individual students of all races that paint a very different and more positive picture of the effects of racial diversity on university campuses. But such testimony, however eloquent, is no more convincing in and of itself than reports of racial incidents in providing a solid empirical basis for assessing the impact of diversity on the development of students. At this point, such an accounting is overdue. A sense of the educational value of diversity led Justice Powell in the *Bakke* case to affirm the continued use of race in admissions decisions. Writing in 1976, he was willing to rely on the statements of university officials. Valuable as

---

[23] Thernstrom and Thernstrom 1997, pp. 386–87.

such declarations are, the time has come, after twenty years, to test them against the views and impressions of those who have actually experienced racial diversity first-hand.

The findings in this chapter have been presented in an effort to provide such an accounting. As one would expect, our survey contains a variety of opinions. Overall, however, there is no mistaking the predominantly favorable impression that students of all races share about the value of diversity in contributing to their education.

These positive responses in no way contradict the existence of many problems and tensions, which are part of the process of bringing students of different races to live and work together. The incidents that critics describe are real. Moreover, every dean knows that beyond the highly publicized racial disputes that occasionally flare up on campus, countless smaller episodes continually take place that illustrate the problems of learning to live with people different from oneself. White students frequently try, sometimes clumsily and patronizingly, to reach out to black classmates, only to be rebuffed; blacks are snubbed by white dormmates, or even greeted occasionally with racial insults pasted on their doors.

Occurrences of this sort have to be placed in a proper educational perspective. Many encounters between students of different races can be unpleasant and hurtful. But if the experience of racial diversity on campus were all kindness and understanding, the college experience would not resemble real life, and little true learning would take place. Unfortunate as such incidents may seem, it is often through racial slights, misunderstandings, and disagreements that minds are opened and the understanding of differences enlarged. Every experienced administrator who has tried to find ways to increase racial tolerance knows that most students will discuss the subject honestly and openly with students of other races only after some unpleasant incident has made the subject impossible to ignore. In this sense, the growth in tolerance and understanding described in this chapter has occurred not in spite of racial incidents and tensions but to no small degree *because* of them. One Wellesley student's recollection of the riots in Los Angeles following the Rodney King verdict (see box) illustrates the point.

A white woman in the '89 cohort at Wellesley:

During the Rodney King riots, a lot of the black students, including my roommate, really wanted to go to Ethos (the black women's house). And she looked at me and said: "I can't look at white people right now. I'm sorry, I like you, I love you, you're my roommate, you're my friend, but I need to absent myself." So she went over to this house with her other African American friends. And at the time it took me a lot of time to understand it and I think a lot of the white students were bewildered. And we had a speakout in the senate. That was when I began to understand that sometimes you have to go back to people who are like you to gain strength to deal with the fact that the world is hostile to people who are like you. . . . It made sense.

The ultimate test of diversity as an educational policy, therefore, is not whether episodes of friction and misunderstanding occur, but what students think of their total experience after traveling the sometimes bumpy road toward greater tolerance and understanding. On this score, the findings discussed in this chapter speak for themselves. Of the many thousands of former matriculants who responded to our survey, the vast majority believe that going to college with a diverse body of fellow students made a valuable contribution to their education and personal development. There is overwhelming support for the proposition that the progress made over the last thirty years in achieving greater diversity is to be prized, not devalued.

CHAPTER 9

Informing the Debate

THE PURPOSE of this study has been to build a firmer foundation of fact on which to conduct the on-going debate about the race-sensitive admissions policies employed by almost all selective colleges and professional schools in the United States. Throughout, our aim has been to convey a more accurate picture of the long and complicated process—more akin to movement along a river than to a smooth passage through a pipeline—by which young people are educated, and then pursue careers and assume responsibilities in their communities. Having explored the contours of the river in some detail, we can now point out how our findings bear upon the arguments commonly made on both sides of the controversy. Of course, information alone cannot resolve all of the issues, since many of them involve differences of values or legal interpretation. Nevertheless, facts often help to confirm some arguments and undermine others. In what ways, then, can the results of this study clarify and advance a debate that has become so heated, so predictable, and yet so inconclusive?

ASSESSING THE PERFORMANCE OF MINORITY STUDENTS

The data assembled in this volume should dispel any impression that the abilities and performance of the minority students admitted to selective colleges and universities have been disappointing. On the contrary, our findings contain abundant evidence that these minority students had strong academic credentials when they entered college, that they graduated in large numbers, and that they have done very well after leaving college.

In our intensive study of applications to five selective colleges, more than 75 percent of the black applicants had higher math SAT scores than the national average for white test-takers, and 73 percent had higher verbal SAT scores. Qualifications of black matriculants have improved dramatically: at the SEL-1 colleges and universities, the percentage with combined SAT scores over 1100 rose from 50 percent for the '76 entering cohort to 73 percent for the '89 cohort. Minority students enter selective colleges with test scores and high school grades substantially below those of most of their classmates. Nevertheless, this gap does not prove that they are deficient by any national standard; rather, it reflects the extraordinary quality of the white and Asian applicants who have been attracted to leading institutions in ever greater numbers.

Of the black students who matriculated in 1989 at the twenty-eight selective colleges in the C&B database, 75 percent graduated from the college they first entered within six years, and another 4 percent transferred and graduated from some other college within this same period. These figures are far above the averages for all NCAA Division I schools, not only for blacks (of whom only 40 percent graduated from their first school) but also for whites (of whom 59 percent graduated). Graduation rates for black students from professional schools are even more impressive. At leading schools of law, business, and medicine, approximately 90 percent of black students complete their studies successfully.

Our research also documents the success of black College and Beyond graduates after they finished college. They were more than five times as likely as all black college graduates nationwide to earn professional degrees or PhDs. Moreover, they were as likely as their white classmates to receive degrees in law, business, or medicine.[1] The attainment of graduate and professional degrees has led large numbers of black graduates into highly productive careers.

Twenty years after entering college, black men who graduated from these selective colleges earned an average of $82,000—*twice* the average earnings of all black men with BAs nationwide; black women graduates of C&B schools earned an average of $58,500—80 percent more than the average earnings of all black women with BAs (see Figure 6.8; these estimates of average annual earnings are for all graduates, not just full-time workers). Earnings for black 1976 matriculants at C&B schools were higher than the average earnings of the "A" students of all races (the top 11 percent of all students in our national control group) who entered colleges nationwide in the same year.

In addition to their economic success, C&B black matriculants have been extensively involved in a wide range of civic and community activities. According to our survey, 1976 black matriculants at selective colleges, especially men, subsequently participated at a higher rate than their white classmates in community and civic undertakings. Black men

---

[1] We also found that impressionistic reports about black students failing to fulfill their educational aspirations were both partially accurate (because the black C&B population entered college with much higher degree attainment goals than those of their white classmates) and misleading (because, in the end, equal percentages of black and white students were attaining advanced degrees, including the most sought after graduate and professional degrees).

in this sample are also much more likely than whites to hold leadership positions in civic and community organizations, especially those involving social service, youth, and school-related activities. These findings appear to bear out the assumption of selective institutions that minority students have unusual opportunities to make valuable contributions to their communities and the society. Even more encouraging is the evident willingness of these matriculants to accept such responsibilities.

By any standard, then, the achievements of the black matriculants have been impressive. Even so, critics continue to challenge the central premises of race-sensitive admissions. Some question whether admitting minority applicants to selective colleges actually benefits these students either in college or in later life. Some dispute the claims of educators that diversity on campus increases racial understanding. Still others argue that any admissions policy that attaches special weight to the race of an applicant aggravates tensions in the larger society.

DO RACE-SENSITIVE ADMISSIONS POLICIES HARM THE INTENDED BENEFICIARIES?

Several opponents of race-sensitive admissions claim that such policies harm the minority students they purport to help. This broad line of argument needs to be examined along a number of dimensions, ranging from the academic performance and graduation rates of black matriculants to their record in obtaining advanced degrees and their subsequent careers.

Graduation Rates

Stephan and Abigail Thernstrom assert correctly that "the college dropout rate for black students is at least 50 percent higher than it is for whites."[2] They then add that "misguided affirmative action policies may have done a lot to create the problem. . . . The point is simple. When students are given a preference in admission because of their race or some other extraneous characteristic, it means that they are jumping into a competition for which their academic achievements do not qualify them and many find it hard to keep up."[3]

In fact, the data show that "the point" is anything but "simple." If race-sensitive admissions in selective colleges lead to more dropouts, it is more than a little puzzling that in our sample of twenty-eight selective schools,

---

[2] Thernstrom and Thernstrom 1997, pp. 405–6.
[3] Ibid., p. 406.

none had a dropout rate for minority students anywhere near as high as the average attrition of 60 percent for black students at all NCAA Division I colleges, many of which are not selective. Black dropout rates are low at all of the C&B schools (averaging just over 25 percent); moreover, *the more selective the college attended, the lower the black dropout rate.*

Since the C&B schools differ among themselves in their degree of selectivity, as measured by the average SAT score of their students, we were able to perform a much more conclusive test of the claim that black students will do better at schools with average SAT scores more nearly like their own (sometimes called the "fit" hypothesis). We compared how black students *with equivalent test scores* performed at colleges where the average score for all students was much higher than their own scores and at colleges where their scores were more like the average score for the entire school (where the "fit" between the black student and the school was presumably better). The results are completely contrary to the claims made by the critics. The higher the average SAT score of the college in question, the *higher* the graduation rate of black students *within each SAT interval* (including the intervals for students with only very modest SAT scores). More generally, when we predicted graduation rates for black students within the C&B universe on an "other things equal" basis (holding constant socioeconomic status, high school grades and test scores), we found that graduation rates were highest for those who attended the most selective schools.[4] We also found that black students who did drop out were not embittered or demoralized, as some critics of race-sensitive admissions have alleged. On the contrary, of the relatively small number of black students who dropped out of the most selective schools, a surprisingly large percentage were "very satisfied" with their college experience—indeed, black dropouts from these schools were more likely than white dropouts to be "very satisfied."

A broader test of the effect of race-sensitive admissions on graduation rates was carried out by Thomas Kane. His results confirm our findings. When Kane compared the graduation rates of black students who attended a much wider range of schools, including some that were not selective at all, he found that blacks admitted to selective schools graduated at significantly *higher* rates than blacks with equivalent test scores,

---

[4] Some critics claim that graduation rates for minorities are overstated because they are more likely than other students to choose allegedly "soft" majors such as Afro-American studies. One of these critics, Lino Graglia, suggests that: "When the specially admitted students discover . . . that they cannot compete with their classmates, no matter how hard they try, . . . they will insist . . . that the game be changed. Thus are born demands for black studies and multiculturalism" (1993, p. 135). Our data indicate that, in general, minority students chose the same array of traditional majors as non-minority students. This tendency seems to have become even more pronounced in recent years.

high school grades, and family backgrounds who attended non-selective schools.[5]

Incentive Effects

Another complaint sometimes made against race-sensitive admissions practices is that they weaken the incentives for minority students to work hard at their studies because they know that they can gain admission to selective colleges and professional schools with lower grades than those of their white classmates. As Jay B. Howd has put it: "At the college and university level, minorities cannot be expected to focus on maximizing their own efforts when rewarded for factors independent of those efforts."[6]

We know of no way to measure directly the effect that race-sensitive admissions policies have on the motivation of minority students. Nevertheless, various findings in our study cast doubt on claims such as Howd's. Even under race-sensitive admissions programs, black applicants have little reason to be complacent about their chances of entering a selective institution. Our analysis of admissions patterns in five selective colleges reveals that less than half of the black applicants were admitted. Approximately 25 percent of blacks with SAT scores between 1350 and 1500 were rejected, although such scores put these students in the top 2 percent of all black test-takers in the nation. In the face of such facts, no sensible black applicant could afford to relax and assume that entry to a selective college would come easily.

Much the same is true of the incentives facing students during their college and professional school years. Most minority students enter selective colleges aspiring to earn a graduate degree, often in law, business or medicine, but competition for admission to such programs is very keen for all applicants. Using national data, Linda Wightman has found that more than half of all black applicants fail to gain acceptance to any law school.[7] The pattern is the same for black applicants to medical school.[8] Once admitted to a professional school, minority students presumably know that the leading law firms and corporations do not seriously consider employing students below the top half, or top third, or even top tenth of the class. It is at least as hard for blacks and Hispanics to achieve these levels of academic achievement as it is for their white classmates, and they presumably focus their efforts accordingly.

---

[5] Kane (forthcoming).

[6] Howd 1992, p. 451.

[7] Wightman 1997, p. 16.

[8] Association of American Medical Colleges 1996, p. 69.

The general tenor of these conclusions is supported by other findings. Our results show that black students in the top third of the class are more likely to earn an advanced degree than students in the middle third of their class, while the latter are much more likely than students in the bottom third to obtain such degrees. Moreover, college grades are clearly and positively correlated with subsequent earnings for blacks and whites alike. In fact, blacks appear to pay an even greater financial penalty than whites for receiving low grades in college. For these reasons, there would seem to be ample incentives for blacks and other members of minority groups to do as well as they can academically, both during their undergraduate years and in the course of their graduate and professional studies.

Demoralization and Its Possible Effect on Grades

According to some opponents of race-sensitive admissions, there is yet another way in which such policies harm the very students they purport to help. Knowing that they have been admitted to selective institutions with lower grade averages and test scores than their white classmates, minority students may become demoralized. According to Shelby Steele, "The effect of preferential treatment—the lowering of normal standards to increase black representation—puts blacks at war with an expanding realm of debilitating doubt, so that the doubt itself becomes an unrecognized preoccupation that undermines their ability to perform, especially in integrated situations."[9]

Yet if minority students were truly demoralized, one would expect that they would be less likely than whites to succeed in graduate and professional schools, less likely to appreciate their college experience, and less inclined to report that they benefited intellectually by having attended a selective school. None of these results appears in our data. Blacks are just as likely as whites to attend the most demanding, competitive professional schools. They are as likely as their white classmates to become doctors, lawyers, and business executives. They are just as appreciative of their college experience, and they tend to believe that they gained more from their undergraduate experience than do their white classmates. Also, contrary to what critics who support the "fit" hypothesis would predict, we found that the more selective the college attended, the *more* satisfied black matriculants were with their college experience—a pattern that holds even for those students with relatively low test scores. As we observed in Chapter 7, if black students admitted to the most academically demanding schools suffered as a result, they certainly don't seem to know it.

[9] Steele 1994, p. 42.

There is one kind of evidence, however, that can be read to support claims of demoralization or diminished motivation. A number of studies (including our own) have found that minority students, especially blacks, perform at significantly lower levels academically than their test scores would predict.[10] Indeed, our data show that underperformance plays a slightly greater role than test scores in explaining why the average rank in class for black students is lower than that of whites. Why does this underperformance occur? Could it reflect some form of demoralization resulting from a realization on the part of minority students that they are less qualified academically than their white classmates?

Some experimental evidence does suggest that vulnerability to racial stereotypes helps to explain underperformance by minority students.[11] If this is so, however, it seems likely that such stereotypes are less a product of race-sensitive admissions policies than of deep-seated prejudices that long antedate these policies and still exist in our society. Another piece of evidence from our study casts further doubt on the hypothesis that *admissions policies* account for underperformance. At least at the SEL-1 schools, underperformance appears to increase as the test scores of black students rise. In other words, it is the *most* academically talented black students (who could be admitted even under a race-blind policy, and who have the *least* reason to feel outmatched intellectually) who perform the furthest below their potential.

Perhaps the fairest conclusion to draw is that no one has yet shown definitively why minority students tend to underperform, although various plausible theories have been advanced to account for this phenomenon (see Chapter 3). Whatever the explanation, several schools appear to have succeeded in creating programs that have substantially eliminated the problem, even in such academically demanding fields as science and engineering. The success of these programs suggests that the existence of academic underperformance does not justify doing away with race-sensitive admissions. Rather, this evidence illustrates what is

---

[10] For an early statement of this proposition, see Klitgaard (1985, pp. 116–31). More recent evidence is cited in Chapter 3 of this study. These findings have an important bearing on the argument made by some proponents of race-sensitive admissions that differences in test scores should be disregarded because standardized tests, such as the SAT, are culturally biased against members of minority groups. To buttress this claim, opponents of these tests often call attention to particular questions that seem to call for familiarity with words or phrases that have little or no currency in poor urban neighborhoods or minority communities. We have no desire to enter the dense thickets of controversy surrounding the use of standardized tests. What is clear is that the evidence cited here shows that, far from being biased *against* minority students, standardized admissions tests consistently predict higher levels of academic performance than most blacks actually achieve.

[11] See, e.g., Steele and Aronson (forthcoming).

possible when schools institute programs designed explicitly to bring the academic achievements of minority students fully in line with their academic potential.

Do Race-Sensitive Admissions Policies Harm Minority Graduates in Their Careers?

Another argument against race-sensitive admissions challenges the claim that colleges and universities can help build stronger leadership for the professions and for society by educating more minority students. According to some critics, race-sensitive policies actually hamper the progress of minorities later in life by inducing them to attend schools for which they were not really qualified and perpetuating the stigma that they are not really as able as whites. In Charles Murray's words, "That is the evil of preferential treatment. It perpetuates the impression of inferiority."[12] By this reasoning, minority graduates would have achieved more in the long run had they attended colleges with students of comparable ability, where they could have performed better academically and avoided any impression that their academic credentials were inferior to those of whites.

Looking at patterns of graduate study provides an initial test of this argument. Our study of the interrelationships among SAT scores, college grades, and attainment of advanced degrees (Chapter 4) shows that black matriculants at the most selective schools, including those with modest SAT scores and only average grades in college, were highly successful in earning advanced degrees, far more successful than black men and women in the sample of those who graduated from all four-year institutions. Judged by this criterion, black students who attended the most academically competitive schools do not appear to have been penalized.

Detailed examination of job histories and a considerable amount of earnings data leads to the same conclusion. We find that black graduates of the most selective colleges have done very well indeed in the marketplace. Among black women and black men with modest SAT scores, those who enrolled at the most selective C&B schools had appreciably higher average earnings than those who attended less selective C&B schools; other things being equal, black matriculants appear to have been well advised to attend the most selective school that would admit them. Moreover, black C&B graduates as a group earned far more than other black college graduates. Similarly, Thomas Kane, using national

[12] Murray 1994, p. 207.

data, has shown that black students who graduate from selective colleges and universities earn more than blacks with similar grades, test scores, and family backgrounds who attended non-selective institutions.[13]

At the same time, black men earn less than white men who graduate from the same selective institutions (a pattern that does not exist for women). In fact, black men earn less than their white classmates even when they have the same grades, college majors, and socioeconomic backgrounds. This persistent earnings gap is troubling,[14] but we have no reason to believe that it has been exacerbated by race-sensitive admissions. On the contrary, the evidence summarized above shows that black matriculants do better in their careers, both absolutely and relative to whites, the more competitive the academic environment. This finding holds within the C&B universe of schools, even after controlling for other variables, and it also holds when we compare C&B graduates as a group with all black graduates nationwide.[15]

One can readily explain why blacks have benefited from attending academically selective colleges and universities. Apart from the quality of education they provide, selective institutions give employers, graduate schools, and others a better-known, more credible basis for judging the capacities of their students. A law school admissions office, a corporate recruiter, or a hospital seeking residents will all give greater weight to transcripts from a selective institution because they are likely to have a clearer sense of what such records mean. The more selective the institution, the more reliance employers tend to place on its records of performance ("grade inflation" notwithstanding).

At the same time, race-sensitive admissions policies result in costs as well as benefits for at least some of the intended beneficiaries. The very existence of a process that gives explicit consideration to race can raise

---

[13] Kane (forthcoming).

[14] It is beyond the scope of this study to analyze the underlying causes of this pattern. There is little doubt that racial discrimination still exists to some degree in the United States and that blacks and Hispanics often suffer the burdens of prejudice and stereotyping on the part of some people with whom they have contact in their working lives. However, Glenn Loury has argued that "imperfect information may be a more pervasive and intractable cause of racial discrimination today than is behavior based on agents' purported distaste for associating with blacks" (1998, p. 1).

[15] These consistent findings rebut assertions that "racial preferences in college admissions systematically mismatch talent and opportunity. . . . Many beneficiaries of preferences have no hope of excelling against their supposed peers, struggle hard merely to keep up, get discouraged, perform poorly by their own standards, and even drop out of school altogether. The modestly successful middle class career they would have enjoyed if they had attended a first-rate second-class school is lost to them, perhaps forever" (O'Sullivan 1998, p. 41).

questions about the true abilities of even the most talented minority students ("stigmatize" them, some would say). The possibility of such costs is one reason why selective institutions have been reluctant to talk about the degree of preference given black students. Such reticence may be due in part to the desire to avoid criticism and controversy, but some of these institutions may also be concerned that the standing of black students in the eyes of white classmates would be lowered if differences in test scores and high school grades were publicized. More than a few black students unquestionably suffer some degree of discomfort from being beneficiaries of the admissions process (as do some athletes and legacies, even though they are generally less "visible"). It is for this reason that many high-achieving black graduates continue to seek reassurance that they have "made it on their own" and why they complain when job interviewers presume that even the most outstanding black student may well have been helped in this way.

The judgment that has to be made is whether, at the end of the day, it is worth accepting these costs, which are all too real, in exchange for the benefits received. The black matriculants themselves—who are, after all, the ones most affected by any stigmatizing effects—are presumably in the best position to weigh the pros and cons. The C&B survey data are unequivocal. Black students do not seem to *think* they have been harmed as a result of attending selective colleges with race-sensitive policies. Were it otherwise, one would suppose that the ablest black students would be resentful of these policies and the colleges that adopted them. Yet our results show that 75 percent of 1989 black matriculants who scored over 1300 on their SATs believe that their college should place "a great deal" of emphasis on racial diversity. Similarly, 77 percent of black graduates who ranked in the top third of their class were "*very* satisfied" with their undergraduate educational experience; only 1 percent were dissatisfied.

The charge that race-sensitive admissions stigmatize blacks, and therefore hurt them rather than help them, is an argument that critics frequently make against affirmative action programs of all kinds. If it were true, those who suffered from the stigma would presumably be the ones most likely to feel its effects. Yet Jennifer Hochschild reports that successful blacks do not feel that they have suffered: "Overall, 55 percent of well-off blacks think affirmative action programs help recipients, and only 4 percent think such programs hurt recipients."[16] In the eyes of those best positioned to know, any putative costs of race-based policies have been overwhelmed by the benefits gained through enhanced access to excellent educational opportunities.

[16] Hochschild 1995, p. 101.

DOES DIVERSITY INCREASE RACIAL UNDERSTANDING?

Still another group of arguments holds that racial diversity, when it is deliberately achieved through an institution's admissions policies, does not necessarily enhance the value of education or contribute to the tolerance and understanding of students. Indeed, some critics suggest that such policies help to poison race relations within the larger society.

Effects of Diversity on Campus Life

In their most modest form, these arguments merely note that little or no persuasive evidence exists to show that a racially diverse student body has positive effects on the education of students. We would agree that such evidence has heretofore been limited; this deficiency was an important reason for conducting this study. Most critics of race-sensitive admissions, however, go further, suggesting that the diversity produced by race-sensitive admissions policies tends to aggravate racial tensions and to result in a segregation of blacks and whites that increases hostility and misunderstanding among students.

Stephan and Abigail Thernstrom have made this argument most forcefully. Pointing to racial problems at Stanford University, they observed: "[Stanford] not only instituted an aggressive affirmative action admissions policy; it trained students in racial sensitivity, created dorms with an ethnic 'theme,' and drastically altered the curriculum to meet minority demands. The result was more minorities on campus; a curriculum that included courses on such subjects as black hair; frustrated, bewildered white students; and blacks who felt more alienated, more culturally black, and perhaps more hostile to whites than when they arrived."[17] From this account of a particular period of racial tension on a single campus, the authors proceed to draw much more sweeping conclusions: "The result is precisely that resegregation of campus life so clearly and appallingly on display at Stanford—but certainly not confined to that school. Without an admissions system involving racial preferences, the picture would be quite different."[18]

What light does our study throw on arguments of this kind? Clearly, racial incidents occur periodically on many campuses; feelings occasionally run high, and administrators can make unwise decisions.[19] Such

[17] Thernstrom and Thernstrom 1997, p. 386.

[18] Ibid., p. 388.

[19] The media sometimes give a misleading impression of the prevalence of such incidents. For a critique of the evidence underlying inflated claims of racial tension on campus, see Bernstein (1994, pp. 203–10).

episodes are unfortunate. But they tend to be uncommon, and when they do occur, they sometimes serve as a catalyst to provoke greater thought and understanding among students about problems of race.[20] Rather than focus exclusively on such incidents in isolation, it is more helpful to ask what the entire undergraduate experience of diversity has contributed to those who have lived it. To this end, our surveys record what diversity in its totality has meant to some thirty thousand former students reflecting on their experience at a wide range of selective colleges during two separate periods in the past twenty-five years. These opinions sum up the entire four years of college, and hence presumably include times of racial harmony as well as episodes of tension and misunderstanding.

The results of these surveys speak very clearly and strongly to the value of racial diversity in college. A large number of both white and black respondents felt that their undergraduate experience made a significant contribution to their ability to work with and get along well with members of other races (a 4 or a 5 on a five-point scale where 5 equals "a great deal"). Moreover, in contradiction to claims that racial diversity leads to a rigid self-segregation, 56 percent of white '89 matriculants reported that at college they "knew well" at least two blacks, and 26 percent said they "knew well" at least two Hispanics, even though each of these minority groups made up less than 10 percent of the total undergraduate student body. Blacks were even more likely to know students of other races; 88 percent knew well two or more of their white classmates, and 54 percent reported being similarly well acquainted with two or more Hispanic students.

Other investigators using different methods likewise report that diversity has a number of positive effects for students. The most comprehensive of these investigations surveyed more than twenty-seven thousand students attending a wide range of colleges and tested the effects of 192 separate variables in the campus environment.[21] Of all the items examined, the extent of racial diversity and racial interaction among students turned out to be among the three most influential factors associated with increased student acceptance of other cultures, participation in community service programs, and growth in other aspects of civic responsibility. The weight of the evidence, therefore, points clearly in one direction. As educators have long surmised, racial diversity does appear to bring

[20] Forty to fifty years ago, when the '51 C&B cohort was enrolled, these campuses were free from racial friction, for the simple reason that there were too few black students on campus to allow for much conflict.

[21] Sax and Astin 1997. (See our discussion in Chapter 8 of the limitations of all studies of this kind.)

about positive results in increasing the mutual understanding of whites and minority students, enhancing their ability to live and work together successfully.

Effects on Racial Tensions in the Society

A somewhat similar argument against utilizing race in the admissions process maintains that efforts of any kind that treat people differently because of their race only tend to increase racial animosities in the larger society. Claims of this kind are largely conjectural, since there is no way of knowing what the effect might be on racial tensions in the United States if colleges and universities did *not* practice race-sensitive admissions. Current admissions policies unquestionably create resentment in some families. But it seems at least as plausible to suppose that racial tensions will increase even more if the vast majority of top jobs in government, business, and the professions continue to be held by whites, while one-third of the population is composed of blacks and Hispanics who are largely relegated to less remunerative, less influential positions.

Paul Sniderman and Edward Carmines have reported some experimental evidence to the effect that affirmative action does produce negative reactions among whites that carry over to affect attitudes toward blacks generally.[22] This phenomenon was neither proved nor disproved by our study, since we were not directly concerned with the society as a whole but only with the effects of race-sensitive admissions policies on students at selective institutions. What we did do, however, was to test whether students turned down by their first-choice selective college were more opposed to racial diversity than their classmates, on the assumption that individuals rejected by the college they most wanted to attend would be especially likely to believe that racial diversity should be emphasized less. Our results indicated no tendency of this sort whatsoever.

It is also worth noting that racial attitudes in the society as a whole have continued to improve during the twenty-five to thirty years in which race-sensitive admissions have been widely practiced.[23] Whites may oppose certain policies to deal with racial problems, such as school busing, minority set-asides, or even race-sensitive admissions policies. On questions of racial discrimination, living in integrated neighborhoods, interracial dating, and intermarriage, however, whites have become more tolerant, not less so, since 1970. One can always argue that progress would have been even faster had colleges not made special efforts to diversify their student bodies. Such claims cannot easily be proved or disproved. But if

[22] Sniderman and Carmines 1997, ch. 2.
[23] Schuman et al. 1997; Page and Shapiro 1992, pp. 68–81.

race-sensitive admissions were truly poisoning race relations, one might expect to see some evidence of growing disaffection among the white alumni/ae who were most exposed to these policies and most likely to have experienced them when they applied to graduate school. In fact, the very opposite is true. Support for an institutional emphasis on enrolling a diverse student body is high among both black and white alumni/ae of selective colleges and appears to have grown steadily, not diminished, from the class beginning college in 1951 to the class that enrolled in 1976 and, finally, to the class that entered thirteen years later.

IS THERE A BETTER WAY?

The final cluster of arguments—apart from those involving issues of "fairness" and "merit," which we discuss at length in the concluding chapter—comes from representatives on both sides of the affirmative action debate who claim that there are ways of admitting students to achieve a racially diverse student body that do not accord different treatment to members of different races in the admissions process.

More Vigorous Recruitment

An early argument along these lines was expressed in 1972 by Thomas Sowell of the Hoover Institute, who declared that selective institutions were simply not trying hard enough to find qualified minority applicants. In his words, "The belief that there is no substantial pool of capable black students might be understandable if the various colleges, foundations and special programs were seeking the academically ablest black students they could possibly find and were failing to turn up what they were looking for. In fact, however, their recruiting efforts are seldom directed toward ferreting out the most academically accomplished black students and many are explicitly *not* looking for any such thing."[24]

Whether or not this statement was accurate when made, it is almost certainly no longer valid. Professional school and college admissions offices can and regularly do obtain reports of every student in the country who meets whatever academic profile the admissions officers select. Thus a law school can write to the Law School Admissions Council and obtain the names of every black student in the United States with a college grade point average over 3.25 and an admissions test score above 130. A college can obtain from the Educational Testing Service a similar printout containing the names of all minority students with, say, SAT scores above

[24] Sowell 1972, pp. 133–34.

1100 and high school grade point averages over 3.0. Admissions officers regularly use these lists to contact promising minority students by mail or by phone and to schedule recruiting visits to high schools and colleges where such candidates are regularly found. Because of such lists, together with the extensive efforts made by most selective institutions to recruit minority candidates, it is highly doubtful that any significant number of black and Hispanic students who are qualified by conventional criteria are overlooked by selective colleges and universities.

Considering Class Rather Than Race

Another argument frequently advanced by participants in the debate over race-sensitive admissions is that universities could attract a suitably diverse class without taking account of race if they simply gave preference to applicants from economically disadvantaged families regardless of race. Such a policy would be based on the generally accepted notion that young people from economically deprived backgrounds have greater obstacles to overcome than do students who grow up in more comfortable circumstances. Because blacks and Hispanics are much more heavily represented among the poor than they are in the population as a whole, proponents argue that a policy based on economic class will automatically result in a significant number of minority students. In the words of Richard Kahlenberg, "Class-based affirmative action is a remedy to the moral and political thicket of affirmative action, a way of meeting the goals racial preferences seek to achieve while avoiding the problems racial preferences create."[25]

Almost every selective institution is committed to the principle that talented students from all income groups should be able to attend regardless of ability to pay the tuition. Indeed, colleges and professional schools make great efforts to act on this principle by raising as much money as they can for scholarships and other forms of financial aid. But it is most unlikely that shifting from race-sensitive to class-based admissions would allow institutions to admit student bodies nearly as racially diverse as they are today. Admitting genuinely poor students is very costly, since such students have few if any resources of their own. As a practical matter, therefore, most selective institutions could not find enough additional financial aid to increase the number of poor students by more than a limited amount. But even if such an approach could be paid for, it would add little to minority student enrollments, because children from poor black and Hispanic families make up less than half of all poor children

---

[25] Kahlenberg 1996, p. xii. For an opposing point of view, see Malamud 1996.

and are much less likely than poor whites to excel in school. As we saw in Chapter 2, Kane found that among all students from families with incomes under $20,000 *who also finished in the top tenth of their high school class,* only one in six is black or Hispanic.

Shifting from race-sensitive admissions to class-based admissions, therefore, would substantially reduce the minority enrollments at selective institutions while changing dramatically their overall student profiles. Our data show that students with low socioeconomic backgrounds are less likely than students of equivalent ability from high socioeconomic backgrounds to complete their studies, attain professional or doctoral degrees, and earn high incomes. As a result, although a class-based system might reward applicants handicapped by poor schools, troubled neighborhoods, and similar burdens, it would surely hinder selective institutions in attempting to prepare the most talented minority students for eventual positions of leadership in government, business, and the professions.

Emphasizing Grades, Not Test Scores

The last suggestion for avoiding an explicitly race-sensitive admissions policy has been advanced by proponents of affirmative action. Such advocates argue that selective institutions should abandon the use of standardized tests and admit all students on the basis of their high school class rank or (in the case of graduate schools) their college class rank.[26] The Texas legislature, in the wake of the *Hopwood* decision, has adopted a variant of this approach. Under legislation passed in 1997, the state's premier public universities are required to admit the top 10 percent of seniors from every public high school in Texas; the remaining offers of admission will be based, as they have been in the past, "on applicants' grades, test scores, essays, and other academic and personal factors."[27]

---

[26] For a detailed discussion of law school admissions and the weaknesses of traditional indicia, especially the Law School Admissions Test (LSAT), see Sturm and Guinier 1996. More recently, Lani Guinier (1998, p. A25) has written in support of the Texas legislature's emphasis on high school grades rather than test scores, an approach which we discuss below.

[27] Healy 1998, p. A29. University officials are cited as expecting members of the 10-percent-cohort to receive about 43 percent of offers to freshmen. They also recognize (in personal correspondence) that it remains to be seen how many slots will actually be filled by those receiving acceptances based on class rank; since there are no limits to the number of places allotted by this policy, it is possible that over time, as the policy becomes more widely known within the state, a very large percentage of the class could be filled by this method.

It is too soon to be able to estimate the effects of this policy on the number of minority students who will attend the most selective universities in Texas and even harder to gauge the potential effects of such a policy in other locales. Nationally, we know that blacks are only half as likely as whites to finish in the top 10 percent of the high school class and less than 40 percent as likely to earn an A average.[28] However, as the article in the *Chronicle* cited earlier indicates, such a policy could give many minority students who attend high schools that are *de facto* segregated a much *better* chance of gaining admission to a premier public university than they had before.

One example given is W. H. Adamson High School in Dallas, where 86 percent of the students are Hispanic. In such situations, the actual effects of the "10 percent plan" will depend on the advice given by guidance counselors, one of whom is said to have told her seniors in the top 10 percent: "You can get into the University of Texas at Austin, but do you really want to go there? Do you feel prepared and confident enough to compete?" Another guidance counselor is quoted as warning her students to focus on "where they can graduate, not where they can attend and then feel discouraged and drop out." Also, how many minority students end up enrolling at a school like the University of Texas at Austin will depend on money, since many minority students, in particular, who rank in the top 10 percent of their class cannot afford to attend college in Austin without a state scholarship program that is either race-based itself or sufficiently generous to benefit all those from lower income families who are admitted to the leading universities. As a guidance counselor asked: "Where's the money? Many of our top kids aren't going to go someplace where they don't get a scholarship."[29]

In effect, much of the responsibility for deciding which students are capable of handling the academic work at a university such as the University of Texas at Austin has now passed from the admissions officers at the university to the guidance counselors at high schools and the prospective students themselves. The likelihood of mistakes being made, simply through lack of knowledge, lack of experience in making such determinations, and the absence of comparative data, would seem to be all too real. At the same time, other students, including minority students, who attended highly competitive high schools but did not finish in the top 10

[28] Thernstrom and Thernstrom 1997, p. 402. Presumably, selective colleges could further increase the percentage of minority students in a way that did not rely overtly on race by giving extra points to students with high GPAs from disadvantaged high schools (i.e., schools with average parental incomes below a certain level). But such strategies only underscore the inequalities *in fact* of utilizing policies of this kind.

[29] Healy 1998, p. A29.

percent of their class, may now be turned down even though they would have been admitted under the previous policy. Having failed to make the 10 percent cutoff, these students will have to compete "at large" for far fewer places even though they possess greater academic ability than many of those who were automatically admitted by virtue of their rank in class. So long as high schools differ so substantially in the academic abilities of their students and the level of difficulty of their courses, treating all applicants alike if they finished above a given high school class rank provides a spurious form of equality that is likely to damage the academic profile of the overall class of students admitted to selective institutions far more than would anything accomplished through race-sensitive admissions policies.

Incentive effects also need to be considered in thinking about the long-term consequences for teaching and learning at all levels. If so much depends on being in the top 10 percent of one's class, many high school students are likely to shy away from tough courses and concentrate even more than they do now simply on "getting good grades." There is also an incentive for parents to find some way to enroll their children in less demanding schools, where they will have a better chance of being in the top 10 percent.

Is a policy of this kind, whatever its shortcomings turn out to be, likely to end controversy over race-sensitive admissions? Some obviously hope so. As the *Chronicle* article noted: "The Texas policy's popularity among both liberal and conservative politicians—who are usually divided over affirmative action—is one of its intriguing qualities." But the article goes on to observe: "The reality, of course, is that new admissions policies create new sets of winners and losers." Already, some applicants from the most competitive high schools are saying that the policy is unfair because it doesn't take account of differences between high schools and is just "another form of affirmative action."[30] As the effects of the new procedure become clear, the debate over appearances versus realities—and over the unintended consequences of the policy—may become even more heated.

We conclude that basing admissions to academically selective institutions on any simple criterion such as being in the top 10 percent of one's high school class (or the top 3 or 4 percent, which would be the required cut-off in situations in which the competition for admission is even more intense than it is in Texas) is unlikely to be an effective substitute for race-sensitive admissions policies. On the contrary, this approach could well have the effect of lowering minority graduation rates from college and

---

[30] Ibid.

diminishing the pool of students who can compete effectively for positions of leadership in business, government, and the professions.

———————

The evidence summarized in this chapter calls into question many of the arguments most frequently made in the debate over race-sensitive admissions. Refuting such arguments, however, does not necessarily resolve the ultimate question of whether or not these admissions policies are desirable. Efforts to answer this question need to take account of the kinds of facts produced by this study. But facts alone are not sufficient for the task. Wise policy decisions require a larger view of the present and future needs of the society, the values that deserve greatest emphasis, the varied missions of leading educational institutions, and an appreciation of where responsibility for educational policy-making should reside. It is to these fundamental concerns that the final chapter is directed.

CHAPTER 10

Summing Up

> Here was a piece of river which was all down in my
> book, but I could make neither head nor tail of it;
> you understand, it was turned around. I had seen
> it when coming upstream, but I had never faced
> about to see how it looked when it was behind me.
> My heart broke again, for it was plain that I had
> got to learn this troublesome river *both* ways.
> —Mark Twain, *Life on the Mississippi*

THE "RIVER" that is the subject of this book can never be "learned" once and for all. The larger society changes, graduates of colleges and universities move from one stage of life to another, and educational institutions themselves evolve. Similarly, there is much yet to be learned about the future lives of those who have attended selective colleges and professional schools over the last thirty years. This study, then, does not purport to provide final answers to questions about race-sensitive admissions in higher education. No piece of this river can ever be considered to be "all down" in anyone's book. But we are persuaded of the value of examining each piece "*both* ways"—when "coming upstream," as students enroll in college, and "when it was behind me," as graduates go on to pursue their careers and live their lives.

So much of the current debate relies on anecdotes, assumptions about "facts," and conjectures that it is easy for those who have worked hard to increase minority enrollments to become defensive or disillusioned. It is easy, too, for black and Hispanic graduates, as well as current minority students, to be offended by what they could well regard as unjustified assaults on their competence and even their character. Some of the critics of affirmative action may also feel aggrieved, sensing that they are unjustly dismissed as Neanderthals or regarded as heartless. In short, the nature of the debate has imposed real costs on both individuals and institutions just as it has raised profound questions of educational and social policy that deserve the most careful consideration. In the face of what seems like a veritable torrent of claims and counterclaims, there is much to be said for stepping back and thinking carefully about the implications of the record to date before coming to settled conclusions.

On inspection, many of the arguments against considering race in admissions—such as allegations of unintended harm to the intended beneficiaries and enhanced racial tensions on campus—seem to us to lack substance. More generally, our data show that the overall record of accomplishment by black students after graduation has been impressive. But what more does this detailed examination of one sizable stretch of the river suggest about its future course? What wide-angle view emerges?

THE MEANING OF "MERIT"

One conclusion we have reached is that the meaning of "merit" in the admissions process must be articulated more clearly. "Merit," like "preference" and "discrimination," is a word that has taken on so much baggage we may have to re-invent it or find a substitute.

Still, it is an important and potentially valuable concept because it reminds us that we certainly do not want institutions to admit candidates who *lack* merit, however the term is defined. Most people would agree that rank favoritism (admitting a personal friend of the admissions officer, say) is inconsistent with admission "on the merits," that no one should be admitted who cannot take advantage of the educational opportunities being offered, and that using a lottery or some similar random numbers scheme to choose among applicants who are over the academic threshold is too crude an approach.

One reason why we care so much about who gets admitted "on the merits" is because, as this study confirms, admission to the kinds of selective schools included in the College and Beyond universe pays off handsomely for individuals of all races, from all backgrounds. But it is not individuals alone who gain. Substantial additional benefits accrue to society at large through the leadership and civic participation of the graduates and through the broad contributions that the schools themselves make to the goals of a democratic society. These societal benefits are a major justification for the favored tax treatment that colleges and universities enjoy and for the subsidies provided by public and private donors. The presence of these benefits also explains why these institutions do not allocate scarce places in their entering classes by the simple expedient of auctioning them off to the highest bidders. The limited number of places is an exceedingly valuable resource—valuable both to the students admitted and to the society at large—which is why admissions need to be based "on the merits."

Unfortunately, however, to say that considerations of merit should drive the admissions process is to pose questions, not answer them. There are no magical ways of automatically identifying those who merit admission on the basis of intrinsic qualities that distinguish them from all others. Test scores and grades are useful measures of the ability to do good work, but they are no more than that. They are far from infallible indicators of other qualities some might regard as intrinsic, such as a deep love of learning or a capacity for high academic achievement. Taken together, grades and scores predict only 15–20 percent of the variance among all students in academic performance and a smaller percentage among black students (see Appendix Table D.3.6). Moreover, such quantitative measures are even less useful in answering other questions relevant to the admissions process, such as predicting which applicants will contribute most in later life to their professions and their communities.[1]

Some critics believe, nevertheless, that applicants with higher grades and test scores are more deserving of admission because they presumably worked harder than those with less auspicious academic records. According to this argument, it is only "fair" to admit the students who have displayed the greatest effort. We disagree on several grounds.

To begin with, it is not clear that students who receive higher grades and test scores have necessarily worked harder in school. Grades and test scores are a reflection not only of effort but of intelligence, which in turn derives from a number of factors, such as inherited ability, family circumstances, and early upbringing, that have nothing to do with how many hours students have labored over their homework. Test scores may also be affected by the quality of teaching that applicants have received or even by knowing the best strategies for taking standardized tests, as coaching schools regularly remind students and their parents. For these reasons, it is quite likely that many applicants with good but not outstanding scores and B+ averages in high school will have worked more diligently than many other applicants with superior academic records.

More generally, selecting a class has much broader purposes than simply rewarding students who are thought to have worked especially hard. The job of the admissions staff is not, in any case, to decide who has earned a "right" to a place in the class, since we do not think that admission to a selective university is a right possessed by anyone. What admissions officers must decide is which set of applicants, *considered individually and collectively,* will take fullest advantage of what the college has to offer, contribute most to the educational process in college, and be most successful in using what they have learned for the benefit of the larger society. Admissions processes should, of course, be "fair," but "fairness" has to be understood to mean only that each individual is to be judged according to a consistent set of criteria that reflect the objectives of the college or university. Fairness should not be misinterpreted to mean that

---

[1] Martin Luther King, Jr., now regarded as one of the great orators of this century, scored in the bottom half of all test-takers on the verbal GRE (Cross and Slater 1997, p. 12).

a particular criterion has to apply—that, for example, grades and test scores must always be considered more important than other qualities and characteristics so that no student with a B average can be accepted as long as some students with As are being turned down.

Nor does fairness imply that each candidate should be judged in isolation from all others. It may be perfectly "fair" to reject an applicant because the college has already enrolled many other students very much like him or her. There are numerous analogies. When making a stew, adding an extra carrot rather than one more potato may make excellent sense—and be eminently "fair"—if there are already lots of potatoes in the pot. Similarly, good basketball teams include both excellent shooters and sturdy defenders, both point guards and centers. Diversified investment portfolios usually include some mix of stocks and bonds, and so on.

To admit "on the merits," then, is to admit by following complex rules derived from the institution's own mission and based on its own experiences educating students with different talents and backgrounds. These "rules" should not be thought of as abstract propositions to be deduced through contemplation in a Platonic cave. Nor are they rigid formulas that can be applied in a mechanical fashion. Rather, they should have the status of rough guidelines established in large part through empirical examination of the actual results achieved as a result of long experience. How many students with characteristic "x" have done well in college, contributed to the education of their fellow students, and gone on to make major contributions to society? Since different institutions operate at very different places along our metaphorical river (some placing more emphasis on research, some with deeper pools of applicants than others), the specifics of these rules should be expected to differ from one institution to another. They should also be expected to change over time as circumstances change and as institutions learn from their mistakes.

Above all, merit must be defined in light of what educational institutions are trying to accomplish. In our view, race is relevant in determining which candidates "merit" admission because taking account of race helps institutions achieve three objectives central to their mission—identifying individuals of high potential, permitting students to benefit educationally from diversity on campus, and addressing long-term societal needs.

Identifying Individuals of High Potential

An individual's race may reveal something about how that person arrived at where he or she is today—what barriers were overcome, and what the individual's prospects are for further growth. Not every member of a minority group will have had to surmount substantial obstacles. More-over, other circumstances besides race can cause "disadvantage." Thus colleges and universities should and do give special consideration to the hard-working son of a family in Appalachia or the daughter of a recent immigrant from Russia who, while obviously bright, is still struggling with the English language. But race is an important factor in its own right, given this nation's history and the evidence presented in many studies of the continuing effects of discrimination and prejudice.[2] Wishing it were otherwise does not make it otherwise. It would seem to us to be ironic indeed—and wrong—if admissions officers were permitted to consider all other factors that help them identify individuals of high potential who have had to overcome obstacles, but were proscribed from looking at an applicant's race.

Benefiting Educationally from Diversity on the Campus

Race almost always affects an individual's life experiences and perspec-tives, and thus the person's capacity to contribute to the kinds of learning through diversity that occur on campuses. This form of learning will be even more important going forward than it has been in the past. Both the growing diversity of American society and the increasing interaction with other cultures worldwide make it evident that going to school only with "the likes of oneself" will be increasingly anachronistic. The advantages of being able to understand how others think and function, to cope across racial divides, and to lead groups composed of diverse individuals are certain to increase.

To be sure, not all members of a minority group may succeed in expanding the racial understanding of other students, any more than all those who grew up on a farm or came from a remote region of the United

---

[2] One of the most compelling findings of this study is that racial gaps of all kinds remain after we have tried to control for the influences of other variables that might be expected to account for "surface" differences associated with race. We have described and discussed black-white gaps in SAT scores, socioeconomic status, high school grades, college gradua-tion rates, college rank in class, attainment of graduate and professional degrees, labor force participation, average earnings, job satisfaction, marital status, household income, civic participation, life satisfaction, and attitudes toward the importance of diversity itself. In short, on an "other things equal" basis, race is a statistically significant predictor of a wide variety of attributes, attitudes, and outcomes. People will debate long and hard, as they should, whether particular gaps reflect unmeasured differences in preparation and pre-vious opportunity, patterns of continuing discrimination, failures of one kind or another in the educational system itself, aspects of the culture of campuses and universities, individual strengths and weaknesses, and so on. But no one can deny that race continues to matter.

States can be expected to convey a special rural perspective. What does seem clear, however, is that a student body containing many different backgrounds, talents, and experiences will be a richer environment in which to develop. In this respect, minority students of all kinds can have something to offer their classmates. The black student with high grades from Andover may challenge the stereotypes of many classmates just as much as the black student from the South Bronx.

Until now, there has been little hard evidence to confirm the belief of educators in the value of diversity. Our survey data throw new light on the extent of interaction occurring on campuses today and of how positively the great majority of students regard opportunities to learn from those with different points of view, backgrounds, and experiences. Admission "on the merits" would be short-sighted if admissions officers were precluded from crediting this potential contribution to the education of all students.

Imposition of a race-neutral standard would produce very troubling results from this perspective: such a policy would reduce dramatically the proportion of black students on campus—probably shrinking their number to less than 2 percent of all matriculants at the most selective colleges and professional schools. Moreover, our examination of the application and admissions files indicates that such substantial reductions in the number of black matriculants, with attendant losses in educational opportunity for all students, would occur without leading to any appreciable improvement in the academic credentials of the remaining black students and would lead to only a modest change in the overall academic profile of the institutions.[3]

Addressing Long-Term Societal Needs

Virtually all colleges and universities seek to educate students who seem likely to become leaders and contributing members of society. Identifying such students is another essential aspect of admitting "on the merits,"

[3] While it is, of course, possible for an institution to be so committed to enrolling a diverse student population that it enrolls unprepared candidates who can be predicted to do poorly, we do not believe that this is a consequential problem today in most academically selective institutions. Three pieces of evidence are relevant: (1) the close correspondence between the academic credentials of those students who would be retrospectively rejected under a race-neutral standard and those who would be retained; (2) the modest associations (within this carefully selected population) of the test scores and high school grades of black matriculants at the C&B schools with their in-college and after-college performance; and (3) the remarkably high graduation rates of black C&B students—judged by any national standard.

and here again race is clearly relevant. There is widespread agreement that our country continues to need the help of its colleges and universities in building a society in which access to positions of leadership and responsibility is less limited by an individual's race than it is today.

The success of C&B colleges and universities in meeting this objective has been documented extensively in this study. In this final chapter, it is helpful to "look back up the river" from a slightly different vantage point. Some of the consequences of mandating a race-neutral standard of admission can be better understood by constructing a rough profile of the approximately 700 black matriculants in the '76 entering cohort at the C&B schools whom we estimate would have been rejected had such a standard been in effect. Our analysis suggests that:[4]

- Over 225 members of this group of retrospectively rejected black matriculants went on to attain professional degrees or doctorates.
- About 70 are now doctors, and roughly 60 are lawyers.
- Nearly 125 are business executives.
- Well over 300 are leaders of civic activities.
- The average earnings of the individuals in the group exceeds $71,000.
- Almost two-thirds of the group (65 percent) were *very* satisfied with their undergraduate experience.

Many of these students would have done well no matter where they went to school, and we cannot know in any precise way how their careers would have been affected as a result. But we do know that there is a statistically significant association, on an "other things equal" basis, between attendance at the most selective schools within the C&B universe and a variety of accomplishments during college and in later life. Generally speaking, the more selective the school, the more the student achieved subsequently. Also, we saw that C&B students as a group earned appreciably more money than did the subgroup of students in our national control with mostly As, which suggests that going to a C&B school conferred a considerable premium on all C&B students, and probably an especially high premium on black students. Black C&B students were

---

[4] We constructed these estimates using the simulation technique described in Chapter 2. We first estimated how many black C&B matriculants within each SAT interval would have been "bumped" from each selectivity tier of C&B schools, and then used the "average" characteristics of each of the cells to estimate the numbers of retrospectively rejected students who are now doctors, and so on. This estimation process is explained further in Appendix B. Even more black students in the '89 cohort would have been retrospectively rejected, and a similar mode of analysis suggests that many of these recent matriculants are already making a mark in graduate schools and civic activities.

also more likely than black college graduates in general to become leaders of community and social service organizations. These findings suggest that reducing the number of black matriculants at the C&B schools would almost certainly have had a decidedly negative effect on the subsequent careers of many of these students and on their contributions to civic life as well.

Even more severe effects would result from insisting on race-neutral admissions policies in professional schools. In law and medicine, all schools are selective. As a consequence, the effect of barring any consideration of race would be the exclusion of more than half of the existing minority student population from these professions. Race-neutral admissions policies would reduce the number of black students in the most selective schools of law and medicine to less than 1 percent of all students. Since major law firms and medical centers often limit their recruitment to the most selective schools, this outcome would deal a heavy blow to efforts to prepare future black leaders for the professions.

But what about the other students (most of them presumably white) who would have taken the places of these retrospectively rejected black students in selective colleges and professional schools? There is every reason to believe that they, too, would have done well, in school and afterwards, though probably not as well as the regularly admitted white students (who were, after all, preferred to them in the admissions process). Still, on the basis of the evidence in this study, the excluded white male students might have done at least as well as their retrospectively rejected black classmates, and probably even better in terms of average earnings.[5] On the other hand, fewer of the "retrospectively accepted" white women would have been employed, and those who were employed would have earned about the same amount of money as the retrospectively rejected black women. Fewer of the additional white students, women and men, would have been involved in volunteer activities, especially in leadership positions.

Would society have been better off if additional numbers of whites and

___

[5] The fact that white male C&B graduates continue to command a modestly higher level of earnings than their black classmates who graduated with the same grades, majors, and so on, is worthy of much more study. At least as intriguing is the fact that black male graduates of C&B schools earn, on average, *more than twice* as much as black graduates nationwide. In short, the C&B earnings premium is much higher for black male matriculants than for whites. This striking finding has led one commentator on our manuscript to suggest that C&B schools are underinvesting in talented black students, since the apparent value added is so high. We are reluctant to come to this strong a conclusion, since many factors need to be taken into account in explaining the differences in earnings premiums. But the extremely high black C&B premium is surely highly suggestive.

Asian Americans had been substituted for minority students in this fashion? That is the central question, and it cannot be answered by data alone.

Fundamental judgments have to be made about societal needs, values, and objectives. When a distinguished black educator visited the Mellon Foundation, he noted, with understandable pride, that his son had done brilliantly in college and was being considered for a prestigious graduate award in neuroscience. "My son," the professor said, "needs no special consideration; he is so talented that he will make it on his own." His conclusion was that we should be indifferent to whether his son or any of the white competitors got the particular fellowship in question. We agreed that, in all likelihood, all of these candidates would benefit from going to the graduate school in question and, in time, become excellent scientists or doctors. Still, one can argue with the conclusion reached by the parent. "Your son will do fine," another person present at the meeting said, "but that isn't the issue. *He may not need us, but we need him!* Why? Because there is only one of him."

That mild exaggeration notwithstanding, the relative scarcity of talented black professionals is all too real. It seemed clear to a number of us that day, and it probably seems clear to many others, that American society needs the high-achieving black graduates who will provide leadership in every walk of life. This is the position of many top officials concerned with filling key positions in government, of CEOs who affirm that they would continue their minority recruitment programs whether or not there were a legal requirement to do so, and of bar associations, medical associations, and other professional organizations that have repeatedly stressed the importance of attracting more minority members into their fields. In view of these needs, we are not indifferent to which student gets the graduate fellowship.

Neither of the authors of this study has any sympathy with quotas or any belief in mandating the proportional representation of groups of people, defined by race or any other criterion, in positions of authority. Nor do we include ourselves among those who support race-sensitive admissions as compensation for a legacy of racial discrimination.[6] We agree emphatic-

---

[6] Justice Thurgood Marshall made such an argument in the *Bakke* case in urging his colleagues on the Supreme Court to uphold the racial quotas provided by the University of California, Davis Medical School; in his view, such programs were simply a way "to remedy the effects of centuries of unequal treatment. . . . I do not believe that anyone can truly look into America's past and still find that a remedy for the effects of that past is impermissible" (438 U.S. at p. 402). Understandable as this argument may seem against a historical background of slavery and segregation, it did not prevail because the remedy is not precise enough to be entirely just in its application. Not every minority student who is admitted will

ally with the sentiment expressed by Mamphela Ramphele, vice chancellor of the University of Cape Town in South Africa, when she said: "Everyone deserves opportunity; no one deserves success."[7] But we remain persuaded that present racial disparities in outcomes are dismayingly disproportionate. At the minimum, this country needs to maintain the progress now being made in educating larger numbers of black professionals and black leaders.

Selective colleges and universities have made impressive contributions at both undergraduate and graduate levels. To take but a single illustration: since starting to admit larger numbers of black students in the late 1960s, the Harvard Law School has numbered among its black graduates more than one hundred partners in law firms, more than ninety black alumni/ae with the title of Chief Executive Officer, Vice President, or General Counsel of a corporation, more than seventy professors, at least thirty judges, two members of Congress, the mayor of a major American city, the head of the Office of Management and Budget, and an Assistant U.S. Attorney General. In this study, we have documented more systematically the accomplishments of the nearly 1,900 black '76 matriculants at the twenty-eight C&B schools, and the evidence of high achievement is overwhelming—there is no other word for it. These individuals are still in their late thirties, having entered college just over twenty years ago. We shall be very surprised if their record of achievement is not magnified many times as they gain seniority and move up various institutional ladders.[8] If, at the end of the day, the question is whether the most selective colleges and universities have succeeded in educating sizable numbers of minority students who have already achieved considerable success and seem likely in time to occupy positions of leadership throughout society, we have no problem in answering the question. Absolutely.

---

have suffered from substantial discrimination, and the excluded white and Asian applicants are rarely responsible for the racial injustices of the past and have sometimes had to struggle against considerable handicaps of their own. For these reasons, a majority of justices in the *Bakke* case rejected Marshall's reasoning, although similar arguments continue to be heard.

[7] Ramphele 1996.

[8] The widely perceived need for more black executives and professionals creates one danger that should be recognized explicitly: some black candidates may be "over-promoted" by firms or individuals too eager to "do the right thing" or even to "look good." No one benefits when this happens. Fortunately, this potential problem has been helped by the increase in the number of well-qualified black candidates and the experience gained by many institutions in judging people's abilities. The obverse problem—a reluctance to give black candidates a chance to succeed or fail in demanding positions—is probably still the more serious one.

We commented earlier on the need to make clear choices. Here is perhaps the clearest choice. Let us suppose that rejecting, on race-neutral grounds, more than half of the black students who otherwise would attend these institutions would raise the probability of acceptance for another white student from 25 percent to, say, 27 percent at the most selective colleges and universities. Would we, as a society, be better off? Considering both the educational benefits of diversity and the need to include far larger numbers of black graduates in the top ranks of the business, professional, governmental, and not-for-profit institutions that shape our society, we do not think so.[9]

How one responds to such questions depends very much, of course, on how important one thinks it is that progress continues to be made in narrowing black-white gaps in earnings and in representation in top-level positions. As the United States grows steadily more diverse, we believe that Nicholas Katzenbach and Burke Marshall are surely right in insisting that the country must continue to make determined efforts to "include blacks in the institutional framework that constitutes America's economic, political, educational and social life."[10] This goal of greater inclusiveness is important for reasons, both moral and practical, that offer all Americans the prospect of living in a society marked by more equality and racial harmony than one might otherwise anticipate.

We recognize that many opponents of race-sensitive admissions will also agree with Katzenbach and Marshall, but will argue that there are better ways of promoting inclusiveness. There is everything to be said, in our view, for addressing the underlying problems in families, neighborhoods, and primary and secondary schools that many have identified so clearly. But this is desperately difficult work, which will, at best, produce results only over a very long period of time. Meanwhile, it is important, in

---

[9] This emphasis on the consequences of rejecting race-neutral policies will seem misplaced to some of the most thoughtful critics of affirmative action, who will argue that their objection to race-based policies is an objection in principle: in their view, no one's opportunities should be narrowed, even by an iota, by reference to the individual's race. We respect this line of argument. However, we do not agree, "in principle," that colleges and universities should ignore the practical effects of one set of decisions or another when making difficult decisions about who "merits" a place in the class. The clash here is principle versus principle, not principle versus expediency. As we argued earlier in the chapter, in making admissions decisions, what is right in principle depends on how one defines the mission of the educational institution involved. For us, the missions of colleges and universities have strong educational and public policy aspects and do not consist solely of conferring benefits on particular individuals.

[10] Katzenbach and Marshall 1998, p. 45.

our view, to do what can be done to make a difference at each educational level, including colleges and graduate and professional schools.

The alternative seems to us both stark and unworthy of our country's ideals. Turning aside from efforts to help larger numbers of well-qualified blacks gain the educational advantages they will need to move steadily and confidently into the mainstream of American life could have extremely serious consequences. Here in the United States, as elsewhere in the world, visible efforts by leading educational institutions to make things better will encourage others to press on with the hard work needed to overcome the continuing effects of a legacy of unfair treatment. Leon Higginbotham spoke from the heart when, commenting on the aftermath of the *Hopwood* decision, he said, "I sometimes feel as if I am watching justice die."[11] To engender such feelings, and a consequent loss of hope on the part of many who have not attained Judge Higginbotham's status, seems a high price to pay for a tiny increase in the probability of admission for white applicants to academically selective colleges and universities.

THE IMPORTANCE OF INSTITUTIONAL AUTONOMY

Who should decide how much consideration to give to race in the admissions process? One of the great advantages of the American system of higher education is that it is highly decentralized, allowing a great deal of experimentation and adaptation to suit the varying needs of society, students, and the marketplace. Even among the relatively similar institutions included in the C&B universe, colleges and universities differ enormously in their traditions, circumstances, and priorities. Especially in considering as complex a set of issues as those we have been discussing, there is much to be said for allowing different institutions to come to different conclusions as to what is the right approach *for them*.

The risk of demonstrably foolish decisions always exists, but it is surely minimal. University faculties and administrators know that they will have to live with their mistakes, and this realization acts as a restraint on hasty, ill-conceived policies. The admissions practices of colleges and professional schools are highly visible, and there is no lack of individuals and entities ready to criticize their results.[12] Trustees have perspectives and

---

[11] Higginbotham 1998, p. 28.

[12] For example, some faculty members argue that colleges are wrong to give special weight to *any* characteristics that are not related to academic ability, such as athletic talent or legacy status. Others have sought to justify race-sensitive admissions policies on the

experiences that often lead them to challenge the judgments of academics, and all colleges and universities are dependent on external sources of support, both private and public. Life in such settings has been described by using the analogy of the fishbowl, and the current debates over race in admissions can only heighten the scrutiny given to whatever policies are followed.

As a society, we should think very carefully before reducing the authority of these institutions to make their own determinations (and occasionally their own mistakes) in an area of decision-making so closely bound up with their missions, values, and views of how best to educate students. An important reason why American higher education has become preeminent in the world is the greater willingness of the government to respect the autonomy of colleges and universities and to refrain from imposing its own judgments on what Justice Felix Frankfurter once described as "the four essential freedoms of a university—to determine for itself on academic grounds who may teach, what may be taught, how it should be taught, and who may be admitted to study."[13]

Outside intervention, whether legislative or judicial, is problematic not only philosophically but pragmatically. Educational institutions and their constituencies are capable of finding many paths toward outcomes that they desire. Closing off one path, such as direct consideration of race in the admissions process, can lead to movements down other paths that may have consequences that are both unintended and perhaps undesirable. For reasons noted in Chapter 9, we are highly skeptical of the wisdom of the approach taken by the Texas legislature in declaring all students in the top 10 percent of their high school classes eligible for admission to the state universities. California appears to have decided to spend more resources on pre-collegiate preparation of minority students and on vigorous programs of recruitment. Such programs may be entirely worthwhile, but it requires some ingenuity to conclude that they do

---

grounds that the favorable treatment of athletes and legacies establishes a precedent for taking account of factors other than test scores and grades (see Greider 1994, p. 189). We do not agree with this line of reasoning. In our view, preferences for athletes and legacies rest on grounds (presumed benefits to the institution of athletic competitions and sustained alumni/ae loyalty) sufficiently different from those relating to minority applicants that they cannot serve as a justification for race-sensitive admissions. Such preferences do serve, however, as clear examples of how an institution's conception of its own mission affects its admissions policy. Without necessarily endorsing the admissions policies practiced by all institutions toward athletes and legacies, we believe that individual institutions should have broad discretion to make judgments of this kind.

[13] Sweezy v. New Hampshire, 354 U.S. 234, 263 (1957).

not represent a form of "racial preference."[14] Class-based programs are another type of response that also, for reasons discussed at length in Chapters 2 and 9, will not have appreciable effects on racial diversity (and could also be very costly and harmful to academic standards, depending on how they are implemented).

In reflecting further on experiences in California, one strong supporter of Proposition 209 (John Yoo, an acting professor at Boalt Hall, the Berkeley law school) has been quoted as saying: "I had never looked to see what the effect of 209 would be on admissions. I didn't realize the score gaps were so huge." Other, less direct, effects also surprised Yoo:

> What I didn't realize was how entrenched the desire to have racial diversity for its own sake was in the university system, and how much pressure was going to be asserted to preserve that goal. . . . I didn't realize until Proposition 209 went into effect that affirmative action, as it was applied by the schools, allowed you to have some racial diversity and at the same time to maintain intellectual standards for the majority of your institutions. It was a form of limiting the damage. Now that you have to have race-neutral methods, if you still want to get African-Americans and Hispanics in, you have to redefine the central mission of the research university in a way that lowers standards for everybody. That's an unintended consequence of Proposition 209, and it's unfortunate.[15]

Similar arguments have been advanced by three University of Texas law professors. In a brief filed in October 1997 in the *Piscataway* case, they urged the Court to preserve existing policies for eminently practical reasons: "If affirmative action is ended, inevitable political, economic, and legal forces will pressure the great public universities to lower admission standards as far as necessary to avoid resegregation."[16] It is likewise hard to imagine private universities, such as Columbia and Vanderbilt, or private colleges such as Smith and Swarthmore, passively accepting reductions in the number of black matriculants so large that they would again seem like white enclaves in a multiracial world.

The broader point is that it is very difficult to stop people from finding a path toward a goal in which they firmly believe. Race-sensitive admis-

[14] The wording of legislation and of regulations may lead some to believe that there is a substantive difference between taking account of race in the admissions process and devising policies that will increase the number of minority applicants. To economists and others, however, both approaches have a key element in common: the disproportionate expenditure of scarce resources on a particular group. It would be better, in our view, to recognize this symmetry and decide which approach (or combination of approaches) best serves the goals of the society.

[15] Quoted in Rosen 1998, pp. 60, 62–64.

[16] Wright et al. 1997.

sions policies were adopted by colleges and universities to address what are clearly race-based problems in ways that seemed to them sound educationally. Barring these institutions from considering race directly and forthrightly is likely to bring forth ingenious efforts to minimize the consequent loss of diversity by adopting seemingly race-neutral policies that can have a wide variety of other consequences, not all of them benign. Moreover, once prohibitions are put in place, someone has to determine whether they are being respected. Judges could well confront a Hobson's choice: either to probe ever more closely into the admissions process (and quite possibly the recruitment process as well) to discover whether the institution was in fact applying a truly race-neutral standard or to accept at more or less face value a presumed equality of treatment that might be both spurious and less satisfying than the current situation from every point of view.

HOW FAST ARE WE HEADING DOWNSTREAM?

Final questions to ponder concern a longer sweep of the river. What is our ultimate objective? How much progress has been made? How far do we still have to go? Along with many others, we look forward to a day when arguments in favor of race-sensitive admissions policies will have become unnecessary. Almost everyone, on all sides of this debate, would agree that in an ideal world race would be an irrelevant consideration. As a black friend said almost thirty years ago: "Our ultimate objective should be a situation in which every individual, from every background, feels *unselfconsciously included.*"

Many who agree with Justice Blackmun's aphorism, "To get beyond racism, we must first take account of race," would be comforted if it were possible to predict, with some confidence, when that will no longer be necessary. But we do not know how to make such a prediction, and we would caution against adopting arbitrary timetables that fail to take into account how deep-rooted are the problems associated with race in America.

At the same time, it is reassuring to see, even within the C&B set of institutions, the changes that have occurred between the admission of the '76 and '89 cohorts. Over that short span of time, the average SAT scores of black matriculants at the C&B schools went up 68 points—a larger gain than that of white matriculants. The overall black graduation rate, which was already more than respectable in the '76 cohort (71 percent), rose to 79 percent. Enrollment in the most highly regarded graduate and professional schools has continued to increase. The '89 black matriculants are even more active in civic affairs (relative to their white classmates) than were the '76 black matriculants. Appreciation for the education they received and for what they learned from diversity is voiced even more strongly by the '89 cohort than by their '76 predecessors.

Whatever weight one attaches to such indicators, and to others drawn from national data, the trajectory is clear. To be sure, there have been mistakes and disappointments. There is certainly much work for colleges and universities to do in finding more effective ways to improve the academic performance of minority students. But, overall, we conclude that academically selective colleges and universities have been highly successful in using race-sensitive admissions policies to advance educational goals important to them and societal goals important to everyone. Indeed, we regard these admissions policies as an impressive example of how venerable institutions with established ways of operating can adapt to serve newly perceived needs. Progress has been made and continues to be made. We are headed downstream, even though there may still be miles to go before the river empties, finally, into the sea.

The College and Beyond Database*

THE COLLEGE AND BEYOND database was assembled by research staff at The Andrew W. Mellon Foundation between 1995 and 1997 to facilitate study of the long-term consequences of attending academically selective colleges and universities in the United States. The core database consists of two primary components: an institutional data file and a survey data file. Because of promises of confidentiality made to participating institutions and individuals, this is a "restricted access database." The core database is linked to two secondary data files provided by the College Entrance Examination Board and the Higher Education Research Institute at the University of California, Los Angeles.[1] In addition, a control group study was conducted by the National Opinion Research Center (NORC) in the spring and summer of 1996.

THE INSTITUTIONAL DATA FILE

The complete institutional data file contains admissions and transcript records of 93,660 full-time students who entered thirty-four colleges and universities in the fall of 1951, 1976, and 1989. Six institutions were not included in the research for this book and are therefore omitted from Table A.1,[2] which summarizes the number of students in the 1976 and 1989 entering cohorts at the remaining twenty-eight institutions. This latter group includes thirteen private universities, four public univer-

---

*Appendix A was prepared by Thomas I. Nygren and Stacy Berg Dale.

[1] In the text, references to the "College and Beyond database" generally encompass all of its components, including the secondary data files.

[2] Four of these institutions are historically black colleges and universities (HBCUs): Howard University, Morehouse College, Spelman College, and Xavier University of Louisiana. Analysis of the data from these four institutions was beyond the scope of this study, which is concerned only with colleges and universities that enroll substantial numbers of white students as well as minority students. Data for the other two institutions, the University of Notre Dame and Georgetown University, were incomplete when our analysis was conducted. The 1951 entering cohort is not shown in Table A.1 since this study focuses almost exclusively on the two younger cohorts; in all twenty-eight institutions, less than 1 percent of the 1951 matriculants were known to be minority students.

TABLE A.1

Entering Cohort Sizes of College and Beyond Institutions, 1976 and 1989

Institution	Size of Entering Cohort/Sample	
	1976	*1989*
Public universities		
Miami University (Ohio)	2,027	1,999
University of Michigan (Ann Arbor)	1,990	1,998
University of North Carolina (Chapel Hill)	2,000	1,998
Pennsylvania State University	1,953	3,273
All	7,970	9,268
Private universities		
Columbia University	726	1,054
Duke University	1,653	1,614
Emory University	437	1,020
Northwestern University	1,731	1,861
University of Pennsylvania	1,994	2,272
Princeton University	1,105	1,140
Rice University	633	581
Stanford University	1,567	1,532
Tufts University	1,029	1,111
Tulane University	1,346	1,512
Vanderbilt University	1,269	1,335
Washington University	1,057	1,187
Yale University	1,302	1,275
All	15,849	17,494
Coeducational liberal arts colleges		
Denison University	604	558
Hamilton College	435	392
Kenyon College	429	431
Oberlin College	748	831
Swarthmore College	337	317
Wesleyan University	567	679
Williams College	493	519
All	3,613	3,727
Women's colleges		
Barnard College	444	479
Bryn Mawr College	466	325
Smith College	773	606
Wellesley College	589	592
All	2,272	2,002
All institutions	29,704	32,491

Source: College and Beyond.

Notes: For public universities (except for Pennsylvania State University in 1989), the numbers reported represent the sample size, not the cohort size; see text for explanation. The sizes of the entering cohorts at the public universities in 1976 and 1989 were (respectively): Miami—3,324 and 3,085; Michigan—4,431 and 4,628; UNC—2,806 and 3,187; Penn State—3,760 and 3,273. For Bryn Mawr College, the 1976 entering cohort also includes matriculants who entered in 1977.

sities, four women's colleges, and seven coeducational liberal arts colleges.[3] One reason for selecting these particular institutions was the availability of data; several other institutions that had hoped to participate in the study did not have sufficiently complete records, especially for the 1951 entering cohort.

The three entering cohorts—1951, 1976, and 1989—were selected to allow researchers to track the major changes that have taken place in American higher education over the past four decades. The 1951 cohort provides a baseline reference point. By the early 1950s, veterans enrolled through the G.I. Bill had mostly passed through undergraduate colleges, but the sweeping institutional changes of the 1960s, including substantial enrollment growth at most of the C&B institutions, still lay ahead. The 1976 entering cohort was selected as a "midpoint" of the study for several reasons. By this time, the turmoil of the late 1960s and early 1970s, including the controversies associated with the Vietnam War, had largely subsided. Furthermore, most of the institutions that were going to become coeducational had done so and were enrolling substantial numbers of women. Finally, and most important from the standpoint of this study, essentially all of the C&B institutions had already embarked on determined efforts to diversify their student bodies and were enrolling sizable numbers of minority students. The 1989 entering cohort was chosen because, when the study began in 1995, it represented the most recent set of matriculants who would have had at least six years to complete college.

At all institutions other than the four public universities, data were collected for all students who enrolled as freshmen in the fall of each year of the study (students who transferred from other institutions were excluded).[4] At the four public universities, a sample of approximately 2,000 entering students was selected, composed of all known minority students, all athletic letter winners, all students with combined SAT scores of 1350 or above, and a random sample of the other members of the entering cohort.[5] (To represent the overall student population prop-

[3] In 1989, all seven colleges were coeducational; in 1951 four of the colleges admitted only men (Hamilton, Kenyon, Wesleyan, and Williams), as did four of the universities (Emory, Princeton, Columbia, and Yale). By 1976, only Columbia remained all male.

[4] Identifying the members of entering cohorts was not always an easy task, since most schools organize their records by graduating class, not entering cohort. In a number of cases, freshman directories or telephone listings were the only source of this information.

[5] In 1951, no sampling of students was used, since all institutions had entering cohorts of fewer than 2,000 students. For Penn State, the complete 1989 entering cohort was included.

erly, institutional sample weights, equal to the inverse of the probability of being sampled, were employed.)

All twenty-eight C&B institutions have had selective admissions policies. Such schools constitute only a small segment of the broad range of four-year colleges and universities in the United States. Moreover, the C&B database does not contain any two-year colleges, which in 1975 enrolled about 26 percent of all U.S. full-time college students (and about 35 percent of all students, including those attending part-time).[6] Table A.2 places the 1976 cohort of the C&B database in a national context by showing the total number of entering freshmen in each of the institutional selectivity categories used in this study.[7] Within the two most selective categories, the C&B database represents a significant portion of all freshmen entering four-year colleges in 1976 (40 percent of SEL-1 matriculants and 34 percent of SEL-2 matriculants). In the third category, the percentage is lower (7 percent), and the lowest two selectivity categories are not represented in the C&B database at all. (A companion control group study, described below, was designed to provide a set of national benchmarks for the C&B database.)

At the very beginning of the project, a decision was made to construct the institutional data file from individual student records, rather than requesting institutions to provide data in summary form. This decision turned out to be critically important. Although building the database from the "ground up" entailed significantly more work (most of the data were laboriously hand-entered from paper documents), this approach allowed us to ensure the consistency and accuracy of the data and, even more important, it made it possible to link the institutional records to the other data sources described below, including the C&B survey file, the data provided by the College Entrance Examination Board, and the survey results collected by the Cooperative Institutional Research Program administered by the Higher Education Research Institute.

The data in the institutional portion of the C&B database were compiled on a confidential basis in collaboration with the participating institutions. They came from two primary sources, college applications and transcripts. Applications provided information on matriculants' pre-college characteristics: gender, race, home state or country, citizenship, place of birth, size and type of high school (private, public, parochial), high school class rank, standardized test scores (SAT, ACT, Achievement Tests), and family background (usually one or both parents' occupation and education). In some cases, information on financial aid was also

---

[6] U.S. Department of Education 1989, p. 174.

[7] See Appendix B for a definition of the categories and a list of institutions included in each category.

TABLE A.2

Full-Time Freshman Enrollment at Four-Year Undergraduate Institutions, by Institutional Selectivity and Race, 1976

		Black			White			All Races	
Mean SAT Score of Freshmen	National (N)	C&B (N)	C&B Share of Nat'l Total (%)	National (N)	C&B (N)	C&B Share of Nat'l Total (%)	National (N)	C&B (N)	C&B Share of Nat'l Total (%)
SEL-1 1250+	876	385	44	13,531	5,311	39	15,672	6,290	40
SEL-2 1150–1249	1,784	740	41	34,875	11,510	33	39,000	13,180	34
SEL-3 1000–1149	11,124	735	7	227,964	15,959	7	253,317	17,172	7
SEL-4 900–999	20,096	0	0	290,168	0	0	328,749	0	0
SEL-5 <900	62,777	0	0	261,962	0	0	345,561	0	0
All	96,657	1,860	2	828,500	32,780	4	982,299	36,642	4

Source: National Center for Education Statistics (Higher Education General Information Survey and Integrated Postsecondary Education Data System).

Notes: Institutional average SAT scores are based on 1978 estimates provided by the Higher Education Research Institute. These scores differ slightly from the C&B data, and the institutional selectivity categories used in this table have been modified accordingly. The C&B share represents total enrollment at the 28 C&B institutions as reported by the National Center for Education Statistics, not the size of the C&B sample.

available. Transcripts provided information on matriculants' achievements and experiences during college, including grades, choice of major, whether or not the student graduated (and in a few cases the reason for not graduating), date of graduation (or date of withdrawal, transfer, etc.), and academic honors earned (such as Phi Beta Kappa).

Secondary sources of data were used for information about students' participation in selected extracurricular activities. Athletic department records provided lists of varsity letter winners, and yearbooks and alumni/ae offices were sources for information on participation in other activities, such as drama, journalism, music, debate, and student government. In some cases, lists of participants were obtained directly from the records of student organizations (e.g., the mastheads of student newspapers). Since the availability of records differed from school to school and from activity to activity, the data on participation in extracurricular activities are far from comprehensive.[8]

Because the records kept by each institution were unique, ensuring the completeness and consistency of the institutional data file was a significant challenge. Even at the same school, the format of applications and transcripts typically changed dramatically over the course of thirty-seven years. In the 1950s many transcripts were handwritten; by 1989 most records were available electronically, at least in part. Data describing high school records and family background were especially likely to be inconsistent in both availability and format. For example, some college applications asked whether the applicant's parents *attended* college, and others asked whether the parents *graduated* from college. Surprisingly, information about students' ethnicity was often incomplete for the 1976 entering cohort; that question on the application was often conspicuously marked "optional." Fortunately, many of these "holes" in the database were filled by the data provided by the College Entrance Examination Board (described below). In the end, only a very small amount of information for key variables was missing. For example, SAT or ACT scores were available for 96 percent of 1976 matriculants and 99 percent of 1989 matriculants (missing cases were primarily foreign students). Cumulative undergraduate GPA was available for over 97 percent of matriculants in both cohorts, date of graduation for 97 percent in 1976 and 94 percent in 1989, and major for 90 percent of the '76 matriculants and 97 percent of the '89 matriculants.

---

[8] For example, yearbooks from the 1970s often had photographs of participants in various activities, but frequently did not identify their names (matching people on the basis of their photographs was impractical if not impossible). Even in the best of circumstances, it is not easy to determine the completeness of yearbook records.

THE SURVEY DATA FILE

The survey data file contains the results of a survey of matriculants from the institutions represented in the institutional data file. Initially, all matriculants in the 1951 and 1976 entering cohorts were surveyed; later, a smaller sample of the 1989 entering cohort was also surveyed. The principal purpose of the survey was to understand the long-term outcomes of attending this set of selective colleges and universities. The result is a database containing detailed "life histories" of 45,184 individuals, including information on educational and occupational histories, retrospective views of college, personal and household income, civic participation, and satisfaction with life.

The C&B survey, which was conducted by Mathematica Policy Research, Inc. (MPR) in Princeton, New Jersey, was designed in early 1995 by a team of researchers from the Mellon Foundation, MPR, and the Survey Research Center at Princeton University. The survey was designed to gather data that could be understood in the context of other national data. To this end, questions concerning income, occupation, and sector of employment were designed to fit the categories used in the U.S. Census; questions concerning life satisfaction were modeled on those used by the General Social Survey; questions concerning the importance placed upon various skills and the contribution that college made to these skills were derived from surveys designed by the Consortium on Financing Higher Education (COFHE); questions about civic participation were similar to those asked in the High School and Beyond survey.[9] A complete copy of the questionnaire sent to members of the 1976 entering cohort is reproduced at the end of this appendix (Exhibit A.1).

The 1951 and 1976 Entering Cohorts

The survey of the 1951 and 1976 entering cohorts was tested on a number of focus groups and then redesigned before a pilot study of five institutions (known as "Wave 1") was launched in May 1995. Our intent was to see whether such an effort could attain high response rates and to test whether the questionnaire itself seemed to be useful. Following a thorough review of the questionnaire, including advice from an outside ad-

[9] For information on the General Social Survey, see National Opinion Research Center (1997). For the COFHE survey, see Consortium on Financing Higher Education (1992). For High School and Beyond, see U.S. Department of Education (1986).

visory panel,[10] the remaining schools in the 1951 and 1976 cohorts were surveyed in two waves ("Wave 2a" and "Wave 2b"), the first beginning in January 1996 and the second beginning in April 1996.

An important goal of the survey was to attain an unusually high response rate, and a target of 75 percent was set. Such goals are often met by employing some sort of incentive (usually cash) to encourage people to respond. We chose not to use a cash incentive, and other incentives tried in the pilot phase proved to be ineffective.[11] We hoped that the reputation of the schools and interest in the content of the survey would encourage people to respond. We decided at the beginning that, while the support of the participating institutions was essential (and their names would be invoked in correspondence with survey recipients), the survey would be framed as coming from the Mellon Foundation rather than from the schools themselves. This was important to encourage responses from those who might have felt less inclined to speak candidly to the schools, and also to differentiate the C&B study from other research or fund-raising appeals being launched by participating institutions. Survey respondents were assured that their responses would be confidential and that individuals' responses would not be provided to the institutions.

The management of the survey and the level of follow-up were crucial to attaining high response rates. The survey was preceded by a letter from William G. Bowen, president of the Mellon Foundation, informing people about the survey. This mailing also served as a way of updating addresses for those whose letters were returned as undeliverable. In the next stage, people received the survey, along with a cover letter and a postage-paid return envelope. About one week later, a postcard was sent to thank those who had already mailed in their completed questionnaires and to encourage those who had not yet responded to do so at their earliest convenience. Then, approximately one month after the first questionnaire had been mailed, another questionnaire was sent to those who had not yet responded, this time in a U.S. Postal Service

[10] The major change that was made to the questionnaire following the Wave 1 pilot study was the addition of more detailed questions pertaining to various domains of satisfaction with life. A question about applications to other colleges was also substantially revised. Other changes clarified question language and simplified skip patterns.

[11] One-half of the respondents in the Wave 1 pilot study were asked to check off whether they would like a $5 donation made to either their school's alumni/ae fund or one of four national charities. Response rates for matriculants who were offered the incentive were no higher than response rates for other matriculants, so the idea of using this kind of incentive was dropped.

Priority Mail envelope. After another "breather," non-respondents received a letter from the president of their college or university (or, in some cases, from another respected figure at the school). This letter was designed to "add another voice to the choir" of support.[12] Soon after this letter, phone calls were initiated to remind people to send in the survey.[13] After several reminder calls, non-respondents deemed unlikely to respond by mail were given the option of responding to the survey over the telephone (17 percent of respondents in the '76 cohort and 25 percent of respondents in the '89 cohort did so). One additional mailing was developed to encourage people to respond—a "results postcard," which displayed the average response rate for the schools with the highest response rates and compared the response rate of the individual's school. Most of the follow-up was completed by the end of 1996 (with a break during the summer months), although some phoning continued into the first half of 1997.

The 1989 Entering Cohort

In December 1996, we decided to survey a sample of the 1989 matriculants. This decision was made for three reasons. First, since more than seven years had now elapsed since they entered college, most would have had time to complete their degrees; many would have been out of school for four years by the time they received the questionnaire and would have found first jobs and/or returned to school to pursue an advanced degree. Second, we thought that a survey of the '89 matriculants would provide a useful benchmark for possible future surveys by capturing their attitudes and views at this early post-college juncture. Third, with this study of race-sensitive admissions in mind, we hoped to elicit information related to the extent of interaction among people from various backgrounds.

Because of time and budgetary constraints, we decided to work with a subsample of the C&B schools and students rather than attempt to survey every individual represented in the institutional data file, as we had done with the earlier cohorts. In the end, we decided to survey matriculants from twenty-one of the thirty-four C&B institutions, including seventeen

[12] An additional letter was sent to African Americans in Waves 2a and 2b from William Gray, president of the UNCF/The College Fund.

[13] In the survey of the 1989 entering cohort, a significant number of individuals had either no phone numbers or unlisted phone numbers, although their addresses were thought to be valid. This group received another reminder postcard, individualized with the name of their school.

of the twenty-eight colleges and universities that form the main database used in this book.[14] Included in this subsample of institutions were all four of the public universities and a mix of liberal arts colleges and private universities representing a range of institutional selectivity, geographical locations, and campus racial mixes. At the liberal arts colleges, all members of the entering cohorts were surveyed. At both the public and private universities, the survey sample consisted of all black, Hispanic, and Native American students; all identified student athletes; and a random sample of 500 other students. (We created survey weights equal to the inverse of the probability of being sampled. At the public universities, the survey sample was drawn from the institutional sample; therefore, when analyzing survey data we weight the responses by the product of the institutional weight and the sample weight.) The total number of 1989 respondents to the survey was 9,549. The survey was launched in March 1997 and largely completed by the late fall of 1997, using the same follow-up procedures described above for the 1951 and 1976 cohorts.

The questionnaire used for the 1989 cohort was essentially the same as the one used for the other two cohorts, with one significant exception: on the '89 survey, we included new questions about interactions among students from different backgrounds, both during their undergraduate years and after leaving college (copies of the interaction questions are reproduced at the end of this appendix, in Exhibit A.2).[15] The wording was designed to avoid (as much as possible) leading questions. For example, we decided against using questions that asked about the extent to which the diversity of the student body affected the respondent's classroom experiences. Instead, we asked whether or not respondents got to know people from various groups (including those with different political views, from different economic backgrounds, from different parts of the country or different parts of the world, and with different racial or ethnic origins). We also asked where these interactions occurred (in class, dorms, sports, or other extracurricular activities, in graduate school, on the job, or in community activities). Finally, in an effort to differentiate those who had experienced a more extensive level of interaction, we asked whether the respondent knew two or more of these people well. We did not try to define what it means to know someone

---

[14] These seventeen institutions are: Bryn Mawr College, Duke University, Kenyon College, University of Miami (Ohio), University of Michigan (Ann Arbor), University of North Carolina (Chapel Hill), Oberlin College, University of Pennsylvania, Pennsylvania State University, Princeton University, Stanford University, Vanderbilt University, Washington University, Wellesley College, Wesleyan University, Williams College, and Yale University.

[15] There were a few other minor changes; for example, there were questions about two post-college jobs, not three, as in the first questionnaire.

"well," but left that judgment to each respondent. This approach was designed to discourage a rote checking off of expected answers. We were concerned that some people might be inclined simply to assume they knew people with different backgrounds and perspectives; we hoped this additional step would force them to stop and reflect on the *number* of people they knew from each group, where they had met them, and whether or not they knew these people *well*. The data from these interaction questions are the evidence underlying much of Chapter 8.

Follow-up Interviews

In October 1997, after initial analysis of the data, we decided to conduct follow-up interviews with individuals from the sample in order to amplify findings documented in the research and to provide a more textured view of some of the findings. A letter was sent to a sample of black and white members of the '76 and '89 cohorts inviting them to participate in follow-up interviews for use in a study of race and higher education, to be written by William G. Bowen and Derek Bok. Approximately sixty-five interviews were conducted by Mathematica Policy Research and by Mellon Foundation staff. Since respondents to the letter were self-selected (i.e., they sent in a card only if they were willing to be interviewed), and because the interview format was intended to be free-flowing rather than structured, these interviews were not intended to be used for scientific analysis. Comments from the interviews have been interspersed in the text when they seemed to illustrate trends identified in the empirical analysis or to offer possible explanations for our findings.

Response Rates

Table A.3 shows two sets of survey response rates, each based on a different denominator. The *cohort response rate* was calculated by dividing the number of survey responses by the total number of matriculants in the entering cohort.[16] Despite considerable effort, it was not possible to locate some matriculants whose records were in the institutional file. The denominator of the *sample response rate* is the number of matriculants who

---

[16] For the schools at which we sampled the entering cohort (in 1976, the four public universities, and in 1989, all schools except the liberal arts colleges), the denominator is the number of matriculants in the sample.

TABLE A.3

Cohort and Sample Response Rates, by Institutional Type, 1976 and 1989 Entering Cohorts

Institutional Type	1976 Entering Cohort			1989 Entering Cohort		
	Number of Respondents	Cohort Response Rate (%)	Sample Response Rate (%)	Number of Respondents	Cohort Response Rate (%)	Sample Response Rate (%)
Public universities	5,757	72.2	80.3	2,584	72.3	79.9
Private universities	10,652	67.2	78.2	4,325	77.2	84.5
Coed liberal arts colleges	2,607	72.2	82.3	1,924	78.9	87.4
Women's colleges	1,646	72.4	86.9	716	78.1	86.9
All matriculants	20,662	69.6	79.9	9,549	76.3	84.0

Source: College and Beyond.

Notes: "Cohort Response Rate" is the number of respondents divided by the number of matriculants in the entering cohort (or in the sample—see footnote 16). "Sample Response Rate" is the number of respondents divided by the number of matriculants presumed to have been located. See text for more detail.

were presumed to have actually been located.[17] In other words, the sample response rate is the number of people who responded to the survey divided by the number who had an opportunity to respond. Some of the matriculants included in the base of the cohort response rate presumably would have responded had we been able to locate them; others either would have chosen not to respond or could not have responded (because, for example, they were deceased). If one assumes that matriculants we were unable to locate would have responded at a somewhat lower rate than those we did locate, the two response rates can be thought of as upper and lower bounds of the "true" response rate.

As shown in the table, the overall cohort response rate was 70 percent for the 1976 entering cohort and 76 percent for the 1989 entering cohort. Overall sample response rates for the two cohorts were 80 percent and 84 percent, respectively. There were modest variations in response rates by type of institution, with the universities having slightly lower rates than the colleges. The lowest cohort response rate for an individual school was 54 percent (for the '76 cohort at a women's college), and the lowest sample response rate was 67 percent (the same cohort at a private university). The highest cohort response rate for an individual school was 85 percent (the '89 cohort at a liberal arts college), and the highest sample response rate was 93 percent (the '89 cohort at a women's college).

SURVEY RESPONSE BIAS

In any survey, the degree of response bias is critically important. That is, were the people who responded to the survey systematically different from the people who did not respond? For example, it is possible in a survey such as this one that individuals dissatisfied with their college experience are disproportionately represented among non-respondents. If so, that would bias the results by overstating the level of satisfaction with the college.

Measuring Response Bias

In most surveys, it is (by definition) very difficult to find out anything about non-respondents. The C&B survey is unusual in that the institu-

---

[17] In some cases it is difficult to be certain whether or not a matriculant was located. For example, if a questionnaire was not returned "undeliverable" by the post office and if no phone number was listed for the individual at that location, we presumed he or she did not live there. However, it is possible that the person really was at that address but did not have a phone.

tional data file provides fairly detailed baseline information about *all* matriculants, respondents and non-respondents alike. This allows us to compare the two groups on the basis of their pre-college and in-college characteristics and experiences. Table A.4 examines a number of these attributes, showing both cohort response rates and sample response rates. The data are organized to highlight differences in black and white response rates.

Looking first at the cohort response rates, we see that while the rates for the 1989 entering cohort are generally a few percentage points higher than those for the 1976 cohort, the patterns in both cohorts are quite similar. White matriculants responded at a somewhat higher rate than did blacks (an overall gap of 12 percentage points in 1976 and 15 in 1989), and women responded at a higher rate than did men (a gap of 4 to 7 percentage points). Matriculants with mid or high parental socioeconomic status (SES)[18] responded at about the same rate, but those with low socioeconomic status responded at a rate that was 9 to 15 percentage points lower. Because of the correlation between SAT scores and undergraduate GPA, both characteristics exhibit similar response rate patterns, with students at the top of the class or with high SAT scores responding at higher rates. But by far the largest gap is between graduates and non-graduates: in both entering cohorts, the cohort response rate for non-graduates was more than 20 percentage points lower than the rate for graduates.

The lower cohort response rate for non-graduates was expected, given that the initial source of contact information for matriculants was institutional alumni/ae offices; it would not be surprising if alumni/ae offices had lost contact with a disproportionately larger number of non-graduates (many of whom transferred to other institutions).[19] This hypothesis is confirmed when we compare the cohort response rates with the sample response rates, which include in the denominator only matriculants who were located. The gap in *sample* response rates between graduates and non-graduates is only about half of the gap in the *cohort* response rates (11 percentage points versus 22 percentage points in the 1976 cohort and 13 versus 21 percentage points in the 1989 cohort). In general, the differences in response rates described above are much more modest when we look at sample response rates, indicating that a substantial portion of the gaps in cohort response rates is due to difficulty

[18] As explained in Chapter 2 and Appendix B, socioeconomic status is based on parental income and education.

[19] As described in the section above, attempts were made to track down *all* matriculants, even those who had no current address on file with the alumni/ae office, using any information available.

TABLE A.4
Cohort and Sample Response Rates, by Selected Characteristics and Race, 1976 and 1989 Entering Cohorts

	1976 Entering Cohort						1989 Entering Cohort					
	Cohort Response Rate			Sample Response Rate			Cohort Response Rate			Sample Response Rate		
	Black	White	All	Black	White	All	Black	White	All	Black	White	All
Gender												
Female	64	76	74	78	85	84	69	83	80	80	88	87
Male	57	70	67	74	78	76	62	79	76	74	84	83
Socioeconomic status												
Low	60	69	65	77	78	78	55	76	64	73	82	78
Mid	65	75	74	77	82	82	68	81	78	78	87	85
High	67	73	73	79	81	81	70	81	79	78	86	85
SAT score												
1300+	71	76	75	88	84	83	75	83	82	86	88	87
1200–1299	60	74	73	75	82	81	71	81	79	79	86	85
1100–1199	63	72	70	78	80	79	77	80	78	88	85	85
1000–1099	65	70	68	79	79	78	63	79	75	74	84	82
<1000	59	67	61	75	79	76	60	75	66	72	81	77
Class rank												
Bottom half of class	60	70	67	75	80	79	65	78	74	76	84	82
Top half of class	74	75	73	83	82	81	78	84	83	89	89	88
Graduation status												
Non-graduate	45	57	53	65	73	71	47	65	59	63	77	73
Graduate	68	76	75	80	83	82	72	83	80	80	87	86
All	61	73	70	76	81	80	66	81	78	77	86	86

Source: College and Beyond.

Notes: See notes to Table A.3 for definitions of cohort and sample response rates. See Appendix B for definition of socioeconomic status. Graduates include "first-school" graduates only.

in locating matriculants. The same pattern holds for the differences between black and white matriculants: the overall cohort response rate gap of 12 percentage points in the 1976 cohort drops to a gap in the sample rate of 5 percentage points; similarly, the gap of 15 points in the '89 cohort drops to 9 points, again indicating that much of the gap is due to greater difficulty in locating black matriculants. In some cases the black-white gap in cohort response rates all but disappears in the sample response rates (see, for example, the SES rows for the 1976 cohort and the "top half of class" row for the 1989 cohort in Table A.4).

Nonetheless, there is clearly evidence of some degree of response bias in the data, whether it is a result of difficulty in locating matriculants or for other reasons, especially among non-graduates. Of particular significance to this study is the fact that black response rates are lower.[20] Moreover, the black-white gap is greater for non-graduates than for graduates, for students in the bottom half of the class compared to those in the top half, and, in the 1989 cohort, for low-SAT and low-SES students.

Estimating the Effects of Response Bias: Graduates versus Non-Graduates

It is difficult to estimate how much effect response bias has on the results presented in this study. In light of the fact that non-graduates have the lowest response rate of any group examined, and since they might be more likely to have had disappointing experiences in college (and in life), and therefore to have unfavorable views of their undergraduate institutions, estimating the survey outcomes of non-respondents who did not graduate is one way to obtain a sense of the magnitude of the bias. As a first step in the analysis, we compared the responses of graduates and non-graduates, since non-graduates who *did* respond are presumably most similar to those who did not respond. Because of the way the survey was conducted, it is possible to go one step further. As described earlier, matriculants were first contacted with a series of mailings. Those who did not respond, even after receiving six mailings and several telephone reminder calls, were contacted by telephone and asked if they would be willing to complete the questionnaire over the telephone. Thus those who answered by telephone responded later and after considerably more persuasion than those who responded by mail, and it is not unreasonable to assume that they are more similar to non-respondents than are respondents in general (after all, they would have been nonrespondents had there been no additional efforts to reach them). Table A.5 compares

[20] For information on the generally lower patterns of survey response rates among African Americans, see Krysan et al. 1994.

TABLE A.5
Selected Characteristics of Survey Respondents, by Graduation Status and
Race, Mail and Telephone Respondents, 1976 Entering Cohort

	All Graduate Respondents	*Non-Graduates Responding by Mail*	*Non-Graduates Responding by Telephone*
Mean personal income			
Black	$65,550	$47,969	$39,202
White	$71,129	$52,506	$58,304
All	$71,493	$52,427	$55,141
Mean household income			
Black	$98,356	$73,381	$65,910
White	$120,553	$92,357	$92,587
All	$120,084	$91,570	$88,959
Percentage earning advanced degree			
Black	56%	13%	3%
White	55%	28%	21%
All	55%	27%	18%
Mean rating of satisfaction with college			
Black	1.48	2.22	1.97
White	1.44	2.16	2.02
All	1.44	2.16	2.02
Mean rating of satisfaction with life			
Black	2.00	2.18	1.93
White	1.73	1.85	1.72
All	1.75	1.86	1.76

Source: College and Beyond.
Notes: Graduates include "first-school" graduates only. Mean personal income is calculated for all respondents, not only those who work full-time. Personal and household
income are for 1995. Satisfaction with college and satisfaction with life ratings are on a scale
of 1 ("very satisfied") to 5 ("very dissatisfied").

selected survey outcomes for three groups of respondents (focusing on
the 1976 entering cohort[21]): graduates, non-graduates who responded by
mail, and non-graduates who responded by telephone (on the assumption that the last group is most likely to be similar to non-graduates who
did not respond).

---

[21] We performed the same analysis for the 1989 entering cohort and found results that
were substantively similar.

Not surprisingly, average personal and household income are much lower for non-graduates than for graduates, as are the percentages earning an advanced degree (the percentages for non-graduates are as high as they are because some of the non-graduates transferred to other schools). Of greater interest is the difference between mail respondents and telephone respondents among the non-graduates. For black non-graduates, both personal income and household income are lower for telephone respondents, suggesting that the most reluctant respondents have been less successful financially. But for white non-graduates, both personal income and household income are higher for telephone respondents. This suggests that two counteracting forces may be at work: some matriculants may not have responded out of a sense of not "measuring up" to their classmates, but others may simply have been too busy to respond or too difficult to reach.

A similar pattern emerges when we examine satisfaction with college. Again, not surprisingly, the non-graduates are less satisfied than the graduates. But the telephone respondents are *more* satisfied than the mail respondents, suggesting that reluctant responders are not necessarily more dissatisfied with their college experience. The same is true of satisfaction with life. In any case, the fact that the outcomes for phone respondents are not dramatically different than the outcomes for mail respondents leads us to believe that the effects of response bias are likely to be modest.

As a final test of the effect of response bias due to fewer non-graduates responding, we examined the potential impact on one outcome variable, personal earned income. Since we knew that non-graduates were less likely to receive a survey,[22] and that those who did receive a survey were less likely to respond, we divided the nonrespondents into four groups within each race and gender category (i.e., white men, white women, black men, black women):

- *Non-graduates who did not receive a survey.* We have no reason to believe that this group is much different from non-graduates who received a survey, so we assigned this group the same mean income as that of all non-graduates.
- *Graduates who did not receive a survey.* Likewise, we assigned this group the same mean income as that of all graduates.
- *Non-graduates who received a survey.* As explained above, we believe this group is most like the telephone respondents. We make the arbitrary assumption, which we believe is reasonable, that this

---

[22] Overall, 93 percent of graduates and 79 percent of non-graduates received surveys.

TABLE A.6
Estimated Effect of Response Bias on Mean Personal Income,
by Race and Gender, 1976 Entering Cohort (1995 dollars)

	Black		White	
	Women	*Men*	*Women*	*Men*
Mean personal income of survey respondents	54,762	72,741	45,443	94,397
Mean estimated personal income adjusted for response bias due to fewer non-graduates responding.	51,887	68,400	44,787	91,750

Source: College and Beyond.

Notes: Mean personal income is derived from income ranges reported by all survey respondents, including those who were not working full time. See text for explanation of method of adjustment for response bias due to fewer non-graduates responding.

group's mean income was 10 percent lower than that of non-graduate phone respondents.[23]

- *Graduates who received a survey.* Using the same assumption, we assigned this group a mean income 10 percent lower than that of phone respondents who graduated from college.

Table A.6 shows our revised estimates of average personal income using these assumptions and compares them to the actual averages reported by respondents. In general, the effect of adjusting for response bias is fairly modest for both black and white matriculants. The adjusted figure for black C&B women is about $3,000 lower than the unadjusted figure—a difference of 5 percent. The difference between the unad-

[23] Some relevant information was gathered from three institutions with extensive supplemental alumni/ae records. We asked them to provide any information they had about the occupations and advanced degrees of non-respondents. Not coincidentally, many of the survey non-respondents had also lost contact with their undergraduate institution. However, these institutions did have employment information for 41 to 53 percent of the non-respondents, and many of the non-respondents held occupational titles that indicated high-paying positions (for example, cardiologist, neurologist, senior software engineer, etc.). Furthermore, about 25 percent of these non-respondents reported to their undergraduate institutions that they had received an advanced degree. We also know from MPR's experience in trying to contact non-respondents that some of the hardest individuals to reach were in the medical profession, because of busy schedules and assistants who prevented access to their superiors. From this admittedly anecdotal evidence, we infer that it was not simply lack of educational or occupational success that prevented many non-respondents from answering the survey.

justed and adjusted figures for black men is only slightly larger—less than $5,000, or about 6 percent. The differences for white women and white men are smaller yet—less than $1,000 for the women (1 percent) and less than $3,000 for the men (3 percent).

In interpreting these results, it is important to remember that:

- the percentage of non-graduates is small (roughly 20 percent among all 1976 matriculants); and
- the overall cohort response rate is very high (70 percent for the entire '76 cohort, including those who could not be located), and the sample response rate is even higher (80 percent).

It is this combination of factors that is mainly responsible for such modest estimates of the effects of response bias. (In the '89 cohort, the percentage of non-graduates was lower yet, and the cohort response rate was higher.) These results, combined with the similarity in the responses of the mail and phone respondents to the surveys, give us considerable confidence in the validity of the overall pattern of results obtained from the C&B surveys.

NATIONAL SURVEY CONTROL GROUP STUDY

Since the C&B survey is restricted to matriculants at a small group of twenty-eight selective colleges and universities, a control group study was conducted to provide a set of national benchmarks. In the spring and summer of 1996, the National Opinion Research Center (NORC) at the University of Chicago conducted a survey of a nationally representative sample of individuals who were approximately eighteen years of age in either 1951 or 1976 (the 1989 entering cohort was not included in the control group study). The survey differed from the C&B survey in that it was conducted entirely over the phone, but the content of the questions was the same.

The control group was designed to consist of 4,000 people, half in the older cohort and half in the younger, with equal representation of men and women. The sample was further divided into two broad educational groups: those who first matriculated at a four-year college or university (whether or not they earned a bachelor's degree), and those who did not, a category that included those who never went to college (and may not even have graduated from high school) and those who first matriculated at a community college. Ideally, the 4,000 cases would have been distributed as 2,000 individuals in each of the two cohorts, and, within the cohorts, 1,000 in each educational group—500 men and 500 women. In fact, the number of respondents in the older cohort was 1,884, and the

TABLE A.7
Control Group Sample Sizes, by Race, Gender, and Matriculation at
Four-Year College, Younger Cohort (1976)

	Matriculated at a Four-Year College	Did Not Matriculate at a Four-Year College	All Respondents
Men			
Black	19	43	62
White	376	605	981
Other	31	76	107
All men	426	724	1,150
Women			
Black	32	45	77
White	350	531	881
Other	28	43	71
All women	410	619	1,029
All men and women			
Black	51	88	139
White	726	1,136	1,862
Other	59	119	178
All	836	1,343	2,179

Source: National Control Group Study.

Notes: The "Younger Cohort" consists of individuals born between 1957 and 1959. Respondents who first matriculated at a two-year school and later matriculated at a four-year one were assigned to the "Did not matriculate at a four-year college" category.

number in the younger cohort was 2,179. The distribution of the younger (1976) cohort by race and gender is shown in Table A.7. Because the number of black respondents was fairly small, the control group study could not be used for fine-grained comparisons between blacks and whites.

NORC attempted to contact an initial telephone sample of 14,429 households. Of these, 7,541 were determined to be ineligible for the study (mainly because the interviewer could not identify a person in the household in the correct age range and education category). Of the 6,888 eligible households, 4,063 completed the interview, an overall sample response rate of 59 percent. The response rate for the younger cohort was also 59 percent. Within this group, there was little variation by gender or level of education (response rates by race were not available): the highest rate was for women with twelve or fewer years of education (63 percent), and the lowest rate was for men with more than twelve years of education (58 percent).

NORC also conducted an analysis of non-respondents to try to obtain basic demographic information about them, such as gender, race, educational level, occupation, and income. A sample of 456 households was selected at random from the non-respondent population. After considerable effort, including phone interviews, mail surveys, and a variety of incentives, 259 responses were elicited (a response rate of 71 percent, since 92 of the cases were found to be ineligible). Compared to respondents, a slightly higher percentage of non-respondents were men and a slightly lower percentage were minorities, but both of these differences were found to be statistically insignificant. However, differences in educational level and income were statistically significant. Non-respondents were split about evenly between those who were high school graduates or less and those who had some college, but 63 percent of respondents had at least some college. The mean income for non-respondents was $31,500 and the mean income for respondents was $54,000.[24]

This gap in personal income between the NORC respondents and non-respondents is appreciably larger than our implicit estimate of the corresponding gap among C&B matriculants (see Table A.6). Also, and even more important, the number of non-respondents in the NORC study is much higher, relatively speaking, than the number of non-respondents in the C&B study (the sample response rate obtained by the NORC control group study was 59 percent, as compared with a rate of 84 percent for the C&B matriculants). Thus, if we were to correct the NORC earnings data for response bias in the same way that we corrected the C&B earnings data, we would find that the earnings differential favoring the C&B graduates increases greatly. Stated differently, the C&B-NORC earnings differential evident in the raw responses that assume no response bias (reported in Chapter 5) is much smaller than the differential that would be obtained after adjusting both sets of figures for response bias.

SECONDARY DATA SOURCES

Two secondary data sources were used to supplement the core C&B institutional data file: one from the College Entrance Examination Board and one from the Higher Education Research Institute at the University of California, Los Angeles.

[24] NORC's conclusion that respondents had higher income than non-respondents is borne out by comparisons we made between the control group sample and data from the 1990 U.S. Census: mean income and educational levels of comparable groups in the Census were generally somewhat lower. Part of the explanation may be that NORC's sample excluded people without telephones, which would tend to give an upward socioeconomic bias to the sample.

College Entrance Examination Board

The source of the data provided by the College Entrance Examination Board was the Student Descriptive Questionnaire (SDQ) completed by high school students when they applied to take the SAT test conducted by the Educational Testing Service. Since almost all matriculants at the C&B colleges and universities in 1976 and 1989 were required to take the SAT test in their junior or senior year in high school, this is an unusually comprehensive source of information.[25] The SDQ includes questions about students' academic preparation for college (including subjects studied in high school, grade point average, high school class rank, size and type of high school), participation in high school and community activities, and college preferences (type and size of college, degree goals, likely major, interest in extracurricular activities, etc.). It also provides basic demographic information, including gender, ethnicity, citizenship, and parental income and education. In addition to SDQ data, the College Entrance Examination Board provided students' verbal and math SAT scores and their Achievement (now called SAT II) scores.

The College Entrance Examination Board's data were matched to records in the 1976 and 1989 cohorts of the C&B institutional file by means of an algorithm developed by the Educational Testing Service that maintained the confidentiality of the data. Not all of the records in the institutional file could be matched successfully. Some students did not take the SAT, and in some cases the information needed to make a confirmed match was incomplete in the institutional file. The overall match rate was 75 percent for the 1976 entering cohort, and 90 percent for the 1989 entering cohort.

Higher Education Research Institute

A second data file was provided by the Higher Education Research Institute (HERI) at the University of California, Los Angeles, based on data from the Cooperative Institutional Research Program (CIRP). The CIRP freshman questionnaire is administered each year to approximately 350,000 entering freshmen at a nationally representative sample of some seven hundred two-year and four-year colleges and universities across the United States.[26] The questionnaire is extensive and, in addition to basic demographic information about the student and his or her parents,

---

[25] The main exceptions are some foreign students and some applicants to institutions in the Midwest that accept either ACT (administered by the American College Testing Program) or SAT scores.

[26] For a full description of this ongoing research project, see Astin et al. (1997).

gathers responses to detailed questions regarding college preparation, reasons for attending college, college goals and degree aspirations, career goals and reasons for selecting a career, personal goals and values, self-ratings of abilities in a range of areas, activities during the past year, use of time during the past week, probable future activities, and opinions on current topics.

Not all of the institutions in the C&B database were part of the HERI study. For the 1976 entering cohort, data for twenty-one of the twenty-eight C&B institutions were available from HERI (four private universities, two liberal arts colleges, and one women's college were missing), and for the 1989 cohort, data for twenty-four institutions were available (one public university and three private universities were missing). As with the data from the College Entrance Examination Board, records were matched by HERI using an algorithm that protected the confidentiality of the records. For the 1976 cohort, 75 percent of the records of the twenty-one institutions in the institutional file were matched, and for the '89 cohort, 70 percent of the records of the twenty-four institutions were matched. Some records did not match because of incomplete information in one of the two data files.

EXHIBIT A.1
College and Beyond Survey (1976 Entering Cohort)

College and Beyond

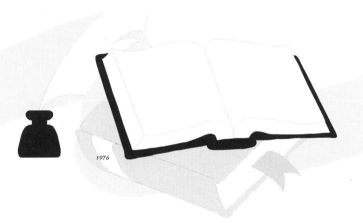

Conducted for:

The Andrew W. Mellon Foundation
New York, New York

By

Mathematica Policy Research, Inc.
Princeton, New Jersey

INSTRUCTIONS

Thank you for taking the time to complete this questionnaire. Directions for filling it out are provided with each question. Because not all questions will apply to everyone, you may be asked to skip certain questions.

- Follow all "SKIP" instructions AFTER marking a box. If no "SKIP" instruction is provided, you should continue to the NEXT question

- Either a pen or pencil may be used

- When answering questions that require marking a box, please use an "X"

- If you need to change an answer, please make sure that your old answer is either completely erased or clearly crossed out

Thank you again for your participation.

SECTION A: EDUCATION

A1. **Do you have a bachelor's degree or higher?**

  1 ☐ Yes
  2 ☐ No → *SKIP to A4*   110

A2. **When did you complete your bachelor's degree?**   111:114

  |___|___| 19 |___|___|
    Month   Year

A3. **At which college or university did you complete your bachelor's degree?**

  • *If you have more than one bachelor's degree, answer for the school at which you completed your first bachelor's degree.*

  School Name: _____ City: _____ State: _____

A4. **Back when you were applying to undergraduate schools, which school did you most want to attend, that is, what was your first choice school?**

  1 ☐ School at which you completed your bachelor's degree (school entered at A3) → *SKIP to A5*   115
  2 ☐ Another school
  ➤ School Name: _____ City: _____ State:_____

A4a. **Thinking about the school you most wanted to attend, which of the following statements best applies . . .**

  Mark (X) one box
  1 ☐ You did not apply to your first choice school,   116
  2 ☐ You applied to the school but were not accepted, or
  3 ☐ You applied to the school and were accepted
  8 ☐ Can't recall

A5. **Did you seriously consider any other schools when you were applying to undergraduate institutions?**

  1 ☐ Yes   117
  2 ☐ No → *SKIP to A6, page 2*

A5a. In rough order of preference, please list the other undergraduate schools you seriously considered. If there were more than three, list the three of most interest to you.

  • *For Each School Listed: Please indicate whether you applied. If you applied to a school, indicate whether you were accepted.*

	Applied? Mark (X) one for each school			Accepted? Mark (X) one for each school		
	Yes	No	Can't Recall	Yes	No	Can't Recall
School Name: _____ City/State: _____	1 ☐	2 ☐	8 ☐	1 ☐	2 ☐	8 ☐
School Name: _____ City/State: _____	1 ☐	2 ☐	8 ☐	1 ☐	2 ☐	8 ☐
School Name: _____ City/State: _____	1 ☐	2 ☐	8 ☐	1 ☐	2 ☐	8 ☐
			118:120			121:123

A6. **Have you taken any college or university courses since completing your undergraduate degree?** *If you left before completing an undergraduate degree, mark "yes" if you have taken any courses since that time.*

   1 ☐ Yes

   2 ☐ No → *SKIP to the box at the top of page 3*

124

A7. **Please indicate the subject areas in which you took these subsequent college or university courses.**

- *"Coursework Only" Box*: Mark this box for subject areas where you took courses but did <u>not</u> complete a degree.
- *"Degree Received" Box*: Mark this box for subject areas where you took courses and received a degree. Please remember to record the year you received the degree, along with the name and location of the school.

Subject Area	A Further Schooling			B School Information	
(Do not count honorary degrees.)	Coursework Only	Degree Received	Year Received	School Name	City/State
Bachelor's Degree/Coursework					
1. (Second) Bachelor's degree	1 ☐	2 ☐ ▸	19 |_|_|	_____	_____
Master's Degree/Coursework					
2. Architecture	1 ☐	2 ☐ ▸	19 |_|_|	_____	_____
3. Biological sciences	1 ☐	2 ☐ ▸	19 |_|_|	_____	_____
4. Business	1 ☐	2 ☐ ▸	19 |_|_|	_____	_____
5. Divinity/Theological Studies	1 ☐	2 ☐ ▸	19 |_|_|	_____	_____
6. Education	1 ☐	2 ☐ ▸	19 |_|_|	_____	_____
7. Engineering, other applied science .	1 ☐	2 ☐ ▸	19 |_|_|	_____	_____
8. Humanities or arts	1 ☐	2 ☐ ▸	19 |_|_|	_____	_____
9. Physical sciences	1 ☐	2 ☐ ▸	19 |_|_|	_____	_____
10. Social sciences (including public/international affairs)	1 ☐	2 ☐ ▸	19 |_|_|	_____	_____
11. Other master's degree - *Specify:* _____	1 ☐	2 ☐ ▸	19 |_|_|	_____	_____
Other Professional Degree/Coursework					
12. Law (LLB or JD)	1 ☐	2 ☐ ▸	19 |_|_|	_____	_____
13. Medicine (MD, DDS, DVM, etc.) ...	1 ☐	2 ☐ ▸	19 |_|_|	_____	_____
14. Other - *Specify:* _____	1 ☐	2 ☐ ▸	19 |_|_|	_____	_____
Doctoral Degree/Coursework					
15. Biological sciences	1 ☐	2 ☐ ▸	19 |_|_|	_____	_____
16. Divinity/Theological Studies	1 ☐	2 ☐ ▸	19 |_|_|	_____	_____
17. Education	1 ☐	2 ☐ ▸	19 |_|_|	_____	_____
18. Engineering, other applied sciences	1 ☐	2 ☐ ▸	19 |_|_|	_____	_____
19. Humanities or arts	1 ☐	2 ☐ ▸	19 |_|_|	_____	_____
20. Physical sciences	1 ☐	2 ☐ ▸	19 |_|_|	_____	_____
21. Social sciences	1 ☐	2 ☐ ▸	19 |_|_|	_____	_____
22. Other doctoral degree - *Specify:* _____	1 ☐	2 ☐ ▸	19 |_|_|	_____	_____

125:146   147:220

Questions A8-A14a ask about the <u>undergraduate school at which you first enrolled</u>, even if you were only there for a short time or didn't receive a degree from that school.

A8. Overall, how satisfied have you been with the undergraduate education you received at the school at which you first enrolled?

Mark (X) one box

1 ☐ Very satisfied
2 ☐ Somewhat satisfied   221
3 ☐ Neither satisfied nor dissatisfied
4 ☐ Somewhat dissatisfied
5 ☐ Very dissatisfied

A9. Imagine that you had your life to live over again and were graduating from high school. Knowing what you do now, how likely is it that you would:

Mark (X) one for each

	Very Likely	Somewhat Likely	Not At All Likely
a. Choose the same undergraduate school?	1 ☐	2 ☐	3 ☐
b. Major in the same field of study?	1 ☐	2 ☐	3 ☐ 222:223

A10. Imagine that you had your life to live over and were an undergraduate again. Knowing what you do now, how much time would you be likely to devote to each of these activities:

- *If you did not take part in an activity as an undergraduate and would not again, mark "About the Same."*

Mark (X) one for each

	More Time	About The Same	Less Time
a. Studying	1 ☐	2 ☐	3 ☐
b. Social life	1 ☐	2 ☐	3 ☐
c. Extra-curricular activities (excluding athletics)	1 ☐	2 ☐	3 ☐
d. Intramural athletics	1 ☐	2 ☐	3 ☐
e. Intercollegiate athletics	1 ☐	2 ☐	3 ☐
f. Working at a job for pay	1 ☐	2 ☐	3 ☐ 224:229

A11. While you were an undergraduate, did anyone associated with your school, other than fellow students, take a special interest in you or your work--that is, was there someone you could turn to for advice or for general support or encouragement?

1 ☐ Yes   230
2 ☐ No → *SKIP to A13, page 4*

A12. (IF YES) Who was that?

Mark (X) all that apply

1 ☐ Faculty member
2 ☐ Teaching assistant   231
3 ☐ Resident advisor
4 ☐ College dean or other administrator
5 ☐ Athletic coach
6 ☐ Alumnus
7 ☐ Other - *Specify:*
_____

A13. Please indicate how important each of the following has been in your life since college.

Importance in Your Life

Mark (X) one for each

		Very Important				Not At All Important
a.	Analytical and problem-solving skills/ ability to think critically	5 ☐	4 ☐	3 ☐	2 ☐	1 ☐
b.	Knowledge of a particular field/discipline	5 ☐	4 ☐	3 ☐	2 ☐	1 ☐
c.	Leadership abilities	5 ☐	4 ☐	3 ☐	2 ☐	1 ☐
d.	Active interest in community service	5 ☐	4 ☐	3 ☐	2 ☐	1 ☐
e.	Ability to work independently	5 ☐	4 ☐	3 ☐	2 ☐	1 ☐
f.	Ability to form and retain friendships	5 ☐	4 ☐	3 ☐	2 ☐	1 ☐
g.	Ability to have a good rapport with people holding different beliefs	5 ☐	4 ☐	3 ☐	2 ☐	1 ☐
h.	Ability to work effectively and get along well with people from different races/cultures	5 ☐	4 ☐	3 ☐	2 ☐	1 ☐
i.	Religious values	5 ☐	4 ☐	3 ☐	2 ☐	1 ☐
j.	Ability to communicate well orally	5 ☐	4 ☐	3 ☐	2 ☐	1 ☐
k.	Competitiveness	5 ☐	4 ☐	3 ☐	2 ☐	1 ☐
l.	Ability to work cooperatively	5 ☐	4 ☐	3 ☐	2 ☐	1 ☐
m.	Ability to relax and enjoy leisure	5 ☐	4 ☐	3 ☐	2 ☐	1 ☐
n.	Ability to write clearly and effectively	5 ☐	4 ☐	3 ☐	2 ☐	1 ☐
o.	Ability to adapt to change	5 ☐	4 ☐	3 ☐	2 ☐	1 ☐

232:246

A13a. How much did your undergraduate experience help you develop in these same areas? *If you attended more than one undergraduate school*, remember, we are asking about the school at which you first enrolled.

- *If unable to determine, mark "Uncertain."*

Contribution of Your Undergraduate Experience

Mark (X) one for each

	A Great Deal				None At All	Uncertain
a. Analytical and problem-solving skills/ ability to think critically	5 ☐	4 ☐	3 ☐	2 ☐	1 ☐	0 ☐
b. Knowledge of a particular field/discipline	5 ☐	4 ☐	3 ☐	2 ☐	1 ☐	0 ☐
c. Leadership abilities	5 ☐	4 ☐	3 ☐	2 ☐	1 ☐	0 ☐
d. Active interest in community service	5 ☐	4 ☐	3 ☐	2 ☐	1 ☐	0 ☐
e. Ability to work independently	5 ☐	4 ☐	3 ☐	2 ☐	1 ☐	0 ☐
f. Ability to form and retain friendships	5 ☐	4 ☐	3 ☐	2 ☐	1 ☐	0 ☐
g. Ability to have a good rapport with people holding different beliefs	5 ☐	4 ☐	3 ☐	2 ☐	1 ☐	0 ☐
h. Ability to work effectively and get along well with people from different races/cultures	5 ☐	4 ☐	3 ☐	2 ☐	1 ☐	0 ☐
i. Religious values	5 ☐	4 ☐	3 ☐	2 ☐	1 ☐	0 ☐
j. Ability to communicate well orally	5 ☐	4 ☐	3 ☐	2 ☐	1 ☐	0 ☐
k. Competitiveness	5 ☐	4 ☐	3 ☐	2 ☐	1 ☐	0 ☐
l. Ability to work cooperatively	5 ☐	4 ☐	3 ☐	2 ☐	1 ☐	0 ☐
m. Ability to relax and enjoy leisure	5 ☐	4 ☐	3 ☐	2 ☐	1 ☐	0 ☐
n. Ability to write clearly and effectively	5 ☐	4 ☐	3 ☐	2 ☐	1 ☐	0 ☐
o. Ability to adapt to change	5 ☐	4 ☐	3 ☐	2 ☐	1 ☐	0 ☐

247:261

> **If you attended more than one undergraduate school**, remember, Questions A14 and A14a are asking about the school at which you first enrolled.

A14.   Please indicate how much emphasis you believe your undergraduate school <u>currently</u> places on:

- *If uncertain, mark "No Current Knowledge".*

<u>Current Emphasis</u>

Mark (X) one for each

	A Great Deal				Very Little/ None	No Current Knowledge
a. Faculty research	5 ☐	4 ☐	3 ☐	2 ☐	1 ☐	0 ☐
b. Teaching undergraduates	5 ☐	4 ☐	3 ☐	2 ☐	1 ☐	0 ☐
c. A broad liberal arts education	5 ☐	4 ☐	3 ☐	2 ☐	1 ☐	0 ☐
d. Intercollegiate athletics	5 ☐	4 ☐	3 ☐	2 ☐	1 ☐	0 ☐
e. Extra-curricular activities other than intercollegiate athletics	5 ☐	4 ☐	3 ☐	2 ☐	1 ☐	0 ☐
f. A commitment to intellectual freedom ...	5 ☐	4 ☐	3 ☐	2 ☐	1 ☐	0 ☐
g. A racially/ethnically diverse student body	5 ☐	4 ☐	3 ☐	2 ☐	1 ☐	0 ☐
h. Quality of residential life	5 ☐	4 ☐	3 ☐	2 ☐	1 ☐	0 ☐
i. Alumni/alumnae concerns	5 ☐	4 ☐	3 ☐	2 ☐	1 ☐	0 ☐

262:270

A14a.   How much emphasis do you think your undergraduate school <u>should</u> place on each of these areas?

- *If uncertain, mark "Don't Know".*

<u>Emphasis Should Be</u>

Mark (X) one for each

	A Great Deal				Very Little/ None	Don't Know
a. Faculty research	5 ☐	4 ☐	3 ☐	2 ☐	1 ☐	0 ☐
b. Teaching undergraduates	5 ☐	4 ☐	3 ☐	2 ☐	1 ☐	0 ☐
c. A broad liberal arts education	5 ☐	4 ☐	3 ☐	2 ☐	1 ☐	0 ☐
d. Intercollegiate athletics	5 ☐	4 ☐	3 ☐	2 ☐	1 ☐	0 ☐
e. Extra-curricular activities other than intercollegiate athletics	5 ☐	4 ☐	3 ☐	2 ☐	1 ☐	0 ☐
f. A commitment to intellectual freedom	5 ☐	4 ☐	3 ☐	2 ☐	1 ☐	0 ☐
g. A racially/ethnically diverse student body	5 ☐	4 ☐	3 ☐	2 ☐	1 ☐	0 ☐
h. Quality of residential life	5 ☐	4 ☐	3 ☐	2 ☐	1 ☐	0 ☐
i. Alumni/alumnae concerns	5 ☐	4 ☐	3 ☐	2 ☐	1 ☐	0 ☐

271:279

80=2

SECTION B: WORK HISTORY

Because space is limited, this section only asks about a few of the jobs you might have held since college.

First Job Held Six Months or Longer

B1. Think back to your first job for pay that lasted for six months or longer after leaving undergraduate school (or graduate school, if you chose to continue your education at that time). When did that job begin?

> 0 ☐ Never worked for pay
>   or profit → *SKIP to C1, page 12*   310

- *Full-time military service counts as a job.*

- *Include a job held in college if you still held that job for at least 6 months after leaving college.*

DATE FIRST
JOB BEGAN: |___|___| 19 |___|___| 311:314
　　　　　　　Month　　　　Year

B2. Was your employer on that first job . . .

Mark (X) one box

1 ☐ A FOR-PROFIT company, business or individual, working for wages, salary or commissions

2 ☐ A NOT-FOR-PROFIT, tax-exempt, organization (includes private schools and private colleges/universities)

3 ☐ SELF-EMPLOYED in own business, professional practice, or farm   315

4 ☐ State or local GOVERNMENT (city, county, etc.) (includes public schools and public colleges/universities)

5 ☐ U.S. GOVERNMENT including military

6 ☐ Other - *Specify:*

_____

B3. While you held that job, were you working . . .

Mark (X) one box

1 ☐ Only or mostly full-time   316

2 ☐ Some full-time and some part-time

3 ☐ Only or mostly part-time

B4. What kind of work were you doing on that first job--that is, what was your occupation? *Please be as specific as possible, including any area of specialization.*

Example: High school teacher - Math

_____

B4a. Using the *OCCUPATIONAL FIELD LIST* (Page 17), select the occupational field code that BEST describes that first job.

OCCUPATION CODE |___|___| 317:318

B4b. Did you record occupation code "07" (*Executive, Managerial, Administrative*) in B4a?

1 ☐ Yes

2 ☐ No → *SKIP to B4d*   319

▼

B4c. Using the *EXECUTIVE, MANAGERIAL, ADMINISTRATIVE CODE LIST* (Page 17), select the code that BEST describes that position.

CODE |___|___| 320:321

B4d. Was this first job the only job you've held since college?

1 ☐ Yes → *SKIP to B10d, page 8*   322

2 ☐ No → *CONTINUE with B5, page 8*   SKIP 323:331

April 1995 or Last Job

B5. Did you work for pay (or profit) at any time during April 1995? This includes being self-employed or temporarily absent from a job (e.g., illness, vacation, or parental leave).

- 1 ☐ Yes → *SKIP to "PLEASE READ" Box Below*
- 2 ☐ No, was retired   332
- 3 ☐ No, did not work for other reasons

B6. When did your last job **prior to** April 1995 end?

JOB
ENDED: |___|___| 19 |___|___| 333:336
     Month   Year

PLEASE READ:

- *If working during April 1995, answer the following questions about your principal job that month.*

- *If not working during April 1995, answer the following questions about your last job prior to April 1995.*

B7. Was your April 1995 job (or your last job prior to April 1995) with the same employer as your first job?

- 1 ☐ Yes → *SKIP to B9*   337
- 2 ☐ No

B8. Was your employer on your principal job during April 1995 (or your last job prior to April 1995) . . .

Mark (X) one box

- 1 ☐ A FOR-PROFIT company, business or individual, working for wages, salary or commissions
- 2 ☐ A NOT-FOR-PROFIT, tax-exempt, organization (includes private schools and private colleges/universities)
- 3 ☐ SELF-EMPLOYED in own business, professional practice, or farm   338
- 4 ☐ State or local GOVERNMENT (city, county, etc.) (includes public schools and public colleges/universities)
- 5 ☐ U.S. GOVERNMENT including military
- 6 ☐ Other - *Specify:*
  _____

B9. While holding this job, were you working . . .

Mark (X) one box

- 1 ☐ Only or mostly full-time   339
- 2 ☐ Some full-time and some part-time
- 3 ☐ Only or mostly part-time

B10. What kind of work were you doing on this job-- that is, what was your occupation? *Please be as specific as possible, including any area of specialization.*

Example: High school teacher - Math

_____

B10a. Using the *OCCUPATIONAL FIELD LIST* (Page 17), select the occupational field code that BEST describes that job.

OCCUPATION CODE |___|___| 340:341

B10b. Did you record occupation code "07" (*Executive, Managerial, Administrative*) in B10a?

- 1 ☐ Yes   342
- 2 ☐ No → *SKIP to B10d*

B10c. Using the *EXECUTIVE, MANAGERIAL, ADMINISTRATIVE CODE LIST* (Page 17), select the code that BEST describes that position.

CODE |___|___| 343:344

B10d. Overall, how satisfied were you with your April 1995 job (or your last job prior to April 1995)?

- 1 ☐ Very satisfied   345
- 2 ☐ Somewhat satisfied
- 3 ☐ Neither satisfied nor dissatisfied
- 4 ☐ Somewhat dissatisfied
- 5 ☐ Very dissatisfied

Job Held the Longest

B11. Was the job you held the longest . . .

Mark (X) one box

1 ☐ One of the jobs you've already described, or

2 ☐ Some other job? → *SKIP to B11b*

346

B11a. Which job have you held the longest . . .

Mark (X) one box

1 ☐ Your first job held 6 months or longer,

2 ☐ Your April 1995 job, or   ➤ *SKIP to B15, page 10*

3 ☐ Your last job prior to April 1995?

347

B11b. When did this job begin?

JOB
BEGAN: |___|___| 19 |___|___| 348:351
　　　　　Month　　　Year

B11c. And when did this job end, or are you still working at this job?

JOB
ENDED: |___|___| 19 |___|___| 352:355
　　　　　Month　　　Year

0 ☐ Still working at the job   356

B12. Is (or was) your employer on the job you held the longest . . .

Mark (X) one box

1 ☐ A FOR-PROFIT company, business or individual, working for wages, salary or commissions

2 ☐ A NOT-FOR-PROFIT, tax-exempt, organization (includes private schools and private colleges/universities)

3 ☐ SELF-EMPLOYED in own business, professional practice, or farm   357

4 ☐ State or local GOVERNMENT (city, county, etc.) (includes public schools and public colleges/universities)

5 ☐ U.S. GOVERNMENT including military

6 ☐ Other - *Specify:*

_____

B13. While holding that job, are you (or were you) working . . .

Mark (X) one box

1 ☐ Only or mostly full-time   358

2 ☐ Some full-time and some part-time

3 ☐ Only or mostly part-time

B14. What kind of work are you (or were you) doing on the job you held the longest; that is, what is (or was) your occupation? *Please be as specific as possible, including any area of specialization.*

Example: High school teacher - Math

_____

B14a. Using the *OCCUPATIONAL FIELD LIST* (Page 17), select the occupational field code that BEST describes that job you held the longest.

OCCUPATION CODE |___|___| 359:360

B14b. Did you record occupation code "07" (*Executive, Managerial, Administrative*) in B14a?

1 ☐ Yes   361

2 ☐ No → *SKIP to B14d*

B14c. Using the *EXECUTIVE, MANAGERIAL, ADMINISTRATIVE CODE LIST* (Page 17), select the code that BEST describes that position.

CODE |___|___| 362:363

B14d. Overall, how satisfied are you (or were you) with the job you held the longest?

1 ☐ Very satisfied

2 ☐ Somewhat satisfied   364

3 ☐ Neither satisfied nor dissatisfied

4 ☐ Somewhat dissatisfied

5 ☐ Very dissatisfied

B15. When thinking about a job, how important is each of the following to you:

	Very Important	Somewhat Important	Not Important
a. Intellectual challenge	3 ☐	2 ☐	1 ☐
b. Independence/autonomy	3 ☐	2 ☐	1 ☐
c. Flexible schedule	3 ☐	2 ☐	1 ☐
d. High level of responsibility	3 ☐	2 ☐	1 ☐
e. Low stress	3 ☐	2 ☐	1 ☐
f. Pleasant working environment	3 ☐	2 ☐	1 ☐
g. Job security	3 ☐	2 ☐	1 ☐
h. Adequate employer-supported child care .	3 ☐	2 ☐	1 ☐
i. Fair treatment of women and minorities ..	3 ☐	2 ☐	1 ☐
j. High income	3 ☐	2 ☐	1 ☐
k. Good benefits	3 ☐	2 ☐	1 ☐
l. Good promotion opportunities	3 ☐	2 ☐	1 ☐
m. Service to society	3 ☐	2 ☐	1 ☐

365:377
80=3

B15a. Using these same criteria, please rate your satisfaction with your principal job during April 1995 (or, if you were not working during April 1995, your last job prior to that date).

	Very Satisfied	Somewhat Satisfied	Not Satisfied
a. Intellectual challenge	3 ☐	2 ☐	1 ☐
b. Independence/autonomy	3 ☐	2 ☐	1 ☐
c. Flexible schedule	3 ☐	2 ☐	1 ☐
d. High level of responsibility	3 ☐	2 ☐	1 ☐
e. Low stress	3 ☐	2 ☐	1 ☐
f. Pleasant working environment	3 ☐	2 ☐	1 ☐
g. Job security	3 ☐	2 ☐	1 ☐
h. Adequate employer-supported child care .	3 ☐	2 ☐	1 ☐
i. Fair treatment of women and minorities ..	3 ☐	2 ☐	1 ☐
j. High income	3 ☐	2 ☐	1 ☐
k. Good benefits	3 ☐	2 ☐	1 ☐
l. Good promotion opportunities	3 ☐	2 ☐	1 ☐
m. Service to society	3 ☐	2 ☐	1 ☐

410:422

PERIODS NOT WORKING

B16.   Including retirement or being a full-time student, have you had any periods lasting 6 months or longer when you were not working for pay since leaving undergraduate school?

1 ☐   Yes   423

2 ☐   No → *SKIP to Section C, page 12*

B16a. Please provide the following information for each period lasting 6 months or longer. Your best guess on the dates is fine.

DATES		REASONS FOR NOT WORKING - *Mark (X) all that apply*							
FROM	**TO**	Retired ↓	Layoff/ Job ended/ Company closed ↓	Full-time student not working ↓	Family responsi- bilities ↓	Chronic illness or permanent disability ↓	Suitable job not available ↓	Did not need or want to work ↓	Other ↓
Month Year	Month Year								
1. |_|_| 19 |_|_|	|_|_| 19 |_|_|	1 ☐	2 ☐	3 ☐	4 ☐	5 ☐	6 ☐	7 ☐	8 ☐
2. |_|_| 19|_|_|	|_|_| 19 |_|_|	1 ☐	2 ☐	3 ☐	4 ☐	5 ☐	6 ☐	7 ☐	8 ☐
3. |_|_| 19|_|_|	|_|_| 19 |_|_|	1 ☐	2 ☐	3 ☐	4 ☐	5 ☐	6 ☐	7 ☐	8 ☐
4. |_|_| 19|_|_|	|_|_| 19 |_|_|	1 ☐	2 ☐	3 ☐	4 ☐	5 ☐	6 ☐	7 ☐	8 ☐
5. |_|_| 19|_|_|	|_|_| 19 |_|_|	1 ☐	2 ☐	3 ☐	4 ☐	5 ☐	6 ☐	7 ☐	8 ☐

424:443   444:463   464:468
                                                                                         80=4

SECTION C: CIVIC ACTIVITIES

C1. To what extent have you participated as a volunteer in <u>each</u> of the following activities since college? (By volunteer, we mean you were not an employee of the group.)

Mark (X) all that apply

	Participation During 1994-1995		Participation Prior to 1994		Have Never Participated
	Member/ Participant	Leadership Role	Member/ Participant	Leadership Role	
a. Youth organizations--such as Little League coach, scouting, etc.	5 ☐	4 ☐	3 ☐	2 ☐	1 ☐
b. Professional or trade associations	5 ☐	4 ☐	3 ☐	2 ☐	1 ☐
c. Political clubs or organizations or local government activities	5 ☐	4 ☐	3 ☐	2 ☐	1 ☐
d. Religious activities (not including worship services)	5 ☐	4 ☐	3 ☐	2 ☐	1 ☐
e. Community centers, neighborhood improvement or social-action associations or civil rights groups	5 ☐	4 ☐	3 ☐	2 ☐	1 ☐
f. Social service or social welfare volunteer work--such as on a hospital planning board, hospital volunteering, etc.	5 ☐	4 ☐	3 ☐	2 ☐	1 ☐
h. Sports teams or sports clubs	5 ☐	4 ☐	3 ☐	2 ☐	1 ☐
i. Literary, art, discussion, music, or study groups; museum board, cultural or historical societies	5 ☐	4 ☐	3 ☐	2 ☐	1 ☐
j. Educational organizations--such as PTA, school board, school trustee, etc.	5 ☐	4 ☐	3 ☐	2 ☐	1 ☐
k. Service organizations--such as Rotary, Junior Chamber of Commerce, Veterans, etc.	5 ☐	4 ☐	3 ☐	2 ☐	1 ☐
l. Alumni activities--such as fund raising, student recruiting, etc. (for any school attended)	5 ☐	4 ☐	3 ☐	2 ☐	1 ☐
m. National charities--such as The American Cancer Society, The American Red Cross, etc.	5 ☐	4 ☐	3 ☐	2 ☐	1 ☐
n. Environmental or conservational activities	5 ☐	4 ☐	3 ☐	2 ☐	1 ☐
o. Another group in which you participate as a volunteer - *Specify:* _____	5 ☐	4 ☐	3 ☐	2 ☐	1 ☐

510:523

C2. Did you vote in the 1992 Presidential election?

1 ☐ Yes   524

2 ☐ No

C3. Thinking about your views concerning economic and social issues, where would you place yourself on the scale below:

Mark (X) one for each

	Very Liberal				Very Conservative	
a. Economic issues	1 ☐	2 ☐	3 ☐	4 ☐	5 ☐	525
b. Social issues	1 ☐	2 ☐	3 ☐	4 ☐	5 ☐	526

D1. In general, how satisfied would you say you are with your life right now? Would you say you are . . .

Mark (X) one box

1 ☐ Very satisfied

2 ☐ Somewhat satisfied   527

3 ☐ Neither satisfied nor dissatisfied

4 ☐ Somewhat dissatisfied

5 ☐ Very dissatisfied

D2. The next several questions ask about your satisfaction with different areas of your life. For each area of life listed, indicate how much <u>satisfaction</u> you get from the area.

D2a. How much satisfaction do you get from the city or place you live in?

Mark (X) one box

1 ☐ A very great deal

2 ☐ A great deal   528

3 ☐ Quite a bit

4 ☐ A fair amount

5 ☐ Some

6 ☐ A little, or

7 ☐ None

D2b. How much satisfaction do you get from your non-working activities--hobbies and so on?

Mark (X) one box

1 ☐ A very great deal

2 ☐ A great deal   529

3 ☐ Quite a bit

4 ☐ A fair amount

5 ☐ Some

6 ☐ A little, or

7 ☐ None

D2c. How much satisfaction do you get from your family life?

Mark (X) one box

1 ☐ A very great deal

2 ☐ A great deal   530

3 ☐ Quite a bit

4 ☐ A fair amount

5 ☐ Some

6 ☐ A little, or

7 ☐ None

D2d. How much satisfaction do you get from your friendships?

Mark (X) one box

1 ☐ A very great deal

2 ☐ A great deal   531

3 ☐ Quite a bit

4 ☐ A fair amount

5 ☐ Some

6 ☐ A little, or

7 ☐ None

D2e. How much satisfaction do you get from your health and physical condition?

Mark (X) one box

1 ☐ A very great deal

2 ☐ A great deal   532

3 ☐ Quite a bit

4 ☐ A fair amount

5 ☐ Some

6 ☐ A little, or

7 ☐ None

D3. Are you . . .

Mark (X) one box

1 ☐ Married

2 ☐ Living with someone in a marriage-like relationship

3 ☐ Widowed

4 ☐ Separated ➤ *SKIP to D6*   533

5 ☐ Divorced

6 ☐ Never married

D4. What is the highest level of education your spouse or partner has attained?

Mark (X) one box

1 ☐ Less than a high school graduate

2 ☐ High school graduate

3 ☐ Some college/vocational school   534

4 ☐ Bachelor's degree

5 ☐ Some graduate school

6 ☐ Master's degree

7 ☐ Law degree (LLB, JD)

8 ☐ Medical degree (MD, DDS, DVM, etc.)

9 ☐ Doctoral degree

10 ☐ Other - *Specify:* _____

D5. Did your spouse or partner work for pay (or profit) at any time during April 1995? This includes being self-employed or temporarily absent from a job (e.g., illness, vacation, or parental leave).

1 ☐ Yes   535

2 ☐ No

D6. How many children (including adopted and stepchildren) have you ever had?

0 ☐ None   536

_____ NUMBER OF CHILDREN   537:538 SKIP 539:551

D7. Please mark the category below which best represents <u>YOUR OWN earned income for 1995, before taxes</u>. Please include income from jobs, net income from business, farm or rent, pensions or social security payments.

• *Do <u>NOT</u> include income from dividends, interest, or other family members such as a spouse or partner--these are included in the next question.*

Mark (X) one box

01 ☐ Less than $1,000

02 ☐ $1,000 to $9,999

03 ☐ $10,000 to $19,999

04 ☐ $20,000 to $29,999   552

05 ☐ $30,000 to $49,999

06 ☐ $50,000 to $74,999

07 ☐ $75,000 to $99,999

08 ☐ $100,000 to $149,999

09 ☐ $150,000 to $199,999

10 ☐ $200,000 or more

D8. Please mark the category below that best represents <u>your total household income for 1995 before taxes</u>.

• *Include all the sources listed in D7 and <u>also</u> include income from dividends or interest and income earned by your spouse or partner.*

Mark (X) one box

01 ☐ Less than $1,000

02 ☐ $1,000 to $9,999

03 ☐ $10,000 to $19,999

04 ☐ $20,000 to $29,999   553

05 ☐ $30,000 to $49,999

06 ☐ $50,000 to $74,999

07 ☐ $75,000 to $99,999

08 ☐ $100,000 to $149,999

09 ☐ $150,000 to $199,999

10 ☐ $200,000 or more

D9. Were you working full-time for pay or profit during all of 1995?

- *This includes being self-employed or temporarily absent from a job (e.g., illness, vacation, or parental leave).*

  1 ☐ Yes → *SKIP to D10*   554

  2 ☐ No

D9a. What was the last year in which you worked full-time for pay or profit for the entire year?

19 |___|___| 555:556
   Year

D9b. Please mark the category below which best represents <u>YOUR OWN earned income before taxes for the year you indicated in D9a.</u>

- *Include only those sources listed in D7.*

Mark (X) one box

01 ☐ Less than $1,000

02 ☐ $1,000 to $9,999

03 ☐ $10,000 to $19,999

04 ☐ $20,000 to $29,999

05 ☐ $30,000 to $49,999

06 ☐ $50,000 to $74,999   557

07 ☐ $75,000 to $99,999

08 ☐ $100,000 to $149,999

09 ☐ $150,000 to $199,999

10 ☐ $200,000 or more

D10. As of April 1995, were you a . . .

Mark (X) one box

<u>U.S. Citizen</u>

  1 ☐ Native born   558

  2 ☐ Naturalized

<u>Non-U.S. Citizen</u>

  3 ☐ With a permanent U.S. resident visa

  4 ☐ With a temporary U.S. resident visa

  5 ☐ Living outside the United States

D11. Do you consider yourself . . .

Mark (X) one box

  1 ☐ Black, not Hispanic

  2 ☐ Black, Hispanic   559

  3 ☐ White, not Hispanic

  4 ☐ White, Hispanic

  5 ☐ Asian or Pacific Islander

  6 ☐ Native American or Alaskan Native

D12. Are you:

  1 ☐ Male   560

  2 ☐ Female

D13. Next we have a few questions about your parents at the time you were applying to undergraduate schools (e.g., your senior year in high school).

During your senior year in high school, what was the highest level of education your <u>father</u> had attained?

Mark (X) one box

01 ☐ Less than a high school graduate

02 ☐ High school graduate

03 ☐ Some college/vocational school

04 ☐ Bachelor's degree

05 ☐ Some graduate school

06 ☐ Master's degree

07 ☐ Law degree (LLB, JD)

08 ☐ Medical degree (MD, DDS, DVM, etc.)   561:562

09 ☐ Doctoral degree

10 ☐ Other - *Specify:*

_____

11 ☐ Don't know

D13a. Was your father working for pay at anytime during your senior year in high school?

  1 ☐ Yes   563

  2 ☐ No → *SKIP to D14, page 16*

D13b. What kind of work was your father doing, that is, what was his occupation at that time? *Please be as specific as possible, including any area of specialization.*

Example: High school teacher - Math.

_____

D14. During your senior year in high school, what was the highest level of education your <u>mother</u> had attained?

Mark (X) one box

01 ☐ Less than a high school graduate

02 ☐ High school graduate

03 ☐ Some college/vocational school

04 ☐ Bachelor's degree

05 ☐ Some graduate school

06 ☐ Master's degree

07 ☐ Law degree (LLB, JD)

08 ☐ Medical degree (MD, DDS, DVM, etc.)

09 ☐ Doctoral degree

10 ☐ Other - *Specify:*

_____

11 ☐ Don't know

564:565

D14a. Was your mother working for pay at anytime during your senior year in high school?

1 ☐ Yes

2 ☐ No → **SKIP to D15**

566

D14b. What kind of work was your mother doing, that is, what was her occupation at that time? *Please be as specific as possible, including any area of specialization.*

Example: High school teacher - Math.

_____

D15. After the data have been collected and analyzed we will prepare a summary of the findings for distribution. Would you like us to send you a copy of the findings?

1 ☐ Yes

2 ☐ No

567
580=5

D16. Questionnaires often don't allow respondents to tell us about their experiences in their own words. Since you may have had experiences at college which had a major effect on your life, but about which we did not ask, please use this space to tell us about these additional college experiences. Any other thoughts or comments about college are also welcomed and appreciated. Attach another sheet if necessary.

Thank you for completing the questionnaire.

Please return the completed form in the postage-paid envelope provided. If you have lost the envelope, our address is:

The Andrew W. Mellon Foundation
c/o Mathematica Policy Research, Inc.
P.O. Box 2393
Princeton, NJ 08543-2393

OCCUPATIONAL FIELD LIST

01   **Clergy, other religious worker, social worker**
02   **Clerical/support** occupation (e.g., secretary, receptionist, office manager, bookkeeper, bank teller, data entry)
03   **Computer** occupation
**   **Consultant** → select the code that comes closest to your usual area of consulting
04   **Education**--preschool/elementary/secondary school (teaching, coaching)
05   **Education**--postsecondary (faculty, teaching, coaching)
06   **Engineering and architecture** (including engineering technology and technician)
07   **Executive**/managerial/administrative
08   **Financial services** (e.g., banker, stockbroker, investment manager)
09   **Health** occupation - physician, dentist, veterinarian
10   **Other health** occupations (e.g., nurse, therapist, pharmacist, health technologist)
11   **Insurance**
12   **Law** (e.g., lawyer, judge)
13   **Management consultant**
14   **Marketing and sales** (advertising, real estate sales, retail sales and service)
15   **Military** service
16   **Natural science** and **mathematical** occupations (e.g., chemist, biologist, statistician)--excluding teaching and medicine--See codes 04 and 05 for teachng; 09 and 10 for medicine

**   **Research** associate/assistant → select the code that comes closest to your field

17   **Social science** occupations (e.g., sociologist, economist, librarian)--excluding teaching--See codes 04 and 05 for teaching

18   **Writing, editing, artist, performer,** and **athlete**

19   **Other** occupations (e.g., firefighter, police officer, cook, construction, mechanic, tailor, etc.)

EXECUTIVE, MANAGERIAL, ADMINISTRATIVE CODE LIST

20   Top executive (CEO, COO)

21   General management

22   Finance

23   Profit center head

24   Manufacturing/engineering/MIS

25   Marketing/sales

26   Human resources

27   Legal

28   Public/community/government relations

29   Research and development

30   Other--executive/management/administrative

EXHIBIT A.2
Interaction Questions on 1989 Survey

A13. Undergraduate school can be a place for meeting people from different backgrounds. Based on your own undergraduate school experiences, did you get to know any of the following types of people? *People who fit more than one category (e.g., a very wealthy roommate from Italy) can be noted more than once.*

	PART A — Where did you meet these students? *Mark All Settings That Apply for Each Category Marked "YES"*					PART B — Did you get to know 2 or more of these students *well* while in school? *Mark "NO" if you only knew one person well in a category*	
While in undergraduate school, did you get to know any students who were: • *Please indicate "YES" or "NO" for each category below. For each category marked "YES," please answer Parts A and B.* NO OR DON'T KNOW / YES	Class or Study Groups	Same Dorm or Roommate	Playing Sports *(Any Level)*	Parties/ Other Social Activities	Other Extra-Curricular Activities	NO	YES
1. From a different region of the *USA*? .... 2☐ 1☐ →	1☐	2☐	3☐	4☐	5☐	2☐	1☐
2. From a different *country*? .... 2☐ 1☐ →	1☐	2☐	3☐	4☐	5☐	2☐	1☐
3. From a family much *wealthier* than yours? ... 2☐ 1☐ →	1☐	2☐	3☐	4☐	5☐	2☐	1☐
4. From a family much *poorer* than yours? ...... 2☐ 1☐ →	1☐	2☐	3☐	4☐	5☐	2☐	1☐
5. Politically much more *conservative* than you? . 2☐ 1☐ →	1☐	2☐	3☐	4☐	5☐	2☐	1☐
6. Politically much more *liberal* than you? .... 2☐ 1☐ →	1☐	2☐	3☐	4☐	5☐	2☐	1☐
7. From a *racial group* other than your own *(Leave your own racial group blank):*							
a. *African American* or *Black*? .... 2☐ 1☐ →	1☐	2☐	3☐	4☐	5☐	2☐	1☐
b. *Asian* or *Asian American*? .... 2☐ 1☐ →	1☐	2☐	3☐	4☐	5☐	2☐	1☐
c. *Hispanic*? .... 2☐ 1☐ →	1☐	2☐	3☐	4☐	5☐	2☐	1☐
d. *Native American*? ... 2☐ 1☐ →	1☐	2☐	3☐	4☐	5☐	2☐	1☐
e. *White*? .... 2☐ 1☐ →	1☐	2☐	3☐	4☐	5☐	2☐	1☐
	310:320	321:331					332:342

A16. Since leaving undergraduate school, did you get to know any of the following types of people? *People who fit more than one category (e.g., a politically liberal co-worker from Bali) can be noted more than once.*

- *Please indicate "YES" or "NO" for each category below. For each category marked "YES," please answer Parts A and B.*

PART A

Where did you meet these people?

Mark All Settings That Apply for Each Category Marked "YES"

PART B

Did you get to know 2 or more of these people *well*?

Mark "NO" if you only knew one person well in a category

	NO OR DON'T KNOW / YES		In Graduate or Professional School	In Any Job Since College	In Community or Other Activities Since College	NO	YES
1. From a different region of the *USA*?	₂☐ ₁☐ →		₁☐	₂☐	₃☐	₂☐	₁☐
2. From a different *country*?	₂☐ ₁☐ →		₁☐	₂☐	₃☐	₂☐	₁☐
3. From a family much *wealthier* than yours?	₂☐ ₁☐ →		₁☐	₂☐	₃☐	₂☐	₁☐
4. From a family much *poorer* than yours?	₂☐ ₁☐ →		₁☐	₂☐	₃☐	₂☐	₁☐
5. Politically much more *conservative* than you?	₂☐ ₁☐ →		₁☐	₂☐	₃☐	₂☐	₁☐
6. Politically much more *liberal* than you?	₂☐ ₁☐ →		₁☐	₂☐	₃☐	₂☐	₁☐
7. From a *racial group* other than your own (*Leave your own racial group blank*):							
a. *African American* or *Black*?	₂☐ ₁☐ →		₁☐	₂☐	₃☐	₂☐	₁☐
b. *Asian* or *Asian American*?	₂☐ ₁☐ →		₁☐	₂☐	₃☐	₂☐	₁☐
c. *Hispanic*?	₂☐ ₁☐ →		₁☐	₂☐	₃☐	₂☐	₁☐
d. *Native American*?	₂☐ ₁☐ →		₁☐	₂☐	₃☐	₂☐	₁☐
e. *White*?	₂☐ ₁☐ →		₁☐	₂☐	₃☐	₂☐	₁☐

428:438   439:449   450:460

Notes on Methodology*

APPENDIX B describes the methods of analysis used in this study. The first section deals with general methodological issues that affect the study as a whole. The other sections address issues specific to particular chapters.

GENERAL METHODOLOGICAL ISSUES

This section begins with a note on the use of sample weights and definitions of two central constructs employed in the study—institutional selectivity and socioeconomic status. Next, we discuss regression analysis and our method of computing adjusted probabilities. At the end of the section, we describe our general approach to building regression models.

Sample Weights

As explained in Appendix A, both the institutional data file and the survey data file included the entire entering cohorts at most C&B schools but were constructed from samples at some institutions. All tabulations and regression analyses presented in the text use appropriate sample weights so that the results accurately represent the entire entering cohort at each institution. Both the institutional weights and the survey weights equal the inverse of the probability of being sampled. The institutional weight is used in all analyses where the outcome of interest is an institutional variable (for example, percentile rank in class, choice of major, etc.). For all tabulations and regression analyses involving survey variables (for example, income, satisfaction with life, etc.), we use a weight equal to the product of the survey weight and the institutional weight. (The survey sample was drawn from the institutional sample, so the probability of being selected for the survey is conditional on being selected for the institutional sample.) For implications of using sample weights in regression analysis, see DeMouchel and Duncan (1983).

---

*Appendix B was prepared by Thomas I. Nygren and Stacy Berg Dale.

Institutional Selectivity

The twenty-eight College and Beyond institutions are grouped into three selectivity categories based on the mean combined SAT score of entering freshmen.[1] Although SAT scores are not the only possible measure of selectivity, they were the most consistent and widely available, and we believe they are a reasonably accurate measure of the overall academic quality of an institution's entering class. The average SAT score of the entering class also serves as a proxy for other characteristics of the school. In general, schools that attract students with high SAT scores have more financial resources at their disposal than do other schools, which is likely to affect the provision of financial aid and other support services, as well as class size and library and laboratory facilities. The SAT scores of entering students can also be expected to correlate positively with the general quality of the faculty. Thus, the relationship between school selectivity and outcomes of various kinds (graduation rates, advanced degrees attained, earnings, and so on) is presumably affected by this entire set of factors, not just average SAT scores per se.

We selected the SAT cutoff points between categories by ranking the twenty-eight schools and identifying the "natural" breakpoints that would create the most homogeneous groupings (recognizing that such classifications inevitably run the risk of arbitrariness).[2] The categories are defined as follows:

- *SEL-1:* Institutions at which the average combined SAT score of the entering class was 1250 or higher in 1976 and 1300 or higher in 1989;
- *SEL-2:* Institutions at which the average combined SAT score of the entering class was at least 1125 but less than 1250 in 1976, and at least 1150 but less than 1300 in 1989;
- *SEL-3:* Institutions at which the average combined SAT score of the entering class was below 1125 in 1976 and below 1150 in 1989.

---

[1] The mean SAT score of matriculants at each school was computed from SAT data in the C&B institutional data file (using institutional sample weights where appropriate). All SAT scores in the C&B database are prior to the recentering of scores that took place in 1995. ACT scores were converted to an approximately equivalent combined SAT score. Either SAT or ACT scores were available for 96 percent of 1976 matriculants in the database and 99.5 percent of 1989 matriculants.

[2] An alternative approach to using three categories would be to assign each institution its own mean combined SAT score, in effect creating twenty-eight selectivity categories. Besides making tabular presentations difficult, we believe this approach would place too much weight on fine distinctions among schools that are, in practical terms, at roughly the same selectivity level.

The institutions in each category are listed in Table B.1.[3] The definitions of the categories shift upwards by 25–50 points between the two cohorts because of the increase in selectivity of the C&B schools that occurred between 1976 and 1989. The list of particular schools falling into each category also varies slightly between the two cohorts.

Socioeconomic Status

We created three socioeconomic status (SES) categories—low, middle, and high—which were intended to capture, at least roughly, the socio-economic environment in which a student was raised. We used two criteria to assign each student to an SES category, family income and parental education. Our low-SES category consists of students from families in which neither parent graduated from college *and* family income was less than $10,000 in 1976, or less than $22,000 in 1989; the high-SES category consists of students from families in which at least one parent was a college graduate *and* family income was more than $30,000 in 1976, or more than $70,000 in 1989.[4] The middle-SES category[5] consists of all other students for whom SES information was available (i.e., those who did not meet both criteria for either the high- or the low-SES category).

In order to gather SES information for as many C&B matriculants as possible, we pooled the parental income and education data from C&B institutional records, the C&B survey, the Cooperative Institutional Research Program (CIRP) questionnaire administered by the Higher Education Research Institute, and the College Entrance Examination Board's Student Descriptive Questionnaire (see Appendix A for a description of these data sources). By using all four sources, we were able to

[3] The mean scores we report may not correspond to published sources, which are generally based on data self-reported by institutions.

[4] The low-income thresholds for both years are at about the 30th percentile of the national income distribution for families of 16- to 18-year-olds. (For the sake of comparison, the federally defined poverty levels for a family of four in 1976 and 1989 were $5,815 and $12,674, respectively.) Although the cutoffs are somewhat arbitrary, they have the advantage of being at least roughly comparable with federal eligibility limits for the need-based Pell Grant program. They are also comparable to the limits used by Kane (forthcoming) in his definition of low socioeconomic status.

The high-income thresholds were selected for a pragmatic reason: they were the highest categories students could select on the 1976 and 1989 ETS Student Descriptive Questionnaires, which were the most complete sources of parental income data available to us. For both years, they are at about the 85th percentile of the national income distribution for families of 16- to 18-year-olds.

[5] In both text and tables, we use the terms "middle SES" and "mid SES" interchangeably.

TABLE B.1

Institutions in Each Institutional Selectivity Category, 1976 and 1989
Entering Cohorts

	1976 Entering Cohort	*1989 Entering Cohort*
SEL-1	Bryn Mawr College	Bryn Mawr College
	Princeton University	Duke University
	Rice University	Princeton University
	Stanford University	Rice University
	Swarthmore College	Stanford University
	Wesleyan University	Swarthmore College
	Williams College	Williams College
	Yale University	Yale University
SEL-2	Barnard College	Barnard College
	Columbia University	Columbia University
	Duke University	Emory University
	Hamilton College	Hamilton College
	Kenyon College	Kenyon College
	Northwestern University	Northwestern University
	Oberlin College	Oberlin College
	Smith College	Smith College
	Tufts University	Tufts University
	University of Pennsylvania	University of Pennsylvania
	Vanderbilt University	Vanderbilt University
	Washington University	Washington University
	Wellesley College	Wellesley College
		Wesleyan University
SEL-3	Denison University	Denison University
	Emory University	Miami University (Ohio)
	Miami University (Ohio)	Pennsylvania State University
	Pennsylvania State University	Tulane University
	Tulane University	University of Michigan
	University of Michigan	(Ann Arbor)
	(Ann Arbor)	University of North Carolina
	University of North Carolina	(Chapel Hill)
	(Chapel Hill)	

Source: College and Beyond.

Notes: For 1976, "SEL-1," "SEL-2," and "SEL-3" indicate institutions whose matriculants had mean combined SAT scores of 1250 or higher, 1125–1249, and below 1125, respectively. For 1989, "SEL-1," "SEL-2," and "SEL-3" indicate institutions whose matriculants had mean combined SAT scores of 1300 or higher, 1150–1299, and below 1150, respectively.

determine both family income and parental education for 71 percent of the 1976 entering cohort and 82 percent of the 1989 entering cohort.[6] Students for whom either parental education or family income data were missing were assigned to the "SES not available" category. Because the percentages with missing SES information were sizable (29 percent for the '76 cohort and 18 percent for the '89 cohort), we included a variable for "SES not available" in all of our regression analyses.

To construct national benchmarks, we used the 1990 and 1980 U.S. Censuses to determine the SES distribution of the families of 16- to 18-year-olds, using the same two criteria. Because the 1980 U.S. Census reports 1979 household income, we inflated the 1976 income thresholds, using the Consumer Price Index; the revised low-income threshold for the 1980 Census population was $12,800, and the revised high-income threshold was $38,300. (The 1990 Census reports 1989 income, so no adjustments were necessary.) Table B.2 shows the percentages of the C&B population and the corresponding national population that are in each SES category, as well as the percentages meeting each of the individual SES criteria.

Regression Analysis

In the text, we often use multivariate regression analysis to estimate the effect that each explanatory, or independent, variable has on a given dependent variable, holding the effect of other variables constant. For example, if we want to estimate whether men or women get better grades, other things equal, it is important to control for SAT scores since we know that men and women perform differently on standardized tests. Most of the explanatory variables we use are categorical, such as gender (men or women) or socioeconomic status (low, mid, or high). When constructing a model with categorical explanatory variables, one category must be omitted from the regression model to serve as the baseline group to which the other categories are compared. Parameter estimates should be interpreted relative to the baseline group. Thus, the parameter estimate for FEMALE (which is assigned a value of 1 for women and 0 for men) should be interpreted relative to the omitted category, MALE. Likewise, the parameter estimates for socioeconomic status, HighSES and LowSES, should be interpreted relative to the omitted category, MidSES.

---

[6] There were some cases in which students reported different parental information on different surveys. In these cases, we used the highest reported income and/or level of education.

TABLE B.2

Socioeconomic Status Criteria, by Race, College and Beyond Matriculants and National College-Age Students, 1976 and 1989 Entering Cohorts (percent of cohort)

	College and Beyond			National		
	Black	White	All	Black	White	All
	1976 Entering Cohort					
Low SES						
Percentage meeting first criterion (neither parent has BA)	54	24	26	95	82	85
Percentage meeting second criterion (low income)	35	6	8	49	22	28
Percentage low SES (meeting both criteria)	26	4	5	48	21	27
High SES						
Percentage meeting first criterion (at least one parent has BA)	46	76	74	5	18	15
Percentage meeting second criterion (high income)	12	43	40	6	21	18
Percentage high SES (meeting both criteria)	11	40	38	1	9	7
Middle SES (neither low SES nor high SES)	63	56	57	51	70	66
	1989 Entering Cohort					
Low SES						
Percentage meeting first criterion (neither parent has BA)	36	15	17	89	75	79
Percentage meeting second criterion (low income)	20	3	6	51	23	30
Percentage low SES (meeting both criteria)	14	2	3	50	22	28
High SES						
Percentage meeting first criterion (at least one parent has BA)	64	85	83	11	25	21
Percentage meeting second criterion (high income)	15	46	43	6	18	15
Percentage high SES (meeting both criteria)	15	44	41	3	11	9
Middle SES (neither low SES nor high SES)	71	54	56	47	67	63

Sources: U.S. Census (1980 and 1990) and College and Beyond.

Notes: National SES characteristics are based on data for the families of 16- to 18-year-olds in the 1980 and 1990 U.S. Censuses. High income is defined as more than $30,000 in 1976 or more than $70,000 in 1989. Low income is defined as less than $10,000 in 1976 or less than $22,000 in 1989. Respondents for whom SES data were missing were excluded from these tabulations. See text for details.

Some of our dependent variables are continuous, such as income or percentile rank in class; others are binary (i.e., they have two values, like "graduating" versus "not graduating" or "being very satisfied" versus "not being very satisfied"). When we analyze continuous variables, we use ordinary least squares (OLS) regression analysis. The coefficients estimated in an OLS model tell us the change in the dependent variable associated with a change in the independent variable, holding the effect of the other variables in the model constant. For example, in the OLS model predicting percentile rank-in-class, the coefficient for FEMALE is 8.2, which implies that if a woman and a man have the same SAT scores, SES, and other characteristics, the woman will have a percentile rank in class that is 8.2 points higher than the man, on average.

When we analyze dependent variables that are not continuous, but binary, we use logistic regression models. The logistic model is based on the cumulative logistic probability function and is specified as

$$\text{Probability } [Y_i = 1] = P_i = \frac{1}{1 + e^{-(\alpha + \beta X_i)}} \tag{1}$$

where P_i is the probability that Y, the outcome in question (e.g. graduating), will take place for the ith individual, e represents Euler's constant (which is approximately equal to 2.718), α is the intercept parameter (or constant term), X_i is a vector of explanatory (independent) variables, and β is a vector of parameter estimates for each of the independent variables in the vector X_i.[7] Dividing the expected probability that an event will occur by the probability that it will not occur, and transforming this equation by taking logs results in:

$$\text{logit}(P_i) = \log\left(\frac{P_i}{1 - P_i}\right) = \alpha + \beta X_i \tag{2}$$

To obtain the parameters α and β, maximum likelihood estimation is used to find the set of parameters that make it most likely that the observed outcomes would have occurred.[8] The logarithm of the odds that a particular outcome will occur (sometimes referred to as the log odds ratio) is a linear function of the independent variables.

If P is the probability of an individual graduating, a typical (simplified) logistic model might be:

$$\text{logit}(P) = \alpha + \beta_1 \text{FEMALE} + \beta_2 \text{LowSES} + \beta_3 \text{HighSES} \tag{3}$$

---

[7] This section is based on Pindyck and Rubinfeld 1991, pp. 258–281.

[8] See Pindyck and Rubinfeld 1991, pp. 279–281 for further details about the maximum-likelihood estimation of logit models.

where FEMALE equals one for women and zero for men, and LowSES and HighSES equal one for students from low-SES and high-SES backgrounds, respectively, and zero for all others. The parameters α, β_1, β_2, and β_3 can be estimated with statistical software, and the results allow us to predict the logarithm of the odds of graduating. This can be converted to an estimate of the probability of graduating by using equation (1).

In the example above, the parameters α, β_1, β_2, and β_3 were estimated as 1.22, 0.03, -0.35, and 0.23, respectively, so the probability of graduating for a male with low SES is 0.70, calculated as follows (using equations (3) and (1), respectively):

$$\text{logit}(P) = 1.22 + (0.03 \times 0) + (-0.35 \times 1) + (0.23 \times 0) = 0.87$$

$$P = \frac{1}{1 + e^{-0.87}} = 0.70$$

In a logistic model, the parameter estimates (β) do not have a simple intuitive interpretation because the dependent variable is expressed in "log odds." To give a clearer meaning, independent categorical parameter estimates can be converted to "odds ratios." First, we calculate the odds of an event occurring, which is the probability of an outcome occurring divided by the probability that it will *not* occur [$P/(1 - P)$]. In the example above, the odds of graduating for a man with low SES are 2.3 to 1 (0.70/0.30). This must be compared to the baseline case, which is a man with middle SES. His probability of graduating is 0.77 (calculated as above, except setting all independent variables to zero), so his odds of graduating are 3.4 to 1. To calculate an odds ratio, we divide the first odds (2.3 to 1) by the second odds (3.4 to 1) to obtain 0.68.[9] In other words, the odds of a low-SES man graduating are 68 percent as great as the odds of a middle-SES man graduating.[10] In appendix tables presenting the results of logistic regression models, we show both parameter estimates and odds ratios. To identify the baseline case, we also list the omitted categories for all categorical variables in the notes to the table.

[9] It can be shown that the odds ratio is, conveniently, equal to e raised to the power of the estimated coefficient; that is, $e^{-0.35} = 0.68$. The odds ratio for a negative parameter estimate will always be less than one.

[10] Note that reporting an odds ratio of 0.68 is *not* the same as saying that a low-SES man is 68 percent as likely to graduate as a high-SES man. As we calculated above, the probability of a low-SES man graduating is 0.70 and the probability of a high-SES man graduating is 0.77, so a low-SES man is actually 91 percent as likely to graduate as a high-SES man. This difference between odds ratios and the ratios of probabilities is one reason we generally avoid the use of odds ratios in presenting results. "Adjusted probabilities" (explained below) have a clearer intuitive meaning.

At the bottom of each logistic regression table in Appendix D, we report several numbers that can be used to measure the model's goodness of fit. We report the -2 log likelihood statistics for both the "restricted" model (estimated with no parameters) and the "unrestricted" model (estimated with all parameters). By subtracting the -2 log likelihood of the unrestricted model from the -2 log likelihood of the restricted model, we calculate the chi-square test-statistic. This chi-square test-statistic can be used to test whether the unrestricted model's independent variables are jointly significant. In ordinary least squares regression tables, we report the conventional R^2, which is the percentage of variance in the dependent variable explained by the model. In both logistic and ordinary least squares regression tables, we report the standard errors of parameter estimates and show in bold type all parameters that are significantly different from zero at the 5 percent level (i.e., there is less than a 5 percent chance of this occurring by chance alone).[11] In the text, we sometimes test whether two variables in a model (such as two SAT categories) are significantly different from each other by constructing 95 percent confidence intervals for each variable; if the intervals overlap, the differences are insignificant.

Adjusted Probabilities

In Chapters 3 through 8, we often compare actual percentages (such as the percentage of matriculants who graduate within six years) with "adjusted" probabilities. The purpose of calculating adjusted probabilities (which are simply alternative presentations of results derived from regressions) is to provide an intuitively understandable method of controlling for other factors that might systematically affect certain groups in a particular way. For instance, women graduate at a higher rate than men. Thus, if some colleges have a higher proportion of women, their graduation rates will be higher than the graduation rates for comparable institutions that enroll fewer women. It is desirable to "adjust" graduation rates to control for this fact. When we compare adjusted rates for blacks and whites, as we frequently do, we are able to analyze outcomes for the two groups on the assumption that they are equivalent in all respects except for their race. Observing that black and white matriculants graduate at different rates, we can answer a question such as the following: If the two

[11] In general, we do not test whether "raw" differences in the descriptive statistics we report in tables and figures are significant. Instead, we rely on our regression results, which allow us to test whether or not differences are significant when controlling for other relevant factors.

groups had the same proportions of men and women, if they had similar socioeconomic backgrounds, if they had identical distributions of SAT scores and majored in the same subjects (and so on for all the other variable in our equation), would they still graduate at different rates?

We calculate adjusted probabilities using the results of the logistic regression analysis described above.[12] To compute an overall adjusted probability (for the "average" person in a particular model) we use equation (1), substituting the parameter estimates for each element in the vector β and multiplying them by each variable's mean value. In Table B.3 we illustrate our methodology with two examples, the first calculating the overall adjusted probability of graduating from college, and the second calculating the adjusted probability of high-SES students graduating from college. In both examples, we use the data for black students only.

Example 1. Column A of the table shows the parameter estimates, and Column B shows the mean values of each variable. The means can be interpreted as follows: 59 percent of the matriculants were female, 6 percent had combined SAT scores of 1300 or above, 13 percent had combined SAT scores between 1200 and 1299, and so on. Column C is simply the product of Columns A and B. The products in Column C are summed at the bottom of the column (step 1), and immediately beneath that we add the intercept (step 2). We have now calculated the "log odds," $\log(P/1 - P)$ as shown in equation (2). The only remaining step (step 3) is to convert the log odds to a probability, by substituting the result from step 2 into equation (1). The result, 0.76, is the overall probability of graduating for a student with average characteristics.[13]

Example 2. This example is identical to the previous one except for one step: rather than assigning means to *all* the variables, in Column D, we assign the high-SES variable a value of one and the low-SES variable a value of zero. The result, 0.83, is the overall probability of graduating

[12] We also calculate adjusted outcomes when we use ordinary least squares regression models in Chapters 3 and 5. The methodology is conceptually the same as the one described for logistic models (except it is simpler because there is no need to convert the result from a log odds to a probability).

[13] One might expect the overall adjusted mean (0.76) to be equal to the *actual* mean (i.e., the simple percentage of black students graduating from college). In fact, that is not necessarily the case when using logistic regressions, and this fact must be taken into consideration when interpreting the results. In this particular example, the actual rate was 0.75. Westoff and Rodriguez (1993) go one step further than we do and adjust the intercept to ensure that the two results are consistent. In the adjusted results presented in the text, the actual means and the overall adjusted probabilities rarely differ by more than two or three percentage points, so for the sake of simplicity we do not make this final refinement.

TABLE B.3

Two Examples of Calculating the Adjusted Probability of Graduating from College, Black Only, 1989 Entering Cohort

		Example 1		Example 2	
Variable	A Parameter Estimate	B Mean Value	C Product of Parameter Estimate and Mean	D Mean Value, or 0 or 1	E Product of Parameter Estimate and Mean
Intercept	0.46				
Female	0.26	0.59	0.16	0.59	0.16
SAT > 1299	0.13	0.06	0.01	0.06	0.01
SAT 1200–1299	0.23	0.13	0.03	0.13	0.03
SAT 1100–1199	0.31	0.20	0.06	0.20	0.06
SAT 1000–1099	0.14	0.20	0.03	0.20	0.03
SAT Not Available	0.05	0.02	0.00	0.02	0.00
Top 10% of High School Class	0.31	0.35	0.11	0.35	0.11
High School Class Rank Not Available	−0.07	0.21	−0.01	0.21	0.00
High SES	0.56	0.13	0.07	1.00	0.50
Low SES	−0.30	0.13	−0.04	0.00	0.00
SES Not Available	0.03	0.14	0.00	0.00	0.00
SEL-1	0.71	0.22	0.16	0.22	0.17
SEL-2	0.28	0.36	0.10	0.36	0.10
Women's College	0.16	0.04	0.01	0.04	0.01
Step 1: Sum the products to obtain βX_i			0.69		1.17
Step 2: Add the intercept (0.46) to obtain $\alpha + \beta X_i$			1.15		1.62
Step 3: Convert to adjusted probability by using equation (1)			0.76		0.84

Source: College and Beyond.

Note: See text for explanation of steps one through three.

from college for high-SES students who are black but have average characteristics in all other respects. The same method can be used to calculate adjusted probabilities for groups defined by other variables in the model. In Appendix D, we provide tables that display the variable means used in our calculations of adjusted probabilities in each chapter (Appendix Tables D.3.7, D.4.5, D.5.7, D.6.9, and D.7.11).

Use of Successive Regression Models

In presenting regression models, we generally begin with a model that includes only pre-collegiate student characteristics and then create successive models that add sets of additional variables. Although results for every model are not always reported because of space limitations, we do show all steps of the process in the models in Chapter 5 used to predict income. The five models described there are similar to the ones used in other chapters, and they illustrate our approach (see Appendix Tables D.5.2 through D.5.5 for the regression results):

- Model 1 includes only those variables known at the time a student applied for admission to college: race, gender, SAT scores, high school grades, and the family's socioeconomic status.
- Model 2 adds only the selectivity of the school attended (SEL-1, SEL-2, SEL-3).
- Model 3 adds two "in-school" measures: the student's major field of study and rank in class.
- Model 4 adds information on the highest degree attained: bachelor's only, master's, law, medicine, business, or PhD.
- Model 5 adds information on sector of employment (private, self-employed, not-for-profit, and government).

By adding variables sequentially, we observe how the relationship between a particular independent variable (such as socioeconomic status) and the dependent variable (earned income, for example) changes as other variables are added to the regression. For example, in Model 1 we can investigate the association between socioeconomic status and earned income while holding constant only the effects of the other pre-collegiate variables (race, gender, SAT scores, and high school grades). Socioeconomic status is related to the type of college that students attend (with students from high-SES backgrounds somewhat more likely to attend SEL-1 schools), and Model 2 shows the association between SES and earnings after we also control for the effects of this relationship between SES and school selectivity. Similarly, Models 3, 4, and 5 show how the addition of other variables that may be related to socioeconomic status affects the "net" relationship between socioeconomic status and earnings.[14]

The model that is most relevant depends on the independent variable being studied and the particular question of interest. Since many of the independent variables have much of their impact on earnings via their effects on other independent variables, it is important not to "over-control" for such interrelationships. For example, if we want to estimate the effect of school selectivity on earnings, we should focus on Model 2, which controls only for variables such as parental socioeconomic status and test scores that were present when the student entered college. However, we do not want to control for variables, such as advanced degree attainment, that both affect earnings and are themselves affected, in some measure, by the selectivity of the school that the student attended. That is, attendance at a highly selective school is associated with increased income partly because it increases the probability of earning an advanced degree. To answer other questions, however, we want to use all of the control variables available to us, including both advanced degrees attained and sector of employment, and we therefore focus on Model 5. For example, we are interested in knowing if black matriculants at the C&B schools earn less than their white classmates because of factors associated with race itself or because of interrelationships between race and other variables (rank in class, socioeconomic status, and so on). Model 5 is appropriate in this instance because it allows us to estimate how much of the black-white difference in average earnings would persist even if blacks and whites came from the same socioeconomic backgrounds, chose the same schools, had the same grades in college, were as likely to earn advanced degrees, worked in the same sector of employment, and so on.

As we explain in detail in Chapters 4 and 5, the interpretation of the relationship between SAT scores and various outcome measures (advanced degrees attained and earnings) depends on which model one believes to be most appropriate. For example, in examining the relationship between SAT scores and advanced degrees attained, it would be inappropriate, in our view, to control for rank in class; students with better grades are more likely to earn advanced degrees, and SAT scores surely exert part

[14] Unobserved forces, such as motivation, may help determine the independent variables (e.g., the type of school attended, the field of study chosen, and grades) *and* the dependent variable, such as earned income. Ideally, we would like to estimate a model that accounts for these interrelationships, and one approach would be to use a two-stage least squares regression model. To do so, one would need to find an instrumental variable that is correlated with the independent variables and the dependent variable, but not with the error term. This level of analysis is beyond the scope of this study.

of their impact on advanced degree attainment via their effect on rank in class. The sequential models help us to understand such connections.

CHAPTER 2: THE ADMISSIONS PROCESS AND "RACE-NEUTRALITY"

National Simulation of Race-Neutral Admissions

Beginning with this section, we discuss methodological issues specific to particular chapters. To estimate the effect of race-neutral admissions on college enrollment, we performed a simulation that combines national data on SAT scores with enrollment patterns for all twenty-eight of the C&B institutions. We assume that under a race-neutral regime, black students within defined SAT intervals would apply, be accepted, and attend schools at each level of selectivity in the same proportions as white students (we explore the plausibility of these assumptions in the next section). This set of assumptions implies that the ratio of blacks to whites within each SAT interval at a given set of schools should correspond to the ratio of black to white test-takers within the same SAT interval in the national population.

Table B.4 shows the calculations underlying the 1989 simulations.[15] From national data, we calculated the ratio of black to white test-takers within 100-point SAT intervals. We multiplied these ratios by the number of white matriculants within each SAT interval at the SEL-1, SEL-2, and SEL-3 schools to estimate the hypothetical number of blacks who would matriculate at each of these groups of schools if admissions were race-neutral. Because combined SAT scores were not available in national data, we ran two separate simulations, one using verbal scores and one using math scores. The results of the simulations are shown in Table B.5.

Application and Attendance Patterns

The simulation described above assumes that under a race-neutral regime, blacks and whites with similar SAT scores would apply to selective institutions at similar rates, and would be equally likely to attend a selective school if they were accepted. Unfortunately, we cannot fully test these assumptions because black students' decisions about where to apply and whether to attend schools might change if college admissions were mandated to be race-neutral. However, using the 1989 survey re-

---

[15] We performed a similar simulation for 1976 but do not show the underlying calculations.

TABLE B.4

Simulations of Race-Neutral College Admissions, 1989 Entering Cohort

	National ETS Data			Current Number of Whites			Hypothetical Number of Blacks				Actual Number of Blacks			
	Number of Whites	Number of Blacks	Ratio of Blacks to Whites	SEL-1	SEL-2	SEL-3	SEL-1	SEL-2	SEL-3	All	SEL-1	SEL-2	SEL-3	All
Simulation Using Verbal SAT Scores														
700+	7,273	91	0.013	1,608	698	355	20	9	4	33	35	6	4	45
600–699	59,314	1,536	0.026	3,435	3,819	2,738	89	99	71	259	229	109	68	406
500–599	166,231	6,673	0.040	1,188	3,055	5,840	48	123	234	405	277	256	245	778
400–499	271,629	20,501	0.075	174	585	3,435	13	44	259	317	96	180	398	674
300–399	199,855	37,438	0.187	11	43	376	2	8	71	81	8	31	206	245
200–299	47,955	30,376	0.633	2	3	6	1	2	4	7	1	3	19	23
All	752,257	96,615	0.128	6,418	8,203	12,750	173	285	643	1,101	646	585	940	2,171
Simulation Using Math SAT Scores														
700+	33,445	381	0.011	3,431	2,195	1,888	39	25	22	86	74	21	17	112
600–699	115,616	2,826	0.024	2,448	4,044	5,312	60	99	130	289	235	145	111	491
500–599	208,212	10,834	0.052	501	1,770	4,268	26	92	222	340	270	277	321	868
400–499	226,768	25,503	0.112	37	190	1,179	4	21	133	158	59	120	374	553
300–399	140,822	39,407	0.280	1	4	98	0	1	27	29	8	22	113	143
200–299	27,394	17,664	0.645	0	0	6	0	0	4	4	0	0	4	4
All	752,257	96,615	0.128	6,418	8,203	12,750	129	238	537	901	646	585	940	2,171

Sources: College and Beyond and tabulations provided by the College Entrance Examination Board.

Notes: See text for explanation of simulations. See notes to Table B.1 for definition of institutional selectivity categories (SEL-1, SEL-2, and SEL-3).

TABLE B.5

Hypothetical Effect of Race-Neutral Admissions on Percentage of Blacks in Class, 1989 Entering Cohort

	Results of Simulation Based on Verbal SAT Scores				Results of Simulation Based on Math SAT Scores			
	SEL-1	*SEL-2*	*SEL-3*	*All*	*SEL-1*	*SEL-2*	*SEL-3*	*All*
Actual number of blacks	646	585	940	2,171	646	585	940	2,171
Hypothetical number of blacks	173	285	643	1,101	129	238	537	901
Total number of students	8,275	10,111	14,197	32,583	8,275	10,111	14,197	32,583
Actual percentage of blacks	7.8%	5.8%	6.6%	6.7%	7.8%	5.8%	6.6%	6.7%
Hypothetical percentage of blacks	2.1%	2.8%	4.5%	3.4%	1.6%	2.4%	3.8%	2.8%

Sources and notes: Same as Table B.4.

sults, we were able to test whether there were differences in application and attendance patterns between blacks and whites under current admissions policies.

The C&B survey asked those respondents who did not attend their first-choice school to list the school they had most wanted to attend, and whether they had applied to and been accepted by that school. (Those who attended their first-choice school are instructed to skip this question. See Exhibit A.1 at the end of Appendix A.) Then the survey asked all respondents to list up to three other undergraduate schools that they had seriously considered, and whether they had applied to and been accepted by these schools. Thus respondents could provide information about three or four other schools to which they had applied.

We used data from the Higher Education Research Institute to determine the mean combined SAT score of each institution to which the survey respondents applied. These mean SAT scores were used to assign each of these institutions to one of our selectivity categories.[16]

We then calculated the average number of applications that respondents submitted to schools other than the ones that they attended. (These averages are somewhat understated since respondents could list a maximum of four other schools to which they applied, their first-choice school and three other schools.) Overall, we found that respondents averaged 1.6 applications to other schools. Next we tested whether there were racial differences in application patterns by selectivity level. We found that, on average, blacks who attended SEL-1 schools submitted slightly more applications to other SEL-1 schools than did whites (an average of 0.94 versus 0.87), but this difference was not statistically significant. Blacks who attended SEL-2 schools submitted an average of about 0.16 fewer applications to SEL-2 schools than did whites, and blacks who attended SEL-3 schools submitted about 0.13 fewer applications to SEL-3 schools than did whites; the magnitude of these differences is small, but they are statistically significant.

We next tested whether blacks were as likely as whites to attend the most selective schools to which they were accepted. According to our definition, a student attended the most selective school he or she could have attended if the mean combined SAT score of the most selective school to which the student was accepted was no more than 100 points greater than the mean combined SAT score of the school at which he or she matriculated. Under this definition, 89 percent of blacks and 90

---

[16] We had to modify the SAT cutoff points for our selectivity categories slightly because the HERI file provides the institution's mean SAT score in 1982, not 1989.

percent of whites attended the most selective schools to which they were admitted.

Finally, we tested the effect of socioeconomic status on college application and attendance patterns. Since blacks are overrepresented in the low-SES category and underrepresented in the high-SES category, any effect that SES has on application or attendance patterns might persist as a racial difference even in a "race-neutral" world. We found that high-SES students at SEL-1 schools submitted (on average) 0.15 more applications than mid-SES students to other SEL-1 schools, and that high-SES students at SEL-3 schools submitted 0.12 more applications to other SEL-3 schools than mid-SES students (there was no statistically significant difference for SEL-2 schools). We also found that low-SES students were slightly more likely than mid-SES or high-SES students to attend the most selective schools to which they were admitted.

In summary, we found slight differences in black and white application patterns and in high-SES and low-SES attendance patterns at selective schools. Even if these differences did persist in a race-neutral world, their magnitude is so small that we would need to make only slight modifications in our initial assumptions that blacks and whites would apply and be accepted to selective schools at the same rate. Thus we believe that the results of our national simulation would remain essentially the same.

CHAPTER 3: ACADEMIC OUTCOMES

Graduation Rates

Two different graduation rates are discussed in Chapter 3: "first-school" graduation rates, which include only students who graduated from the schools at which they first matriculated, and "overall" graduation rates, which also include students who transferred to other schools and earned degrees there ("transfer graduates"). Thus, by definition, first-school rates are always less than or equal to overall rates, and overall rates equal the sum of first-school rates and "transfer" graduation rates. Both first-school and overall graduation rates can be found in Appendix Tables D.3.1 and D.3.2.

First-school graduation rates were calculated from records for individual students supplied by all twenty-eight C&B schools and therefore report quite precisely and completely how many matriculants received a bachelor's degree within six years. Since information about transfer graduates is available only for individuals who responded to the C&B survey, we employed the following three assumptions to estimate the transfer graduation rate:

1. For matriculants who responded to the survey, we used self-reported information from the survey on whether or not they obtained a bachelor's degree from another institution within six years of matriculation.
2. For matriculants who were part of the survey population but did not respond, we assumed (rather arbitrarily) that the transfer graduation rate was half the transfer graduation rate of survey respondents.
3. For matriculants who were not part of the survey population, or for whom graduation status was missing from both institutional and survey records, we assumed that the transfer graduation rate was equivalent to the transfer graduation rate of survey respondents.

Undergraduate Majors

In Chapter 3, and in regression models in other chapters, undergraduate majors are grouped into five categories. Examples of the majors included in each category are given below. This list is not intended to be comprehensive, but it includes the great majority of all undergraduate majors.

- *Humanities:* American studies, art, art history, classics, English literature, foreign languages and literature, history, letters, music, theater, philosophy, and religion;
- *Social science:* Anthropology, area studies, economics, political science, government, psychology, sociology, and statistics;
- *Natural science:* Astronomy, atmospheric sciences, biological sciences, chemistry, geological sciences, mathematics, and physics;
- *Engineering:* All branches of engineering plus computer and information sciences;
- *Other professional:* Agriculture, architecture, environmental design, business, management, communications, education, and health sciences.

CHAPTER 4: ADVANCED STUDY: GRADUATE AND PROFESSIONAL DEGREES

Multiple Advanced Degrees

One complication in analyzing the attainment of advanced degrees is that respondents often received more than one degree. When examining advanced degrees earned in separate fields, we count each degree individually; in other words, a respondent with a business degree and a law degree would be counted in both categories. But in regression analysis we count each individual once, using the following rules:

- Those with a master's degree (except for an MBA) and a professional or doctoral degree were assigned the professional or doctoral degree.
- Those with multiple professional degrees (including MBAs) and/or doctoral degrees were assigned the latest degree they earned.

For example, a person who first earned a medical degree and later a law degree would be assigned to the law degree category. But someone who first earned a medical degree and later earned a master's in public health would be assigned to the medical degree category.

Top-Rated Professional Schools

In Chapter 4, we discuss the percentages of C&B matriculants attending top-rated professional schools. The schools included in this category were defined as follows:

- *Law Schools.* John Wehrli, a graduate student at the University of California at Berkeley, has computed composite rankings for law schools, using a combination of published rankings, a measure of student quality, and job placement data.[17] First, Wehrli averages the rankings in each publication for every available year but the most recent (generally since the late 1980s). For each school, this historical average rank is averaged with the rank for the most recent year assigned by that publication to produce the publication's overall average rank. Wehrli then averages the rankings from all of the publications, adjusting for publications that do not rank every school in the nation. For the top thirty schools, a measure of student caliber is calculated by using LSAT scores, grade

---

[17] At present these rankings are available only on the Internet, at http://wehrli. ilrg.com.

point average, and yield. A placement rank is determined by averaging the median starting salary rank for the most recent class and the percentage of students with jobs six months after graduation from a law school. Finally, a composite ranking of the top thirty schools is determined by assigning a 70 percent weight to the average published ranking, a 20 percent weight to the student quality ranking, and a 10 percent weight to the placement ranking. On the basis of a study of variances about the mean according to the published rankings, Wehrli found a clear division between the law schools ranked 1 through 8, those ranked 9 through 17, and those ranked 18 through 30. "Top tier," as used in the text, refers to the top eight law schools schools as determined by Wehrli's composite ranking.

- *Business Schools.* Wehrli also has computed a composite ranking for business schools based on published rankings and a measure of "student caliber." Similar to the methodology used for law schools, Wehrli averages the historical and current year published rankings, giving a 50 percent weight to the average historical rank and a 50 percent weight to the publication's most recent ranking. He then calculates a "caliber of student" ranking using median GPA, median GMAT score, and published student selectivity rankings. A composite ranking is determined by assigning an 80 percent weight to the average published ranking and a 20 percent weight to the caliber of student ranking. Based on a study of the variances about the mean, he found a statistical division between business schools ranked 1 through 6, those ranked 7 through 19, and those ranked 20 through 30. "Top tier," as used in the text, refers to the top six business schools.

- *Medical Schools.* To rank medical schools, we averaged the 1997 *U.S. News & World Report* Top 25 and the 1989 Gourman Report Rankings. First, the schools were sorted according to their average ranking, and a percentile rank was calculated for each school. "Top-tier," as used in the text, refers to the twelve schools ranked in the top quartile.

The same quality tiers were used for both the 1976 and the 1989 C&B entering cohorts. Studies have shown that the ranking of programs has been quite consistent over different time periods.[18]

[18] Webster 1983.

CHAPTER 5: EMPLOYMENT, EARNINGS, AND
JOB SATISFACTION

Estimation of Income

The C&B survey did not ask respondents to report their exact income. Instead, respondents were asked to mark one of the following ten categories (the same categories were used for both earned income and household income): less than $1,000; $1,000 to $9,999; $10,000 to $19,999; $20,000 to $29,999; $30,000 to $49,999; $50,000 to $74,999; $75,000 to $99,999; $100,000 to $149,999; $150,000 to $199,999; and $200,000 or more.[19] Respondents from the 1951 and 1976 entering cohorts were asked to provide their pre-tax 1995 income,[20] and those from the 1989 entering cohort were asked for their pre-tax 1996 income.

In general, we converted the income categories to a linear scale by assigning income values equal to the midpoint of each income range (we assumed the lowest possible earned income was zero, so the midpoint of the lowest category was $5,000). However, because the highest income category has no upper limit, we needed to estimate the average income for those C&B workers who earned over $200,000. To do this, we first learned from income data in the 1990 U.S. Census (inflated to 1995 dollars by using the Consumer Price Index) that the average income of all national college graduates aged 36–38 who earned more than $200,000 was $248,000. Because C&B graduates tend to earn more than all graduates, we assumed that this estimate would understate the income of the top C&B earners. Specifically, we know that the average income for C&B graduates who earned less than $200,000 was approximately $17,000 greater than the average income for all national graduates who earned less than $200,000. Therefore, we added $17,000 to our Census estimate of $248,000 to reach our final estimate that C&B workers in the top income category earned an average of $265,000.

We used the same procedure to estimate the average income of households earning over $200,000. The corresponding Census average was $273,000, to which we added a C&B differential of $17,000 to reach our final estimate of $290,000.

To determine how sensitive our calculations of mean income are to changes in the top income category, we experimented with four different

[19] In Wave 1 of the survey (an initial pilot study of five institutions), the lowest two categories were combined into a single category. To make the data consistent for all institutions, the lowest two categories were also combined for institutions surveyed after Wave 1 into a single "less than $10,000" category.

[20] The Wave 1 survey differed slightly in that it asked for 1994 income. Since this discrepancy affected only five schools, we ignored it.

values for the top category: $225,000, $250,000, $265,000, and $300,000. Not surprisingly, the effect on men is greater than the effect on women. For all men, estimates of mean income ranged from $93,400 to $101,500, and for all women, they ranged from $63,000 to $65,200. We performed similar tests in our regression analysis, and found that our results were qualitatively similar regardless of which estimate was used.

Most of our income analysis includes only people who worked full-time for the entire year. For national comparisons from the U.S. Census, we defined full-time, full-year workers as anyone who worked at least fifty weeks of the year, and at least thirty-five hours per week. For the C&B population, respondents identified themselves as full-time, full-year workers by their responses to the questionnaire.

CHAPTER 6: CIVIC PARTICIPATION AND SATISFACTION WITH LIFE

Estimation of Spouse's Income

We needed to estimate the income of respondents' spouses in order to understand better women's labor force participation rates. To estimate spouse's income, we subtracted the respondent's own income from household income. Then we assigned each respondent to one of four spousal income categories: less than $30,000; $30,000 to $74,999; $75,000 to $149,999; and $150,000 or greater. This approach involves two approximations. First, household income includes both spouse's income and other non-earned income, such as dividends and capital gains. Thus, spouse's income is overstated for anyone with substantial income from non-earned sources, although we suspect that most people would remain in the same category. Second, because the top income category on the survey questionnaire for household income was "greater than $200,000," the spouse's income category cannot be determined for individuals with high personal income. For example, if the respondent's personal income is $150,000, and his or her household income is greater than $200,000, then his or her spouse's income could be any amount above $50,000. Because of this problem, we excluded these indeterminate cases from the regression model in Appendix Table D.6.1. An alternative approach we tested was to leave the indeterminate cases in the model but flag them with a dummy variable. The results were qualitatively the same.

CHAPTER 10: SUMMING UP

Estimating Outcomes for Retrospectively Rejected Black Matriculants

In our admissions simulation (see Chapter 2 notes above), we estimated the hypothetical number of black students who would have been admitted under a race-neutral regime. In Chapter 10, we took this simulation one step further. First, we calculated the number who would have been "retrospectively rejected" by subtracting the number of "hypothetical" black enrollees from the number of black students who were in fact enrolled (see Table B.6).[21] Next, we estimated outcomes, such as income, for these "retrospectively rejected" black men and women. To do this, we assumed that all black students within each 100-point SAT range in each selectivity category had the same outcomes. Then, the outcomes for the "retrospectively rejected" population were calculated as weighted averages, with the weights equal to the relative numbers of "retrospectively rejected" students within each SAT range and selectivity category.[22]

To illustrate our approach, Table B.7 shows how we calculated the number of black matriculants currently pursuing medical degrees who would have been "retrospectively rejected" from the 1989 C&B entering cohort. Within each SAT range and selectivity category, we multiplied the portion of actual black matriculants pursuing medical degrees by the number of "retrospective rejections" (taken from Table B.6). The sum of these products, 80, is our estimate of the number of black matriculants who would have been rejected from C&B schools under race-neutral admissions and who are now pursuing medical degrees.

[21] A negative number of retrospective rejections indicates that there would be more black students in that SAT/selectivity category under race-neutral admissions.

[22] There is, of course, no way of knowing which individual black students within each SAT range would have been kept and which rejected, which is why we adopted an approach that assumes the outcomes are the same within each SAT interval.

TABLE B.6

Numbers of Hypothetical, Actual, and "Retrospectively Rejected" Black Matriculants, 1989 Entering Cohort

Verbal SAT	Hypothetical Black Matriculants			Actual Black Matriculants			"Retrospectively Rejected" Black Matriculants		
	SEL-1	SEL-2	SEL-3	SEL-1	SEL-2	SEL-3	SEL-1	SEL-2	SEL-3
700+	20	9	4	35	6	4	15	–3	0
600–699	89	99	71	229	109	68	140	10	–3
500–599	48	123	234	277	256	245	229	133	10
400–499	13	44	259	96	180	398	83	136	139
300–399	2	8	71	8	31	206	6	23	135
200–299	1	2	4	0	1	3	–1	–1	–1
All	173	285	643	645	583	924	472	298	280

Sources: College and Beyond and tabulations provided by the College Entrance Examination Board.

Notes: "Retrospectively Rejected" black matriculants are the difference between actual and hypothetical black matriculants in each SAT range and selectivity category. See Table B.4 and the corresponding text for an explanation of hypothetical black matriculants.

TABLE B.7
Estimation of Number of "Retrospectively Rejected" Black Matriculants Pursuing Medical Degrees, 1989 Entering Cohort

Verbal SAT	Percentage of Black Matriculants Pursuing Medical Degrees			Number of "Retrospectively Rejected" Black Matriculants			Number of "Retrospectively Rejected" Black Matriculants Pursuing Medical Degrees			
	SEL-1	SEL-2	SEL-3	SEL-1	SEL-2	SEL-3	SEL-1	SEL-2	SEL-3	All
700+	0	0	0	15	-3	0	0	0	0	0
600–699	8	8	20	140	10	-3	11	1	-1	11
500–599	13	7	7	229	133	10	30	9	1	40
400–499	12	5	6	83	136	139	10	7	8	25
300–399	0	0	3	6	23	135	0	0	4	4
200–299	0	0	0	-1	-1	-1	0	0	0	0
All	11	6	5	472	298	280	51	17	13	80

Source: Same as Table B.6.

Notes: The number of "retrospectively rejected" black matriculants is derived in Table B.6. See text for explanation.

Earnings in Relation to Advanced Degrees, Sector of Employment, and Occupation

IN THIS APPENDIX, we describe in detail the ways in which the earnings of College and Beyond graduates, and especially black graduates, are affected by the advanced degrees they have earned, the sectors in which they have worked, and the jobs that they have held. We focus on graduates, rather than matriculants, and on full-time workers, so that we can make direct comparisons with Census data for comparable individuals who held BAs, worked full-time, and were in the same age range.

ADVANCED DEGREES

To what extent are the high earnings of C&B graduates a reflection of subsequent graduate and professional training rather than the receipt of a BA degree per se?[1] It is a somewhat complex relationship. Undergraduate education at a C&B school has a double-barreled effect on earnings via the acquisition of advanced degrees. Nationwide, holders of professional degrees earned appreciably more, on average, than did college graduates without advanced degrees. In the age range of the '76 matriculants, the earnings premiums range from 65 to 85 percent, depending on race and gender (Figures C.1a and C.1b). And, as we saw previously, exceptionally large numbers of both white and black graduates of the C&B schools earned advanced degrees—especially professional degrees in the well-paying fields of law, medicine, and business. Moreover, holders of professional degrees from C&B schools had appreciably higher average earnings than did all holders of professional degrees; this additional earnings premium ranges from roughly 30 to 55 percent.[2]

---

[1] The effects of various types of advanced degrees on the subsequent earnings of C&B matriculants, on an "other things equal" basis, are estimated in the OLS regressions for Models 4 and 5 presented in Appendix Tables D.5.2–D.5.5. The discussion in this appendix focuses on graduates only and compares the data for C&B graduates with nationwide data for all holders of BAs.

[2] As shown in Appendix Table D.C.2, there are also substantial differences in earnings by type of professional degree held. Later in this appendix we consider earnings by occupation and look specifically at doctors, lawyers, and business executives.

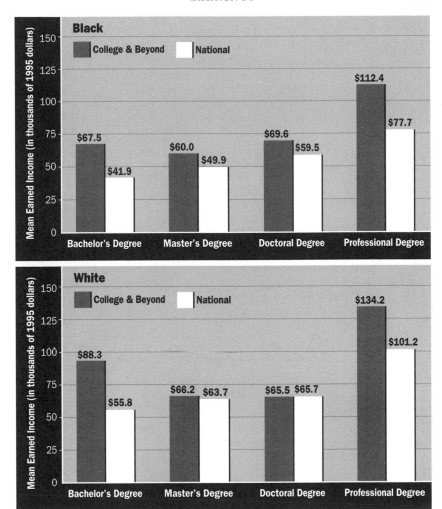

Figure C.1a. Mean Earned Income of Men in 1995, by Type of Degree and Race, College and Beyond Graduates and National Graduates, 1976 Entering Cohort

Sources: College and Beyond and 1990 U.S. Census.

Notes: For College and Beyond graduates, mean earned income is derived from income ranges reported by full-time, full-year workers. For National graduates, the 1989 income of full-time, full-year workers, aged 37 to 39 is inflated to 1995 dollars. See Appendix B for details.

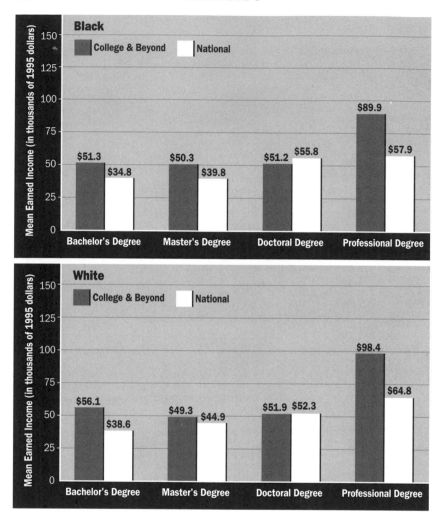

Figure C.1b. Mean Earned Income of Women in 1995, by Type of Degree and Race, College and Beyond Graduates and National Graduates, 1976 Entering Cohort

Sources and notes: Same as Figure C.1a.

These propositions hold for women and men, for blacks and whites. The C&B premiums, however, are relatively larger for blacks than for whites, and for women than for men. Also, while C&B graduates as a group were more likely to have earned professional degrees than other college graduates, this differential in educational attainment was especially pronounced for black graduates.

Graduates of C&B schools who earned *no* advanced degrees also earned appreciably more than did the national "BA-only" population. The earnings premiums enjoyed by C&B graduates with only a BA degree were on the order of 45 to 55 percent; these premiums are similar to those enjoyed by C&B holders of professional degrees.

In contrast, those who received non-professional advanced degrees, both master's degrees and doctorates, exhibited earnings patterns that were, at least on the surface, surprising. Two apparent anomalies stand out. First, while average earnings rose steadily for college graduates nationwide as they ascended the educational attainment ladder (with BAs earning less than MAs, and MAs earning less than holders of doctorates), this neat progression is not found when we examine the C&B population. Within this group, BAs earned more than both MAs and PhDs, and MAs and PhDs earned about the same amount of money. Second, holders of doctorates constituted the only category of any kind identified thus far in this study in which graduates of C&B colleges earned less than their counterparts from other schools.

Both of these apparent anomalies can be explained, however, and made to disappear, by examining the choices C&B graduates made concerning the sectors in which they worked and the kind of work that they did—choices that were influenced by the range of opportunities available to them. In brief, C&B graduates with either master's degrees or doctorates were more likely to work in the not-for-profit sector, and especially in education and research, than were all holders of these types of advanced degrees—who were far more likely to work in the better-paying for-profit sector.

Once we examine these differences by sector and occupation, the C&B earnings advantage reappears. Within the same sector, C&B holders of doctorates had consistently higher average earnings than did all holders of doctorates—roughly 15 percent more in the for-profit sector and about 5 percent more in the not-for-profit sector. Similar relationships are observed at the master's level. Looking at each sector and occupation separately also eliminates the other apparent anomaly: C&B holders of doctorates earned more than C&B holders of master's degrees within the same sector and occupation.[3]

---

[3] We also believe (with less evidence to rely on) that disproportionately large numbers of C&B holders of doctorates took their degrees in fields of study where compensation is relatively low—especially the humanities. Conversely, we suspect that the population at large contains relatively more holders of doctorates in education than does the C&B population, and that some significant number of individuals with EdDs have administrative jobs in education that pay better than most teaching positions. Unfortunately, the Census data do not permit a direct test of either of these hypotheses.

Unraveling these relationships is useful because of the light shed on the interpretation of "raw" earnings differentials. One advantage of advanced training is that it gives individuals more career options. Some individuals undoubtedly made financial sacrifices in order to pursue paths that are more rewarding to them in other respects.

SECTORS OF EMPLOYMENT

It is important to take account of sectors of employment in interpreting earnings differentials of all kinds, not just those associated with certain kinds of advanced degrees.[4] Thus, we now broaden the discussion to consider explicitly, and in detail, how earnings differentials in general are affected by the sectors in which people work. The pronounced overall differences in earnings between C&B graduates and all graduates are in part—but only in part—associated with differences in the sectors in which members of each group have chosen to work. We distinguish three main sectors: (1) *for-profit* businesses and firms (including self-employment); (2) *not-for-profit* entities (which include private schools and private colleges and universities); and (3) *governmental* units (which include federal, state, and local government, the military, and public schools, colleges, and universities).

The distribution of jobs across sectors varies systematically with race and gender (Figure C.2) for a range of reasons, including personal preferences and perceived and real obstacles to fair treatment. Men and whites are more heavily represented in the for-profit sector than women and blacks; conversely, women and blacks are more heavily represented in the governmental sector. There is also a persistent tendency for more women than men to gravitate to the not-for-profit sector, but employment in this sector does not correlate with race in any consistent way.

Against this backdrop, we now ask whether these patterns vary depending on whether individuals went to C&B schools—a question of particular relevance in the case of black holders of BAs. We see in Figure C.2 that the C&B graduates from the '76 cohorts are more likely to work in the for-profit sector—which is generally the highest-paying sector—than graduates nationwide; the bar for C&B graduates is higher than the bar for graduates nationwide in each of the four race/gender quadrants of the figure. This pattern is particularly pronounced among blacks. Among men, two-thirds of black holders of BAs from the C&B schools (67 percent) worked in the for-profit sector, whereas only 56 percent of all black

---

[4] See Appendix Tables D.5.2–D.5.5 for OLS estimates of the effects of sector of employment on the earnings of C&B matriculants, after controlling for other variables, including advanced degrees attained.

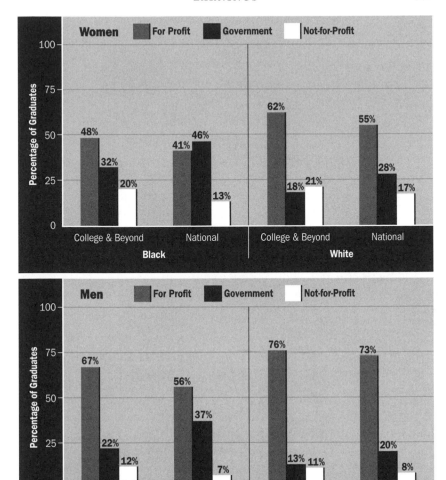

Figure C.2. Percentage of Graduates in Each Employment Sector, by Gender and Race, College and Beyond Graduates and National Graduates, 1976 Entering Cohort

Sources: College and Beyond and 1990 U.S. Census.

Notes: The for-profit sector includes individuals who are self-employed. Percentages may not total 100 due to rounding.

BAs nationwide worked in this sector. Among white male graduates, the percentage that worked in the for-profit sector was also higher among those from the C&B schools, but here the gap is decidedly narrower (76 percent for the C&B graduates versus 73 percent for graduates nationwide). Similar relationships hold for women.

A second noteworthy finding is that graduates from the C&B schools—grouped by both race and gender—were appreciably less inclined to work in the governmental sector than were all BAs nationwide. An extremely high percentage of the national population of black women in this age range with BAs worked for one or another governmental entity (46 percent); the corresponding figure for black women from the C&B schools is 32 percent. Similarly, the percentage of black males nationwide in the governmental sector is 37 percent, as compared with 22 percent of black males from the C&B schools. (Government also attracts lower percentages of white graduates from C&B schools than from schools nationwide.)

Adding information about compensation enriches this picture considerably. As expected, the for-profit sector paid better than either of the other sectors in all eight of the pairwise comparisons shown in Figure C.3. The not-for-profit sector appears to have paid ever so slightly better than the governmental sector in five of the eight comparisons, slightly less well in one (black females nationwide), and quite a bit better in two (black and white male graduates from the C&B schools).

Especially noteworthy are the marked differences in the sector salary differentials between the C&B graduates and graduates nationwide: C&B graduates were paid *much* better to work in the for-profit sector than in the other two sectors (and especially in government), as compared with graduates nationwide. Among the C&B graduates, the differential in average salaries between the for-profit and governmental sectors was $23,000 for black females (+43 percent), $27,000 for white females (+55 percent), $35,000 for black males (+62 percent), and $50,000 for white males (+81 percent). The corresponding salary differentials for all holders of BAs were $3,000 for black females (+8 percent), $8,000 for white females (+21 percent), $10,000 for black males (+24 percent), and $22,000 for white males (+47 percent). The radically different incentives to work in the private sector implied by these sharply divergent salary differentials surely help explain the differences in the distribution of employment by sector. For the national population of black female BA recipients, the financial incentive to enter the private for-profit sector was minimal, only $3,000. No wonder almost half of these women work for the government. Among the C&B population, on the other hand, the corresponding pay differential for black women was $23,000, and many of them appear to have responded accordingly.

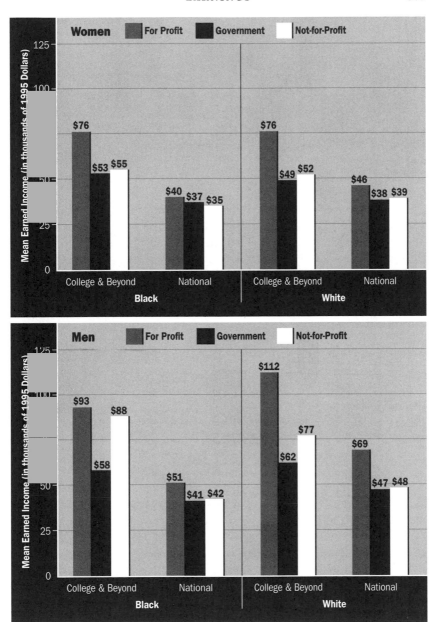

Figure C.3. Mean Earned Income in 1995, by Employment Sector, Gender, and Race, College and Beyond Graduates and National Graduates, 1976 Entering Cohort

Sources and notes: Same as Figure C.1a.

Needless to say, various other factors help explain distributions of employment across sectors. As Freeman noted many years ago in his pathbreaking study of the "Black Elite," the government was ahead of other sectors in welcoming black professionals.[5] (Most black doctors, lawyers, teachers, and ministers had long been expected to practice primarily in their own communities.) Also, as noted in Chapter 5, government jobs have generally been regarded as more secure, with better benefits, than jobs in other sectors. Finally, there are explanations for this pattern rooted in the economic theory of discrimination, which posits that enterprises responding to consumer prejudice and operating in competitive marketplaces might be more likely to discriminate than "monopoly" employers, such as the government.[6]

Black C&B graduates were clearly more likely than black graduates nationwide to work in the for-profit sector and to be paid relatively well. While the data also indicate that white C&B graduates did better yet in the for-profit sector, their exceptional economic success should not obscure the progress made by their black classmates in gaining highly remunerative employment in business and commerce. The earnings data also reveal that black C&B graduates earned roughly the same salaries as their white classmates in the not-for-profit and governmental sectors (actually slightly more in the case of black women). In some ways, the most telling comparison is between black graduates from the C&B schools and the national population of white graduates. In every single category (defined by the combination of gender and sector of employment), the black C&B graduates had appreciably higher average earnings than did the national population of white BA recipients.

OCCUPATIONAL CATEGORIES

Differences between the C&B graduates and BA recipients nationwide are, if anything, even more pronounced when we examine specific occupational categories. Black women and black men from the C&B schools are much more heavily represented in the fields of medicine, law, and higher education than black BA recipients nationwide (see the top left panels of Figures C.4a and C.4b). Black women C&B graduates are five times more likely to work in higher education, six times more likely to be lawyers, and eight times more likely to be doctors than the national

[5] Freeman 1976, ch. 6. Freeman writes: "Public employers, particularly the federal government, offered qualified blacks better job opportunities than the private sector in the new market" (p. 151).

[6] Ehrenberg and Smith 1994 and Cain 1986.

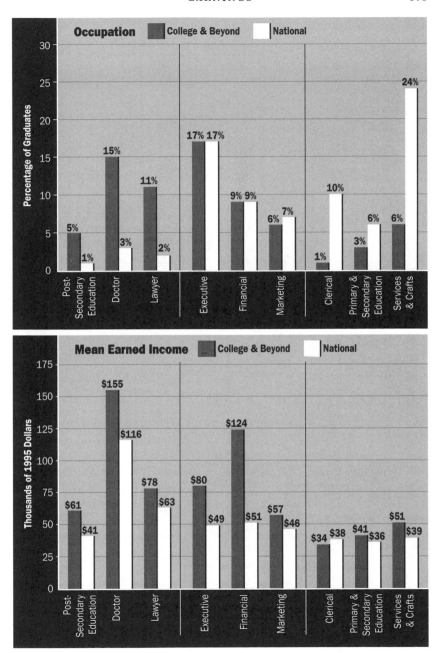

Figure C.4a. Percentage of Black Men in Selected Occupations and Mean Earned Income of Black Men in 1995, by Occupation, College and Beyond Graduates and National Graduates, 1976 Entering Cohort

Sources and notes: Same as Figure C.1a.

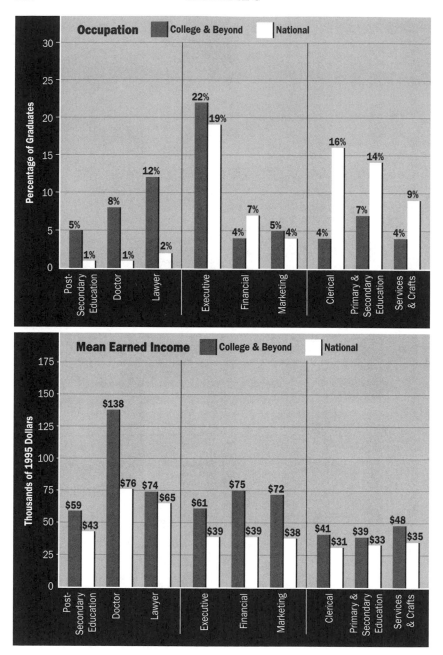

Figure C.4b. Percentage of Black Women in Selected Occupations and Mean Earned Income of Black Women in 1995, by Occupation, College and Beyond Graduates and National Graduates, 1976 Entering Cohort

Sources and notes: Same as Figure C.1a.

population of black women holders of BAs. The ratios for black men are very similar. In contrast, the employment percentages in the main business occupations—executive, finance, and marketing jobs—are much the same for blacks from the C&B schools and black holders of BAs nationwide (see the top middle panels of Figures C.4a and C.4b). Finally, black female and male C&B graduates are far less likely than black graduates nationwide to work in clerical positions, in elementary or secondary education, or in services and crafts (top right panels of Figures C.4a and C.4b). For example, black C&B graduates were between one-eighth and one-tenth as likely to work in clerical positions as black holders of BAs nationwide.[7]

Average earnings by occupation, seen in relation to these employment patterns, reveal several clear patterns:

- Black C&B graduates earned more than black graduates nationwide in seventeen of the eighteen gender/occupational categories shown in Figures C.4a and C.4b (bottom panels).
- As one might have predicted, the C&B earnings premiums tend to be lowest within those occupations least favored by the C&B graduates—especially clerical work and elementary/secondary education.
- Within the "learned" professions, where black C&B graduates are present in very large numbers, the earnings premiums are substantial in both absolute and relative terms. In these professions, black women doctors enjoy the highest premium and black women lawyers the lowest;[8] the C&B premium in higher educa-

[7] The data for all holders of BAs are taken from the 1990 decennial Census. The occupational classifications used in the C&B surveys and by the Census are very similar. Comparative data for an even larger number of occupations are shown in Appendix Tables D.C.1A and D.C.1B, along with data for white women and white men.

[8] The field of law is especially interesting, in large part because lawyers have a wider range of choice regarding sector of employment. The relatively modest overall earnings premium enjoyed by black women lawyers from the C&B schools is largely because many of them work in either the not-for-profit or governmental sector, where salary differentials are more compressed than they are in the private, for-profit sector (where slightly more than a third of black women work). In contrast, two-thirds of the black men from the C&B schools work for private law firms. National comparisons are also revealing. Among all black male lawyers, just over half worked for private firms, and they averaged $65,000 a year, as compared with average annual earnings of $90,000 for black male lawyers from C&B schools who worked in the private sector. These relationships mirror closely the patterns observed earlier when we looked more generally at employment and earnings by sector—the differences are more pronounced here, probably because law is a more narrowly defined occupational category.

tion is much larger than we would have expected (46 percent for men and 30 percent for women).

- The business occupations are in some ways particularly revealing. Even though black C&B graduates are present in these occupations in approximately the same relative numbers as black BA recipients nationwide, the C&B graduates earn much more money: earnings premiums are commonly in the 60+ percent range, reaching a high of 143 percent for black men in financial services. We interpret these results as indicating that there can be great differences in the positions two people may hold even though both are classified as "executives" or "in finance," and that the black C&B graduates who have gravitated to these for-profit jobs have succeeded in obtaining much more remunerative (and, we presume, often more demanding) positions than black graduates in general.

Additional Tables

APPENDIX TABLE D.2.1

Mean Verbal and Math SAT Scores of Applicants to Five Selective Institutions
and National College-Bound Seniors, by Race, 1989

	National		*Five C&B Institutions*	
	Black	*White*	*Black*	*White*
Mean verbal SAT score	351	446	520	611
Mean math SAT score	386	491	545	663

Sources: Admissions data provided by five College and Beyond institutions; national data from College Entrance Examination Board (1989, p. 6).

APPENDIX TABLE D.3.1

Graduation Rates, by Institutional Selectivity, Institutional Type, and Race,
1989 Entering Cohort (percent)

		First-School	*Overall*
SEL-1	Black	84.7	88.7
	Hispanic	91.7	96.4
	Asian	95.4	98.4
	Native American	78.9	78.9
	White	94.8	97.3
	Other	75.0	85.5
	All	93.7	96.5
SEL-2	Black	76.2	80.1
	Hispanic	79.3	91.1
	Asian	86.4	96.4
	Native American	88.7	88.7
	White	85.7	95.4
	Other	76.6	84.0
	All	84.9	94.3
SEL-3	Black	67.9	72.8
	Hispanic	71.2	81.6
	Asian	84.4	93.3
	Native American	71.9	85.9
	White	82.4	90.3
	Other	81.7	88.0
	All	81.3	88.3
All institutions	Black	74.7	79.2
	Hispanic	81.4	90.0
	Asian	88.2	96.2
	Native American	77.9	81.0
	White	85.8	93.7
	Other	78.1	84.9
	All	85.1	92.3
Private	Black	79.1	84.3
	Hispanic	84.9	93.4
	Asian	90.4	95.8
	Native American	82.1	82.1
	White	87.6	95.3
	Other	72.3	99.2
	All	87.1	94.0

APPENDIX TABLE D.3.1 *Continued*

		First-School	*Overall*
Public	Black	67.3	72.2
	Hispanic	71.2	81.5
	Asian	84.6	93.4
	Native American	70.8	85.4
	White	83.6	90.9
	Other	84.2	89.5
	All	82.4	88.9
Liberal arts	Black	77.6	80.9
	Hispanic	82.2	92.7
	Asian	86.0	96.3
	Native American	86.7	86.7
	White	86.5	95.1
	Other	82.2	82.2
	All	85.7	94.3
All institutions	Black	74.7	79.2
	Hispanic	81.4	90.0
	Asian	88.2	96.2
	Native American	77.9	81.0
	White	85.8	93.7
	Other	78.1	84.9
	All	85.1	92.3

Source: College and Beyond.

Notes: "First-School Graduation Rate" counts as graduates only those students who graduated within six years from the same school at which they matriculated as freshmen. "Overall Graduation Rate" also counts those who transferred from their first school and graduated elsewhere. See Appendix B for a more complete definition. "SEL-1" indicates institutions with mean combined SAT scores of 1300 or above; "SEL-2" indicates institutions with mean combined SAT scores between 1150 and 1299; "SEL-3" indicates institutions with mean combined SAT scores below 1150.

APPENDIX TABLE D.3.2
Graduation Rates, by Institutional Selectivity, Institutional Type, and Race,
1976 Entering Cohort (percent)

		First-School	Overall
SEL-1	Black	81.2	85.1
	Hispanic	76.5	79.2
	Asian	90.7	93.5
	Native American	70.0	85.0
	White	87.2	91.8
	Other	56.1	70.4
	All	86.2	90.8
SEL-2	Black	67.4	73.2
	Hispanic	67.2	73.2
	Asian	77.4	84.6
	Native American	63.6	78.4
	White	79.6	89.1
	Other	47.4	55.8
	All	77.7	87.2
SEL-3	Black	56.1	60.7
	Hispanic	54.9	62.9
	Asian	78.1	88.8
	Native American	45.5	52.9
	White	74.1	84.3
	Other	42.5	42.5
	All	72.4	82.6
All institutions	Black	65.9	70.8
	Hispanic	68.1	73.3
	Asian	82.1	88.7
	Native American	56.9	68.6
	White	78.3	87.2
	Other	45.8	49.4
	All	76.8	85.7
Private	Black	72.3	76.3
	Hispanic	70.1	75.9
	Asian	83.5	87.0
	Native American	55.3	69.7
	White	81.0	89.7
	Other	46.9	55.2
	All	79.3	87.8

APPENDIX TABLE D.3.2 *Continued*

		First-School	*Overall*
Public	Black	55.1	60.2
	Hispanic	59.4	61.2
	Asian	77.2	87.9
	Native American	47.4	56.4
	White	75.2	84.2
	Other	45.9	45.9
	All	73.5	82.5
Liberal arts	Black	71.2	77.8
	Hispanic	66.7	75.8
	Asian	81.8	92.4
	Native American	83.3	94.4
	White	78.7	89.2
	Other	28.1	28.1
	All	78.0	88.4
All institutions	Black	65.9	70.8
	Hispanic	68.1	73.3
	Asian	82.1	88.7
	Native American	56.9	68.6
	White	78.3	87.2
	Other	45.8	49.4
	All	76.8	85.7

Source: College and Beyond.

Notes: "First-School Graduation Rate" counts as graduates only those students who graduated within six years from the same school at which they matriculated as freshmen. "Overall Graduation Rate" also counts those who transferred from their first school and graduated elsewhere. See Appendix B for a more complete definition. "SEL-1" indicates institutions with mean combined SAT scores of 1250 or above; "SEL-2" indicates institutions with mean combined SAT scores between 1125 and 1249; "SEL-3" indicates institutions with mean combined SAT scores below 1125.

APPENDIX TABLE D.3.3
Graduation Rates, by Institutional Selectivity, SAT Score, and Race,
1976 and 1989 Entering Cohorts (percent)

Combined SAT Score	*1976 Entering Cohort*							
	Black				White			
	SEL-1	SEL-2	SEL-3	All	SEL-1	SEL-2	SEL-3	All
<1000	83	72	53	63	81	75	69	70
1000–1099	84	62	69	70	89	78	73	75
1100–1199	83	68	65	73	87	79	77	79
1200–1299	73	68	—	69	87	83	78	82
>1299	75	—	—	69	88	81	81	84
All	81	67	56	66	87	80	74	78

Combined SAT Score	*1989 Entering Cohort*							
	Black				White			
	SEL-1	SEL-2	SEL-3	All	SEL-1	SEL-2	SEL-3	All
<1000	88	75	65	68	86	82	78	78
1000–1099	81	76	72	75	89	83	82	83
1100–1199	87	79	72	80	94	87	84	85
1200–1299	87	74	83	81	95	86	83	86
>1299	82	81	—	81	95	86	84	90
All	85	76	68	75	95	86	82	86

Source: College and Beyond.

Notes: Graduation rates are six-year first-school graduation rates, as defined in the notes to Appendix Table D.3.1. For 1989, institutional selectivity categories are as defined in the notes to Appendix Table D.3.1; for 1976, they are as defined in the notes to Appendix Table D.3.2. Dashes represent cells with fewer than 20 observations.

APPENDIX TABLE D.3.4
Logistic Regression Model Predicting Graduation Rates, 1989 Entering Cohort

Variable	All Matriculants			Black Only		
	Parameter Estimate	Standard Error	Odds Ratio	Parameter Estimate	Standard Error	Odds Ratio
Intercept	0.957	0.052	—	0.455	0.112	—
Female	**0.280**	0.031	1.323	**0.265**	0.101	1.303
Black	**−0.513**	0.056	0.599			
Hispanic	**−0.350**	0.080	0.705			
Asian	**0.122**	0.055	1.130			
Other Race	**−0.330**	0.104	0.719			
SAT > 1299	**0.331**	0.059	1.393	0.128	0.248	1.137
SAT 1200–1299	**0.253**	0.055	1.288	0.232	0.179	1.261
SAT 1100–1199	**0.350**	0.053	1.420	**0.308**	0.149	1.361
SAT 1000–1099	**0.192**	0.054	1.211	0.141	0.136	1.151
SAT Not Available	**−0.330**	0.127	0.719	0.048	0.349	1.050
Top 10% of High School Class	**0.342**	0.036	1.407	**0.315**	0.117	1.370
High School Class Rank Not Available	−0.065	0.046	0.937	−0.065	0.148	0.937
High SES	**0.283**	0.036	1.327	**0.557**	0.175	1.746
Low SES	**−0.385**	0.079	0.680	**−0.305**	0.143	0.737
SES Not Available	**0.110**	0.050	1.116	0.031	0.172	1.031
SEL-1	**1.092**	0.058	2.979	**0.712**	0.161	2.038
SEL-2	**0.193**	0.036	1.212	**0.280**	0.119	1.323
Women's College	**−0.299**	0.069	0.742	0.158	0.269	1.171
Number of observations	32,524			2,354		
−2 Log likelihood						
Restricted	31,553			2,667		
Unrestricted	30,160			2,569		
Chi-square	1,393 with 18 d.f.			98 with 14 d.f.		

Source: College and Beyond.

Notes: Bold coefficients are significant at the .05 level; other coefficients are not. The omitted categories in the model are White, Male, SAT < 1000, Bottom 90% of High School Class, Middle SES, SEL-3, Coed Institution. Graduation rates are six-year, first-school graduation rates, as defined in the notes to Appendix Table D.3.1. Institutional selectivity categories are as defined in the notes to Appendix Table D.3.1. See Appendix B for definition of socioeconomic status (SES).

APPENDIX TABLE D.3.5
Percentage of Graduates Majoring in Selected Fields, by Race,
1976 and 1989 Entering Cohorts

	1976 Entering Cohort		1989 Entering Cohort	
	Black	White	Black	White
Social sciences				
Economics	6.8	7.1	5.3	5.7
Psychology	10.5	5.2	9.4	7.0
Sociology	4.4	1.4	3.7	1.3
Political science	10.5	7.0	13.7	10.0
Area and ethnic studies	1.1	0.5	2.7	1.5
Humanities				
History	3.6	5.4	5.1	6.8
English	4.7	5.8	5.6	8.7
Philosophy	1.1	1.1	1.1	1.1
Natural sciences/math				
Biology	10.0	8.4	6.8	7.1
Chemistry	2.0	2.6	1.5	1.7
Mathematics	1.5	1.9	1.5	2.0
Engineering	6.3	10.1	8.9	9.0

Source: College and Beyond.
Note: Includes first-school graduates only.

APPENDIX TABLE D.3.6
Ordinary Least Squares Regression Model Predicting Percentile Rank in Class,
1989 Entering Cohort

Variable	All Matriculants		Black Only	
	Parameter Estimate	Standard Error	Parameter Estimate	Standard Error
Intercept	**−23.937**	1.422	**−26.173**	3.192
Female	**8.159**	0.306	**4.924**	0.881
Black	**−16.183**	0.644		
Hispanic	**−9.002**	0.848		
Asian	**−3.071**	0.495		
Other Race	**−3.378**	1.224		
SAT Score (100-point intervals)	**5.929**	0.118	**5.024**	0.304
Top 10% of High School Class	**10.819**	0.359	**5.524**	0.989
High School Class Rank Not Available	**4.855**	0.472	2.488	1.311
High SES	**2.749**	0.332	**3.400**	1.292
Low SES	−1.798	0.928	0.072	1.320
SES Not Available	**2.939**	0.496	0.028	1.528
SEL-1	**−14.924**	0.476	**15.468**	1.312
SEL-2	**−7.892**	0.367	**−8.098**	1.074
Women's College	−1.131	0.676	−0.441	2.154
Social Science	−0.706	0.404	−0.304	1.191
Natural Science	**−2.131**	0.501	**−4.923**	1.633
Engineering	**−8.092**	0.546	**−9.050**	1.680
Other Major	0.601	0.463	1.890	1.398
Major Not Available	**−14.011**	0.696	**−14.467**	1.820
Number of observations	31,593		2,233	
R^2	0.205		0.190	

Source: College and Beyond.

Notes: Bold coefficients are significant at the .05 level; other coefficients are not. The omitted categories in the model are White, Male, Bottom 90% of High School Class, Middle SES, SEL-3, Coed Institution, and Humanities Major. Institutional selectivity categories are as defined in the notes to Appendix Table D.3.1. See Appendix B for definition of socioeconomic status (SES).

APPENDIX TABLE D.3.7
Means of Independent Variables in Chapter 3 Regression Models,
1976 Entering Cohort

Variable	Means for Regression Models in:			
	Table D.3.4		Table D.3.6	
	All	Black	All	Black
Black	0.06	—	0.06	—
Hispanic	0.03	—	0.03	—
Asian	0.10	—	0.10	—
Other Race	0.02	—	0.01	—
Female	0.51	0.59	0.51	0.59
SAT Score (100-point intervals)	—	—	12.02	10.42
SAT > 1299	0.30	0.06	—	—
SAT 1200–1299	0.23	0.13	—	—
SAT 1100–1199	0.21	0.20	—	—
SAT 1000–1099	0.14	0.20	—	—
SAT Not Available	0.01	0.02	—	—
Top 10% of High School Class	0.51	0.35	0.51	0.35
High School Class Rank Not Available	0.22	0.21	0.21	0.20
High SES	0.34	0.13	0.35	0.13
Low SES	0.03	0.13	0.03	0.12
SES Not Available	0.16	0.14	0.15	0.13
SEL-1	0.20	0.22	0.20	0.23
SEL-2	0.37	0.36	0.37	0.35
Women's College	0.05	0.04	0.05	0.04
Social Science	—	—	0.27	0.35
Natural Science	—	—	0.13	0.10
Engineering	—	—	0.11	0.10
Other Major	—	—	0.19	0.19
Major Not Available	—	—	0.05	0.07

Source: College and Beyond.
Notes: Data include all matriculants, not just survey respondents. Data used in the model for Table D.3.6 exclude matriculants with missing SAT scores, and therefore the means are different from those in the model for Table D.3.4. Dashes represent variables not used in the regression model. See Appendix B for definitions of socioeconomic status (SES) and institutional selectivity (SEL-1, SEL-2, and SEL-3).

APPENDIX TABLE D.4.1
Percentage of Graduates Attaining Advanced Degrees, by Type of Degree, Institutional Selectivity, Gender, and Race, 1976 Entering Cohort

	SEL-1			SEL-2			SEL-3			All C&B Schools		
	Black	White	All	Black	White	All	Black	White	All	Black	White	All
Advanced degree												
Female	61	67	66	61	59	59	50	39	40	57	51	52
Male	62	71	71	53	67	66	49	50	51	54	60	60
All	61	69	69	59	63	63	49	45	45	56	56	56
Master's degree only												
Female	17	23	23	17	24	23	24	20	20	20	22	22
Male	8	14	14	13	14	15	10	14	14	11	14	14
All	13	18	18	16	19	19	19	17	17	16	18	18
Professional degree												
Female	39	34	34	40	29	30	22	16	17	34	24	24
Male	48	46	46	36	46	45	36	32	33	40	40	40
All	43	40	40	39	37	37	28	24	24	36	32	32
Business degree												
Female	8	10	10	14	12	12	9	8	8	11	10	10
Male	18	17	17	16	17	17	15	15	15	16	16	16
All	12	14	14	15	14	14	11	11	11	13	13	13

(Continued)

APPENDIX TABLE D.4.1 *Continued*

	SEL-1			SEL-2			SEL-3			All C&B Schools		
	Black	*White*	*All*	*Black*	*White*	*All*	*Black*	*White*	*All*	*Black*	*White*	*All*
Law degree												
Female	16	14	14	17	11	11	11	5	6	15	9	9
Male	21	18	18	9	17	16	10	10	10	13	14	14
All	18	16	16	14	14	14	10	8	8	14	11	12
Medical degree												
Female	16	9	10	10	6	7	3	3	3	9	5	6
Male	14	11	12	12	13	13	14	8	8	13	10	11
All	15	10	11	10	9	10	7	5	6	11	8	8
Doctoral degree												
Female	4	11	11	4	6	6	3	3	3	4	6	6
Male	8	13	13	3	8	8	3	5	5	5	8	7
All	6	12	12	4	7	7	3	4	4	4	7	7

Source: College and Beyond.

Notes: "Professional degree" includes law, medical, business, and other professional degrees. "Master's degree only" includes those students whose highest degree was a master's degree (other than an MBA). "SEL-1" indicates institutions with mean combined SAT scores of 1250 or above; "SEL-2" indicates institutions with mean combined SAT scores between 1125 and 1249; "SEL-3" indicates institutions with mean combined SAT scores below 1125.

APPENDIX TABLE D.4.2

Logistic Regression Models Predicting Advanced Degree Attainment for Graduates, 1976 Entering Cohort

Variable	All						Black Only					
	Model 2			Model 3			Model 2			Model 3		
	Parameter Estimate	Standard Error	Odds Ratio	Parameter Estimate	Standard Error	Odds Ratio	Parameter Estimate	Standard Error	Odds Ratio	Parameter Estimate	Standard Error	Odds Ratio
Intercept	−1.251	0.063	—	−1.518	0.076	—	−0.611	0.355	—	−1.277	0.413	—
Black	**0.399**	0.075	1.491	**0.618**	0.078	1.856						
Hispanic	**0.284**	0.132	1.328	**0.342**	0.136	1.408						
Asian	**0.310**	0.097	1.363	**0.266**	0.100	1.305						
Other Race	−0.321	0.250	0.726	−0.209	0.260	0.811						
Female	**−0.254**	0.028	0.776	**−0.361**	0.030	0.697	0.160	0.144	1.173	0.128	0.150	1.137
SAT > 1299	**0.988**	0.057	2.685	**0.518**	0.060	1.679	**1.470**	0.564	4.347	**1.200**	0.581	3.319
SAT 1200–1299	**0.770**	0.054	2.160	**0.455**	0.056	1.575	0.262	0.294	1.299	−0.039	0.311	0.962
SAT 1100–1199	**0.507**	0.051	1.660	**0.269**	0.053	1.309	0.220	0.211	1.245	0.035	0.221	1.035
SAT 1000–1099	**0.280**	0.052	1.323	**0.157**	0.054	1.169	0.089	0.182	1.093	−0.029	0.190	0.971
SAT Score Not Available	**0.512**	0.082	1.668	**0.330**	0.086	1.391	0.082	0.417	1.085	−0.045	0.438	0.956
Top 10% of High School Class	**0.249**	0.040	1.282	**0.084**	0.042	1.087	−0.046	0.175	0.956	−0.078	0.183	0.925
High School Class Rank Not Available	0.002	0.041	1.002	−0.068	0.043	0.935	−0.416	0.189	0.659	−0.418	0.195	0.659
High SES	**0.208**	0.034	1.231	**0.194**	0.035	1.214	0.288	0.237	1.334	0.294	0.245	1.342
Low SES	**−0.177**	0.079	0.838	−0.102	0.082	0.903	−0.342	0.187	0.711	−0.344	0.193	0.709
SES Not Available	**0.108**	0.045	1.113	**0.099**	0.046	1.104	0.316	0.222	1.372	0.333	0.229	1.395
Aspired to Advanced Degree	**0.798**	0.046	2.222	**0.674**	0.047	1.961	0.652	0.343	1.920	0.605	0.354	1.832
Degree Aspirations Not Available	**0.623**	0.050	1.864	**0.530**	0.052	1.699	0.636	0.350	1.888	0.626	0.362	1.870

(Continued)

APPENDIX TABLE D.4.2 Continued

| | All | | | | | | Black Only | | | | | |
| | Model 2 | | | Model 3 | | | Model 2 | | | Model 3 | | |
Variable	Parameter Estimate	Standard Error	Odds Ratio	Parameter Estimate	Standard Error	Odds Ratio	Parameter Estimate	Standard Error	Odds Ratio	Parameter Estimate	Standard Error	Odds Ratio
SEL-1	**0.455**	0.045	1.576	**0.557**	0.048	1.746	0.280	0.198	1.323	**0.466**	0.214	1.593
SEL-2	**0.391**	0.034	1.478	**0.476**	0.036	1.609	0.244	0.164	1.276	**0.431**	0.175	1.539
Social Science				**0.295**	0.043	1.344				**0.625**	0.212	1.867
Natural Science				**0.602**	0.051	1.826				**0.865**	0.268	2.376
Engineering				−0.083	0.054	0.920				0.066	0.321	1.068
Other Major				**−0.391**	0.044	0.677				0.244	0.233	1.276
Major Not Available				0.041	0.074	1.042				0.048	0.384	1.049
Top Third of Class				**1.247**	0.040	3.481				**1.275**	0.320	3.577
Middle Third of Class				**0.639**	0.037	1.894				**0.822**	0.172	2.275
Number of Observations	18,840			18,840			888			888		
−2 Log likelihood												
Restricted	31,342			31,342			1,249			1,249		
Unrestricted	29,231			27,688			1,209			1,158		
Chi-square	2,111 with 19 d.f.			3,654 with 26 d.f.			40 with 15 d.f.			91 with 22 d.f.		

Source: College and Beyond.

Notes: Bold coefficients are significant at the .05 level; other coefficients are not. The omitted categories in the model are White, Male, SAT < 1000, Bottom 90% of High School Class, Middle SES, Did Not Aspire to Advanced Degree, SEL-3, Humanities Major, Bottom Third of Class. Institutional selectivity categories (SEL-1, SEL-2, SEL-3) are as defined in the notes to Appendix Table D.4.1.

APPENDIX TABLE D.4.3

Logistic Regression Models Predicting Professional or Doctoral Degree Attainment for Graduates, 1976 Entering Cohort

| | All | | | | | | Black Only | | | | | |
| | Model 2 | | | Model 3 | | | Model 2 | | | Model 3 | | |
Variable	Parameter Estimate	Standard Error	Odds Ratio	Parameter Estimate	Standard Error	Odds Ratio	Parameter Estimate	Standard Error	Odds Ratio	Parameter Estimate	Standard Error	Odds Ratio
Intercept	−1.936	0.064	—	−2.348	0.079	—	−1.339	0.246	—	−2.350	0.338	—
Black	**0.560**	0.079	1.751	**0.729**	0.082	2.073						
Hispanic	**0.432**	0.132	1.540	**0.485**	0.135	1.624						
Asian	**0.240**	0.093	1.271	**0.194**	0.097	1.214						
Other Race	−1.171	0.269	0.843	−0.114	0.279	0.893						
Female	**−0.598**	0.030	0.550	**−0.715**	0.031	0.489	−0.248	0.148	0.780	−0.219	0.156	0.803
SAT > 1299	**1.082**	0.064	2.950	**0.727**	0.067	2.068	0.823	0.434	2.277	0.527	0.461	1.694
SAT 1200–1299	**0.913**	0.061	2.490	**0.677**	0.064	1.967	0.496	0.291	1.642	0.167	0.313	1.182
SAT 1100–1199	**0.627**	0.060	1.891	**0.453**	0.062	1.580	**0.573**	0.211	1.774	0.347	0.222	1.415
SAT 1000–1099	**0.443**	0.062	1.557	**0.356**	0.064	1.428	0.372	0.187	1.451	0.252	0.196	1.286
SAT Score Not Available	**0.523**	0.093	1.687	**0.383**	0.096	1.467	−0.374	0.469	0.688	−0.495	0.494	0.610
Top 10% of High School Class	**0.184**	0.043	1.203	0.033	0.044	1.034	−0.029	0.179	0.971	−0.071	0.188	0.932
High School Class Rank Not Available	−0.016	0.045	0.984	−0.085	0.046	0.919	−0.217	0.195	0.805	−0.190	0.205	0.827
High SES	**0.348**	0.035	1.416	**0.336**	0.036	1.400	0.171	0.237	1.187	0.196	0.246	1.217
Low SES	−0.139	0.088	0.870	−0.080	0.090	0.923	−0.279	0.200	0.756	−0.274	0.207	0.760
SES Not Available	**0.184**	0.047	1.202	**0.180**	0.048	1.197	0.007	0.225	1.007	0.010	0.237	1.010
Aspired to Advanced Degree	**1.074**	0.040	2.926	**0.926**	0.041	2.525	**1.012**	0.216	2.750	**0.870**	0.226	2.387
Degree Aspirations Not Available	**0.609**	0.042	1.838	**0.541**	0.043	1.718	**0.740**	0.223	2.096	**0.710**	0.231	2.034

(Continued)

APPENDIX TABLE D.4.3 *Continued*

	All						Black Only					
	Model 2			Model 3			Model 2			Model 3		
Variable	*Parameter Estimate*	*Standard Error*	*Odds Ratio*	*Parameter Estimate*	*Standard Error*	*Odds Ratio*	*Parameter Estimate*	*Standard Error*	*Odds Ratio*	*Parameter Estimate*	*Standard Error*	*Odds Ratio*
SEL-1	**0.395**	0.045	1.484	**0.487**	0.048	1.627	**0.410**	0.203	1.506	**0.626**	0.222	1.870
SEL-2	**0.333**	0.035	1.395	**0.401**	0.038	1.493	**0.368**	0.172	1.445	**0.568**	0.185	1.765
Social Science				**0.596**	0.044	1.815				**0.931**	0.230	2.537
Natural Science				**0.757**	0.049	2.133				**1.526**	0.280	4.600
Engineering				**-0.128**	0.057	0.880				**0.783**	0.338	2.189
Other Major				**-0.116**	0.048	0.890				0.475	0.257	1.608
Major Not Available				0.134	0.078	1.143				0.013	0.437	1.013
Top Third of Class				**1.011**	0.042	2.748				**1.128**	0.298	3.091
Middle Third of Class				**0.476**	0.040	1.609				**0.794**	0.173	2.211
Number of observations	18,840			18,840			888			888		
-2 Log likelihood												
Restricted	30,295			30,296			1,223			1,223		
Unrestricted	27,279			26,037			1,155			1,090		
Chi-square	3,016 with 19 d.f.			4,259 with 26 d.f.			68 with 15 d.f.			133 with 22 d.f.		

Source: College and Beyond.

Notes: Bold coefficients are significant at the .05 level; other coefficients are not. The omitted categories in the models are: White, Male, SAT < 1000, Bottom 90% of High School Class, Middle SES, Did Not Aspire to Advanced Degree, SEL-3, Humanities Major, Bottom Third of Class. Institutional selectivity categories (SEL-1, SEL-2, SEL-3) are as defined in the notes to Appendix Table D.4.1. See Appendix B for definition of socioeconomic status (SES).

APPENDIX TABLE D.4.4
Percentage of Graduates Attaining Advanced Degrees, by Institutional
Selectivity, Class Rank, and Race, Actual and Adjusted Percentages,
1976 Entering Cohort

	Percentage Attaining Any Advanced Degree		Percentage Attaining Professional or Doctoral Degree	
	Actual	*Adjusted*	*Actual*	*Adjusted*
All graduates				
SEL-1	69	63	51	41
SEL-2	63	62	43	39
SEL-3	45	50	28	30
Top third of class	69	70	49	47
Middle third of class	54	56	35	34
Bottom third of class	41	40	27	24
Black graduates only				
SEL-1	61	61	48	44
SEL-2	59	60	43	42
SEL-3	49	50	31	29
Top third of class	75	78	56	59
Middle third of class	68	69	50	51
Bottom third of class	49	49	34	32

Source: College and Beyond.

Notes: Adjusted rates are estimated by using a logistic regression model controlling for student and institutional characteristics (see Appendix Tables D.4.2 and D.4.3 [Model 3] and Appendix B). Advanced degrees and institutional selectivity categories are as defined in the notes to Appendix Table D.4.1.

APPENDIX TABLE D.4.5
Means of Independent Variables in Chapter 4 Regression Models,
1976 Entering Cohort

Variable	Means for Regression Models in Tables D.4.2 and D.4.3	
	All	Black
Black	0.04	—
Hispanic	0.01	—
Asian	0.02	—
Other Race	0.00	—
Female	0.51	0.63
SAT > 1299	0.24	0.03
SAT 1200–1299	0.21	0.07
SAT 1100–1199	0.21	0.15
SAT 1000–1099	0.17	0.21
SAT Score Not Available	0.04	0.03
Top 10% of High School Class	0.40	0.30
High School Class Rank Not Available	0.40	0.35
High SES	0.30	0.11
Low SES	0.03	0.19
SES Not Available	0.23	0.21
Aspired to Advanced Degree	0.47	0.35
Degree Aspirations Not Available	0.40	0.45
SEL-1	0.20	0.25
SEL-2	0.35	0.41
Social Science	0.22	0.35
Natural Science	0.15	0.13
Engineering	0.11	0.07
Other Major	0.25	0.24
Major Not Available	0.05	0.04
Top Third of Class	0.36	0.07
Middle Third of Class	0.35	0.26

Source: College and Beyond.

Notes: Data exclude those who did not graduate from college. Dashes represent variables not used in the regression model. See Appendix B for definitions of socioeconomic status (SES) and institutional selectivity (SEL-1, SEL-2, and SEL-3).

APPENDIX TABLE D.5.1
Logistic Regression Model Predicting Women's Decision Not to Work,
1976 Entering Cohort

Variable	Parameter Estimate	Standard Error	Odds Ratio
Intercept	−1.494	0.164	—
Black	**−0.910**	0.181	0.402
Hispanic	0.419	0.225	1.520
Asian	0.043	0.178	1.044
Other Race	0.545	0.410	1.725
SAT > 1299	−0.013	0.103	0.987
SAT 1200–1299	−0.022	0.092	0.979
SAT 1100–1199	0.014	0.084	1.015
SAT 1000–1099	0.024	0.083	1.024
SAT Not Available	−0.119	0.138	0.888
Top 10% of High School Class	**−0.186**	0.069	0.830
High School Class Rank Not Available	**−0.173**	0.070	0.841
High SES	0.113	0.059	1.119
Low SES	−0.272	0.162	0.762
SES Not Available	−0.064	0.070	0.938
SEL-1	0.065	0.089	1.067
SEL-2	−0.033	0.063	0.968
Social Science	0.078	0.072	1.081
Natural Science	−0.112	0.096	0.894
Engineering	0.120	0.120	1.127
Other Major	−0.051	0.070	0.951
Major Not Available	0.196	0.109	1.217
Top Third of Class	0.104	0.069	1.109
Middle Third of Class	0.002	0.065	0.998
Less than Bachelor's Degree	**−0.292**	0.103	0.747
Master's Degree	**−0.381**	0.067	0.683
Law Degree	**−0.711**	0.102	0.491
Medical Degree	**−1.803**	0.183	0.165
Business Degree	**−0.440**	0.092	0.644
Doctoral Degree	**−0.991**	0.153	0.371
Spouse's Income $150,000+	**1.205**	0.072	3.337
Spouse's Income $75,000–$149,999	**0.881**	0.065	2.413
Spouse's Income < $30,000	**−1.138**	0.093	0.320
Spouse's Income Not Available	**2.080**	0.120	8.004

(*Continued*)

APPENDIX TABLE D.5.1 *Continued*

Variable	Parameter Estimate	Standard Error	Odds Ratio
Married	**−0.723**	0.145	0.485
Divorced/Widowed	**−0.736**	0.183	0.479
Marital Status Not Available	−0.470	0.350	0.625
Has Children	**1.246**	0.089	3.475
Number of observations	9,981		
−2 Log likelihood			
Restricted	12,450		
Unrestricted	10,367		
Chi-square	2,083 with 37 *d.f.*		

Source: College and Beyond.

Notes: Bold coefficients are significant at the .05 level; other coefficients are not. The omitted categories in the model are White, SAT < 1000, Bottom 90% of High School Class, Middle SES, SEL-3, Humanities Major, Bottom Third of Class, Bachelor's Degree Only, Spouse's Income $30,000–74,999, Single, Without Children. "SEL-1" indicates institutions with mean combined SAT scores of 1250 or above; "SEL-2" indicates institutions with mean combined SAT scores between 1125 and 1249; "SEL-3" indicates institutions with mean combined SAT scores below 1125. See Appendix B for definitions of socioeconomic status (SES) and spouse's income.

APPENDIX TABLE D.5.2

Ordinary Least Squares Regression Models Predicting Income for Men in 1995, 1976 Entering Cohort

	Model 1		Model 2		Model 3		Model 4		Model 5	
Variable	Parameter Estimate	Standard Error	Parameter Estimate	Standard Error	Parameter Estimate	Standard Error	Parameter Estimate	Standard Error	Parameter Estimate	Standard Error
Intercept	76,357	2,662	75,919	2,654	56,849	3,104	65,110	2,971	32,684	3,311
Black	−7,729	3,974	−13,182	3,998	−9,763	3,910	−12,554	3,596	−8,450	3,482
Hispanic	194	6,044	−6,302	6,049	−3,868	5,906	−8,976	5,419	−7,147	5,241
Asian	17,344	4,599	13,409	4,590	10,231	4,487	3,356	4,118	5,054	3,984
Other Race	2,172	12,091	1,388	12,025	3,676	11,725	7,219	10,746	5,770	10,393
SAT > 1299	14,743	2,766	3,843	2,952	−7,039	2,971	−6,868	2,731	−5,855	2,644
SAT 1200–1299	15,296	2,803	8,342	2,871	1,023	2,849	−969	2,616	−1,132	2,531
SAT 1100–1199	10,672	2,796	6,847	2,806	1,602	2,767	−385	2,538	−421	2,455
SAT 1000–1099	3,554	2,905	1,710	2,894	−577	2,830	−2,380	2,594	−4,560	2,510
SAT Not Available	−3,618	4,368	−7,938	4,365	−9,498	4,266	−6,469	3,919	−7,559	3,791
Top 10% of High School Class	5,937	2,034	4,033	2,033	−1,739	2,006	−3,075	1,839	−2,526	1,779
High School Class Rank Not Available	377	2,079	−920	2,073	−3,762	2,026	−4,280	1,857	−4,205	1,796
High SES	20,296	1,726	18,861	1,722	16,974	1,686	11,233	1,554	9,919	1,504
Low SES	−12,243	3,898	−12,123	3,877	−10,658	3,781	−9,761	3,466	−7,960	3,353
SES Not Available	15,344	3,023	12,232	2,046	13,174	1,998	9,925	1,833	9,649	1,773
SEL-1			19,654	2,176	23,419	2,184	20,984	2,020	19,893	1,958
SEL-2			14,937	1,745	18,539	1,742	14,286	1,614	13,528	1,564
Social Science					22,790	2,231	16,280	2,068	15,346	2,002
Natural Science					23,994	2,365	9,874	2,326	7,228	2,254
Engineering					8,679	2,348	10,037	2,196	4,337	2,148
Other Major					15,667	2,282	11,365	2,127	9,559	2,059
Major Not Available					816	3,303	2,262	3,097	312	2,996

(Continued)

APPENDIX TABLE D.5.2 *Continued*

Variable	Model 1 Parameter Estimate	Model 1 Standard Error	Model 2 Parameter Estimate	Model 2 Standard Error	Model 3 Parameter Estimate	Model 3 Standard Error	Model 4 Parameter Estimate	Model 4 Standard Error	Model 5 Parameter Estimate	Model 5 Standard Error
Top Third of Class					**29,712**	1,832	**20,838**	1,798	**20,900**	1,739
Middle Third of Class					**11,884**	1,738	**7,792**	1,639	**7,897**	1,586
Less than Bachelor's Degree							**−16,296**	2,439	**−14,535**	2,361
Master's Degree							**−25,615**	2,158	**−14,226**	2,136
Law Degree							**19,797**	2,272	**20,036**	2,204
Medical Degree							**69,079**	2,575	**77,799**	2,576
Business Degree							**28,768**	2,041	**26,273**	1,980
Doctoral Degree							**−34,048**	2,935	**−14,067**	2,949
For-Profit									**41,177**	1,982
Self-Employed									**41,533**	2,398
Not-for-Profit									3,382	2,572
Other Employment Sector									**17,941**	8,215
Employment Sector Not Available									33,142	6,758
Number of observations	9,238		9,238		9,238		9,238		9,238	
R^2	0.036		0.046		0.095		0.241		0.290	

Source: College and Beyond.

Notes: Data exclude people who did not work full time for the full year. Bold coefficients are significant at the .05 level; other coefficients are not. The omitted categories in the models are White, SAT < 1000, Bottom 90% of High School Class, Middle SES, SEL-3, Humanities Major, Bottom Third of Class, Bachelor's Degree Only, Government Sector. Institutional selectivity categories (SEL-1, SEL-2, SEL-3) are as defined in the notes to Appendix Table D.5.1. See Appendix B for definition of socioeconomic status (SES).

APPENDIX TABLE D.5.3
Ordinary Least Squares Regression Models Predicting Income for Women in 1995, 1976 Entering Cohort

Variable	Model 1 Parameter Estimate	Model 1 Standard Error	Model 2 Parameter Estimate	Model 2 Standard Error	Model 3 Parameter Estimate	Model 3 Standard Error	Model 4 Parameter Estimate	Model 4 Standard Error	Model 5 Parameter Estimate	Model 5 Standard Error
Intercept	47,081	2,014	46,810	2,014	34,626	2,385	40,067	2,364	25,715	2,609
Black	6,295	2,569	2,033	2,625	2,321	2,607	−3,136	2,444	−333	2,388
Hispanic	−2,250	5,476	−7,051	5,501	−5,738	5,470	−8,082	5,029	−8,086	4,891
Asian	22,484	4,064	19,411	4,072	16,358	4,002	14,495	3,730	12,478	3,629
Other Race	−4,948	9,704	−6,879	9,670	−5,144	9,363	−5,311	8,831	2,833	8,601
SAT > 1299	16,080	2,210	8,979	2,435	2,007	2,463	−1,192	2,316	−701	2,254
SAT 1200–1299	11,438	2,176	6,100	2,287	1,426	2,271	−939	2,132	−268	2,074
SAT 1100–1199	6,490	2,079	2,849	2,130	−425	2,095	−1,932	1,963	−2,137	1,910
SAT 1000–1099	5,449	2,123	4,041	2,123	2,628	2,076	826	1,942	565	1,889
SAT Not Available	−769	3,392	−2,703	3,389	−4,094	3,607	−5,005	3,099	−3,926	3,014
Top 10% of High School Class	6,254	1,770	5,555	1,766	2,323	1,704	1,310	1,631	1,062	1,588
High School Class Rank Not Available	3,525	1,844	2,562	1,841	1,520	1,792	1,864	1,688	1,128	1,642
High SES	12,859	1,515	11,547	1,520	11,448	1,487	6,974	1,395	6,228	1,357
Low SES	−3,268	3,016	−3,261	3,005	−3,385	2,946	−2,709	2,742	−2,105	2,668
SES Not Available	5,735	1,776	3,586	1,794	3,919	1,785	1,510	1,641	1,472	1,596
SEL-1			11,867	1,978	14,209	2,018	10,516	1,901	10,858	1,859
SEL-2			9,858	1,517	10,347	1,555	6,923	1,466	7,399	1,435
Social Science					16,341	1,670	11,340	1,649	10,250	1,606
Natural Science					17,700	1,574	8,522	2,063	7,129	2,012
Engineering					27,264	1,764	24,444	2,797	18,612	2,741
Other Major					6,195	2,097	5,200	1,661	5,265	1,616
Major Not Available					6,850	2,995	7,172	2,484	6,572	2,416

(Continued)

APPENDIX TABLE D.5.3 Continued

Variable	Model 1 Parameter Estimate	Model 1 Standard Error	Model 2 Parameter Estimate	Model 2 Standard Error	Model 3 Parameter Estimate	Model 3 Standard Error	Model 4 Parameter Estimate	Model 4 Standard Error	Model 5 Parameter Estimate	Model 5 Standard Error
Top Third of Class					**13,246**	1,778	**8,057**	1,618	**8,397**	1,575
Middle Third of Class					**7,011**	2,628	**3,985**	1,490	**4,077**	1,449
Less than Bachelor's Degree							**−8,224**	2,203	**−7,055**	2,144
Master's Degree							**−8,969**	1,592	−2,001	1,595
Law Degree							**29,305**	2,103	**31,013**	2,057
Medical Degree							**51,636**	2,671	**58,294**	2,647
Business Degree							**33,314**	2,049	**31,091**	1,998
Doctoral Degree							**−9,491**	2,581	698	2,574
For-Profit									**23,565**	1,580
Self-Employed									**10,257**	1,580
Not-for-Profit									−96	1,805
Other Employment Sector									8,219	6,059
Employment Sector Not Available									−3,381	5,808
Number of observations	6,024		6,024		6,024		6,024		6,024	
R^2	0.037		0.046		0.080		0.211		0.254	

Source: College and Beyond.

Notes: Data exclude people who did not work full time for the full year. Bold coefficients are significant at the .05 level; other coefficients are not. Omitted categories are as enumerated in the notes to Appendix Table D.5.2. Institutional selectivity categories (SEL-1, SEL-2, SEL-3) are as defined in the notes to Appendix Table D.5.1. See Appendix B for definition of socioeconomic status (SES).

APPENDIX TABLE D.5.4

Ordinary Least Squares Regression Models Predicting Income for Black Men in 1995, 1976 Entering Cohort

Variable	Model 1 Parameter Estimate	Standard Error	Model 2 Parameter Estimate	Standard Error	Model 3 Parameter Estimate	Standard Error	Model 4 Parameter Estimate	Standard Error	Model 5 Parameter Estimate	Standard Error
Intercept	60,617	5,681	58,513	6,059	41,595	8,433	43,804	8,709	27,539	9,582
SAT > 1299	−10,110	12,489	−14,726	12,909	−23,391	12,694	−22,618	11,843	−25,586	11,637
SAT 1200–1299	30,405	10,880	27,874	11,030	15,628	10,870	19,942	10,103	16,239	9,965
SAT 1100–1199	3,722	8,894	934	9,118	−6,019	8,881	−8,122	8,287	−11,088	8,182
SAT 1000–1099	17,429	6,991	15,512	7,147	6,940	6,950	2,681	6,477	−1,356	6,448
SAT Not Available	−14,441	14,063	−15,376	14,081	−14,505	13,456	−10,811	12,505	−16,287	12,316
Top 10% of High School Class	19,438	7,007	17,332	7,167	10,302	6,936	10,650	6,449	9,079	6,355
High School Class Rank Not Available	−836	7,412	−2,631	7,523	−5,332	7,238	−5,321	6,742	−5,300	6,646
High SES	41,128	10,970	40,762	11,049	31,986	10,611	30,055	9,878	23,929	9,778
Low SES	−7,449	6,978	−6,799	6,995	−7,679	6,641	−4,335	6,248	−4,742	6,152
SES Not Available	18,519	8,162	18,101	8,167	14,675	7,832	16,589	7,279	16,225	7,169
SEL-1			10,699	7,648	17,365	7,603	12,199	7,244	13,996	7,170
SEL-2			5,629	6,550	12,899	6,336	8,995	6,004	11,394	5,942
Social Science					12,653	8,354	8,868	7,911	10,351	7,811
Natural Science					49,537	9,923	16,305	10,200	16,415	10,022
Engineering					11,529	10,465	7,563	9,812	5,082	9,653
Other Major					21,490	8,985	17,204	8,361	16,659	8,245
Major Not Available					−2,717	10,967	−2,240	10,472	−162	10,284
Top Third of Class					34,089	12,263	26,857	11,638	34,133	11,634
Middle Third of Class					19,382	6,943	11,209	6,718	15,698	6,710

(Continued)

APPENDIX TABLE D.5.4 *Continued*

Variable	Model 1		Model 2		Model 3		Model 4		Model 5	
	Parameter Estimate	*Standard Error*	*Parameter Estimate*	*Standard Error*	*Parameter Estimate*	*Standard Error*	*Parameter Estimate*	*Standard Error*	*Parameter Estimate*	*Standard Error*
Less than Bachelor's Degree							−4,192	6,749	−3,931	6,620
Master's Degree							−10,915	9,806	−8,093	9,649
Law Degree							11,804	9,537	12,742	9,460
Medical Degree							**74,180**	10,106	**77,361**	10,423
Business Degree							**23,521**	8,648	**18,751**	8,527
Doctoral Degree							−4,782	14,956	3,928	15,206
For-Profit									**22,649**	6,179
Self-Employed									**26,635**	8,546
Not-for-Profit									923	9,641
Other Employment Sector									−11,018	29,352
Employment Sector Not Available									**46,191**	20,376
Number of observations	402		402		402		402		402	
R^2	0.114		0.119		0.225		0.348		0.385	

Source: College and Beyond.

Notes: Data exclude people who did not work full time for the full year. Bold coefficients are significant at the .05 level; other coefficients are not. The omitted categories in the models are SAT < 1000, Bottom 90% of High School Class, Middle SES, SEL-3, Humanities Major, Bottom Third of Class, Bachelor's Degree Only, Government Sector. Institutional selectivity categories (SEL-1, SEL-2, SEL-3) are as defined in the notes to Appendix Table D.5.1. See Appendix B for definition of socioeconomic status (SES).

APPENDIX TABLE D.5.5
Ordinary Least Squares Regression Models Predicting Income for Black Women in 1995, 1976 Entering Cohort

Variable	Model 1 Parameter Estimate	Model 1 Standard Error	Model 2 Parameter Estimate	Model 2 Standard Error	Model 3 Parameter Estimate	Model 3 Standard Error	Model 4 Parameter Estimate	Model 4 Standard Error	Model 5 Parameter Estimate	Model 5 Standard Error
Intercept	54,302	3,625	47,550	3,978	33,940	5,708	40,359	5,598	32,467	5,915
SAT > 1299	22,630	15,382	15,411	15,282	9,209	14,878	−1,152	13,390	1,545	13,082
SAT 1200–1299	−4,986	8,683	−13,074	8,798	−16,127	8,558	−14,166	7,683	−12,402	7,506
SAT 1100–1199	**16,666**	5,381	8,867	5,669	3,276	5,503	−1,334	5,004	−66	4,901
SAT 1000–1099	8,947	4,915	2,850	5,062	−150	4,897	−3,699	4,468	−3,533	4,354
SAT Not Available	3,375	12,826	−1,240	12,698	−2,771	12,311	1,313	11,025	−2,676	10,897
Top 10% of High School Class	2,147	4,513	−179	4,481	−4,105	4,406	−5,454	3,970	−5,769	3,878
High School Class Rank Not Available	−2,284	4,950	−4,704	4,919	−6,299	4,762	−1,080	4,329	−2,521	4,230
High SES	**22,371**	6,472	**21,272**	6,382	**23,331**	6,118	**14,854**	5,555	**13,904**	5,417
Low SES	−2,538	4,829	−1,642	4,766	−1,904	4,565	−1,447	4,089	−653	4,010
SES Not Available	2,236	5,650	1,314	5,574	1,584	5,386	−4,284	4,839	−2,409	4,733
SEL-1			**20,583**	5,603	**23,671**	5,545	**14,939**	5,040	**13,386**	4,983
SEL-2			**16,021**	4,394	**16,133**	4,340	**9,877**	3,944	**9,410**	3,899
Social Science					10,744	5,351	5,727	4,831	4,567	4,711
Natural Science					37,935	6,913	12,752	6,789	8,987	6,668
Engineering					17,894	8,896	12,746	8,079	8,131	7,924
Other Major					3,512	5,804	−1,925	5,223	−1,615	5,100
Major Not Available					10,452	7,698	13,067	7,199	12,687	7,018
Top Third of Class					27,478	7,512	**21,069**	6,860	**21,560**	6,701
Middle Third of Class					16,006	4,243	10,217	3,937	**9,627**	3,861

(Continued)

APPENDIX TABLE D.5.5 *Continued*

Variable	Model 1 Parameter Estimate	Model 1 Standard Error	Model 2 Parameter Estimate	Model 2 Standard Error	Model 3 Parameter Estimate	Model 3 Standard Error	Model 4 Parameter Estimate	Model 4 Standard Error	Model 5 Parameter Estimate	Model 5 Standard Error
Less than Bachelor's Degree							−11,689	5,361	**−10,762**	5,226
Master's Degree							−2,514	4,714	3,554	4,738
Law Degree							**16,864**	5,361	**21,667**	5,361
Medical Degree							**66,960**	6,920	71,056	6,867
Business Degree							**25,811**	5,874	**24,513**	5,756
Doctoral Degree							−3,066	9,324	4,835	9,198
For-Profit									**17,851**	3,910
Self-Employed									9,863	6,432
Not-for-Profit									−3,660	4,513
Other Employment Sector									3,843	21,092
Employment Sector Not Available									1,902	13,712
Number of observations	523		523		523		523		523	
R^2	0.057		0.088		0.178		0.356		0.392	

Source: College and Beyond.

Notes: Data exclude people who did not work full time for the full year. Bold coefficients are significant at the .05 level; other coefficients are not. Omitted categories are as enumerated in the notes to Appendix Table D.5.4. Institutional selectivity categories are as defined in the notes to Appendix Table D.5.1. See Appendix B for definition of socioeconomic status (SES).

APPENDIX TABLE D.5.6

Logistic Regression Model Predicting Likelihood of Being "Very Satisfied" with
Job, 1976 Entering Cohort

Variable	Parameter Estimate	Standard Error	Odds Ratio
Intercept	− 0.077	0.088	—
Black	**− 0.349**	0.076	0.705
Hispanic	0.119	0.131	1.126
Asian	− 0.107	0.099	0.898
Other Race	0.439	0.260	1.550
Female	**0.211**	0.034	1.235
SAT > 1299	− 0.118	0.063	0.889
SAT 1200–1299	− 0.061	0.060	0.941
SAT 1100–1199	0.001	0.057	1.001
SAT 1000–1099	0.061	0.057	1.063
SAT Not Available	− 0.038	0.089	0.963
Top 10% of High School Class	− 0.034	0.044	0.966
High School Class Rank Not Available	− 0.035	0.044	0.965
High SES	**0.090**	0.037	1.094
Low SES	**− 0.177**	0.079	0.837
SES Not Available	**0.086**	0.043	1.090
SEL-1	**− 0.187**	0.049	0.830
SEL-2	**− 0.158**	0.039	0.854
Social Science	− 0.025	0.047	0.975
Natural Science	0.006	0.055	1.006
Engineering	− 0.034	0.057	0.967
Other Major	− 0.051	0.048	0.950
Major Not Available	− 0.076	0.071	0.927
Top Third of Class	− 0.068	0.043	0.934
Middle Third of Class	− 0.055	0.039	0.946
Less than Bachelor's Degree	0.051	0.059	1.053
Master's Degree	0.060	0.048	1.062
Law Degree	**− 0.332**	0.056	0.718
Medical Degree	− 0.035	0.070	0.965
Business Degree	**− 0.153**	0.051	0.858
Doctoral Degree	**0.162**	0.071	1.176
For-Profit	**− 0.404**	0.047	0.668
Self-Employed	**0.190**	0.059	1.209
Not-for-Profit	0.051	0.056	1.053
Other Employment Sector	0.110	0.186	1.116
Employment Sector Not Available	− 0.278	0.178	0.758

(*Continued*)

APPENDIX TABLE D.5.6 *Continued*

Variable	Parameter Estimate	Standard Error	Odds Ratio
High Income ($150,000+)	**0.984**	0.057	2.675
Middle Income ($75,000–$149,999)	**0.475**	0.040	1.608
Very Low Income (<$30,000)	**−0.528**	0.052	0.590
Income Not Available	**0.859**	0.105	2.360
Married	**0.219**	0.052	1.245
Divorced/Separated/Widowed	0.097	0.076	1.102
Marital Status Missing	**0.495**	0.231	1.641
Has Children	**0.175**	0.038	1.192
Number of observations	15,326		
−2 Log likelihood			
Restricted	25,792		
Unrestricted	24,775		
Chi-square	1,016 with 43 *d.f.*		

Source: College and Beyond.

Notes: Data exclude people who did not work full time for the full year. Bold coefficients are significant at the .05 level; other coefficients are not. The omitted categories in the model are White, Male, SAT < 1000, Bottom 90% of High School Class, Middle SES, SEL-3, Humanities Major, Bottom Third of Class, Bachelor's Degree Only, Government Sector, Own Income $30,000–74,999, Single, Without Children. Institutional selectivity categories (SEL-1, SEL-2, SEL-3) are as defined in the notes to Appendix Table D.5.1. See Appendix B for definition of socioeconomic status (SES).

APPENDIX TABLE D.5.7

Means of Independent Variables in Chapter 5 Regression Models, 1976 Entering Cohort

			Means for Regression Models in:			
Variable	Table D.5.1 (All Women)	Table D.5.2 (All Men)	Table D.5.3 (All Women)	Table D.5.4 (Black Men)	Table D.5.5 (Black Women)	Table D.5.6 (All)
Black	0.05	0.04	0.07	—	—	0.05
Hispanic	0.01	0.01	0.01	—	—	0.01
Asian	0.02	0.02	0.02	—	—	0.02
Other Race	0.00	0.00	0.00	—	—	0.00
Female	—	—	—	—	—	0.40
SAT > 1299	0.18	0.28	0.19	0.05	0.01	0.25
SAT 1200–1299	0.19	0.22	0.19	0.07	0.05	0.21
SAT 1100–1199	0.22	0.21	0.21	0.12	0.16	0.21
SAT 1000–1099	0.19	0.15	0.18	0.23	0.19	0.17
SAT Not Available	0.05	0.04	0.05	0.04	0.02	0.04
Top 10% of High School Class	0.38	0.39	0.41	0.26	0.32	0.39
High School Class Rank Not Available	0.41	0.40	0.39	0.34	0.30	0.40
High SES	0.29	0.29	0.28	0.07	0.10	0.28
Low SES	0.04	0.04	0.05	0.24	0.21	0.04
SES Not Available	0.23	0.22	0.21	0.22	0.17	0.22
SEL-1	0.17	0.20	0.19	0.24	0.22	0.20
SEL-2	0.35	0.33	0.35	0.33	0.43	0.34

(Continued)

APPENDIX TABLE D.5.7 *Continued*

	Means for Regression Models in:					
Variable	*Table D.5.1 (All Women)*	*Table D.5.2 (All Men)*	*Table D.5.3 (All Women)*	*Table D.5.4 (Black Men)*	*Table D.5.5 (Black Women)*	*Table D.5.6 (All)*
Social Science	0.22	0.20	0.22	0.29	0.34	0.21
Natural Science	0.12	0.17	0.13	0.14	0.11	0.15
Engineering	0.05	0.17	0.05	0.12	0.05	0.12
Other Major	0.28	0.21	0.26	0.21	0.25	0.23
Major Not Available	0.07	0.06	0.07	0.10	0.08	0.06
Top Third of Class	0.35	0.32	0.35	0.05	0.06	0.33
Middle Third of Class	0.36	0.32	0.36	0.18	0.24	0.33
Less than Bachelor's Degree	0.09	0.10	0.09	0.27	0.14	0.09
Master's Degree	0.21	0.12	0.19	0.08	0.16	0.15
Law Degree	0.08	0.12	0.10	0.09	0.13	0.11
Medical Degree	0.04	0.10	0.06	0.10	0.08	0.09
Business Degree	0.08	0.14	0.10	0.11	0.09	0.13
Doctoral Degree	0.05	0.06	0.06	0.03	0.03	0.06
For-Profit	—	0.59	0.48	0.53	0.40	0.55
Self-Employed	—	0.16	0.12	0.13	0.07	0.14
Not-for-Profit	—	0.11	0.20	0.10	0.19	0.14
Other Employment Sector	—	0.01	0.01	0.01	0.01	0.01
Employment Sector Not Available	—	0.01	0.01	0.01	0.01	0.01

APPENDIX TABLE D.5.7 *Continued*

	Means for Regression Models in:					
Variable	Table D.5.1 (All Women)	Table D.5.2 (All Men)	Table D.5.3 (All Women)	Table D.5.4 (Black Men)	Table D.5.5 (Black Women)	Table D.5.6 (All)
Spouse's Income > $149,999	0.12	—	—	—	—	—
Spouse's Income $75,000–$149,999	0.17	—	—	—	—	—
Spouse's Income < $30,000	0.40	—	—	—	—	—
Spouse's Income Not Available	0.05	—	—	—	—	—
High Personal Income	—	—	—	—	—	0.12
Middle Personal Income	—	—	—	—	—	0.26
Very Low Personal Income	—	—	—	—	—	0.14
Personal Income Not Available	—	—	—	—	—	0.03
Married	0.79	—	—	—	—	0.79
Divorced/Separated/Widowed	0.07	—	—	—	—	0.06
Marital Status Not Available	0.01	—	—	—	—	0.00
Has Children	0.69	—	—	—	—	0.65

Source: College and Beyond.

Notes: Regression models for Tables D.5.2 through D.5.6 exclude people who did not work full-time for the entire year. Dashes represent variables not used in the regression model. See Appendix B for definitions of socioeconomic status (SES) and institutional selectivity (SEL-1, SEL-2, and SEL-3).

APPENDIX TABLE D.6.1A

Logistic Regression Model Predicting Leadership of Selected Civic Activities in 1995, Model 2, 1976 Entering Cohort

Variable	Youth/Education			Cultural/Alumni/ae			Social/Community		
	Parameter Estimate	Standard Error	Odds Ratio	Parameter Estimate	Standard Error	Odds Ratio	Parameter Estimate	Standard Error	Odds Ratio
Intercept	−1.262	0.057	—	−3.023	0.092	—	−2.605	0.081	—
Black	0.060	0.082	1.061	**0.355**	0.109	1.426	**0.603**	0.095	1.827
Hispanic	−0.249	0.164	0.780	−0.173	0.217	0.841	0.212	0.181	1.236
Asian	**0.516**	0.140	0.597	−0.258	0.165	0.773	−0.083	0.152	0.920
Other Race	−0.110	0.274	0.896	0.420	0.322	1.522	0.066	0.350	1.069
Female	0.065	0.034	1.067	**0.181**	0.047	1.198	**0.121**	0.044	1.129
SAT > 1299	**−0.532**	0.067	0.587	0.079	0.097	1.082	−0.124	0.089	0.884
SAT 1200–1299	**−0.271**	0.061	0.763	0.130	0.094	1.139	0.038	0.084	1.039
SAT 1100–1199	−0.066	0.057	0.937	0.118	0.090	1.126	0.084	0.079	1.087
SAT 1000–1099	−0.033	0.057	0.967	0.153	0.092	1.165	0.150	0.080	1.162
SAT Not Available	−0.105	0.092	0.901	0.115	0.141	1.121	−0.102	0.133	0.903
Top 10% of High School Class	0.037	0.046	1.038	−0.004	0.006	0.996	0.036	0.061	1.036
High School Rank Not Available	−0.029	0.047	0.971	−0.124	0.069	0.883	−0.084	0.063	0.919
High SES	**0.098**	0.040	1.103	**0.264**	0.056	1.302	**0.299**	0.052	1.348
Low SES	**−0.213**	0.094	0.808	−0.151	0.141	0.860	0.000	0.118	1.000
SES Not Available	0.048	0.047	1.050	**0.199**	0.066	1.220	**0.182**	0.062	1.200

APPENDIX TABLE D.6.1A *Continued*

	Youth/Education			Cultural/Alumni/ae			Social/Community		
Variable	*Parameter Estimate*	*Standard Error*	*Odds Ratio*	*Parameter Estimate*	*Standard Error*	*Odds Ratio*	*Parameter Estimate*	*Standard Error*	*Odds Ratio*
SEL-1	**−0.380**	0.056	0.684	**0.633**	0.071	1.883	**0.206**	0.068	1.228
SEL-2	**−0.239**	0.040	0.788	**0.470**	0.058	1.601	**0.153**	0.053	1.165
Number of observations	20,647			20,647			20,647		
−2 Log likelihood									
Restricted	23,614			14,198			15,628		
Unrestricted	23,268			13,990			15,510		
Chi-square	345 with 17 d.f.			208 with 17 d.f.			118 with 17 d.f.		

Source: College and Beyond.

Notes: Bold coefficients are significant at the .05 level; other coefficients are not. The omitted categories in the models are White, Male, SAT < 1000, Bottom 90% of High School Class, Middle SES, SEL-3. "SEL-1," "SEL-2," and "SEL-3" indicate those institutions whose matriculants had mean combined SAT scores of 1250 or above, 1125–1249, and below 1125, respectively.

APPENDIX TABLE D.6.1B

Logistic Regression Model Predicting Leadership in Selected Civic Activities in 1995, Model 5, 1976 Entering Cohort

Variable	Youth/Education			Cultural/Alumni/ae			Social/Community		
	Parameter Estimate	Standard Error	Odds Ratio	Parameter Estimate	Standard Error	Odds Ratio	Parameter Estimate	Standard Error	Odds Ratio
Intercept	-1.317	0.295	—	-2.724	0.351	—	-2.483	0.343	—
Black	0.294	0.088	1.342	0.474	0.113	1.606	0.656	0.099	1.927
Hispanic	-0.229	0.169	0.795	-0.124	0.219	0.884	0.175	0.183	1.191
Asian	-0.404	0.144	0.668	-0.120	0.167	0.887	0.005	0.154	1.005
Other Race	0.031	0.285	1.032	0.410	0.326	1.506	0.041	0.353	1.042
Female	-0.247	0.042	0.781	0.006	0.053	1.006	-0.043	0.051	0.958
SAT > 1299	-0.329	0.072	0.720	0.098	0.102	1.103	-0.080	0.093	0.924
SAT 1200–1299	-0.149	0.065	0.861	0.125	0.096	1.133	0.069	0.086	1.072
SAT 1100–1199	0.014	0.059	1.014	0.116	0.092	1.123	0.104	0.081	1.109
SAT 1000–1099	-0.016	0.059	0.984	0.154	0.093	1.166	0.166	0.081	1.180
SAT Not Available	-0.043	0.096	0.958	0.129	0.143	1.138	-0.049	0.135	0.952
Top 10% of High School Class	0.082	0.048	1.085	0.053	0.068	1.054	0.051	0.062	1.052
High School Class Rank Not Available	-0.011	0.049	0.989	-0.124	0.070	0.884	-0.075	0.064	0.928
High SES	0.043	0.042	1.043	0.167	0.057	1.182	0.204	0.053	1.226
Low SES	-0.156	0.097	0.855	-0.099	0.142	0.906	0.025	0.120	1.025
SES Not Available	0.002	0.049	1.002	0.132	0.067	1.141	0.114	0.063	1.121
SEL-1	-0.318	0.061	0.728	0.359	0.076	1.432	0.090	0.072	1.095
SEL-2	-0.194	0.044	0.824	0.283	0.061	1.326	0.053	0.056	1.054

APPENDIX TABLE D.6.1B *Continued*

Variable	Youth/Education			Cultural/Alumni/ae			Social/Community		
	Parameter Estimate	Standard Error	Odds Ratio	Parameter Estimate	Standard Error	Odds Ratio	Parameter Estimate	Standard Error	Odds Ratio
Social Science	0.098	0.054	1.102	−0.304	0.063	0.738	0.133	0.063	1.142
Natural Science	0.172	0.066	1.188	−0.638	0.088	0.528	−0.184	0.083	0.832
Engineering	0.066	0.068	1.068	−0.822	0.102	0.439	−0.545	0.103	0.580
Other Major	0.200	0.052	1.221	−0.630	0.073	0.533	0.016	0.067	1.016
Major Not Available	0.056	0.081	1.058	−0.355	0.104	0.701	−0.007	0.099	0.993
Top Third of Class	−0.150	0.049	0.861	0.018	0.066	1.018	0.003	0.063	1.003
Middle Third of Class	−0.091	0.044	0.913	0.017	0.062	1.017	0.024	0.058	1.025
Less than Bachelor's Degree	−0.123	0.066	0.884	−0.090	0.098	0.914	0.145	0.087	1.156
Master's and Other Degree	−0.141	0.053	0.868	0.188	0.071	1.206	0.154	0.067	1.166
Law Degree	−0.117	0.066	0.890	0.261	0.079	1.298	0.585	0.072	1.794
Medical Degree	−0.800	0.093	0.449	−0.643	0.128	0.526	−0.036	0.103	0.965
Business Degree	−0.059	0.059	0.942	0.321	0.077	1.378	0.023	0.080	1.023
Doctoral Degree	−0.573	0.102	0.564	0.090	0.115	1.094	−0.290	0.125	0.749
Full-Time	−0.947	0.272	0.388	0.165	0.320	1.179	−0.225	0.315	0.799
Part-Time	−0.449	0.273	0.638	0.447	0.323	1.563	−0.070	0.318	0.932
For-Profit	−0.178	0.059	0.837	−0.009	0.083x	0.991	−0.191	0.075	0.826
Self-Employed	0.090	0.069	1.095	0.398	0.093	1.489	0.307	0.084	1.360
Not-for-Profit	0.014	0.071	1.014	0.288	0.093	1.334	0.283	0.085	1.328
Other Employment Sector	−0.183	0.237	0.833	0.344	0.274	1.410	0.053	0.267	1.054
Employment Sector Not Available	−0.296	0.273	0.744	0.458	0.322	1.580	0.108	0.317	1.114

(Continued)

APPENDIX TABLE D.6.1B *Continued*

Variable	Youth/Education			Cultural/Alumni/ae			Social/Community		
	Parameter Estimate	*Standard Error*	*Odds Ratio*	*Parameter Estimate*	*Standard Error*	*Odds Ratio*	*Parameter Estimate*	*Standard Error*	*Odds Ratio*
High Household Income ($150,000+)	**0.152**	0.053	1.165	**0.503**	0.071	1.653	**0.341**	0.068	1.406
Middle Household Income ($75,000–149,999)	0.021	0.043	1.022	0.071	0.063	1.074	0.094	0.058	1.098
Very Low Household Income (<$30,000)	**−0.291**	0.098	0.747	0.029	0.107	1.029	−0.079	0.109	0.924
Household Income Not Available	**0.324**	0.129	1.382	0.124	0.158	1.132	**0.300**	0.150	1.350
Married	**−0.239**	0.095	0.787	−0.188	0.083	0.829	−0.099	0.085	0.906
Divorced/Separated/Widowed	**−0.260**	0.115	0.771	0.033	0.114	1.034	−0.030	0.115	0.971
Marital Status Not Available	0.175	0.261	1.191	**−1.060**	0.427	0.347	0.164	0.263	1.178
Has Children	**1.539**	0.067	4.662	**−0.190**	0.061	0.827	0.083	0.060	1.086
Number of observations	20,647			20,647			20,647		
−2 Log likelihood									
Restricted	23,614			14,198			15,628		
Unrestricted	21,611			13,597			15,147		
Chi-square	2,003 with 45 *d.f.*			600 with 45 *d.f.*			454 with 45 *d.f.*		

Source: College and Beyond.

Notes: Bold coefficients are significant at the .05 level; other coefficients are not. The omitted categories in the model are White, Male, SAT < 1000, Bottom 90% of High School Class, Middle SES, SEL-3, Humanities Major, Bottom Third of Class, Bachelor's Degree Only, Not Working, Government Employee, Low Household Income ($30,000–74,999) Single, Without Children. "SEL-1" indicates institutions with mean combined SAT scores of 1250 or above; "SEL-2" indicates institutions with mean combined SAT scores between 1125 and 1249; "SEL-3" indicates institutions with mean combined SAT scores below 1125. See Appendix B for definition of socioeconomic status (SES).

APPENDIX TABLE D.6.2

Political Participation and Views, by Race and Gender, College and Beyond Matriculants and National Control Group, 1976 Entering Cohort

	College and Beyond Matriculants									National Control Group	
	Men			Women			All				
	Black	White	All	Black	White	All	Black	White	All	Matriculants	Non-Matriculants
Percentage participating in a political activity in 1995	19%	14%	14%	15%	12%	12%	17%	13%	13%	10%	9%
Percentage leading a political activity in 1995	5%	4%	4%	2%	2%	2%	4%	3%	3%	2%	1%
Percentage ever participating in a political activity	29%	22%	22%	27%	21%	21%	28%	22%	22%	16%	14%
Percentage ever leading a political activity	9%	6%	6%	5%	4%	4%	6%	5%	5%	5%	2%
Percentage voting in 1992 U.S. presidential election	88%	93%	92%	92%	94%	94%	90%	94%	93%	91%	78%
Mean self-rating of economic views	3.02	3.51	3.48	2.71	3.07	3.05	2.84	3.29	3.26	3.41	3.22
Mean self-rating of social views	2.39	2.72	2.71	2.34	2.44	2.44	2.36	2.58	2.57	3.05	3.12

Sources: College and Beyond and National Control Group Study (see Appendix A).
Note: Self-ratings of economic and social views are on a scale of 1 (liberal) to 5 (conservative).

APPENDIX TABLE D.6.3

Cumulative Household Income Distribution in 1995, by Race and Gender, College and Beyond Graduates and National Graduates, 1976 Entering Cohort (percent)

Household Income (1995 dollars)	Men				Women			
	Black		White		Black		White	
	C&B	National	C&B	National	C&B	National	C&B	National
<$10,000	2	7	1	2	1	4	1	2
$10,000–$19,999	4	11	2	4	3	8	2	5
$20,000–$29,999	7	18	4	8	7	18	5	11
$30,000–$49,999	18	41	13	27	28	45	18	32
$50,000–$74,999	40	70	33	57	53	73	39	60
$75,000–$99,999	62	86	52	76	70	89	57	78
$100,000–$149,999	81	96	74	90	86	97	77	92
$150,000–$199,999	90	98	84	95	93	99	86	96
$200,000+	100	100	100	100	100	100	100	100
Mean income	$107,770	$63,390	$125,160	$82,502	$92,877	$63,390	$116,718	$79,156

Sources: College and Beyond and 1990 U.S. Census.

Note: See Appendix B for estimation of mean household income. For national graduates, the 1990 income of households in the appropriate age range is converted to 1995 dollars.

APPENDIX TABLE D.6.4

Mean Household Income of Women in 1995, by Work Status, Marital Status, and Race, 1976 Entering Cohort (1995 dollars)

	Married		Divorced/Separated		Never Married		All	
	Black	White	Black	White	Black	White	Black	White
Full-time	116,058	131,118	64,946	71,084	62,774	68,886	92,400	114,908
Part-time	130,071	114,393	—	72,534	—	31,208	99,834	108,264
Not working	101,591	136,913	—	62,353	—	36,715	88,362	131,154
All	116,602	128,289	63,496	70,474	59,613	63,454	92,877	116,718

Source: College and Beyond.

Note: "Married" includes people living together in a marriage-like relationship. Dashes represent cells with fewer than 20 observations.

APPENDIX TABLE D.6.5

Percentage of Matriculants Deriving "A Great Deal" or "A Very Great Deal" of Satisfaction from Selected Aspects of Life, by Race and Gender, 1976 and 1989 Entering Cohorts

| Satisfaction from: | *1976 Entering Cohort* | | | | | |
| | *Women* | | *Men* | | *All* | |
	Black	*White*	*Black*	*White*	*Black*	*White*
Friendships	62	66	49	47	57	57
Non-working activities	52	59	60	54	55	57
Health and physical condition	47	54	57	49	51	52
Family life	70	79	66	75	69	77
Place of residence	45	56	47	51	46	54

| Satisfaction from: | *1989 Entering Cohort* | | | | | |
| | *Women* | | *Men* | | *All* | |
	Black	*White*	*Black*	*White*	*Black*	*White*
Friendships	67	74	69	69	68	72
Non-working activities	51	57	60	57	54	57
Health and physical condition	51	55	63	53	55	54
Family life	64	70	60	58	62	64
Place of residence	36	50	45	47	40	49

Source: College and Beyond.

APPENDIX TABLE D.6.6

Percentage of Matriculants Satisfied with Life, by SAT Score and Race,
1976 and 1989 Entering Cohorts

	1976 Entering Cohort					
Combined	*Percentage "Very Satisfied"*			*Percentage "Very Satisfied" or "Somewhat Satisfied"*		
SAT Score	*Black*	*White*	*All*	*Black*	*White*	*All*
< 1000	28	45	42	83	90	89
1000–1099	29	46	45	83	90	90
1100–1199	30	45	44	83	89	89
1200–1299	30	44	44	82	89	89
> 1299	25	41	42	81	88	88
All	28	44	43	83	89	89

	1989 Entering Cohort					
Combined	*Percentage "Very Satisfied"*			*Percentage "Very Satisfied" or "Somewhat Satisfied"*		
SAT Score	*Black*	*White*	*All*	*Black*	*White*	*All*
< 1000	22	39	35	76	89	86
1000–1099	29	34	33	81	87	86
1100–1199	31	41	40	80	86	85
1200–1299	29	41	39	79	88	87
> 1299	40	41	40	82	87	86
All	28	40	38	79	87	86

Source: College and Beyond.

APPENDIX TABLE D.6.7

Percentage of Matriculants "Very Satisfied" with Life, by Class Rank and Race, 1976 and 1989 Entering Cohorts

Class Rank	Percentage "Very Satisfied" with Life					
	1976 Entering Cohort			1989 Entering Cohort		
	Black	White	All	Black	White	All
Top third of class	33	46	46	33	44	43
Middle third of class	33	45	44	34	39	38
Bottom third of class	27	41	39	26	35	33
All	28	44	43	28	40	38

Source: College and Beyond.

APPENDIX TABLE D.6.8

Logistic Regression Models Predicting Likelihood of Being "Very Satisfied" with Life, 1976 and 1989 Entering Cohorts

| | 1976 Entering Cohort | | | | | | 1989 Entering Cohort | | | | | |
| | All Matriculants | | | Black Only | | | All Matriculants | | | Black Only | | |
Variable	Parameter Estimate	Standard Error	Odds Ratio	Parameter Estimate	Standard Error	Odds Ratio	Parameter Estimate	Standard Error	Odds Ratio	Parameter Estimate	Standard Error	Odds Ratio
Intercept	−1.724	0.2222	—	0.145	1.255	—	−0.817	0.070	—	−1.101	0.250	—
Female	**0.150**	0.031	1.162	−0.221	0.153	0.802	0.047	0.031	1.048	**−0.364**	0.144	0.695
Black	**−0.425**	0.076	0.654				**−0.414**	0.073	0.661			
Hispanic	−0.007	0.120	0.993				−0.065	0.088	0.937			
Asian	−0.092	0.091	0.913				**−0.560**	0.055	0.571			
Other Race	−0.039	0.220	0.962				−0.055	0.183	0.946			
SAT > 1299	**−0.158**	0.056	0.853	−0.017	0.446	0.983	−0.124	0.066	0.884	0.479	0.313	1.614
SAT 1200–1299	−0.077	0.052	0.926	0.102	0.304	1.108	−0.077	0.062	0.926	−0.045	0.250	0.956
SAT 1100–1199	−0.043	0.049	0.958	0.124	0.229	1.132	0.010	0.059	1.010	0.076	0.216	1.079
SAT 1000–1099	−0.012	0.050	0.989	−0.014	0.197	0.986	**−0.238**	0.063	0.789	0.148	0.208	1.159
SAT Not Available	−0.114	0.078	0.892	0.339	0.413	1.404	0.296	0.168	1.344	0.029	0.630	1.029
Top 10% of High School Class	**0.088**	0.038	1.092	0.149	0.182	1.160	−0.054	0.037	0.947	−0.098	0.159	0.907
High School Class Rank Not Available	0.044	0.039	1.044	0.112	0.193	1.118	**−0.250**	0.051	0.779	0.095	0.225	1.100
High SES	**0.114**	0.033	1.120	0.347	0.244	1.415	**0.283**	0.033	1.326	−0.175	0.206	0.839
Low SES	−0.084	0.075	0.920	−0.209	0.192	0.811	−0.023	0.107	0.977	0.112	0.235	1.118
SES Not Available	0.089	0.038	1.093	−0.301	0.212	0.740	**0.137**	0.051	1.146	−0.382	0.252	0.683
SEL-1	−0.060	0.045	0.942	**−0.594**	0.227	0.552	**0.100**	0.045	1.105	0.329	0.213	1.390
SEL-2	**−0.068**	0.034	0.934	**−0.514**	0.179	0.598	**0.081**	0.039	1.084	**0.647**	0.187	1.909

(*Continued*)

APPENDIX TABLE D.6.8 *Continued*

| | 1976 Entering Cohort | | | | | | 1989 Entering Cohort | | | | | |
| | All Matriculants | | | Black Only | | | All Matriculants | | | Black Only | | |
Variable	Parameter Estimate	Standard Error	Odds Ratio	Parameter Estimate	Standard Error	Odds Ratio	Parameter Estimate	Standard Error	Odds Ratio	Parameter Estimate	Standard Error	Odds Ratio
Social Science	−0.014	0.041	0.986	−0.150	0.220	0.861	**0.085**	0.042	1.089	−0.015	0.193	0.985
Natural Science	−0.032	0.049	0.969	−0.463	0.309	0.630	**0.287**	0.052	1.333	0.032	0.270	1.033
Engineering	−0.044	0.052	0.957	−0.224	0.322	0.799	**0.167**	0.056	1.182	−0.258	0.282	0.773
Other Major	0.054	0.041	1.055	−0.240	0.239	0.786	**0.192**	0.047	1.212	−0.008	0.233	0.992
Major Not Available	0.109	0.062	1.115	0.375	0.301	1.455	0.117	0.076	1.124	−0.264	0.343	0.768
Top Third of Class	0.021	0.038	1.021	−0.318	0.326	0.727	**0.272**	0.040	1.312	0.301	0.286	1.351
Middle Third of Class	0.057	0.035	1.058	0.028	0.183	1.029	**0.146**	0.038	1.157	**0.349**	0.168	1.418
Less than Bachelor's Degree	−0.040	0.053	0.960	−0.169	0.228	0.845	**0.283**	0.078	0.753	−0.218	0.245	0.804
Master's and Other Degree	**0.121**	0.041	1.129	0.516	0.230	1.675	0.033	0.039	1.033	−0.183	0.196	0.833
Law Degree	−0.007	0.050	0.993	0.261	0.261	1.298	**0.178**	0.055	1.195	0.359	0.234	1.432
Medical Degree	**0.205**	0.062	1.228	0.290	0.312	1.337	**0.680**	0.059	1.974	**0.647**	0.280	1.910
Business Degree	0.052	0.046	1.053	0.135	0.256	1.144	**0.536**	0.056	1.709	0.421	0.268	1.523
Doctoral Degree	0.004	0.066	1.004	0.148	0.448	1.160	0.064	0.060	1.066	−0.292	0.318	0.746
Full-Time	0.150	0.205	1.162	−1.205	1.210	0.300						
Part-Time	0.230	0.207	1.259	−0.979	1.223	0.376						
For-Profit	**−0.218**	0.044	0.804	−0.161	0.191	0.851						
Self-Employed	−0.030	0.054	0.971	−0.260	0.281	0.771						
Not-for-Profit	0.077	0.052	1.080	0.371	0.233	1.449						
Other Employment Sector	**−0.419**	0.166	0.657	−0.279	0.906	0.757						
Employment Sector Not Available	0.145	0.205	1.156	−0.819	1.184	0.441						

APPENDIX TABLE D.6.8 Continued

<table>
<tr><th rowspan="3">Variable</th><th colspan="6">1976 Entering Cohort</th><th colspan="6">1989 Entering Cohort</th></tr>
<tr><th colspan="3">All Matriculants</th><th colspan="3">Black Only</th><th colspan="3">All Matriculants</th><th colspan="3">Black Only</th></tr>
<tr><th>Parameter Estimate</th><th>Standard Error</th><th>Odds Ratio</th><th>Parameter Estimate</th><th>Standard Error</th><th>Odds Ratio</th><th>Parameter Estimate</th><th>Standard Error</th><th>Odds Ratio</th><th>Parameter Estimate</th><th>Standard Error</th><th>Odds Ratio</th></tr>
<tr><td>High Household Income ($150,000+)</td><td>0.779</td><td>0.042</td><td>2.179</td><td>1.487</td><td>0.243</td><td>4.423</td><td></td><td></td><td></td><td></td><td></td><td></td></tr>
<tr><td>Middle Household Income ($75,000–149,999)</td><td>0.379</td><td>0.034</td><td>1.460</td><td>0.669</td><td>0.178</td><td>1.952</td><td></td><td></td><td></td><td></td><td></td><td></td></tr>
<tr><td>Very Low Household Income (<$30,000)</td><td>−0.318</td><td>0.075</td><td>0.728</td><td>−0.342</td><td>0.327</td><td>0.710</td><td></td><td></td><td></td><td></td><td></td><td></td></tr>
<tr><td>Household Income Not Available</td><td>0.998</td><td>0.099</td><td>2.713</td><td>1.055</td><td>0.581</td><td>2.873</td><td></td><td></td><td></td><td></td><td></td><td></td></tr>
<tr><td>Married</td><td>0.848</td><td>0.056</td><td>2.335</td><td>0.450</td><td>0.237</td><td>1.568</td><td></td><td></td><td></td><td></td><td></td><td></td></tr>
<tr><td>Divorced</td><td>0.062</td><td>0.079</td><td>1.064</td><td>0.317</td><td>0.292</td><td>1.373</td><td></td><td></td><td></td><td></td><td></td><td></td></tr>
<tr><td>Marital Status Not Available</td><td>0.492</td><td>0.194</td><td>1.636</td><td>0.115</td><td>0.740</td><td>1.121</td><td></td><td></td><td></td><td></td><td></td><td></td></tr>
<tr><td>Has Children</td><td>0.303</td><td>0.036</td><td>1.354</td><td>0.140</td><td>0.186</td><td>1.150</td><td></td><td></td><td></td><td></td><td></td><td></td></tr>
<tr><td>Number of observations</td><td>20,559</td><td></td><td></td><td>1,094</td><td></td><td></td><td>9,531</td><td></td><td></td><td>1,135</td><td></td><td></td></tr>
<tr><td>−2 Log likelihood
Restricted
Unrestricted</td><td>34,341
32,128</td><td></td><td></td><td>1,355
1,234</td><td></td><td></td><td>28,351
27,601</td><td></td><td></td><td>1,360
1,304</td><td></td><td></td></tr>
<tr><td>Chi-square</td><td>2,313 with 45 d.f.</td><td></td><td></td><td>121 with 41 d.f.</td><td></td><td></td><td>750 with 30 d.f.</td><td></td><td></td><td>57 with 26 d.f.</td><td></td><td></td></tr>
</table>

Source: College and Beyond.

Notes: Bold coefficients are significant at the .05 level; other coefficients are not. Omitted categories are as enumerated in the notes to Appendix Table D.6.1. For 1976, "SEL-1" indicates institutions with mean combined SAT scores of 1250 or above; "SEL-2" indicates institutions with mean combined SAT scores between 1125 and 1249; "SEL-3" indicates institutions with mean combined SAT scores below 1125. For 1989, "SEL-1" indicates institutions with mean combined SAT scores of 1300 or above; "SEL-2" incicates institutions with mean combined SAT scores between 1150 and 1299; "SEL-3" indicates institutions with mean combined SAT scores below 1150. See Appendix B for definition of socioeconomic status (SES).

APPENDIX TABLE D.6.9
Means of Independent Variables in Chapter 6 Regression Models,
1976 and 1989 Entering Cohorts

| Variable | Means for Regression Models in Tables D.6.1A, D.6.1B, and D.6.8 | | | |
| | 1976 Entering Cohort | | 1989 Entering Cohort | |
	All	Black	All	Black
Female	0.50	0.59	0.52	0.62
Black	0.05	—	0.05	—
Hispanic	0.01	—	0.03	—
Asian	0.02	—	0.09	—
Other Race	0.00	—	0.01	—
SAT > 1299	0.23	0.03	0.33	0.07
SAT 1200–1299	0.21	0.07	0.22	0.15
SAT 1100–1199	0.21	0.14	0.21	0.21
SAT 1000–1099	0.17	0.20	0.14	0.19
SAT Not Available	0.04	0.03	0.01	0.01
Top 10% of High School Class	0.39	0.28	0.56	0.40
High School Class Rank Not Available	0.40	0.33	0.19	0.17
High SES	0.29	0.09	0.33	0.14
Low SES	0.04	0.21	0.02	0.10
SES Not Available	0.23	0.20	0.15	0.13
SEL-1	0.19	0.22	0.24	0.30
SEL-2	0.35	0.40	0.26	0.25
Social Science	0.21	0.31	0.26	0.35
Natural Science	0.14	0.12	0.14	0.11
Engineering	0.11	0.08	0.11	0.09
Other Major	0.24	0.23	0.21	0.20
Major Not Available	0.07	0.10	0.05	0.07
Top Third of Class	0.34	0.06	0.34	0.07
Middle Third of Class	0.34	0.21	0.34	0.23
Less than Bachelor's Degree	0.09	0.20	0.05	0.13
Master's and Other Degree	0.16	0.13	0.22	0.20
Law Degree	0.10	0.11	0.09	0.10
Medical Degree	0.07	0.08	0.08	0.07
Business Degree	0.11	0.10	0.08	0.07
Doctoral Degree	0.06	0.03	0.07	0.06

APPENDIX TABLE D.6.9 *Continued*

Variable	Means for Regression Models in Tables D.6.1A, D.6.1B, and D.6.8			
	1976 Entering Cohort		1989 Entering Cohort	
	All	Black	All	Black
Full-Time Worker	0.75	0.87	—	—
Part-Time Worker	0.13	0.08	—	—
For-Profit	0.47	0.44	—	—
Self-Employed	0.14	0.10	—	—
Not-for-Profit	0.14	0.15	—	—
Other Employment Sector	0.01	0.01	—	—
Employment Sector Not Available	0.12	0.06	—	—
High Household Income ($150,000+)	0.22	0.13	—	—
Middle Household Income ($75,000–$149,999)	0.36	0.33	—	—
Very Low Household Income (<$30,000)	0.09	0.11	—	—
Household Income Not Available	0.04	0.02	—	—
Married	0.81	0.61	—	—
Divorced/Separated/Widowed	0.06	0.13	—	—
Marital Status Not Available	0.01	0.01	—	—
Has Children	0.69	0.62	—	—

Source: College and Beyond.

Notes: Dashes represent variables not used in the regression model. See Appendix B for definitions of socioeconomic status (SES) and institutional selectivity (SEL-1, SEL-2, and SEL-3).

APPENDIX TABLE D.7.1

Percentage of Students Satisfied with College, by Graduation Status, Race, and Gender, 1976 and 1989 Entering Cohorts

	1976 Entering Cohort						1989 Entering Cohort					
	Very Satisfied	Somewhat Satisfied	Very or Somewhat Satisfied	Somewhat Dissatisfied	Very Dissatisfied	Very or Somewhat Dissatisfied	Very Satisfied	Somewhat Satisfied	Very or Somewhat Satisfied	Somewhat Dissatisfied	Very Dissatisfied	Very or Somewhat Dissatisfied
All matriculants												
Black												
Female	58	31	89	4	1	6	59	33	91	4	1	5
Male	59	27	86	5	2	7	62	31	93	3	1	4
All	58	30	88	5	2	7	60	32	92	4	1	5
White												
Female	62	29	90	4	1	5	67	26	93	4	1	5
Male	62	28	89	4	2	6	64	28	91	4	1	5
All	62	28	90	4	1	6	65	27	92	4	1	5
All races												
Female	62	29	90	5	1	6	66	27	93	4	1	5
Male	62	27	89	4	2	6	64	28	91	4	1	5
All	62	28	90	4	1	6	65	27	92	4	1	5

APPENDIX TABLE D.7.1 *Continued*

	1976 Entering Cohort						1989 Entering Cohort					
	Very Satisfied	Somewhat Satisfied	Very or Somewhat Satisfied	Somewhat Dissatisfied	Very Dissatisfied	Very or Somewhat Dissatisfied	Very Satisfied	Somewhat Satisfied	Very or Somewhat Satisfied	Somewhat Dissatisfied	Very Dissatisfied	Very or Somewhat Dissatisfied
First-school graduates												
Black	65	28	93	3	1	4	66	29	95	2	0	3
White	67	26	93	3	1	4	69	26	95	3	1	3
All	67	26	93	3	1	4	68	26	95	2	1	3
Transfer graduates												
Black	43	33	77	8	4	12	30	46	76	11	8	19
White	39	35	74	11	4	15	33	39	72	13	7	20
All	40	35	75	11	4	15	33	39	72	13	7	19
Non-graduates												
Black	36	37	73	10	5	15	33	47	80	10	3	13
White	31	39	70	12	5	17	30	29	60	20	8	28
All	32	38	71	11	5	16	32	32	64	18	7	24

Source: College and Beyond.

Notes: Data for 1976 entering cohort exclude five schools surveyed in Wave 1 (see Appendix A). "First-school graduates," "Transfer graduates," and "Non-graduates" are defined in Appendix B.

APPENDIX TABLE D.7.2

Logistic Regression Models Predicting Likelihood of Being "Very Satisfied" with College for Graduates, 1976 Entering Cohort

| | All Graduates | | | | | | Black Only | | | | | |
| | Model 3 | | | Model 5 | | | Model 3 | | | Model 5 | | |
Variable	Parameter Estimate	Standard Error	Odds Ratio	Parameter Estimate	Standard Error	Odds Ratio	Parameter Estimate	Standard Error	Odds Ratio	Parameter Estimate	Standard Error	Odds Ratio
Intercept	−0.661	0.077	—	−0.805	0.091	—	−0.189	0.337	—	−0.410	0.392	—
Female	**−0.093**	0.032	0.911	0.010	0.034	1.010	**−0.353**	0.165	0.703	−0.290	0.173	0.748
Black	−0.001	0.081	0.999	−0.051	0.083	0.951						
Hispanic	0.267	0.149	1.306	0.234	0.151	1.264						
Asian	−0.143	0.099	0.867	−0.194	0.100	0.824						
Other Race	−0.061	0.277	0.940	−0.081	0.279	0.922						
SAT > 1299	**−0.129**	0.063	0.879	**−0.164**	0.064	0.849	−0.288	0.494	0.749	−0.368	0.509	0.692
SAT 1200–1299	−0.026	0.059	0.975	−0.062	0.060	0.940	**−0.661**	0.324	0.516	**−0.702**	0.335	0.496
SAT 1100–1199	−0.026	0.056	0.975	−0.049	0.057	0.953	0.314	0.249	1.368	0.361	0.260	1.435
SAT 1000–1099	**0.149**	0.057	1.160	**0.130**	0.058	1.139	0.089	0.206	1.093	0.063	0.216	1.065
SAT Not Available	0.095	0.094	1.099	0.105	0.095	1.111	0.840	0.604	2.316	1.067	0.621	2.906
Top 10% of High School Class	0.085	0.044	1.089	0.082	0.044	1.086	0.017	0.196	1.017	−0.009	0.202	0.991
High School Class Rank Not Available	0.038	0.044	1.039	0.046	0.045	1.047	−0.041	0.207	0.960	0.055	0.214	1.057
High SES	−0.027	0.037	0.973	**−0.104**	0.038	0.901	0.311	0.269	1.365	0.090	0.278	1.094
Low SES	−0.036	0.085	0.964	−0.020	0.086	0.980	0.151	0.209	1.163	0.232	0.216	1.261
SES Not Available	**−0.086**	0.043	0.917	**−0.128**	0.044	0.880	0.017	0.227	1.017	−0.083	0.237	0.920
SEL-1	**0.558**	0.051	1.747	**0.472**	0.052	1.603	**0.756**	0.234	2.129	**0.630**	0.243	1.878
SEL-2	**0.333**	0.039	1.395	**0.265**	0.040	1.304	**0.457**	0.188	1.579	0.291	0.196	1.338

APPENDIX TABLE D.7.2 Continued

	All Graduates						Black Only					
	Model 3			Model 5			Model 3			Model 5		
Variable	Parameter Estimate	Standard Error	Odds Ratio	Parameter Estimate	Standard Error	Odds Ratio	Parameter Estimate	Standard Error	Odds Ratio	Parameter Estimate	Standard Error	Odds Ratio
Social Science	**0.177**	0.046	1.194	0.084	0.047	1.088	−0.374	0.246	0.688	**−0.602**	0.257	0.548
Natural Science	**0.271**	0.052	1.311	**0.158**	0.056	1.172	−0.310	0.295	0.733	**−0.627**	0.331	0.534
Engineering	**0.313**	0.058	1.367	**0.278**	0.060	1.320	**−0.770**	0.347	0.463	**−0.991**	0.363	0.371
Other Major	**0.184**	0.047	1.201	**0.165**	0.048	1.179	−0.190	0.271	0.827	−0.289	0.279	0.749
Major Not Available	0.281	0.148	1.324	0.193	0.151	1.213	−0.456	0.558	0.634	−0.778	0.571	0.460
Top Third of Class	**0.599**	0.042	1.819	**0.462**	0.044	1.587	**0.840**	0.328	2.317	0.588	0.351	1.800
Middle Third of Class	**0.299**	0.039	1.348	**0.233**	0.040	1.263	**1.095**	0.200	2.989	**0.982**	0.207	2.670
First Choice Institution	**0.459**	0.037	1.582	**0.481**	0.037	1.617	**0.365**	0.174	1.440	0.336	0.181	1.400
Choice Not Available	−0.227	0.139	0.797	−0.222	0.141	0.801	−0.811	0.685	0.444	−0.821	0.716	0.440
Had Mentor	**0.786**	0.032	2.195	**0.809**	0.032	2.245	**0.600**	0.156	1.822	**0.524**	0.162	1.688
Master's Degree				0.075	0.045	1.077				0.361	0.237	1.434
Law Degree				**0.521**	0.058	1.684				**1.011**	0.291	2.749
Medical Degree				**0.465**	0.073	1.592				**0.725**	0.340	2.065
Business Degree				**0.273**	0.051	1.314				**0.623**	0.258	1.864
Doctoral Degree				0.289	0.074	1.335				0.344	0.447	1.411
For-Profit				0.061	0.052	1.062				0.031	0.213	1.031
Self-Employed				−0.088	0.061	0.916				0.074	0.296	1.077
Not-for-Profit				−0.017	0.061	0.983				−0.130	0.263	0.878
Other Employment Sector				**−0.466**	0.187	0.628				−0.129	1.010	0.879
Employment Sector Not Available				−0.060	0.065	0.942				0.212	0.396	1.236

(Continued)

APPENDIX TABLE D.7.2 *Continued*

	All Graduates						Black Only					
	Model 3			Model 5			Model 3			Model 5		
Variable	Parameter Estimate	Standard Error	Odds Ratio	Parameter Estimate	Standard Error	Odds Ratio	Parameter Estimate	Standard Error	Odds Ratio	Parameter Estimate	Standard Error	Odds Ratio
High Household Income ($150,000+)				**0.373**	0.047	1.452				**0.600**	0.276	1.822
Middle Household Income ($75,000–149,999)				**0.171**	0.038	1.186				**0.455**	0.185	1.576
Very Low Household Income (<30,000)				**−0.465**	0.074	0.628				−0.563	0.324	0.569
Household Income Not Available				**0.512**	0.103	1.668				0.734	0.613	2.084
Number of observations	17,252			17,252			840			840		
−2 Log likelihood												
Restricted	26,470			26,470			1,113			1,113		
Unrestricted	25,146			24,795			1,011			969		
Chi-square	1,324 with 27 d.f.			1,675 with 41 d.f.			102 with 23 d.f.			145 with 37 d.f.		

Source: College and Beyond.

Notes: "Graduates" refers to first-school graduates. Bold coefficients are significant at the .05 level; other coefficients are not. The omitted categories in the models are White, Male, SAT < 1000, Bottom 90% of High School Class, Middle SES, SEL-3, Humanities Major, Bottom Third of Class, Not First-Choice School, No Mentor, Bachelor's Degree Only, Government Employee, Low Household Income ($30,000–74,999). "SEL-1" indicates institutions with mean combined SAT scores of 1250 or above; "SEL-2" indicates institutions with mean combined SAT scores between 1125 and 1249; "SEL-3" indicates institutions with mean combined SAT scores below 1125. See Appendix B for definition of socioeconomic status (SES).

APPENDIX TABLE D.7.3

Logistic Regression Models Predicting Likelihood of Being "Very Satisfied" with College for Graduates, 1989 Entering Cohort

| | All Graduates | | | | | | Black Only | | | | | |
| | Model 3 | | | Model 4 | | | Model 3 | | | Model 4 | | |
Variable	Parameter Estimate	Standard Error	Odds Ratio	Parameter Estimate	Standard Error	Odds Ratio	Parameter Estimate	Standard Error	Odds Ratio	Parameter Estimate	Standard Error	Odds Ratio
Intercept	−0.818	0.086	—	−0.852	0.087	—	−0.315	0.314	—	−0.331	0.321	—
Female	0.052	0.034	1.054	**0.089**	0.035	1.093	−0.317	0.163	0.728	−0.321	0.165	0.725
Black	0.009	0.078	1.009	−0.061	0.079	0.941						
Hispanic	0.131	0.102	1.140	0.096	0.103	1.100						
Asian	−0.106	0.058	0.900	**−0.143**	0.058	0.867						
Other Race	0.046	0.212	1.047	0.083	0.213	1.087						
SAT > 1299	**−0.155**	0.074	0.857	**−0.215**	0.075	0.807	0.189	0.402	1.208	0.189	0.405	1.208
SAT 1200–1299	−0.043	0.070	0.958	−0.103	0.070	0.902	0.057	0.277	1.059	−0.028	0.281	0.973
SAT 1100–1199	−0.036	0.067	0.964	−0.086	0.067	0.918	−0.251	0.232	0.778	−0.314	0.235	0.731
SAT 1000–1099	0.040	0.069	1.041	0.016	0.069	1.016	**−0.552**	0.220	0.576	−0.595	0.221	0.551
SAT Not Available	0.022	0.203	1.022	−0.047	0.205	0.954	—	—	—	—	—	—
Top 10% of High School Class	**0.196**	0.041	1.216	**0.186**	0.041	1.204	−0.015	0.171	0.985	−0.047	0.172	0.955
High School Class Rank Not Available	**0.169**	0.057	1.185	**0.167**	0.057	1.182	0.156	0.253	1.169	0.153	0.253	1.165

(Continued)

APPENDIX TABLE D.7.3 Continued

Variable	All Graduates						Black Only					
	Model 3			Model 4			Model 3			Model 4		
	Parameter Estimate	Standard Error	Odds Ratio	Parameter Estimate	Standard Error	Odds Ratio	Parameter Estimate	Standard Error	Odds Ratio	Parameter Estimate	Standard Error	Odds Ratio
High SES	**0.199**	0.038	1.220	**0.162**	0.038	1.176	−0.182	0.221	0.834	−0.244	0.225	0.784
Low SES	**−0.461**	0.114	0.631	**−0.430**	0.115	0.650	0.355	0.268	1.426	0.368	0.270	1.445
SES Not Available	−0.110	0.057	0.896	**−0.147**	0.057	0.863	0.021	0.272	1.021	−0.063	0.275	0.939
SEL-1	**0.620**	0.052	1.859	**0.606**	0.052	1.834	**1.163**	0.240	3.199	**1.147**	0.242	3.149
SEL-2	**0.266**	0.044	1.305	**0.262**	0.044	1.300	**0.567**	0.203	1.763	**0.595**	0.205	1.814
Social Science	**0.282**	0.047	1.325	**0.248**	0.047	1.282	−0.218	0.223	0.804	−0.236	0.224	0.790
Natural Science	0.105	0.056	1.110	0.008	0.059	1.008	**−0.619**	0.285	0.539	**−0.743**	0.306	0.476
Engineering	**0.199**	0.061	1.220	**0.259**	0.062	1.295	**−1.366**	0.306	0.255	**−1.283**	0.308	0.277
Other Major	0.272	0.051	1.313	**0.289**	0.052	1.335	−0.350	0.247	0.705	−0.285	0.250	0.752
Major Not Available	−0.193	0.107	0.825	**−0.245**	0.107	0.783	−0.848	0.454	0.428	−0.832	0.456	0.435
Top Third of Class	**0.695**	0.044	2.004	**0.639**	0.045	1.895	**0.841**	0.330	2.319	**0.801**	0.335	2.227
Middle Third of Class	**0.407**	0.041	1.503	**0.377**	0.041	1.458	**0.707**	0.188	2.028	**0.659**	0.190	1.932
First Choice Institution	**0.380**	0.037	1.462	**0.371**	0.037	1.450	**0.548**	0.165	0.730	**0.565**	0.166	1.759
Choice Not Available	0.059	0.158	1.060	0.100	0.159	1.105	0.773	0.747	2.167	0.793	0.745	2.211
Had Mentor	**0.752**	0.033	2.122	**0.766**	0.034	2.151	0.846	0.160	2.331	**0.830**	0.161	2.293

APPENDIX TABLE D.7.3 *Continued*

| | All Graduates | | | | | | Black Only | | | | | |
| | Model 3 | | | Model 4 | | | Model 3 | | | Model 4 | | |
Variable	Parameter Estimate	Standard Error	Odds Ratio	Parameter Estimate	Standard Error	Odds Ratio	Parameter Estimate	Standard Error	Odds Ratio	Parameter Estimate	Standard Error	Odds Ratio
Master's Degree				0.012	0.042	1.012				−0.084	0.189	0.919
Law Degree				**0.453**	0.065	1.573				0.515	0.276	1.673
Medical Degree				**0.602**	0.072	1.827				0.554	0.334	1.741
Business Degree				**0.556**	0.067	1.744				0.013	0.285	1.013
Doctoral Degree				0.132	0.069	1.141				0.269	0.341	1.308
Number of observations	8,620			8,620			945			945		
−2 Log likelihood												
Restricted	23,999			23,999			1,234			1,234		
Unrestricted	22,564			22,392			1,083			1,076		
Chi-square	1,435 with 27 *d.f.*			1,608 with 32 *d.f.*			147 with 22 *d.f.*			154 with 27 *d.f.*		

Source: College and Beyond.

Notes: "Graduates" refers to first-school graduates. Bold coefficients are significant at the .05 level; other coefficients are not. The omitted categories in the models are White, Male, SAT < 1000, Bottom 90% of High School Class, Middle SES, SEL-3, Humanities Major, Bottom Third of Class, Not First-Choice School, No Mentor, Bachelor's Degree Only. "SEL-1" indicates institutions with mean combined SAT scores of 1300 or above; "SEL-2" indicates institutions with mean combined SAT scores between 1150 and 1299; "SEL-3" indicates institutions with mean combined SAT scores below 1150. See Appendix B for definition of socioeconomic status (SES).

APPENDIX TABLE D.7.4

Percentage of Graduates "Very Satisfied" with College, by Institutional Selectivity, Institutional Type, SAT Score, and Race, 1976 and 1989 Entering Cohorts

	Percentage "Very Satisfied" with College									
	SAT Scores of 1976 Entering Cohort					SAT Scores of 1989 Entering Cohort				
	<1000	1000–1099	1100–1199	1200–1299	>1299	<1000	1000–1099	1100–1199	1200–1299	>1299
Institutional selectivity										
Black										
SEL-1	76	69	78	64	—	—	72	75	79	83
SEL-2	65	62	68	54	—	69	63	65	71	—
SEL-3	55	70	77	—	—	56	45	59	68	—
White										
SEL-1	75	81	71	72	74	77	76	75	74	77
SEL-2	67	68	68	68	68	72	77	71	72	66
SEL-3	61	65	61	64	63	66	66	64	64	68
Institutional type										
Black										
Private	61	64	69	61	65	71	64	67	75	84
Public	56	69	80	—	—	56	45	59	68	—
Liberal arts	78	68	83	—	—	72	80	80	—	—
White										
Private	62	66	66	66	69	68	76	70	72	72
Public	62	66	62	66	64	66	66	64	64	68
Liberal arts	63	69	72	74	77	82	78	75	74	75

Source: College and Beyond.

Notes: "Graduates" refers to first-school graduates. Dashes represent cells with fewer than 20 observations. For 1976, "SEL-1" indicates institutions with mean combined SAT scores of 1250 or above; "SEL-2" indicates institutions with mean combined SAT scores between 1125 and 1249; "SEL-3" indicates institutions with mean combined SAT scores below 1125. For 1989, "SEL-1" indicates institutions with mean combined SAT scores of 1300 or above; "SEL-2" indicates institutions with mean combined SAT scores between 1150 and 1299; "SEL-3" indicates institutions with mean combined SAT scores below 1150.

APPENDIX TABLE D.7.5

Percentage of Graduates "Very Satisfied" with College, by Institutional Selectivity, Institutional Type, and Race, 1976 and 1989 Entering Cohorts

| | Percentage "Very Satisfied" with College | | | | | |
| | 1976 Entering Cohort | | | 1989 Entering Cohort | | |
	Black	White	All	Black	White	All
Institutional selectivity						
SEL-1	73	73	73	78	76	76
SEL-2	65	68	68	68	70	69
SEL-3	59	63	63	55	65	64
All	65	67	67	66	69	68
Institutional type						
Private university	64	67	67	72	72	72
Public university	60	64	64	55	65	64
Liberal arts college	76	73	73	78	75	75
All	65	67	67	66	69	68

Source: College and Beyond.

Notes: "Graduates" refers to first-school graduates. See notes to Appendix Table D.7.4 for definitions of institutional selectivity.

APPENDIX TABLE D.7.6

Percentage of Graduates Who Had a Mentor, by Race and Gender, 1976 and 1989 Entering Cohorts

| | | *1976 Entering Cohort* | | |
| | *Had Mentor* | *Who Was Mentor?* | | |
		Faculty	*Dean*	*Alumni/ae*
Black				
Female	55	69	40	9
Male	56	61	38	14
All	55	66	39	11
White				
Female	48	85	15	6
Male	46	82	15	6
All	47	84	15	6
All Races				
Female	48	84	17	6
Male	46	81	16	6
All	47	82	16	6

| | | *1989 Entering Cohort* | | |
| | *Had Mentor* | *Who Was Mentor?* | | |
		Faculty	*Dean*	*Alumni/ae*
Black				
Female	67	69	40	9
Male	74	70	36	12
All	70	70	39	10
White				
Female	60	83	15	7
Male	57	80	16	8
All	59	81	16	7
All Races				
Female	61	81	19	7
Male	58	80	18	8
All	59	80	18	8

Source: College and Beyond.

Notes: "Graduates" refers to first-school graduates. Respondents were allowed to identify more than one mentor.

APPENDIX TABLE D.7.7

Percentage of Graduates "Very Likely" and "Not Likely" to Choose Same College Again, by Institutional Selectivity, Institutional Type, and Race, 1976 and 1989 Entering Cohorts

| | *Percentage "Very Likely" to Choose Same College* | | | | | |
| | *1976 Entering Cohort* | | | *1989 Entering Cohort* | | |
	Black	*White*	*All*	*Black*	*White*	*All*
Institutional selectivity						
SEL-1	68	71	72	80	81	81
SEL-2	53	58	58	67	63	63
SEL-3	54	66	65	68	76	75
All	57	64	64	72	74	74
Institutional type						
Private university	57	63	63	74	72	73
Public university	57	68	68	68	76	75
Liberal arts college	57	58	59	74	71	71
All	57	64	64	72	74	74

| | *Percentage "Not Likely" to Choose Same College* | | | | | |
| | *1976 Entering Cohort* | | | *1989 Entering Cohort* | | |
	Black	*White*	*All*	*Black*	*White*	*All*
Institutional selectivity						
SEL-1	10	8	8	3	4	4
SEL-2	15	12	12	9	9	9
SEL-3	15	9	9	8	5	6
All	14	10	10	7	6	6
Institutional type						
Private university	13	10	11	5	6	6
Public university	14	8	8	8	5	6
Liberal arts college	15	12	13	10	8	8
All	14	10	10	7	6	6

Source: College and Beyond.

Notes: "Graduates" refers to first-school graduates. See notes to Appendix Table D.7.4 for definition of institutional selectivity.

APPENDIX TABLE D.7.8

Percentage of Graduates "Very Likely" and "Not Likely" to Choose Same Major
Again, by Major and Race, 1976 and 1989 Entering Cohorts

| | *Percentage "Very Likely" to Choose Same Major* | | | | | |
| | *1976 Entering Cohort* | | | *1989 Entering Cohort* | | |
	Black	*White*	*All*	*Black*	*White*	*All*
Social science	30	33	33	51	46	47
Natural science	48	47	47	43	38	39
Engineering	45	51	50	45	54	53
Humanities	38	44	43	54	55	54
All	36	41	41	46	46	46

| | *Percentage "Not Likely" to Choose Same Major* | | | | | |
| | *1976 Entering Cohort* | | | *1989 Entering Cohort* | | |
	Black	*White*	*All*	*Black*	*White*	*All*
Social science	36	26	27	13	13	14
Natural science	24	16	17	22	20	20
Engineering	17	17	17	28	15	14
Humanities	28	18	18	18	11	11
All	29	21	22	19	16	16

Source: College and Beyond.
Note: "Graduates" refers to first-school graduates.

APPENDIX TABLE D.7.9

Percentage of Graduates Who Wish They Had Spent More Time Studying,
by Class Rank and Race, 1976 and 1989 Entering Cohorts

	1976 Entering Cohort	*1989 Entering Cohort*
Top third of class		
Black	—	25
White	17	16
All	17	17
Middle third of class		
Black	43	53
White	46	49
All	46	50
Bottom third of class		
Black	67	75
White	68	69
All	68	70

Source: College and Beyond.

Note: "Graduates" refers to first-school graduates. Dashes represent cells with fewer than 20 observations.

APPENDIX TABLE D.7.10

Mean Self-Ratings of Abilities, College and Beyond Matriculants and
National College-Bound Seniors, 1976 Entering Cohort

	College and Beyond Matriculants			National College-Bound Seniors	Difference
	Black	White	All		
Mathematical	3.19	3.73	3.71	2.85	0.86
Scientific	3.02	3.48	3.46	2.76	0.70
Written expression	3.43	3.58	3.57	3.00	0.57
Creative writing	3.13	3.30	3.29	2.76	0.53
Organizing	3.33	3.57	3.56	3.05	0.51
Spoken expression	3.39	3.45	3.44	2.95	0.49
Leadership	3.63	3.60	3.60	3.16	0.44
Acting	2.30	2.58	2.57	2.37	0.20
Mechanical	2.61	2.63	2.63	2.48	0.15
Get along with others	4.05	3.83	3.84	3.69	0.15
Artistic	2.19	2.42	2.41	2.38	0.03

Source: College Entrance Examination Board and College and Beyond.

Notes: Self-ratings are on a scale of 1 (below average) to 5 (top 1 percent). The "Difference" column is the difference between all College and Beyond matriculants and national college-bound seniors.

APPENDIX TABLE D.7.11

Means of Independent Variables in Chapter 7 Regression Models,
1976 and 1989 Entering Cohorts

| | Means for Regression Models in Tables D.7.2 and D.7.3 | | | |
| | 1976 Entering Cohort | | 1989 Entering Cohort | |
Variable	All	Black	All	Black
Black	0.04	—	0.05	—
Hispanic	0.01	—	0.03	—
Asian	0.02	—	0.09	—
Other Race	0.00	—	0.01	—
Female	0.50	0.62	0.52	0.64
SAT > 1299	0.25	0.03	0.34	0.07
SAT 1200–1299	0.21	0.07	0.22	0.16
SAT 1100–1199	0.21	0.15	0.20	0.22
SAT 1000–1099	0.16	0.21	0.14	0.19
SAT Not Available	0.04	0.03	0.01	0.01
Top 10% of High School Class	0.40	0.30	0.57	0.42
High School Class Rank Not Available	0.40	0.35	0.19	0.17
High SES	0.30	0.11	0.35	0.15
Low SES	0.04	0.19	0.02	0.10
SES Not Available	0.23	0.21	0.15	0.13
SEL-1	0.21	0.25	0.25	0.32
SEL-2	0.35	0.41	0.26	0.26
Social Science	0.24	0.36	0.27	0.37
Natural Science	0.16	0.14	0.14	0.11
Engineering	0.12	0.08	0.11	0.09
Other Major	0.26	0.24	0.22	0.21
Major Not Available	0.01	0.02	0.02	0.03
Top Third of Class	0.37	0.07	0.36	0.07
Middle Third of Class	0.36	0.27	0.36	0.26
First-Choice Institution	0.77	0.74	0.73	0.72
Choice Not Available	0.01	0.01	0.01	0.01
Had Mentor	0.47	0.55	0.59	0.70
Master's Degree	0.18	0.16	0.23	0.24
Law Degree	0.11	0.14	0.09	0.12
Medical Degree	0.08	0.11	0.09	0.08
Business Degree	0.13	0.13	0.08	0.08
Doctoral Degree	0.06	0.04	0.08	0.07

(*Continued*)

APPENDIX TABLE D.7.11 *Continued*

	Means for Regression Models in Tables D.7.2 and D.7.3			
	1976 Entering Cohort		*1989 Entering Cohort*	
Variable	*All*	*Black*	*All*	*Black*
For-Profit	0.47	0.42	—	—
Self-Employed	0.14	0.12	—	—
Not-for-Profit	0.14	0.15	—	—
Other Employment Sector	0.01	0.01	—	—
Employment Sector Not Available	0.12	0.05	—	—
High Household Income ($150,000+)	0.24	0.16	—	—
Middle Household Income ($75,000–149,999)	0.37	0.36	—	—
Very Low Household Income (<$30,000)	0.08	0.09	—	—
Household Income Not Available	0.04	0.02	—	—

Source: College and Beyond.

Notes: Dashes represent variables not used in the regression model. See Appendix B for definitions of socioeconomic status (SES) and institutional selectivity (SEL-1, SEL-2, and SEL-3).

APPENDIX TABLE D.8.1

White Matriculants' Views on Racial Diversity, by Size of Black Population in
Entering Cohort, 1976 and 1989 Entering Cohorts

	Percentage of Respondents Who:			
Percentage of Blacks in Entering Cohort	*Said Getting Along with People of Different Races Was "Very Important"*	*Said College Contributed "A Great Deal" to Getting Along with People of Different Races*	*Said Their Schools Should Emphasize Racial Diversity "A Great Deal"*	*Knew Well Two or More Blacks in College*
1976 Entering Cohort				
1.0 to 3.9%	42	13	32	—
4.0 to 6.9%	42	19	37	—
7.0 to 9.9%	42	21	39	—
1989 Entering Cohort				
2.0 to 4.9%	54	26	42	49
5.0 to 12.9%	55	39	53	60

Source: College and Beyond.

Notes: Schools are grouped into two categories for the 1989 entering cohort because only seventeen institutions were surveyed. The survey of the 1976 entering cohort did not include the "knew well two or more" question.

APPENDIX TABLE D.8.2
White Matriculants' Degree of Interaction in College, by Pre-College Self-Ratings of Personality Traits, 1989 Entering Cohort

	Percentage of White Matriculants Who Knew:		
Pre-College Self-Rating	*No Blacks*	*Some Blacks*	*Well Two or More Blacks*
Popularity			
Below average	24	37	39
Average	8	38	54
Above average	9	34	57
Highest 10%	6	28	65
Self-Confidence (Social)			
Below average	14	42	45
Average	9	38	53
Above average	9	33	58
Highest 10%	6	30	64
Leadership			
Below average	13	42	45
Average	12	38	50
Above average	8	35	57
Highest 10%	6	32	62

Sources: Higher Education Research Institute and College and Beyond.

Notes: Respondents rated their personality traits on a scale of 1 to 5, where 1 = "lowest 10%"; 2 = "below average"; 3 = "average"; 4 = "above average"; and 5 = "highest 10%." In this table, "Below average" combines responses of "1" and "2" because of the small number of responses in those categories.

APPENDIX TABLE D.8.3

White Matriculants' Mean Pre-College Self-Ratings of Personality Traits,
by Institutional Selectivity, 1989 Entering Cohort

	Mean Pre-College Self-Rating		
	Popularity	*Self-Confidence (Social)*	*Leadership*
SEL-1	3.5	3.5	3.9
SEL-2	3.6	3.6	3.9
SEL-3	3.5	3.4	3.7
All	3.5	3.5	3.8

Source: Higher Education Research Institute and College and Beyond.

Notes: Respondents rated pre-college personality traits on a scale of 1 to 5, where
1 = "lowest 10%"; 2 = "below average"; 3 = "average"; 4 = "above average"; and 5 = "highest
10%." "SEL-1" indicates institutions with mean combined SAT scores of 1300 or above;
"SEL-2" indicates institutions with mean combined SAT scores between 1150 and 1299;
"SEL-3" indicates institutions with mean combined SAT scores below 1150.

APPENDIX TABLE D.8.4

Views on Institutional Priorities, by Race, 1976 and 1989 Entering Cohorts

	1976 Entering Cohort (mean rating)				1989 Entering Cohort (mean rating)			
	View of Current Emphasis		Desired Emphasis		View of Current Emphasis		Desired Emphasis	
	Black	White	Black	White	Black	White	Black	White
Faculty research	4.5	4.3	4.0	3.8	4.5	4.4	4.1	3.9
Intellectual freedom	4.1	4.2	4.6	4.5	4.1	4.1	4.7	4.6
Liberal arts education	4.2	4.1	4.4	4.3	4.2	4.1	4.5	4.3
Undergraduate teaching	4.0	4.0	4.8	4.8	3.9	3.8	4.9	4.9
Quality of residential life	3.6	3.7	4.3	4.1	3.9	3.8	4.5	4.3
Extracurricular activities	3.5	3.4	3.8	3.7	3.7	3.7	4.0	3.9
Alumni/ae concerns	3.8	3.7	3.7	3.3	4.0	3.9	3.9	3.6
Intercollegiate athletics	3.8	3.7	3.3	3.1	4.0	3.9	3.5	3.4
Racial diversity	3.0	3.7	4.7	4.0	3.4	3.8	4.8	4.2

Source: College and Beyond.

Notes: Respondents were asked to rate the emphasis they believed their undergraduate schools currently place on each priority, and how much emphasis they thought their schools *should* place on each priority. The responses to both questions were on a scale of 1 ("very little/none") to 5 ("a great deal").

APPENDIX TABLE D.8.5

Views on Institutional Emphasis on Racial Diversity, by Institutional Selectivity, Institutional Type, and Race, 1976 and 1989 Entering Cohorts

| | 1976 Entering Cohort (mean rating) | | | | 1989 Entering Cohort (mean rating) | | | |
| | *View of Current Emphasis* | | *Desired Emphasis* | | *View of Current Emphasis* | | *Desired Emphasis* | |
	Black	*White*	*Black*	*White*	*Black*	*White*	*Black*	*White*
SEL-1	3.3	4.0	4.8	4.0	3.6	4.1	4.8	4.3
SEL-2	2.9	3.8	4.7	4.0	3.5	3.8	4.8	4.3
SEL-3	2.8	3.6	4.7	3.9	3.3	3.7	4.8	4.2
Private university	2.9	3.8	4.7	3.9	3.4	3.8	4.8	4.2
Public university	2.8	3.6	4.8	3.9	3.3	3.7	4.8	4.2
Liberal arts college	3.4	4.0	4.8	4.3	3.9	4.2	4.8	4.6

Source: College and Beyond.

Notes: Respondents were asked to rate the emphasis they believed their undergraduate schools currently place on racial diversity, and how much emphasis they thought their schools *should* place on this priority. The responses to both questions were on a scale of 1 ("very little/none") to 5 ("a great deal"). For 1976, "SEL-1" indicates institutions with mean combined SAT scores of 1250 or above; "SEL-2" indicates institutions with mean combined SAT scores between 1125 and 1249; "SEL-3" indicates institutions with mean combined SAT scores below 1125. For 1989, "SEL-1" indicates institutions with mean combined SAT scores of 1300 or above; "SEL-2" indicates institutions with mean combined SAT scores between 1150 and 1299; "SEL-3" indicates institutions with mean combined SAT scores below 1150.

APPENDIX TABLE D.C.1A

Distribution of Occupations in 1995, by Race and Gender, College and Beyond Graduates and National Graduates, 1976 Entering Cohort (percent)

	Clergy	Clerical	Computer	Primary Education	Post-Secondary Education	Engineer	Executive/ Managerial	Financial Services	Doctor
Black women									
College and Beyond	2.4	4.0	3.8	7.5	4.7	1.8	21.7	3.6	8.4
National	7.9	16.3	1.6	14.2	1.1	7.0	19.0	6.9	1.3
White women									
College and Beyond	1.5	4.0	4.3	7.9	6.0	3.5	20.1	5.3	6.6
National	3.6	11.2	2.0	12.1	1.6	1.4	18.1	7.4	2.2
Black men									
College and Beyond	1.4	1.4	5.8	3.4	5.4	3.0	16.5	8.8	14.6
National	4.5	10.1	10.2	5.5	1.3	5.0	17.4	8.9	3.3
White men									
College and Beyond	0.9	0.6	5.8	2.1	4.3	10.0	21.7	7.9	10.9
National	2.5	4.6	2.1	3.3	1.3	7.1	21.5	9.3	4.7

APPENDIX TABLE D.C.1A *Continued*

	Other Health	Law	Management Consultant	Marketing and Sales	Military	Math/ Science	Social Science	Writers, Artists, Performers	Services and Crafts
Black women									
College and Beyond	5.3	12.2	2.0	5.1	0.4	2.2	4.4	4.0	4.5
National	9.6	2.3	1.3	4.1	1.0	9.0	1.6	2.0	9.1
White women									
College and Beyond	7.5	9.0	1.4	6.4	0.2	3.2	3.3	6.4	2.7
National	12.7	2.8	1.2	6.6	0.1	1.2	2.7	4.5	8.5
Black men									
College and Beyond	1.6	10.8	3.4	6.5	2.0	0.7	2.4	6.8	5.8
National	2.2	2.4	0.7	7.2	1.2	1.4	1.5	2.6	23.8
White men									
College and Beyond	1.4	11.8	1.4	6.4	1.4	3.6	1.4	3.7	3.6
National	2.5	4.7	9.0	11.8	0.7	2.0	1.4	3.0	16.5

Sources: College and Beyond and 1990 U.S. Census.

Note: For definitions of occupations, see "Occupational Field List" at end of Exhibit A.1 in Appendix A.

APPENDIX TABLE D.C.1B

Mean Earned Income in 1995, by Occupation, Race, and Gender, College and Beyond Graduates and National Graduates, 1976 Entering Cohort (1995 dollars)

	Clergy	Clerical	Computer	Primary Education	Post-Secondary Education	Engineer	Executive/ Managerial	Financial Services	Doctor
Black women									
College and Beyond	33,636	40,694	51,912	39,038	58,810	—	60,607	74,844	137,697
National	31,568	31,130	46,909	33,189	42,540	53,396	39,441	39,066	76,477
White women									
College and Beyond	35,369	35,448	64,805	34,651	45,709	63,281	76,871	100,985	111,120
National	31,044	30,777	48,800	32,853	39,585	51,151	49,175	48,061	84,125
Black men									
College and Beyond	—	—	71,637	40,750	61,250	—	79,946	123,942	155,074
National	33,959	38,270	55,703	36,457	41,479	56,917	49,247	51,162	116,365
White men									
College and Beyond	38,728	50,003	75,507	42,813	57,742	73,483	108,053	149,037	169,583
National	32,965	45,274	57,926	39,381	50,011	59,880	68,875	69,941	123,260

APPENDIX TABLE D.C.1B *Continued*

	Other Health	Law	Management Consultant	Marketing and Sales	Military	Math/ Science	Social Science	Writers, Artists, Performers	Services and Crafts
Black women									
College and Beyond	47,188	74,070	—	71,596	—	51,880	54,500	56,528	48,043
National	41,511	65,338	34,122	37,961	44,827	44,982	35,943	36,917	35,273
White women									
College and Beyond	47,999	93,692	100,556	71,596	62,736	50,881	47,294	48,804	40,604
National	40,653	73,807	48,889	45,685	43,782	44,208	43,380	42,824	34,090
Black men									
College and Beyond	—	77,891	58,292	56,806	—	—	—	83,625	51,243
National	44,629	62,998	64,939	45,993	36,997	45,795	46,652	45,800	39,028
White men									
College and Beyond	65,696	119,072	121,777	95,852	56,368	65,726	58,071	65,798	64,762
National	55,502	98,269	70,306	65,608	47,427	51,971	58,944	50,804	45,441

Sources: College and Beyond and 1990 U.S. Census.

Notes: Dashes represent cells with fewer than 10 observations. For definitions of occupations, see "Occupational Field List" at end of Exhibit A.1 in Appendix A. For College and Beyond graduates, mean earned income is derived from income ranges reported by full-time, full-year workers. For National graduates, the 1989 income of full-time, full-year workers aged 37 to 39 is converted to 1995 dollars. See Appendix B.

APPENDIX TABLE D.C.2

Mean Earned Income in 1995, by Type of Degree, Race, and Gender, College and Beyond Graduates and National Graduates, 1976 Entering Cohort (1995 dollars)

	Bachelor's Degree	Master's Degree	Doctoral Degree	Law Degree	Professional Degrees			All Professional Degrees
					Medical Degree	Business Degree		
Black women								
College and Beyond	51,259	50,264	51,176	73,597	127,791	79,700		89,850
National	34,794	39,828	55,795	—	—	—		57,908
White women								
College and Beyond	56,093	49,321	51,926	91,624	112,845	96,317		98,350
National	38,552	44,906	52,322	—	—	—		64,760
Black men								
College and Beyond	67,519	60,000	69,583	87,838	153,134	95,797		112,420
National	41,895	49,867	59,468	—	—	—		77,735
White men								
College and Beyond	88,278	66,162	65,523	119,394	168,551	124,129		134,214
National	55,762	63,733	65,671	—	—	—		101,213

Sources: College and Beyond and 1990 U.S. Census.

Notes: Income by type of professional degree was not available in Census data. For College and Beyond graduates, mean earned income is derived from income ranges reported by full-time, full-year workers. For National graduates, the 1989 income of full-time, full-year workers aged 37 to 39 is converted to 1995 dollars. See Appendix B.

References

Allport, Gordon W. 1979. *The Nature of Prejudice*. (1954; reprint, with introduction by Kenneth Clark and foreword by Thomas Pettigrew, 25th anniversary ed., Reading, Mass.: Addison-Wesley).

Appiah, K. Anthony. 1997. "The Multiculturalist Misunderstanding." *New York Review of Books* 44(15): 30–36.

Arrow, Kenneth J. 1974. *The Limits of Organization*. New York: Norton.

Association of American Medical Colleges. 1996. *Minority Students in Medical Education: Facts and Figures X*. Washington, D.C.: Association of American Medical Colleges.

Astin, Alexander W., Sarah A. Parrott, William S. Korn, and Linda J. Sax. 1997. *The American Freshman: Thirty Year Trends*. Los Angeles: Higher Education Research Institute, UCLA.

Avery, Christopher, Andrew Fairbanks, and Richard Zeckhauser. 1997. "An Assessment of Early Admissions Programs at Highly Selective Undergraduate Institutions." Harvard University, November 6. Duplicated.

Axtell, James. Forthcoming. *The Pleasures of Academe: A Celebration and Defense of Higher Education*. Lincoln: University of Nebraska Press.

Barron's. 1982. *Profiles of American Colleges*. 12th ed. Woodbury, N.Y.: Barron's Educational Series.

Bates, Timothy Mason. 1993. *Banking on Black Enterprise: The Potential of Emerging Firms for Revitalizing Urban Economies*. Washington, D.C.: Joint Center for Political and Economic Studies.

Becker, Gary S. 1993. *Human Capital: A Theoretical and Empirical Analysis, with Special Reference to Education*. Chicago: University of Chicago Press.

Behrman, Jere R., Jill Constantine, Lori Kletzer, Michael S. McPherson, and Morton Owen Schapiro. 1996. "The Impact of College Quality Choices on Wages: Are There Differences Among Demographic Groups?" Discussion Paper no. 38. Williams Project on the Economics of Higher Education.

Bernstein, Richard. 1994. *The Dictatorship of Virtue: Multiculturalism and the Battle for America's Future*. New York: Knopf.

Blackwell, James E. 1987. *Mainstreaming Outsiders: The Production of Black Professionals*. 2d ed. Dix Hills, N.Y.: General Hall.

Bobo, Lawrence, and Susan A. Suh. 1995. "Surveying Racial Discrimination: Analyses from a Multiethnic Labor Market." Working Paper no. 75. Russell Sage Foundation.

Bok, Derek. 1982. *Beyond the Ivory Tower: Social Responsibilities of the Modern University*. Cambridge: Harvard University Press.

———. 1993. *The Cost of Talent: How Executives and Professionals Are Paid and How It Affects America*. New York: Free Press.

———. 1996. *State of the Nation*. Cambridge: Harvard University Press.

Brewer, Dominic, Eric Eide, and Ronald G. Ehrenberg. 1996. *Does It Pay to Attend an Elite Private College? Cross Cohort Evidence on the Effects of College Quality on Earnings.* Santa Monica, Calif.: RAND Corporation.

Bronner, Ethan. 1997. "Colleges Look for Answers to Racial Gaps in Testing." *New York Times,* November 8, sec. A1.

Bruni, Frank. 1998. "Blacks at Berkeley are Offering No Welcome Mat." *New York Times,* May 2, sec. A1.

Cain, Glen G. 1986. "The Economic Analysis of Labor Market Discrimination: A Survey." In *Handbook of Labor Economics,* vol. 1, edited by Orley Ashenfelter and Richard Layard. New York: Elsevier Science Publishers.

Campbell, Angus. 1981. *The Sense of Well-Being in America: Recent Patterns and Trends.* New York: McGraw-Hill.

Campbell, Angus, Philip E. Converse, and Willard L. Rodgers. 1976. *The Quality of American Life: Perceptions, Evaluations, and Satisfactions.* New York: Russell Sage Foundation.

Card, David, and Alan B. Krueger. 1992a. "Does School Quality Matter? Returns to Education and the Characteristics of Public Schools in the United States." *Journal of Political Economy* 100(1): 1–40.

———. 1992b. "School Quality and Black-White Relative Earnings: A Direct Assessment." *The Quarterly Journal of Economics* 107(1): 151–200.

———. 1996. "Labor Market Effects of School Quality: Theory and Evidence." In *Does Money Matter? The Effect of School Measures on Student Achievement and Adult Success,* edited by Gary Burtless. Washington, D.C.: Brookings Institution.

Casper, Gerhard. 1995. "Keeping Open an Avenue Whereby the Deserving May Rise through Their Own Efforts." Statement on Affirmative Action at Stanford University, October 4.

Collins, Randall. 1979. *The Credential Society: An Historical Sociology of Education and Stratification.* New York: Academic Press.

College Entrance Examination Board. 1976. *National Report on College-Bound Seniors, 1975–76.* New York: College Entrance Examination Board.

———. 1990. *College-Bound Seniors: 1989 Profile of SAT and Achievement Test Takers.* New York: College Entrance Examination Board.

Consortium on Financing Higher Education. 1992. Class of '82 Follow-Up Survey. Cambridge, Mass.

Cose, Ellis. 1997. *Color-Blind: Seeing Beyond Race in a Race-Obsessed World.* New York: HarperCollins.

Cross, Theodore, and Robert Bruce Slater. 1997. "Why the End of Affirmative Action Would Exclude All but a Very Few Blacks from America's Leading Universities and Graduate Schools." *Journal of Blacks in Higher Education* 17 (Autumn): 8–17.

Daniel, Kermit, Dan Black, and Jeffrey Smith. 1997. "College Quality and the Wages of Young Men." Research Report no. 9707. Department of Economics, University of Western Ontario.

Davidson, Robert C., and Ernest L. Lewis. 1997. "Affirmative Action and Other Special Consideration Admissions at the University of California, Davis, School of Medicine." *Journal of the American Medical Association* 278(14): 1153–58.

Diener, Ed. 1984. "Subjective Well-Being." *Psychological Bulletin* 95(3): 542–75.

Doermann, Humphrey. 1969. *Crosscurrents in College Admissions: Institutional Response to Student Ability and Family Income.* New York: Teachers College Press.

D'Souza, Dinesh. 1991. *Illiberal Education: The Politics of Race and Sex on Campus.* New York: Free Press.

Duffy, Elizabeth A., and Idana Goldberg. 1998. *Crafting a Class: College Admissions and Financial Aid, 1955–1994.* Princeton, N.J.: Princeton University Press.

Dugan, Mary Kay, et al. 1996. "Affirmative Action: Does It Exist in Graduate Business Schools?" *Selections* 12(2): 11–18.

DuMouchel, William H., and Greg J. Duncan. 1983. "Using Sample Survey Weights in Multiple Regression Analyses of Stratified Samples." *Journal of the American Statistical Association* 78(383): 535–43.

Ehrenberg, Ronald G., and Robert S. Smith. 1994. *Modern Labor Economics: Theory and Public Policy.* New York: HarperCollins.

Executive Leadership Council. 1998. "Diversity: A Business Imperative." A special advertising section in *Forbes,* April 20.

Farley, Reynolds. 1996. *The New American Reality: Who We Are, How We Got Here, Where We Are Going.* New York: Russell Sage Foundation.

Feagin, Joe R., and Melvin P. Sikes. 1994. *Living with Racism.* Boston: Beacon Press.

Fetter, Jean H. 1995. *Questions and Admissions: Reflections on 100,000 Admissions Decisions at Stanford.* Stanford: Stanford University Press.

Fordham, Signithia, and John U. Ogbu. 1986. "Black Students' School Success: Coping with the Burden of 'Acting White.'" *Urban Review* 18(3): 176–206.

Frank, Robert H., and Philip J. Cook. 1995. *The Winner-Take-All Society.* New York: Free Press.

Franklin, John Hope. 1993. *The Color Line: Legacy for the Twenty-First Century.* Columbia: University of Missouri Press.

Freeman, Richard B. 1976. *Black Elite: The New Market for Highly Educated Black Americans.* New York: Carnegie Foundation for the Advancement of Teaching.

Gates, Henry Louis, Jr. 1998. "Are We Better Off?" Essay prepared for *Frontline,* "The Two Nations of Black America." Available: http://www.pbs.org/wgbh/pages/frontline/shows/race/main.html.

Gates, Henry Louis, Jr., and Cornel West. 1996. *The Future of the Race.* New York: Knopf.

Goldin, Claudia Dale. 1990. *Understanding the Gender Gap: An Economic History of American Women.* New York: Oxford University Press.

Goode, William J. 1975. "Toward a Sociological Understanding of the Professions: The Professionalizing Occupations." *General Education Seminar Reports* 3(6): 97–104.

Graglia, Lino A. 1993. "Racial Preferences in Admission to Institutions of Higher Education." In *The Imperiled Academy,* edited by Howard Dickman. New Brunswick, N.J.: Transaction Publishers.

Greider, William. 1994. "The Politics of the Diversion: Blame It on the Blacks." In *Debating Affirmative Action: Race, Gender, Ethnicity, and the Politics of Inclusion,* edited by Nicolaus Mills. New York: Delta.

Guinier, Lani. 1998. "An Equal Chance." *New York Times,* April 23, sec. A25.

Hacker, Andrew, ed. 1983. *U/S: A Statistical Portrait of the American People.* New York: Viking.

Healy, Patrick. 1998. "Admissions Law Changes the Equations for Students and Colleges in Texas." *Chronicle of Higher Education,* April 3, pp. A29–A31.

Heckman, James J., and Solomon Polachek. 1974. "Empirical Evidence on the Functional Form of the Earnings-Schooling Relationship." *Journal of the American Statistical Association* 69(346): 350–54.

Hedges, Larry V., and Amy Nowell. Forthcoming. "Black-White Test Score Convergence: Can Socioeconomic Changes Explain the Trend?" In *The Black-White Test Score Gap,* edited by Christopher Jencks and Meredith Phillips. Washington, D.C.: Brookings Institution.

Herrnstein, Richard J., and Charles Murray. 1994. *The Bell Curve: Intelligence and Class Structure in American Life.* New York: Free Press.

Higginbotham, A. Leon, Jr. 1998. "Breaking Thurgood Marshall's Promise." *New York Times,* January 18, sec. 6.

Hochschild, Jennifer L. 1995. *Facing Up to the American Dream: Race, Class, and the Soul of the Nation.* Princeton, N.J.: Princeton University Press.

Hout, Michael. 1988. "More Universalism, Less Structural Mobility: The American Occupational Structure in the 1980s." *American Journal of Sociology* 93(6): 1358–1400.

Howd, Jay B. 1992. "Race-Exclusive Scholarships in Federally-Assisted Colleges and Universities—Will They Survive?" *Southern Illinois Law Journal* 16: 451.

Hrabowski, Freeman A., Kenneth I. Maton, and Geoffrey L. Greif. 1998. *Beating the Odds: Raising Academically Successful African American Males.* New York: Oxford University Press.

Hungerford, Thomas, and Gary Solon. 1987. "Sheepskin Effects in the Returns to Education." *Review of Economics and Statistics* 69(1): 175–77.

Independent Sector. 1996. *Giving and Volunteering in the United States.* Washington, D.C.: Independent Sector.

Jaeger, David A., and Marianne E. Page. 1996. "Degrees Matter: New Evidence on Sheepskin Effects in the Returns to Education." *Review of Economics and Statistics* 78(4): 733–40.

Jaynes, Gerald D., and Robin M. Williams, Jr., eds. 1989. A *Common Destiny: Blacks and American Society.* Washington, D.C.: National Academy Press.

Jencks, Christopher, and Meredith Phillips, eds. Forthcoming. *The Black-White Test Score Gap.* Washington, D.C.: Brookings Institution.

Johnson, William R., and Derek Neal. Forthcoming. "Basic Skills and the Black-White Earnings Gap." In *The Black-White Test Score Gap,* edited by Christopher Jencks and Meredith Phillips. Washington, D.C.: Brookings Institution.

Kahlenberg, Richard D. 1996. *The Remedy: Class, Race, and Affirmative Action.* New York: Basic Books.

Kane, Thomas J. Forthcoming. "Racial and Ethnic Preferences in College Admission." In *The Black-White Test Score Gap,* edited by Christopher Jencks and Meredith Phillips. Washington, D.C.: Brookings Institution.

Karen, David. 1991. "The Politics of Class, Race and Gender: Access to Higher

Education in the United States, 1960–1986." *American Journal of Education* 99(2): 208–37.

Katchadourian, Herant, and John Boli. 1994. *Cream of the Crop: The Impact of Elite Education in the Decade after College.* New York: Basic Books.

Katzenbach, Nicholas deB., and Burke Marshall. 1998. "Not Color Blind: Just Blind." *New York Times,* February 22, sec. 6.

Keith, Stephen N., et al. 1986. "Effects of Affirmative Action in Medical School: A Study of the Class of 1975." *New England Journal of Medicine* 313(24): 1519–25.

Kendrick, S. A. 1967. "The Coming Segregation of Our Selective Colleges." *College Board Review* 66 (Winter): 6–13.

Kernan, Alvin. Forthcoming. *In Plato's Cave: The Democratization of Higher Education.* New Haven, Conn.: Yale University Press.

Klausner, Stephen E., Stephen B. Hunter, and Samuel Estreicher. 1997. Board of Education of the Township of Piscataway v. Sharon Taxman. No. 96-697. (U.S. filed 1997) (respondent's brief), *appeal withdrawn.*

Klitgaard, Robert. 1985. *Choosing Elites.* New York: Basic Books.

Kluger, Richard. 1975. *Simple Justice: The History of* Brown v. Board of Education *and Black America's Struggle for Equality.* New York: Vintage Books.

Knaplund, Kristine S., and Richard Sander. 1995. "The Art and Science of Academic Support." *Journal of Legal Education* 45(2): 157–234.

Komaromy, Miriam, et al. 1996. "The Role of Black and Hispanic Physicians in Providing Health Care for Underserved Populations." *New England Journal of Medicine* 334(20): 1305–10.

Kravitz, David A., et al. 1996. "Affirmative Action: A Review of Psychological and Behavioral Research." Report prepared by a subcommittee of the Scientific Affairs Committee of the Society for Industrial and Organizational Psychology. Bowling Green, Ohio, October.

Krysan, Maria, Howard Schuman, Lesli Jo Scott, and Paul Beatty. 1994. "Response Rates and Response Content in Mail Surveys versus Face-to-Face Surveys." *Public Opinion Quarterly* 58: 381–99.

Ladd, Everett C. 1996. "The Data Just Don't Show Erosion of America's 'Social Capital.'" *The Public Perspective* 7(4): 5–22.

Lederman, Douglas, Michael Crissey, and Bryan Mealer. 1997. "Impact of Affirmative-Action Ruling in Texas is Less Clear-Cut Than Predicted." *Chronicle of Higher Education,* September 26, p. A32.

Levin, Richard C. 1996. "Preparing for Yale's Fourth Century." Essay prepared for the Association of Yale Alumni Assembly, October 26.

Levy, Frank, and Richard J. Murnane. 1992. "U.S. Earnings Levels and Earnings Inequality: A Review of Recent Trends and Proposed Explanations." *Journal of Economic Literature* 30(3): 1333–81.

Lewis, W. Arthur. 1969. "The Road to the Top Is Through Higher Education— Not Black Studies." *New York Times,* May 11, sec. 6.

Loury, Glenn C. 1995. "The Moral Quandary of the Black Community." In *One by One from the Inside Out: Essays and Reviews on Race and Responsibility in America.* New York: Free Press.

456   REFERENCES

—————. 1998. "Discrimination in the Post–Civil Rights Era: Beyond Market Interactions." Paper presented at meeting of Russell Sage Foundation.

Loury, Linda Datcher, and David Garman. 1995. "College Selectivity and Earnings." *Journal of Labor Economics* 13(2): 289–308.

Lowe, Eugene Y., ed. Forthcoming. *Dilemma and Promise: Incorporating Racial Diversity in Higher Education.* Princeton, N.J.: Princeton University Press.

Malamud, Deborah. 1996. "Class-Based Affirmative Action: Lessons and Caveats." *Texas Law Review* 74: 1847.

Merton, Robert K., George G. Reader, and Patricia L. Kendall, eds. 1957. *The Student Physician: Introductory Studies in the Sociology of Medical Education.* Cambridge: Harvard University Press.

Metzger, Walter P. 1987. "A Spectre Is Haunting American Scholars: The Spectre of 'Professionism.'" *Educational Researcher* 16(6): 10–19.

Miller, L. Scott. 1995. *An American Imperative: Accelerating Minority Educational Advancement.* New Haven, Conn.: Yale University Press.

Mincer, Jacob. 1974. *Schooling, Experience, and Earnings.* New York: National Bureau of Economic Research.

Morris, John E. 1997. "Boalt Hall's Affirmative Action Dilemma." *American Lawyer* 19(9): 4–7, 77–81.

Moy, Ernest, and Barbara A. Bartman. 1995. "Physician Race and Care of Minority and Medically Indigent Patients." *Journal of The American Medical Association* 273(19): 1515–20.

Murphy, Kevin, and Finis Welch. 1989. "Wage Premiums for College Graduates: Recent Growth and Possible Explanations." *Educational Researcher* 18(4):17–26.

Murray, Charles. 1994. "Affirmative Racism." In *Debating Affirmative Action: Race, Gender, Ethnicity, and the Politics of Inclusion,* edited by Nicolaus Mills. New York: Delta.

Nakao, Keiko, and Judith Treas. 1990. *Computing 1989 Occupational Prestige Scores.* General Social Survey Methodological Report no. 70. Chicago: National Opinion Research Center.

National Collegiate Athletic Association. 1996. *NCAA Division I Graduation-Rates Report.*

National Opinion Research Center. 1997. General Social Surveys Cumulative Data File, 1972–1996 (computer file). Chicago, Ill.: National Opinion Research Center (producer). Storrs, Conn.: Roper Center for Public Opinion Research (distributor).

Nettles, Michael T. and Laura W. Perna. 1997. *The African American Education Data Book: Higher and Adult Education.* vol. 1. Fairfax, Va.: Frederick D. Patterson Research Institute of the College Fund/UNCF.

Nettles, Michael T., Laura W. Perna, and Kimberley C. Edelin. Forthcoming. "The Role of Affirmative Action in Expanding Student Access at Selective Colleges and Universities." In *Hopwood, Bakke, and Beyond: Diversity on our Nation's Campuses.* Washington, D.C.: American Association of Collegiate Registrars and Admissions Officers.

Nickens, Herbert W., Timothy P. Ready, and Robert G. Petersdorf. 1994. "Project

3000 by 2000: Racial and Ethnic Diversity in U.S. Medical Schools." *New England Journal of Medicine* 331(7): 472–76.

Oliver, Melvin L., and Thomas M. Shapiro. 1995. *Black Wealth/White Wealth: A New Perspective on Racial Inequality.* New York: Routledge.

O'Neil, Robert M. 1970. "Preferential Admissions: Equalizing Access to Legal Education." *University of Toledo Law Review* (spring/summer): 281–320.

O'Sullivan, John. 1998. In "Is Affirmative Action on the Way Out? Should It Be? A Symposium." *Commentary* 105(3): 40–42.

Page, Benjamin I., and Robert Y. Shapiro. 1992. *The Rational Public: Fifty Years of Trends in Americans' Policy Preferences.* Chicago: University of Chicago Press.

Pascarella, Ernest T., and Patrick T. Terenzini. 1991. *How College Affects Students: Findings and Insights from Twenty Years of Research.* San Francisco: Jossey-Bass.

Patterson, Orlando. 1997. *The Ordeal of Integration: Progress and Resentment in America's "Racial" Crisis.* Washington, D.C.: Civitas/Counterpoint.

Peterson, Marvin W., et al. 1978. *Black Students on White Campuses: The Impacts of Increased Black Enrollments.* Ann Arbor: University of Michigan.

Peterson's Guide to Four-Year Colleges. 1998. Princeton, N.J.: Peterson's.

Phillips, Meredith, James Crouse, and John Ralph. Forthcoming. "Does the Black-White Test Score Gap Widen after Children Enter School?" In *The Black-White Test Score Gap,* edited by Christopher Jencks and Meredith Phillips. Washington, D.C.: Brookings Institution.

Pindyck, Robert S., and Daniel L. Rubinfield. 1991. *Econometric Models and Economic Forecasts.* 3rd ed. New York: McGraw-Hill.

Putnam, Robert D. 1995. "Bowling Alone: America's Declining Social Capital." *Journal of Democracy* 6(1): 65–78.

Rainwater, Lee, and William L. Yancey. 1967. *The Moynihan Report and the Politics of Controversy.* Cambridge: MIT Press.

Ramist, Leonard, Charles Lewis, and Laura McCamley-Jenkins. 1994. "Student Group Differences in Predicting College Grades: Sex, Language, and Ethnic Groups," College Board Report no. 93-1.

Ramphele, Mamphela. 1996. "Equity and Excellence—Strange Bedfellows? A Case Study of South African Higher Education." Paper presented at The Princeton Conference on Higher Education, March 21–23.

Reddy, Marlita A. 1995. *The Statistical Record of Hispanic Americans.* 2d ed. Detroit: Gale Research.

Report of The Andrew W. Mellon Foundation. 1993. New York: The Andrew W. Mellon Foundation.

Riley, Matilda White, Anne Foner, and Joan Waring. 1988. "Sociology of Age." In *Handbook of Sociology,* edited by Neil J. Smelser. Newbury Park, Calif.: Sage Publications.

Rindfuss, Ronald R., S. Philip Morgan, and Kate Offutt. 1996. "Education and the Changing Age Pattern of American Fertility: 1963–1989." *Demography* 33(3): 277–90.

Roberts, Sam. 1995. "Conversations/Kenneth B. Clark: An Integrationist to This Day, Believing All Else Has Failed." *New York Times,* May 7, sec. 4.

Rosen, Jeffrey. 1998. "Damage Control." *New Yorker,* February 23 and March 2, 1998, 58–68.

Rudenstine, Neil L. 1996. "The President's Report on Diversity and Learning." Harvard University.

Sax, Linda J., and Alexander W. Astin. 1997. "The Development of 'Civic Virtue' among College Students." In *The Senior Year Experience: Facilitating Integration, Reflection, Closure, and Transition,* edited by John N. Gardner and Gretchen Van der Veer. San Francisco: Jossey-Bass.

Schön, Donald A. 1983. *The Reflective Practitioner: How Professionals Think in Action.* New York: Basic Books.

Schuman, Howard, et al. 1997. *Racial Attitudes in America: Trends and Interpretations.* Rev. ed. Cambridge: Harvard University Press.

Seglin, Jeffrey L. 1996. "The Happiest Workers in the World." *Inc.* State of Small Business issue.

Shepard, Scott. 1997. "Discussion of Race Must Be Inclusive." *Times of Trenton,* December 29, sec. A.

Smigel, Erwin. 1969. *The Wall Street Lawyer: Professional Organizational Man.* Bloomington: Indiana University Press.

Sniderman, Paul M., and Edward G. Carmines. 1997. *Reaching Beyond Race.* Cambridge: Harvard University Press.

Sowell, Thomas. 1972. *Black Education: Myths and Tragedies.* New York: McKay.

Steele, Claude, and Joshua Aronson. Forthcoming. "Stereotype Threat and the Test Performance of Academically Successful African-Americans." In *The Black-White Test Score Gap,* edited by Christopher Jencks and Meredith Phillips. Washington, D.C.: Brookings Institution.

Steele, Shelby. 1994. "A Negative Vote on Affirmative Action." In *Debating Affirmative Action: Race, Gender, Ethnicity, and the Politics of Inclusion,* edited by Nicolaus Mills. New York: Delta.

Sturm, Susan, and Lani Guinier. 1996. "The Future of Affirmative Action: Reclaiming the Innovative Ideal." *California Law Review* 84: 953.

Sullivan, William M. 1995. *Work and Integrity: The Crisis and Promise of Professionalism in America.* New York: HarperBusiness.

Thernstrom, Stephan, and Abigail Thernstrom. 1997. *America in Black and White: One Nation Indivisible.* New York: Simon & Schuster.

Tinto, Vincent. 1993. *Leaving College: Rethinking the Causes and Cures of Student Attrition.* 2d. ed. Chicago: University of Chicago Press.

Tocqueville, Alexis de. [1840] 1990. *Democracy in America.* New York: Vintage Books.

Turner, Sarah E., and William G. Bowen. Forthcoming. "Choice of Major: The Changing (Unchanging) Gender Gap," *Industrial and Labor Relations Review.*

Twain, Mark. [1883] 1961. *Life on the Mississippi.* Reprint, New York: Penguin Books.

U.S. Bureau of the Census. 1940. *Census of the Population.* Public Use Microdata Sample.

———. 1960. *Census of Population and Housing.* Public Use Sample.

———. 1990. *Census of Population and Housing.* Public Use Sample.

———. 1997. *Statistical Abstract of the United States.* Washington, D.C.: Government Printing Office.

U.S. Bureau of Labor Statistics. 1998. *Employment and Earnings.* (January): tab. 10.

U.S. Department of Education. 1986. *High School and Beyond, 1980: Sophomore and Senior Third Follow-Up* (computer file). 2d. release. Chicago: National Center for Education Statistics (producer); Ann Arbor: Interuniversity Consortium for Political and Social Research (distributor).

———. various years. *Digest of Education Statistics.* Washington, D.C.: Government Printing Office.

Vars, Fredrick and William G. Bowen. Forthcoming. "SAT Scores, Race, and Academic Performance in Academically Selective Colleges and Universities." In *The Black-White Test Score Gap,* edited by Christopher Jencks and Meredith Phillips. Washington, D.C.: The Brookings Institution.

Verhovek, Sam Howe. 1997a. "Houston Voters Maintain Affirmative Action Policy." *New York Times,* November 6, sec. A.

———. 1997b. "In Poll, Americans Reject Means but Not Ends of Racial Diversity." *New York Times,* December 14, sec. 1.

Watters, Ethan. 1995. "Claude Steele Has Scores to Settle." *New York Times,* September 17, sec. 6.

Webster, David S. 1983. "America's Highest Ranked Graduate Schools, 1925–1982." *Change* 15(4): 14–24.

Wehrli, John E. 1998. "Wehrli's Graduate School Rankings: Internet Legal Resource Guide." Available: http://wehrli.ilrg.com.

West, Cornel. 1993. *Race Matters.* Boston: Beacon Press.

Westoff, Charles F., and Germán Rodríguez. 1993. "The Mass Media and Family Planning in Kenya." Demographic and Health Surveys Working Paper No. 4, Columbia, MD.

Wightman, Linda F. 1997. "The Threat to Diversity in Legal Education: An Empirical Analysis of the Consequences of Abandoning Race as a Factor in Law School Admissions Decisions." *New York University Law Review* 72(1): 1–53.

Wilkins, David B., and G. Mitu Gulati. 1996. "Why Are There So Few Black Lawyers in Corporate Law Firms? An Institutional Analysis." *California Law Review* 84(3): 493–626.

Wilson, William Julius. 1987. *The Truly Disadvantaged: The Inner City, the Underclass, and Public Policy.* Chicago: University of Chicago Press.

Wright, Charles Alan, Douglas Laycock, and Samuel Issacharoff. 1997. Board of Education of the Township of Piscataway v. Sharon Taxman. No. 96-679. (U.S. filed 1997) (amicus brief), *appeal withdrawn.*

CASES CITED

Adarand Constructors, Inc. v. Peña, 515 U.S. 200 (1995).

Brown v. Board of Education, 347 U.S. 483 (1954).

City of Richmond v. J. A. Croson Co., 488 U.S. 469 (1989).

Hopwood v. Texas, 78 F.3d 932 (5th Cir. 1996), *cert. denied,* 116 S.Ct. 2582 (1996).

Missouri *ex rel.* Gaines v. Canada, 305 U.S. 337 (1938).

Regents of the University of California v. Bakke, 438 U.S. 265 (1978).

Sweatt v. Painter, 339 U.S. 629 (1950).

Sweezy v. New Hampshire, 354 U.S. 234, 263 (1957).

Index

Page numbers for entries occurring in exhibits are suffixed by an e; those for entries in figures, by an f; those for entries in notes, by an n, with the number of the note following; and those for entries in tables, by a t.

William G. Bowen is President of The Andrew W. Mellon Foundation and former President of Princeton University.

Derek Bok is the 300th Anniversary University Professor at the John F. Kennedy School of Government at Harvard University. He is former President of Harvard University and former Dean of the Harvard Law School.